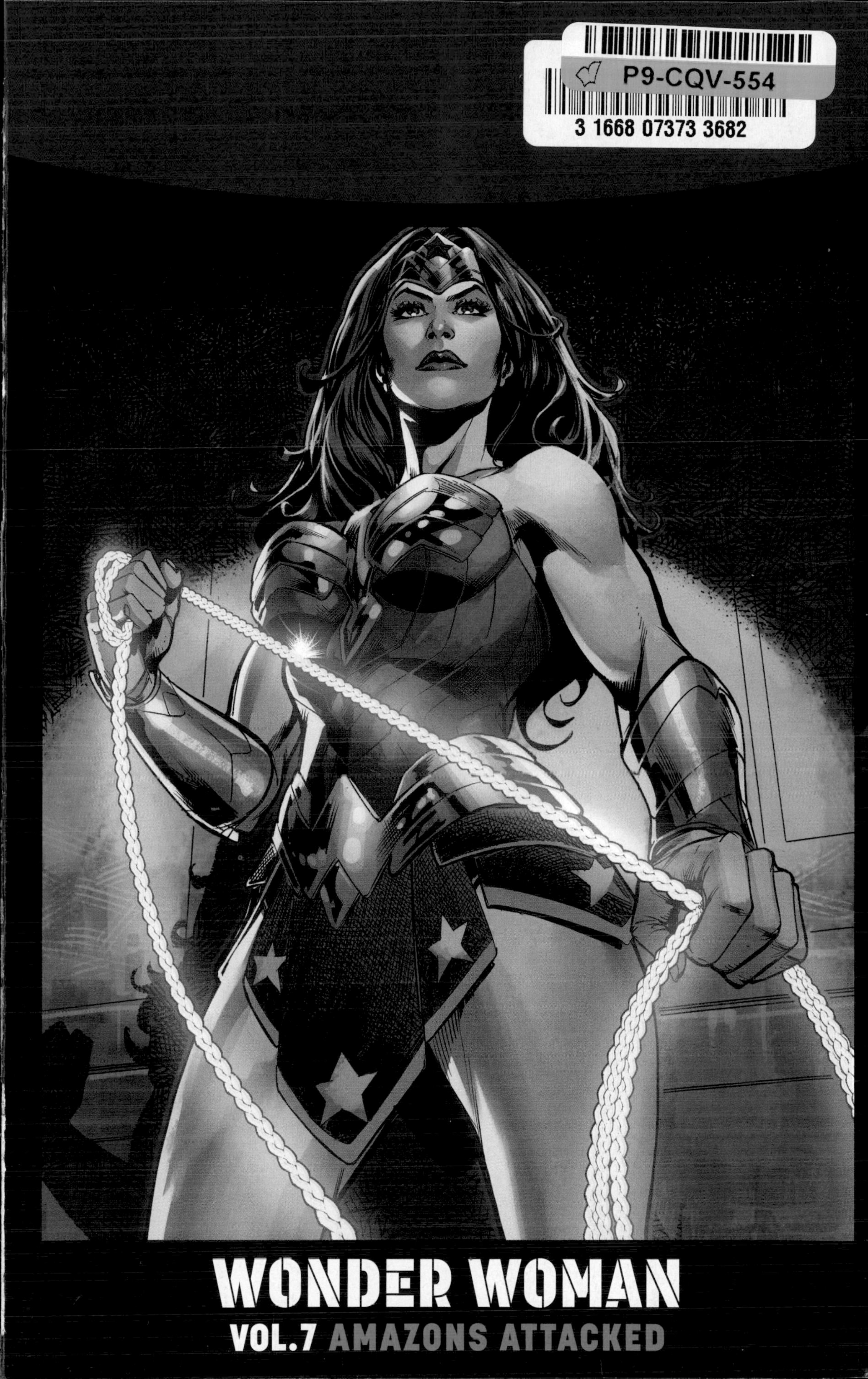

WONDER WOMAN
VOL.7 AMAZONS ATTACKED

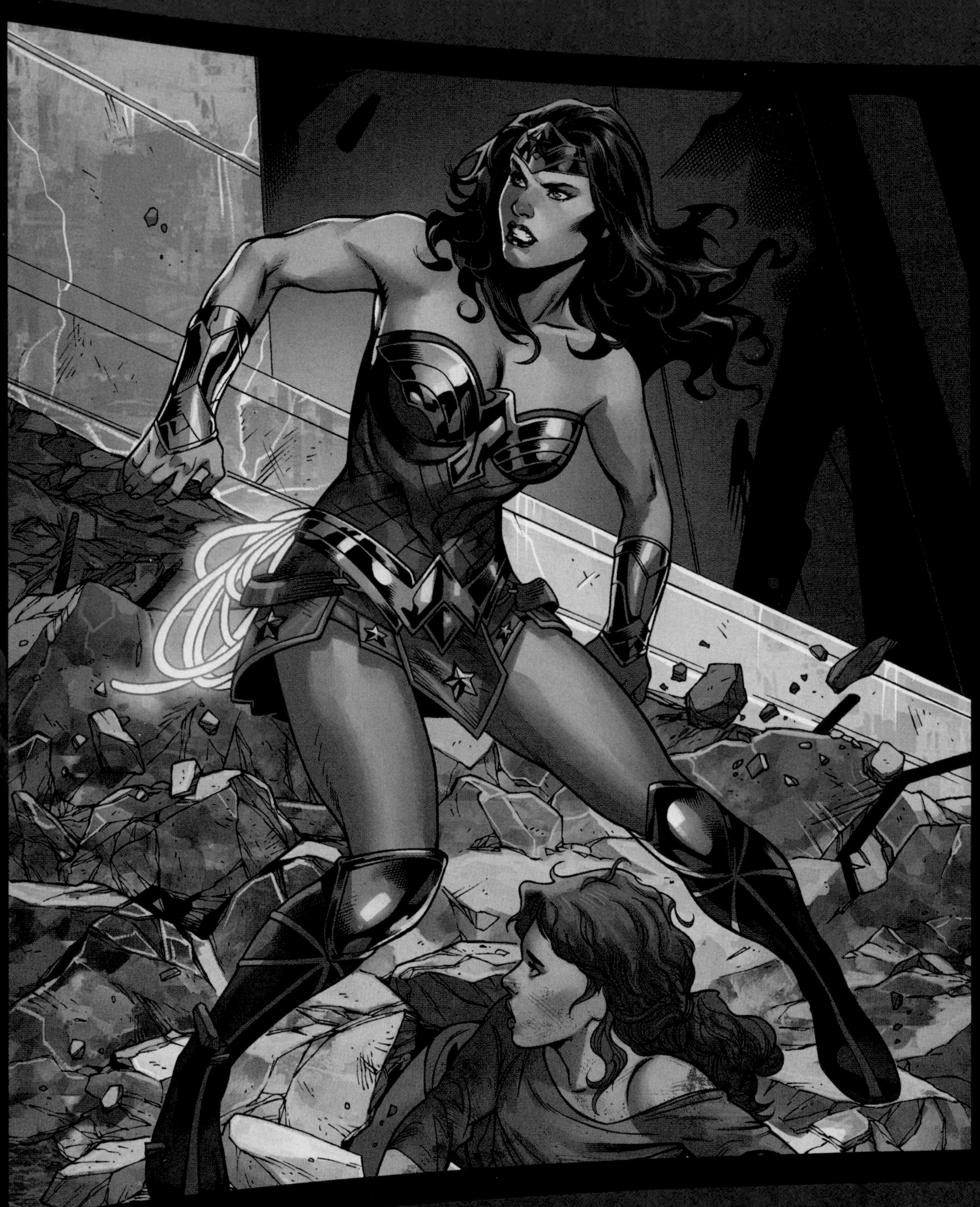

WONDER WOMAN
VOL.7 AMAZONS ATTACKED

JAMES ROBINSON
writer

EMANUELA LUPACCHINO * **RAY McCARTHY**
CARMEN CARNERO * **STEPHEN SEGOVIA**
JESUS MERINO * **MARCO SANTUCCI**
artists

ROMULO FAJARDO JR. * **HI-FI**
colorists

SAIDA TEMOFONTE
letterer

JENNY FRISON
collection cover artist

WONDER WOMAN created by WILLIAM MOULTON MARSTON

CHRIS CONROY Editor - Original Series * **ANDREW MARINO DAVE WIELGOSZ** Assistant Editors - Original Series
JEB WOODARD Group Editor - Collected Editions * **ROBIN WILDMAN** Editor - Collected Edition
STEVE COOK Design Director - Books * **SHANNON STEWART** Publication Design

BOB HARRAS Senior VP - Editor-in-Chief, DC Comics
PAT McCALLUM Executive Editor, DC Comics

DAN DiDIO Publisher * **JIM LEE** Publisher & Chief Creative Officer
AMIT DESAI Executive VP - Business & Marketing Strategy, Direct to Consumer & Global Franchise Management
BOBBIE CHASE VP & Executive Editor, Young Reader & Talent Development * **MARK CHIARELLO** Senior VP - Art, Design & Collected Editions
JOHN CUNNINGHAM Senior VP - Sales & Trade Marketing * **BRIAR DARDEN** VP - Business Affairs
ANNE DePIES Senior VP - Business Strategy, Finance & Administration * **DON FALLETTI** VP - Manufacturing Operations
LAWRENCE GANEM VP - Editorial Administration & Talent Relations * **ALISON GILL** Senior VP - Manufacturing & Operations
JASON GREENBERG VP - Business Strategy & Finance * **HANK KANALZ** Senior VP - Editorial Strategy & Administration
JAY KOGAN Senior VP - Legal Affairs * **NICK J. NAPOLITANO** VP - Manufacturing Administration
LISETTE OSTERLOH VP - Digital Marketing & Events * **EDDIE SCANNELL** VP - Consumer Marketing
COURTNEY SIMMONS Senior VP - Publicity & Communications * **JIM (SKI) SOKOLOWSKI** VP - Comic Book Specialty Sales & Trade Marketing
NANCY SPEARS VP - Mass, Book, Digital Sales & Trade Marketing * **MICHELE R. WELLS** VP - Content Strategy

WONDER WOMAN VOL. 7: AMAZONS ATTACKED

Published by DC Comics. Compilation and all new material Copyright © 2018 DC Comics. All Rights Reserved.
Originally published in single magazine form in WONDER WOMAN 38-45. Copyright © 2018 DC Comics. All Rights Reserved.
All characters, their distinctive likenesses and related elements featured in this publication are trademarks of DC Comics.
The stories, characters and incidents featured in this publication are entirely fictional.
DC Comics does not read or accept unsolicited submissions of ideas, stories or artwork.

DC Comics, 2900 West Alameda Ave., Burbank, CA 91505
Printed by Times Printing, LLC, Random Lake, WI, USA. 11/16/18. First Printing.
ISBN: 978-1-4012-8534-0

Library of Congress Cataloging-in-Publication Data is available.

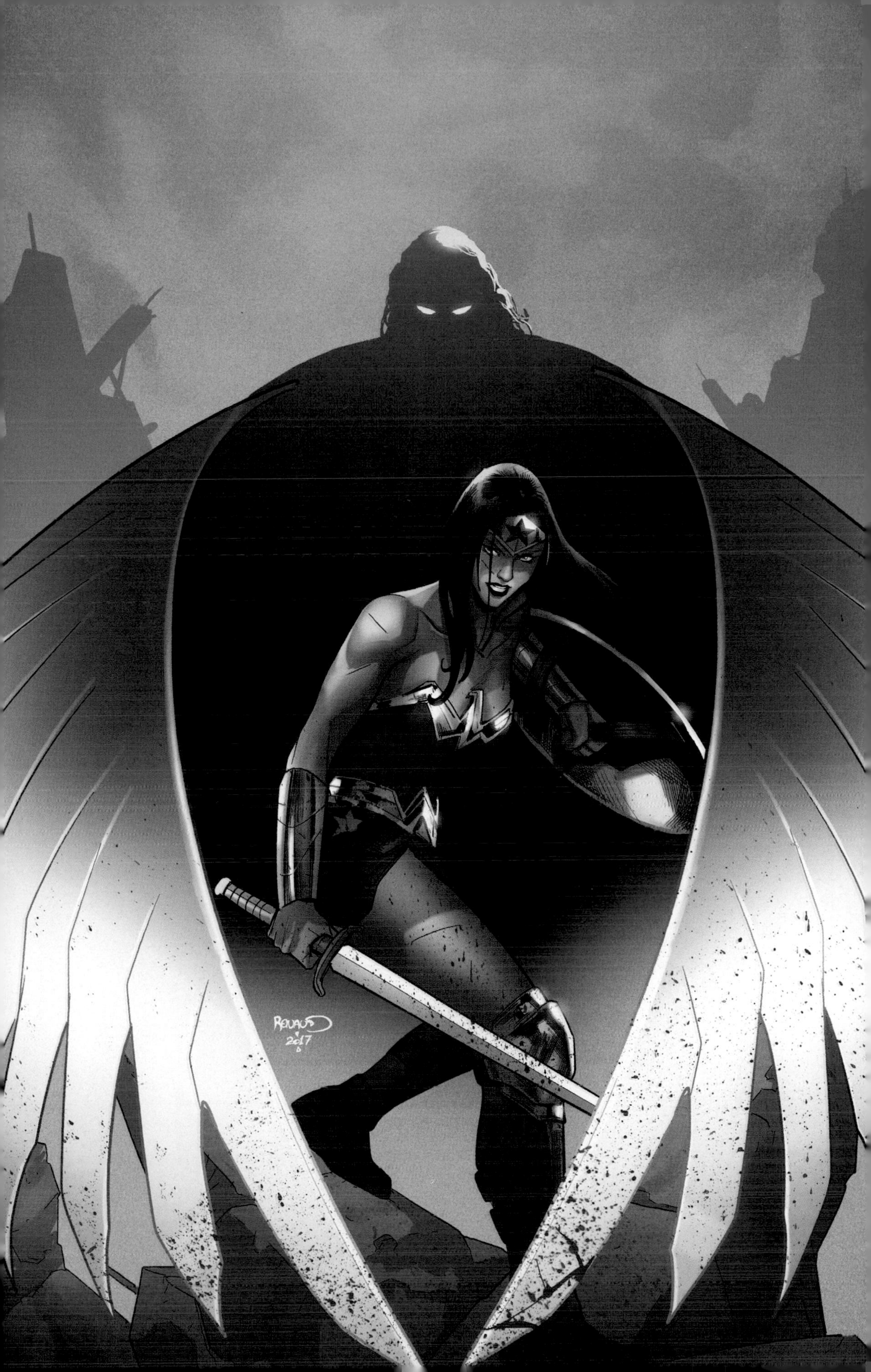

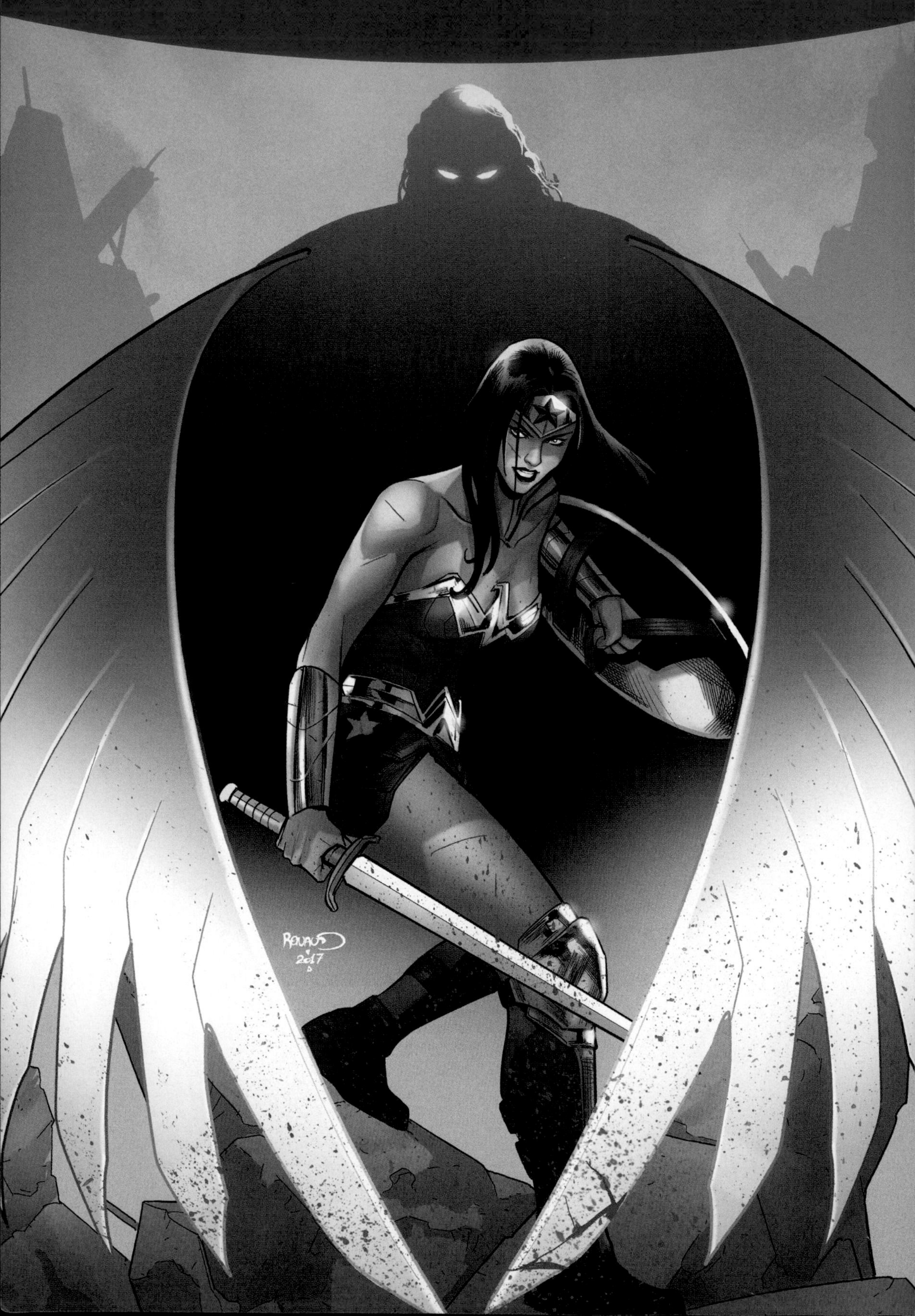

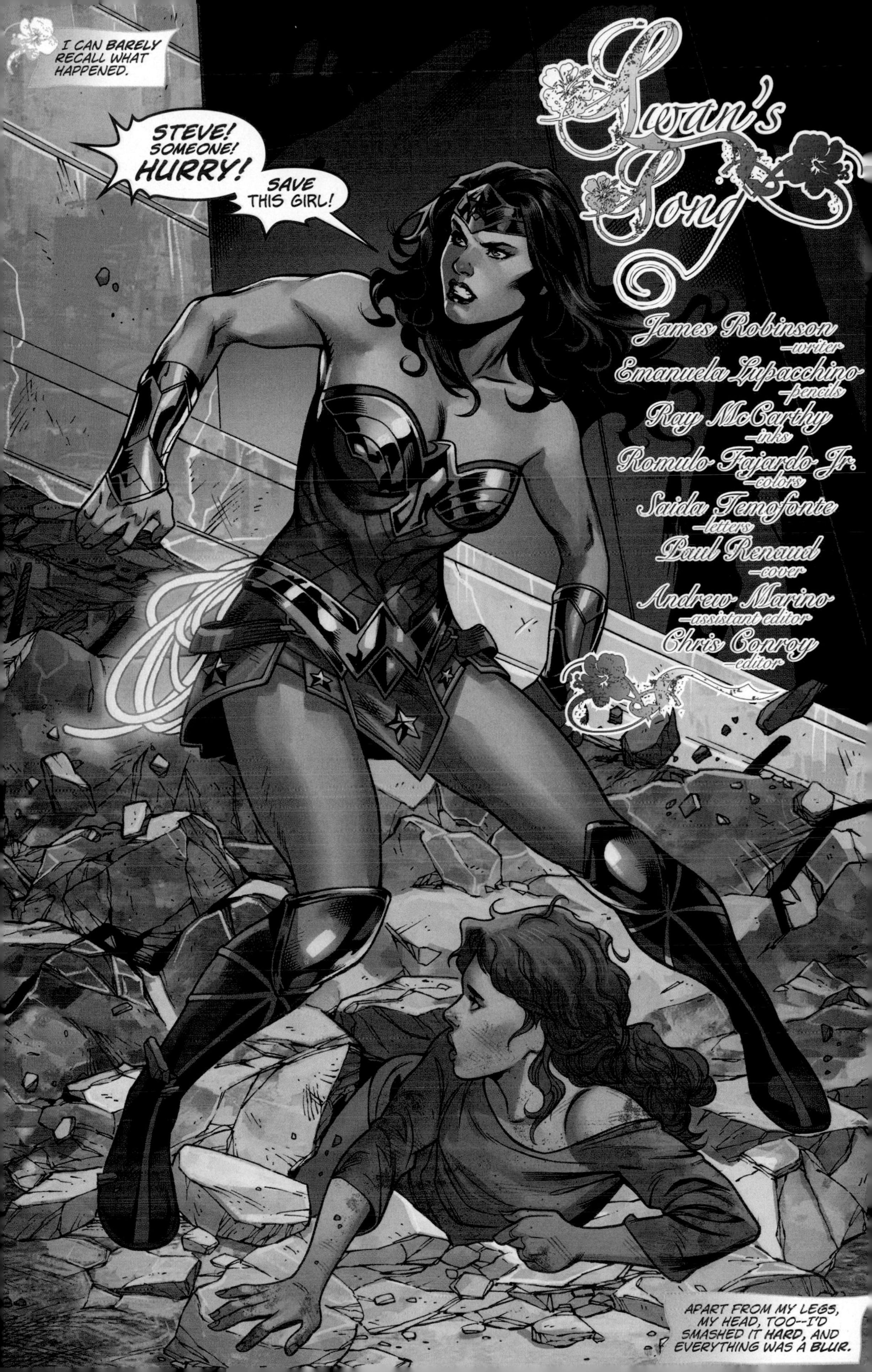
I CAN BARELY RECALL WHAT HAPPENED.
STEVE! SOMEONE! HURRY!
SAVE THIS GIRL!
Swan's Song
James Robinson —writer
Emanuela Lupacchino —pencils
Ray McCarthy —inks
Romulo Fajardo Jr. —colors
Saida Temofonte —letters
Paul Renaud —cover
Andrew Marino —assistant editor
Chris Conroy —editor
APART FROM MY LEGS, MY HEAD, TOO--I'D SMASHED IT HARD, AND EVERYTHING WAS A BLUR.

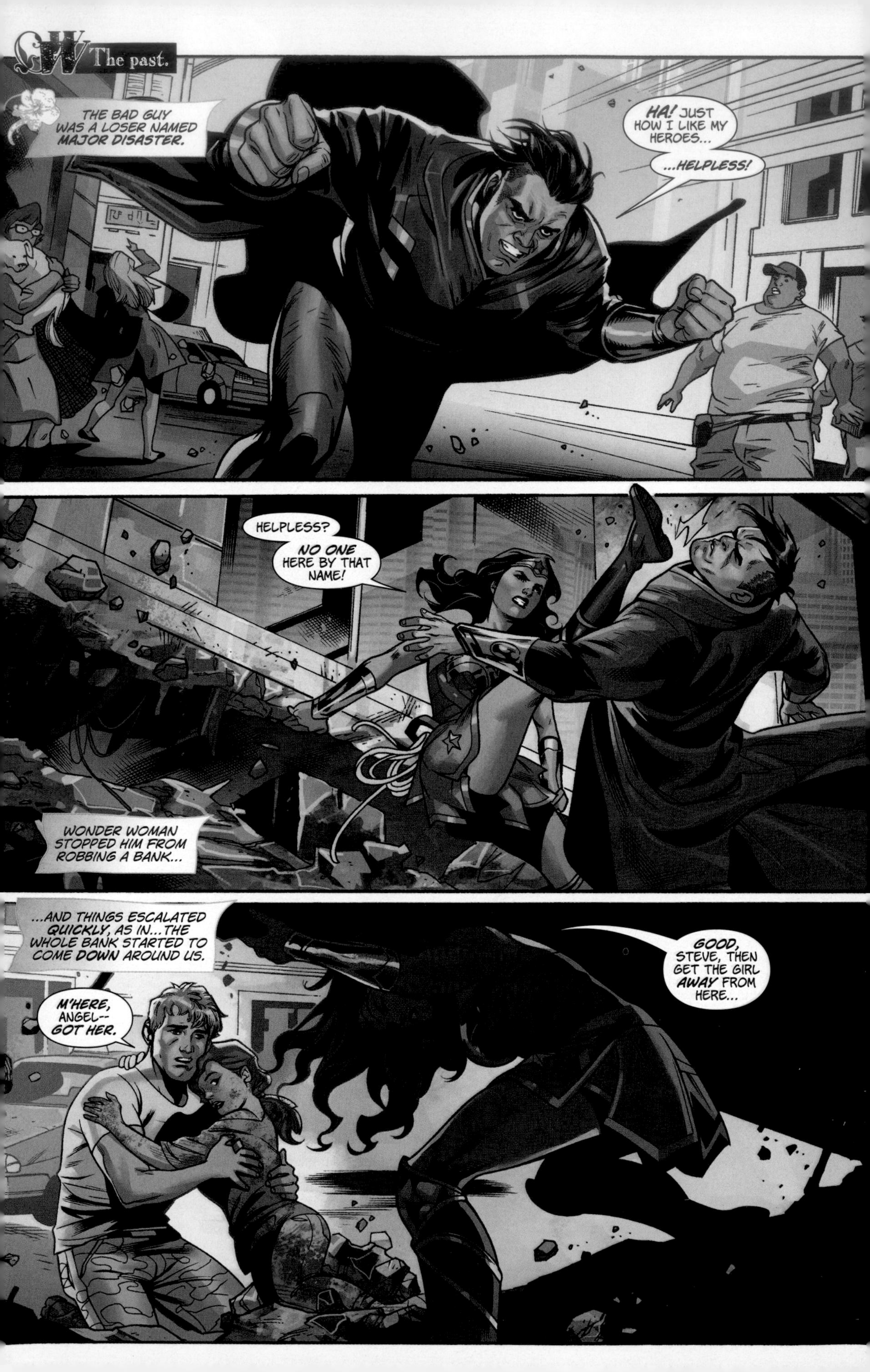

The past.
THE BAD GUY WAS A LOSER NAMED MAJOR DISASTER.
HA! JUST HOW I LIKE MY HEROES...
...HELPLESS!
HELPLESS? NO ONE HERE BY THAT NAME!
WONDER WOMAN STOPPED HIM FROM ROBBING A BANK...
...AND THINGS ESCALATED QUICKLY, AS IN...THE WHOLE BANK STARTED TO COME DOWN AROUND US.
M'HERE, ANGEL-- GOT HER.
GOOD, STEVE, THEN GET THE GIRL AWAY FROM HERE...

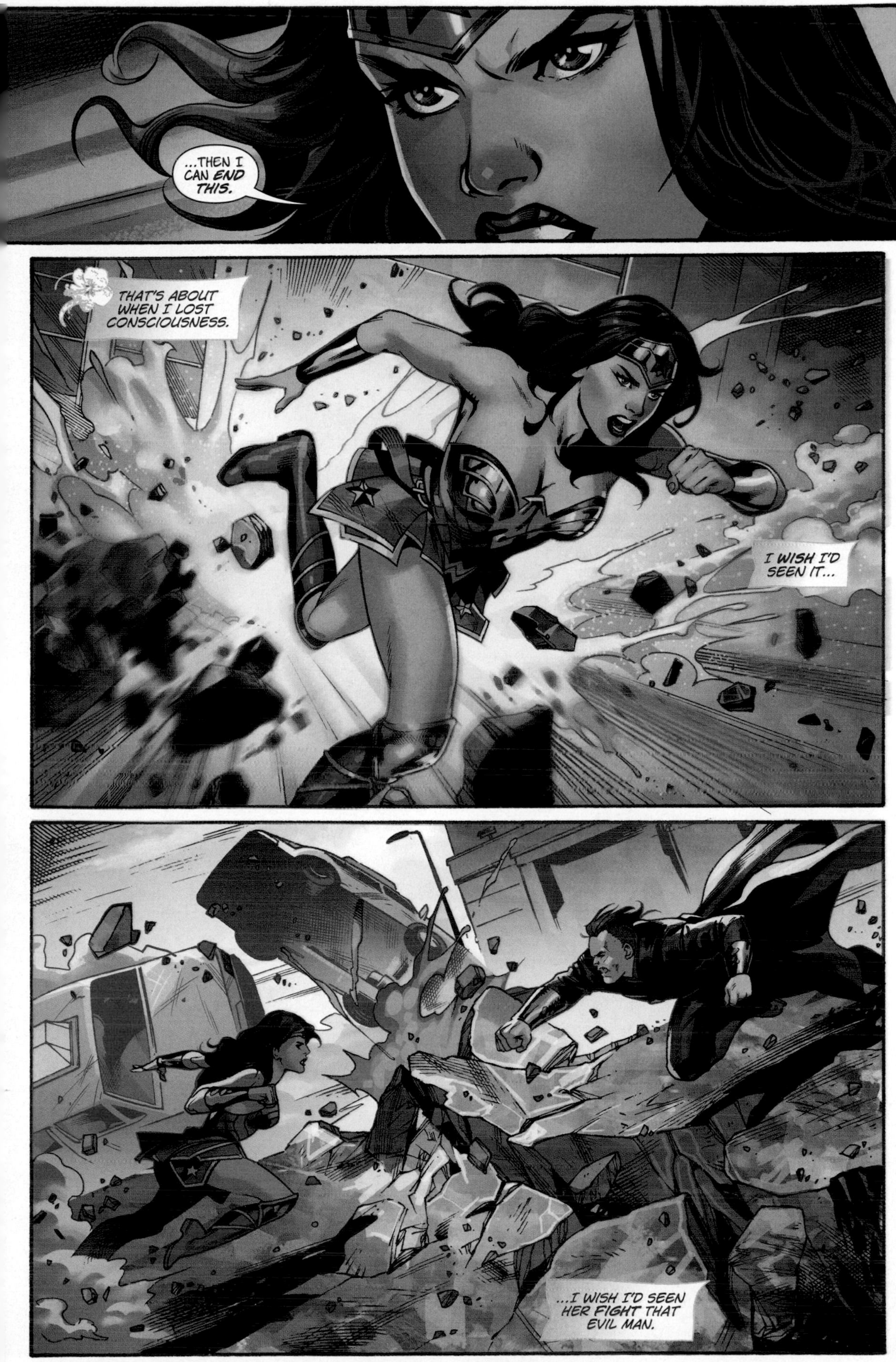
...THEN I CAN END THIS.
THAT'S ABOUT WHEN I LOST CONSCIOUSNESS.
I WISH I'D SEEN IT...
...I WISH I'D SEEN HER FIGHT THAT EVIL MAN.

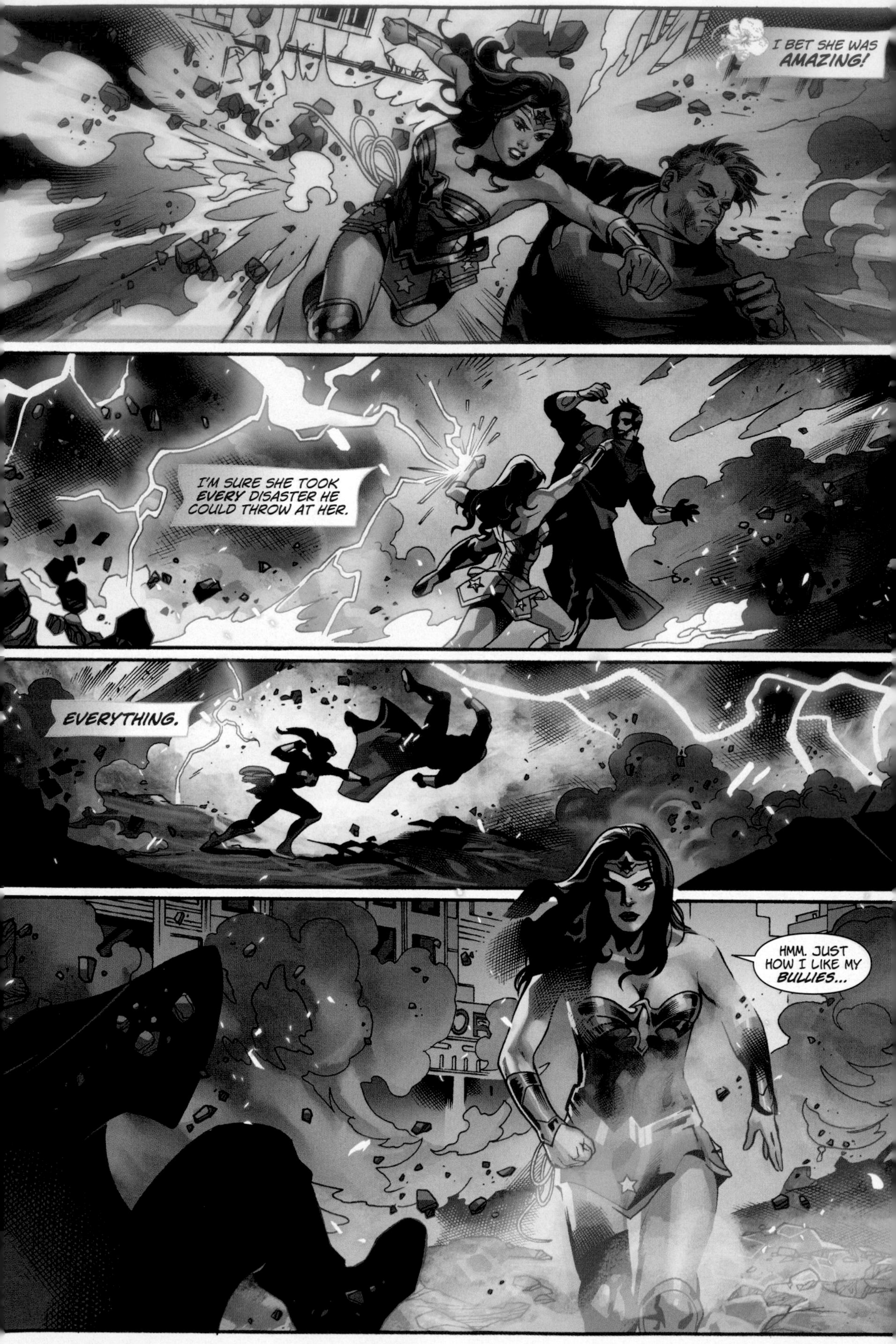
I BET SHE WAS AMAZING!
I'M SURE SHE TOOK EVERY DISASTER HE COULD THROW AT HER.
EVERYTHING.
HMM. JUST HOW I LIKE MY BULLIES...

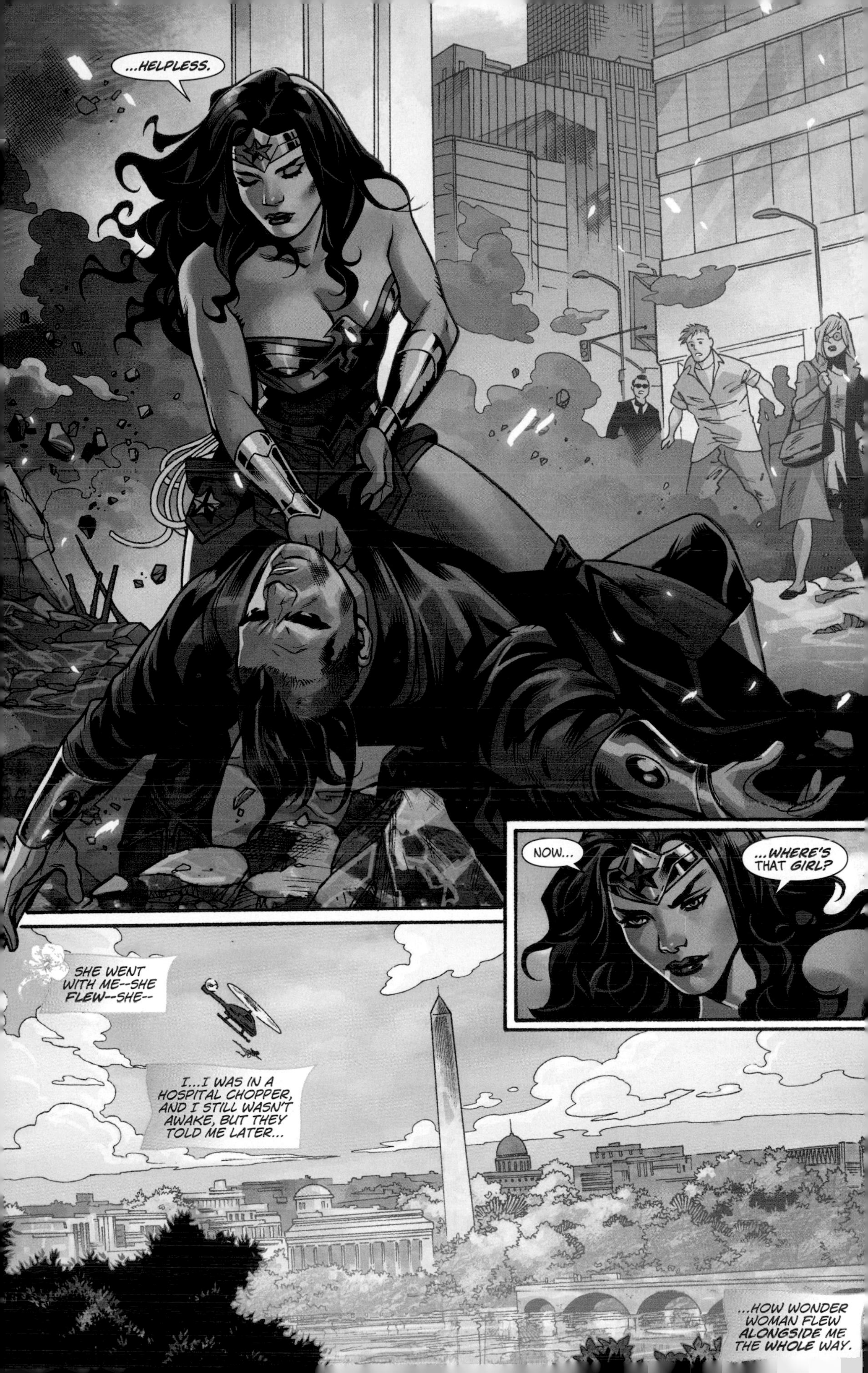
...HELPLESS.
NOW...
...WHERE'S THAT GIRL?
SHE WENT WITH ME--SHE FLEW--SHE--
I...I WAS IN A HOSPITAL CHOPPER, AND I STILL WASN'T AWAKE, BUT THEY TOLD ME LATER...
...HOW WONDER WOMAN FLEW ALONGSIDE ME THE WHOLE WAY.

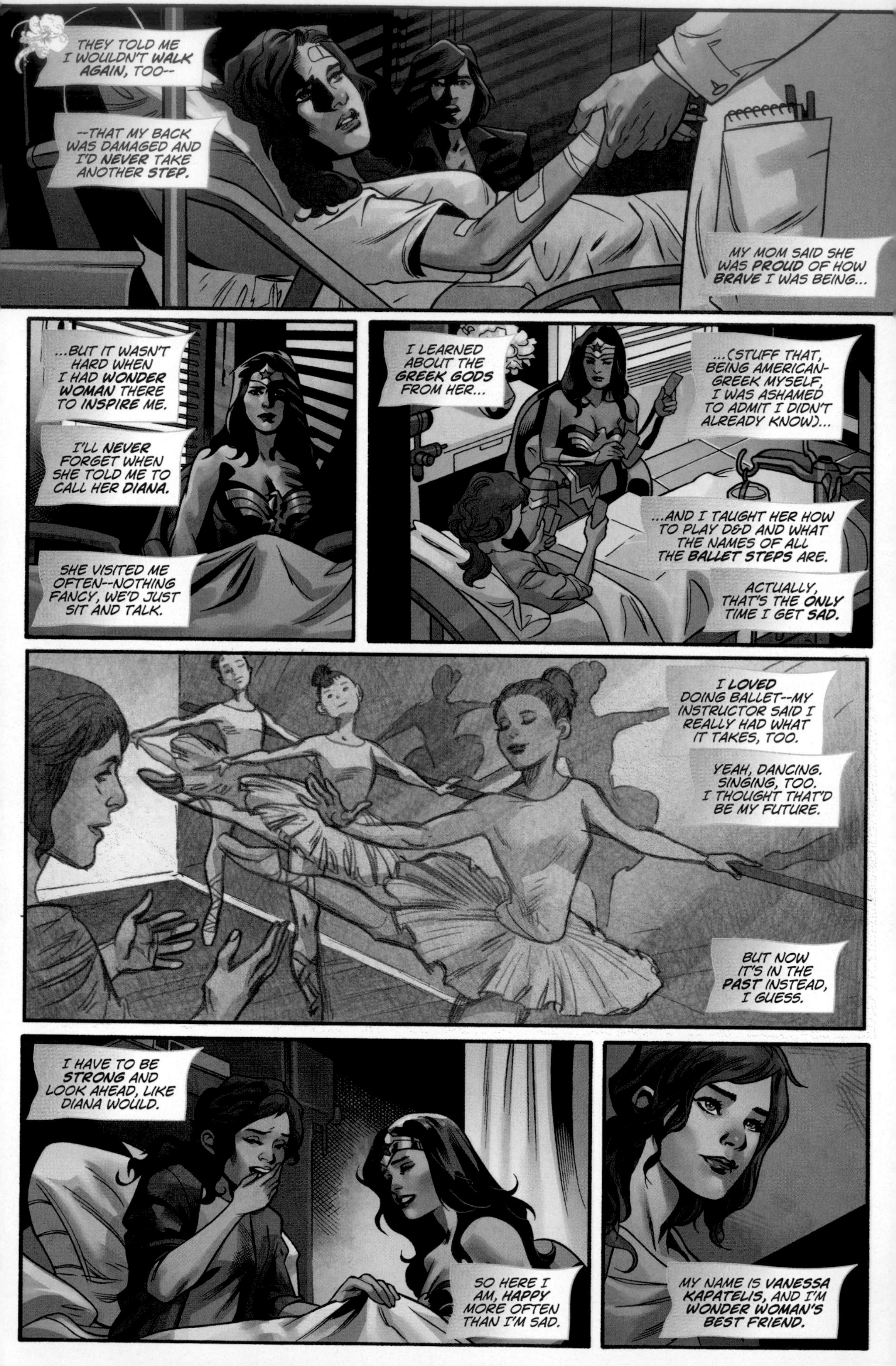
THEY TOLD ME I WOULDN'T WALK AGAIN, TOO--
--THAT MY BACK WAS DAMAGED AND I'D NEVER TAKE ANOTHER STEP.
MY MOM SAID SHE WAS PROUD OF HOW BRAVE I WAS BEING...
...BUT IT WASN'T HARD WHEN I HAD WONDER WOMAN THERE TO INSPIRE ME.
I'LL NEVER FORGET WHEN SHE TOLD ME TO CALL HER DIANA.
SHE VISITED ME OFTEN--NOTHING FANCY, WE'D JUST SIT AND TALK.
I LEARNED ABOUT THE GREEK GODS FROM HER...
...(STUFF THAT, BEING AMERICAN-GREEK MYSELF, I WAS ASHAMED TO ADMIT I DIDN'T ALREADY KNOW)...
...AND I TAUGHT HER HOW TO PLAY D&D AND WHAT THE NAMES OF ALL THE BALLET STEPS ARE.
ACTUALLY, THAT'S THE ONLY TIME I GET SAD.
I LOVED DOING BALLET--MY INSTRUCTOR SAID I REALLY HAD WHAT IT TAKES, TOO.
YEAH, DANCING. SINGING, TOO. I THOUGHT THAT'D BE MY FUTURE.
BUT NOW IT'S IN THE PAST INSTEAD, I GUESS.
I HAVE TO BE STRONG AND LOOK AHEAD, LIKE DIANA WOULD.
SO HERE I AM, HAPPY MORE OFTEN THAN I'M SAD.
MY NAME IS VANESSA KAPATELIS, AND I'M WONDER WOMAN'S BEST FRIEND.

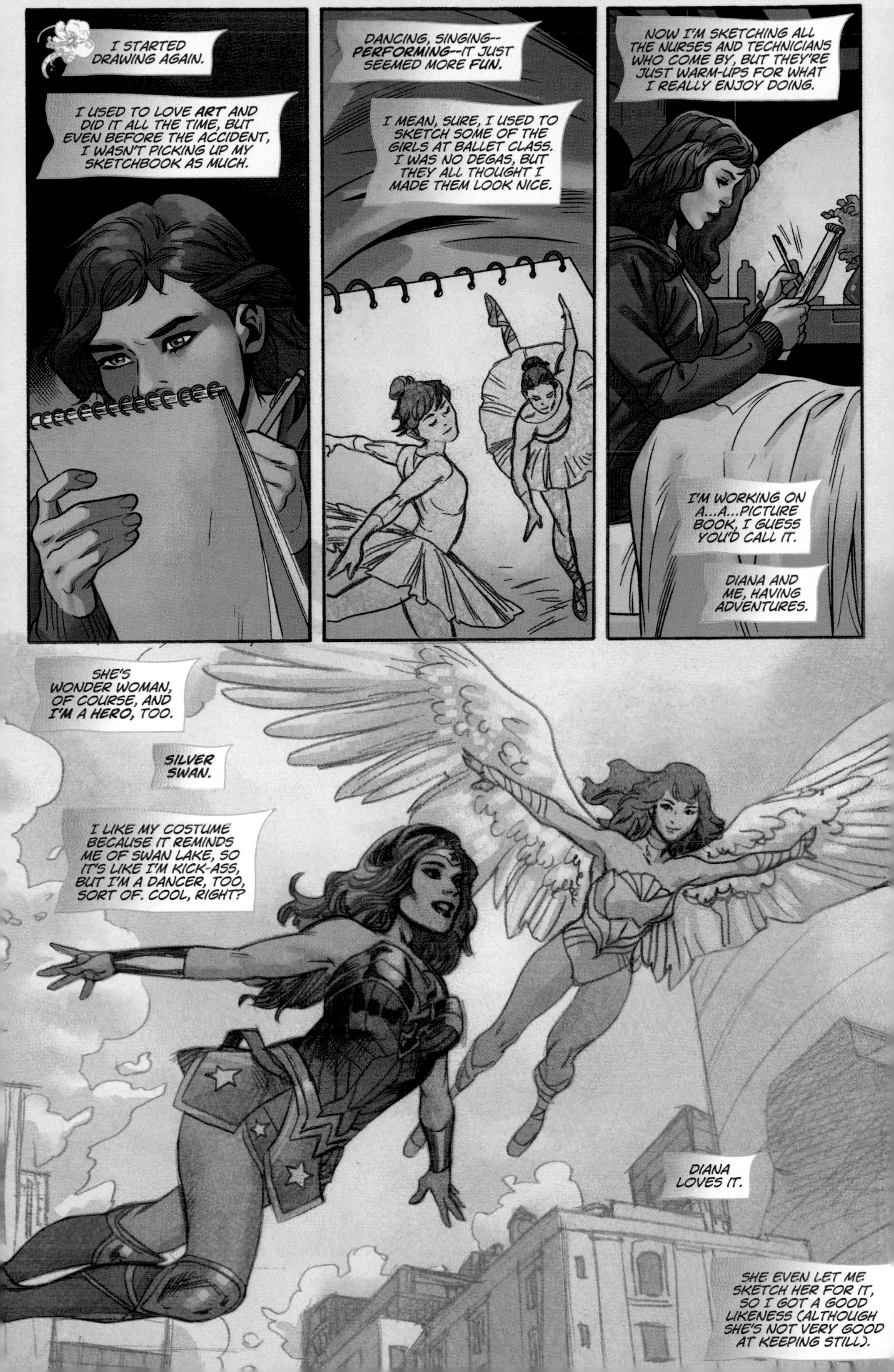
I STARTED DRAWING AGAIN.
I USED TO LOVE **ART** AND DID IT ALL THE TIME, BUT EVEN BEFORE THE ACCIDENT, I WASN'T PICKING UP MY SKETCHBOOK AS MUCH.
DANCING, SINGING-- **PERFORMING**--IT JUST SEEMED MORE **FUN**.
I MEAN, SURE, I USED TO SKETCH SOME OF THE GIRLS AT BALLET CLASS. I WAS NO DEGAS, BUT THEY ALL THOUGHT I MADE THEM LOOK NICE.
NOW I'M SKETCHING ALL THE NURSES AND TECHNICIANS WHO COME BY, BUT THEY'RE JUST WARM-UPS FOR WHAT I REALLY ENJOY DOING.
I'M WORKING ON A...A...PICTURE BOOK, I GUESS YOU'D CALL IT.
DIANA AND ME, HAVING ADVENTURES.
SHE'S WONDER WOMAN, OF COURSE, AND **I'M A HERO,** TOO.
SILVER SWAN.
I LIKE MY COSTUME BECAUSE IT REMINDS ME OF SWAN LAKE, SO IT'S LIKE I'M KICK-ASS, BUT I'M A DANCER, TOO, SORT OF. COOL, RIGHT?
DIANA LOVES IT.
SHE EVEN LET ME SKETCH HER FOR IT, SO I GOT A GOOD LIKENESS (ALTHOUGH SHE'S NOT VERY GOOD AT KEEPING STILL).

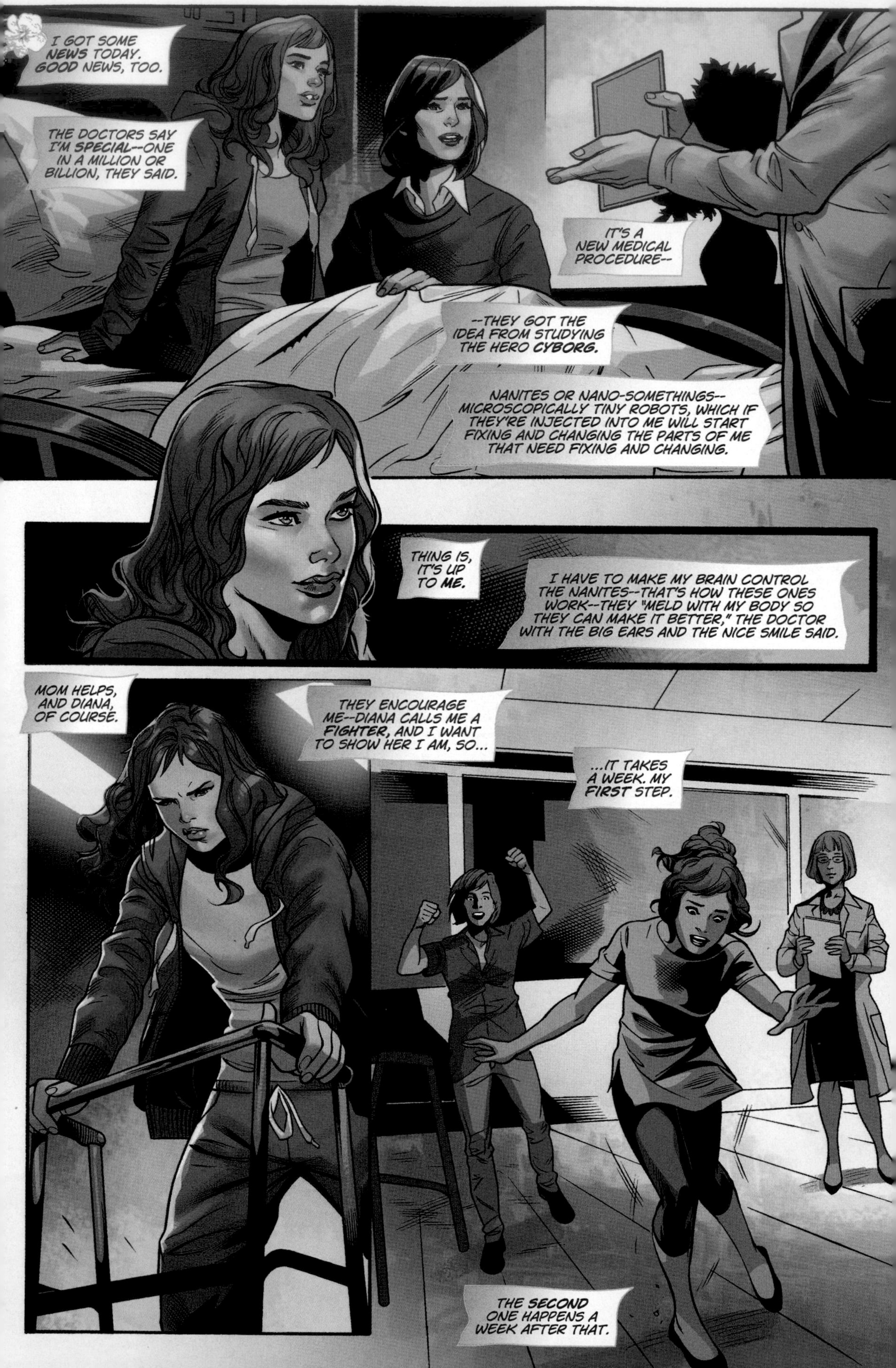
I GOT SOME NEWS TODAY. GOOD NEWS, TOO.
THE DOCTORS SAY I'M SPECIAL--ONE IN A MILLION OR BILLION, THEY SAID.
IT'S A NEW MEDICAL PROCEDURE--
--THEY GOT THE IDEA FROM STUDYING THE HERO CYBORG.
NANITES OR NANO-SOMETHINGS--MICROSCOPICALLY TINY ROBOTS, WHICH IF THEY'RE INJECTED INTO ME WILL START FIXING AND CHANGING THE PARTS OF ME THAT NEED FIXING AND CHANGING.
THING IS, IT'S UP TO ME.
I HAVE TO MAKE MY BRAIN CONTROL THE NANITES--THAT'S HOW THESE ONES WORK--THEY "MELD WITH MY BODY SO THEY CAN MAKE IT BETTER," THE DOCTOR WITH THE BIG EARS AND THE NICE SMILE SAID.
MOM HELPS, AND DIANA, OF COURSE.
THEY ENCOURAGE ME--DIANA CALLS ME A FIGHTER, AND I WANT TO SHOW HER I AM, SO...
...IT TAKES A WEEK. MY FIRST STEP.
THE SECOND ONE HAPPENS A WEEK AFTER THAT.

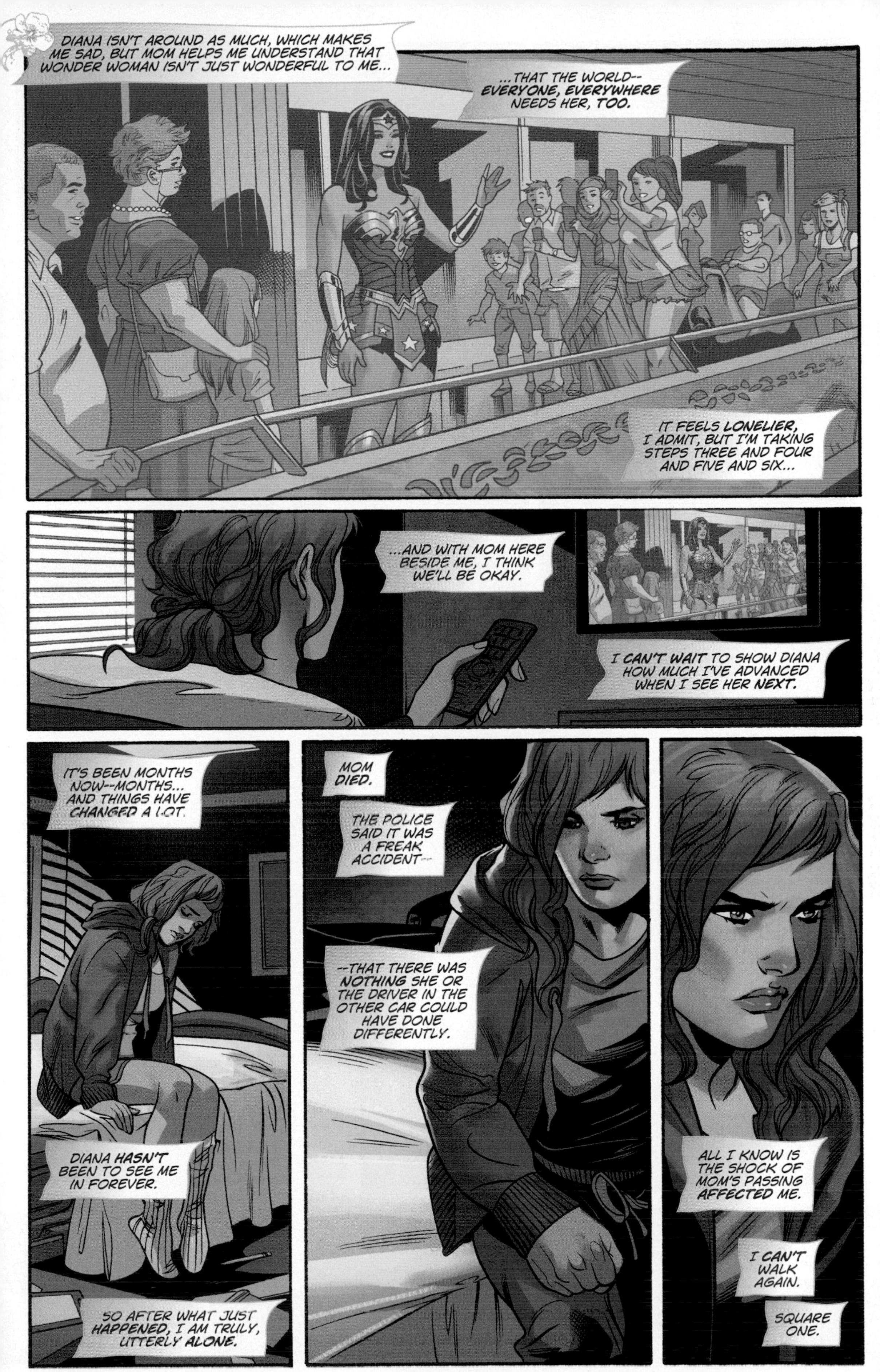
DIANA ISN'T AROUND AS MUCH, WHICH MAKES ME SAD, BUT MOM HELPS ME UNDERSTAND THAT WONDER WOMAN ISN'T JUST WONDERFUL TO ME...
...THAT THE WORLD-- EVERYONE, EVERYWHERE NEEDS HER, TOO.
IT FEELS LONELIER, I ADMIT, BUT I'M TAKING STEPS THREE AND FOUR AND FIVE AND SIX...
...AND WITH MOM HERE BESIDE ME, I THINK WE'LL BE OKAY.
I CAN'T WAIT TO SHOW DIANA HOW MUCH I'VE ADVANCED WHEN I SEE HER NEXT.
IT'S BEEN MONTHS NOW--MONTHS... AND THINGS HAVE CHANGED A LOT.
DIANA HASN'T BEEN TO SEE ME IN FOREVER.
SO AFTER WHAT JUST HAPPENED, I AM TRULY, UTTERLY ALONE.
MOM DIED.
THE POLICE SAID IT WAS A FREAK ACCIDENT--
--THAT THERE WAS NOTHING SHE OR THE DRIVER IN THE OTHER CAR COULD HAVE DONE DIFFERENTLY.
ALL I KNOW IS THE SHOCK OF MOM'S PASSING AFFECTED ME.
I CAN'T WALK AGAIN.
SQUARE ONE.

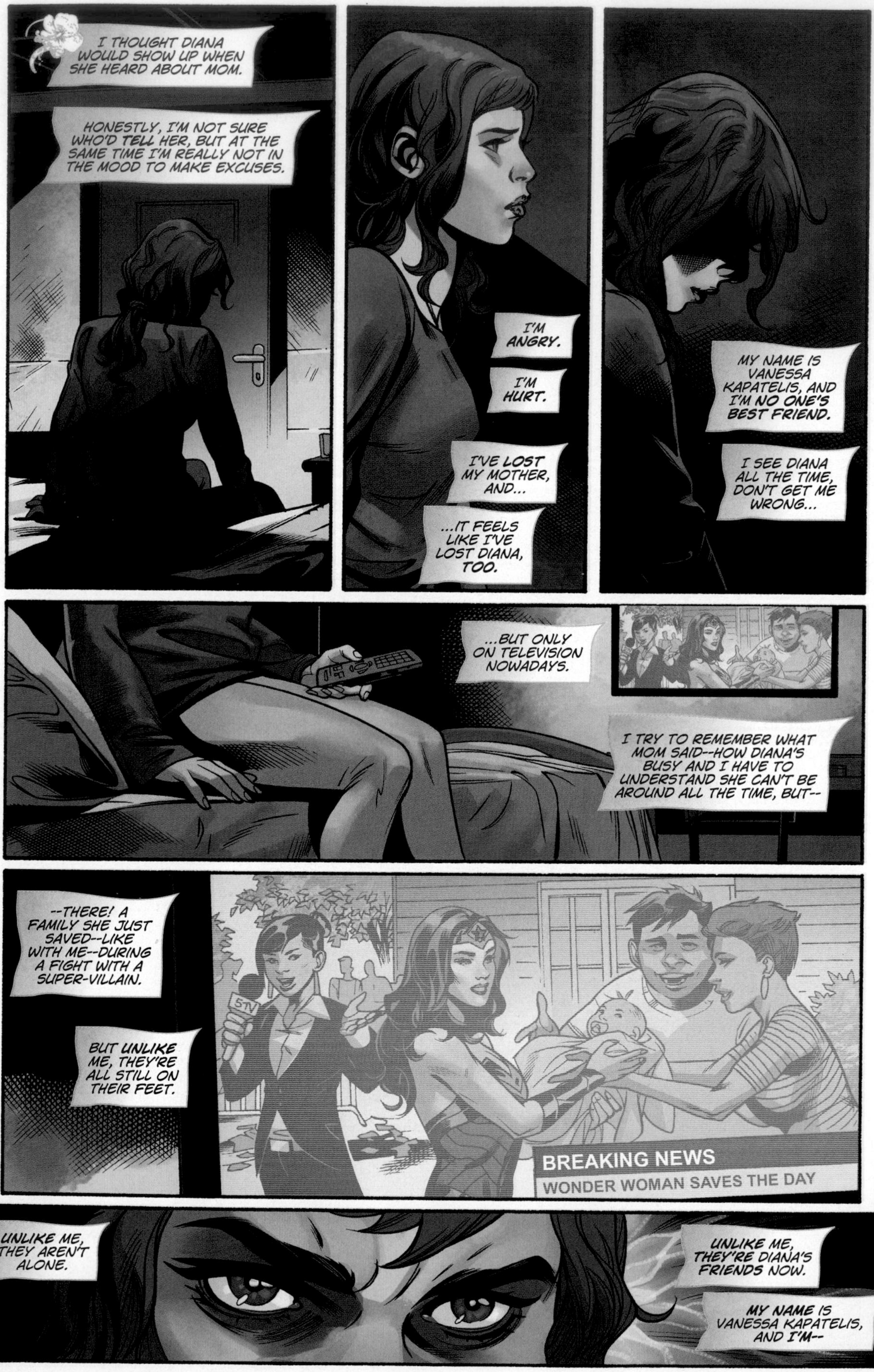
I THOUGHT DIANA WOULD SHOW UP WHEN SHE HEARD ABOUT MOM.
HONESTLY, I'M NOT SURE WHO'D TELL HER, BUT AT THE SAME TIME I'M REALLY NOT IN THE MOOD TO MAKE EXCUSES.
I'M ANGRY.
I'M HURT.
I'VE LOST MY MOTHER, AND...
...IT FEELS LIKE I'VE LOST DIANA, TOO.
MY NAME IS VANESSA KAPATELIS, AND I'M NO ONE'S BEST FRIEND.
I SEE DIANA ALL THE TIME, DON'T GET ME WRONG...
...BUT ONLY ON TELEVISION NOWADAYS.
I TRY TO REMEMBER WHAT MOM SAID--HOW DIANA'S BUSY AND I HAVE TO UNDERSTAND SHE CAN'T BE AROUND ALL THE TIME, BUT--
--THERE! A FAMILY SHE JUST SAVED--LIKE WITH ME--DURING A FIGHT WITH A SUPER-VILLAIN.
BUT UNLIKE ME, THEY'RE ALL STILL ON THEIR FEET.
5TV
BREAKING NEWS
WONDER WOMAN SAVES THE DAY
UNLIKE ME, THEY AREN'T ALONE.
UNLIKE ME, THEY'RE DIANA'S FRIENDS NOW.
MY NAME IS VANESSA KAPATELIS, AND I'M--

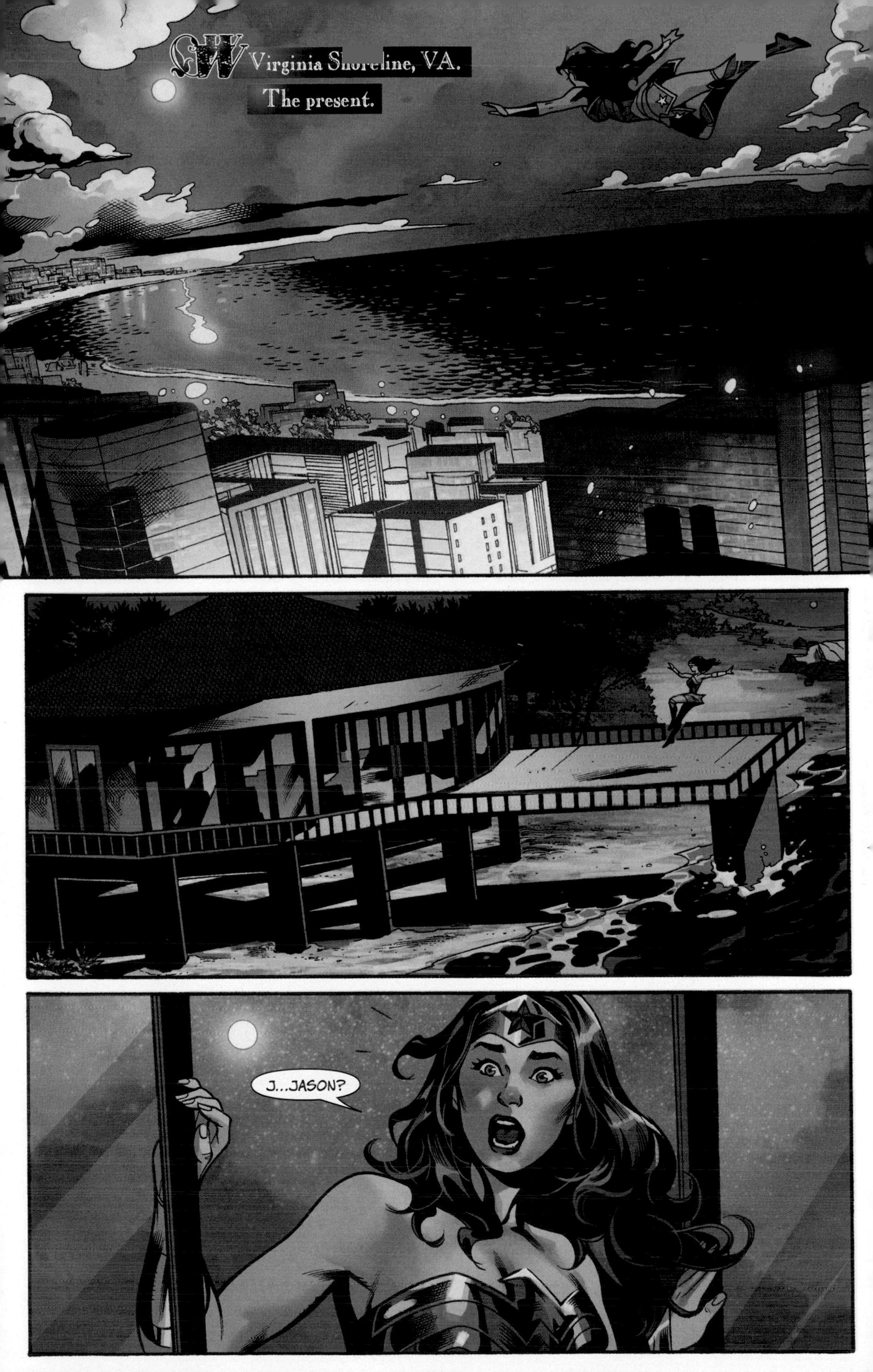
Virginia Shoreline, VA.
The present.
J...JASON?

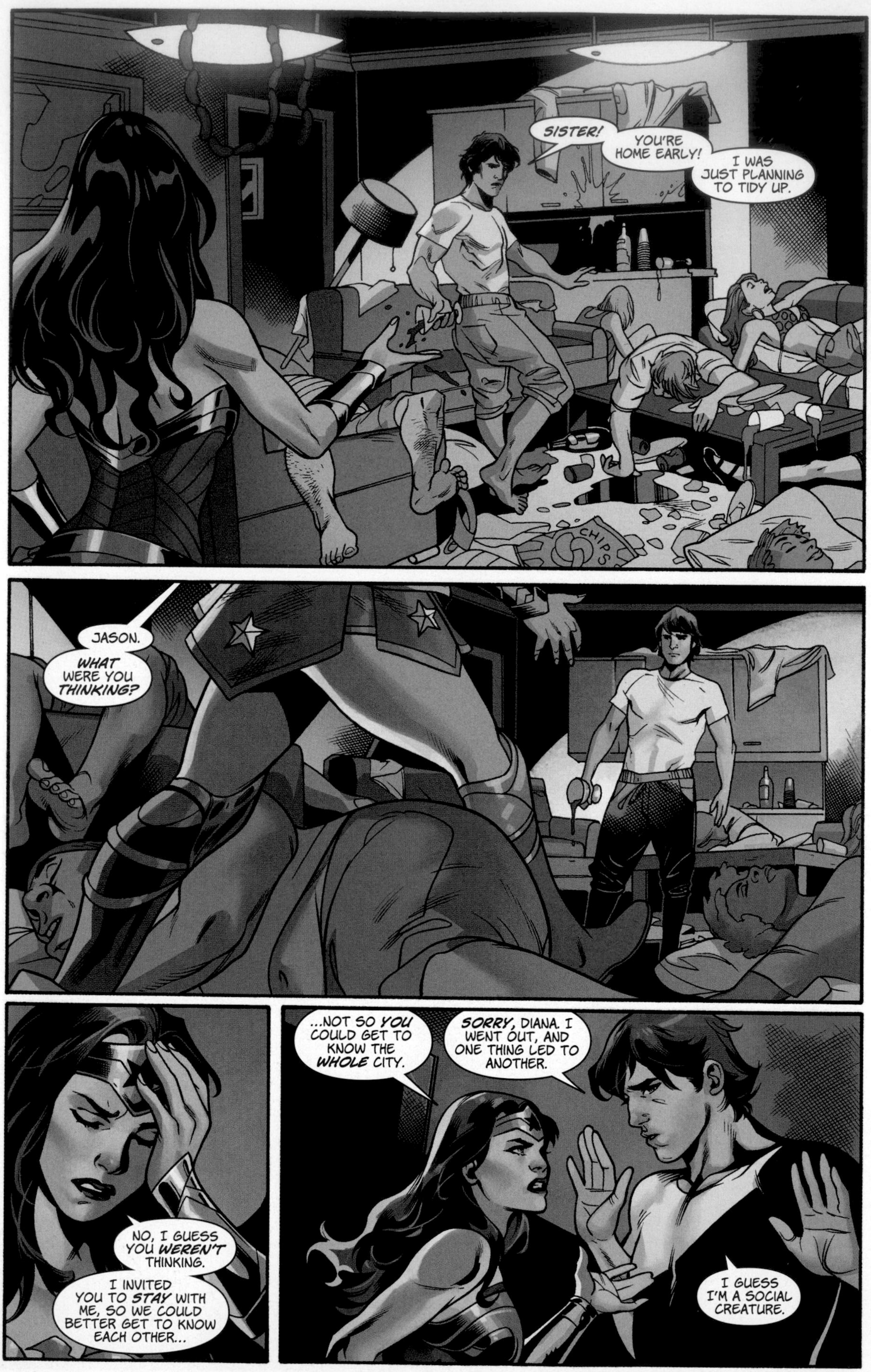
SISTER!
YOU'RE HOME EARLY!
I WAS JUST PLANNING TO TIDY UP.
CHIPS
JASON. WHAT WERE YOU THINKING?
NO, I GUESS YOU WEREN'T THINKING.
I INVITED YOU TO STAY WITH ME, SO WE COULD BETTER GET TO KNOW EACH OTHER...
...NOT SO YOU COULD GET TO KNOW THE WHOLE CITY.
SORRY, DIANA. I WENT OUT, AND ONE THING LED TO ANOTHER.
I GUESS I'M A SOCIAL CREATURE.

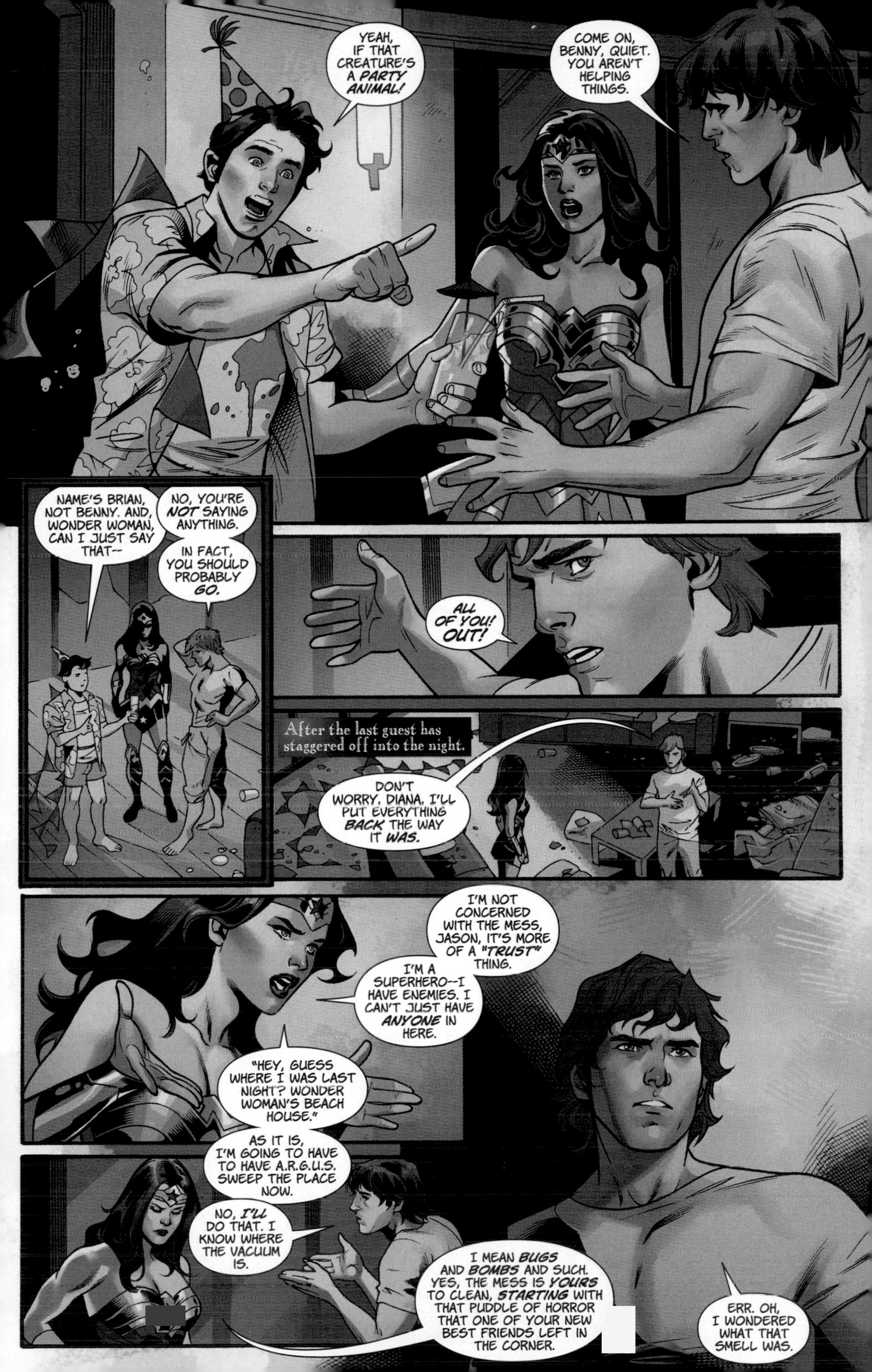
YEAH, IF THAT CREATURE'S A PARTY ANIMAL!
COME ON, BENNY, QUIET. YOU AREN'T HELPING THINGS.
NAME'S BRIAN, NOT BENNY. AND, WONDER WOMAN, CAN I JUST SAY THAT--
NO, YOU'RE NOT SAYING ANYTHING.
IN FACT, YOU SHOULD PROBABLY GO.
ALL OF YOU! OUT!
After the last guest has staggered off into the night.
DON'T WORRY, DIANA. I'LL PUT EVERYTHING BACK THE WAY IT WAS.
I'M NOT CONCERNED WITH THE MESS, JASON, IT'S MORE OF A "TRUST" THING.
I'M A SUPERHERO--I HAVE ENEMIES. I CAN'T JUST HAVE ANYONE IN HERE.
"HEY, GUESS WHERE I WAS LAST NIGHT? WONDER WOMAN'S BEACH HOUSE."
AS IT IS, I'M GOING TO HAVE TO HAVE A.R.G.U.S. SWEEP THE PLACE NOW.
NO, I'LL DO THAT. I KNOW WHERE THE VACUUM IS.
I MEAN BUGS AND BOMBS AND SUCH. YES, THE MESS IS YOURS TO CLEAN, STARTING WITH THAT PUDDLE OF HORROR THAT ONE OF YOUR NEW BEST FRIENDS LEFT IN THE CORNER.
ERR. OH, I WONDERED WHAT THAT SMELL WAS.

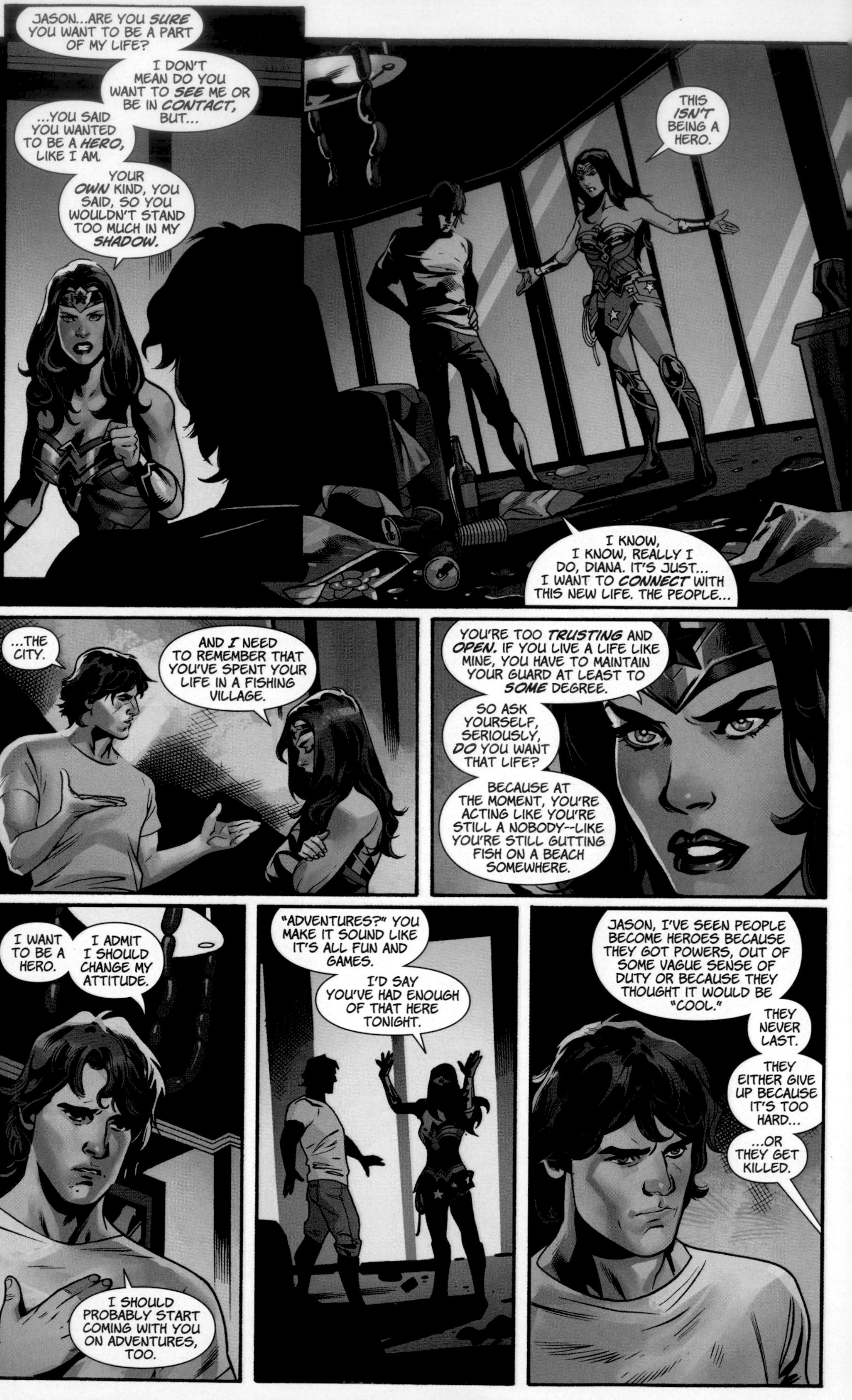

JASON...ARE YOU SURE YOU WANT TO BE A PART OF MY LIFE?
I DON'T MEAN DO YOU WANT TO SEE ME OR BE IN CONTACT, BUT...
...YOU SAID YOU WANTED TO BE A HERO, LIKE I AM.
YOUR OWN KIND, YOU SAID, SO YOU WOULDN'T STAND TOO MUCH IN MY SHADOW.
THIS ISN'T BEING A HERO.
I KNOW, I KNOW, REALLY I DO, DIANA. IT'S JUST... I WANT TO CONNECT WITH THIS NEW LIFE. THE PEOPLE...
...THE CITY.
AND I NEED TO REMEMBER THAT YOU'VE SPENT YOUR LIFE IN A FISHING VILLAGE.
YOU'RE TOO TRUSTING AND OPEN. IF YOU LIVE A LIFE LIKE MINE, YOU HAVE TO MAINTAIN YOUR GUARD AT LEAST TO SOME DEGREE.
SO ASK YOURSELF, SERIOUSLY, DO YOU WANT THAT LIFE?
BECAUSE AT THE MOMENT, YOU'RE ACTING LIKE YOU'RE STILL A NOBODY--LIKE YOU'RE STILL GUTTING FISH ON A BEACH SOMEWHERE.
I WANT TO BE A HERO.
I ADMIT I SHOULD CHANGE MY ATTITUDE.
I SHOULD PROBABLY START COMING WITH YOU ON ADVENTURES, TOO.
"ADVENTURES?" YOU MAKE IT SOUND LIKE IT'S ALL FUN AND GAMES.
I'D SAY YOU'VE HAD ENOUGH OF THAT HERE TONIGHT.
JASON, I'VE SEEN PEOPLE BECOME HEROES BECAUSE THEY GOT POWERS, OUT OF SOME VAGUE SENSE OF DUTY OR BECAUSE THEY THOUGHT IT WOULD BE "COOL."
THEY NEVER LAST.
THEY EITHER GIVE UP BECAUSE IT'S TOO HARD...
...OR THEY GET KILLED.

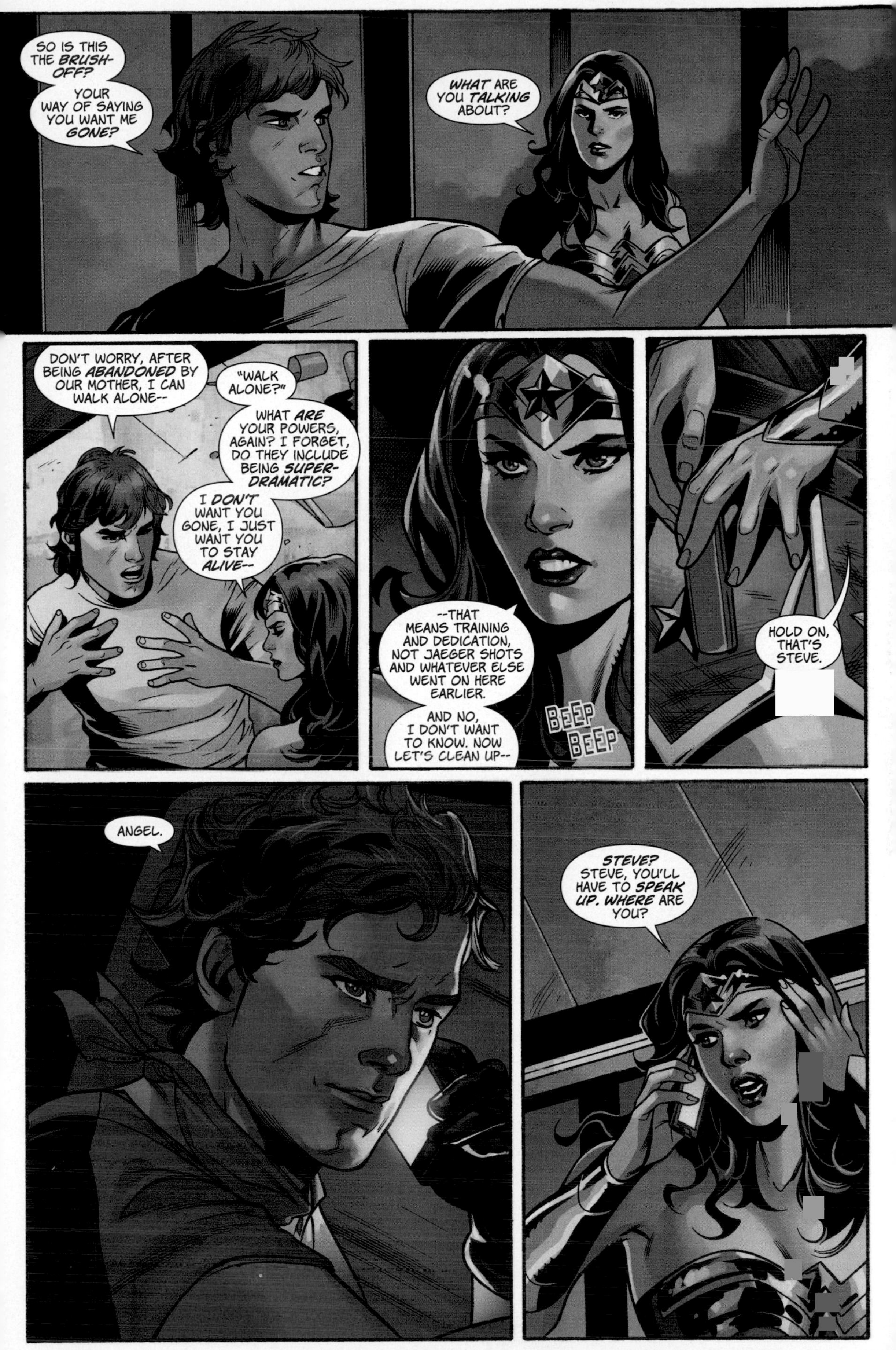
SO IS THIS THE BRUSH-OFF?
YOUR WAY OF SAYING YOU WANT ME GONE?
WHAT ARE YOU TALKING ABOUT?
DON'T WORRY, AFTER BEING ABANDONED BY OUR MOTHER, I CAN WALK ALONE--
"WALK ALONE?"
WHAT ARE YOUR POWERS, AGAIN? I FORGET, DO THEY INCLUDE BEING SUPER-DRAMATIC?
I DON'T WANT YOU GONE, I JUST WANT YOU TO STAY ALIVE--
--THAT MEANS TRAINING AND DEDICATION, NOT JAEGER SHOTS AND WHATEVER ELSE WENT ON HERE EARLIER.
AND NO, I DON'T WANT TO KNOW. NOW LET'S CLEAN UP--
BEEP BEEP
HOLD ON, THAT'S STEVE.
ANGEL.
STEVE? STEVE, YOU'LL HAVE TO SPEAK UP. WHERE ARE YOU?

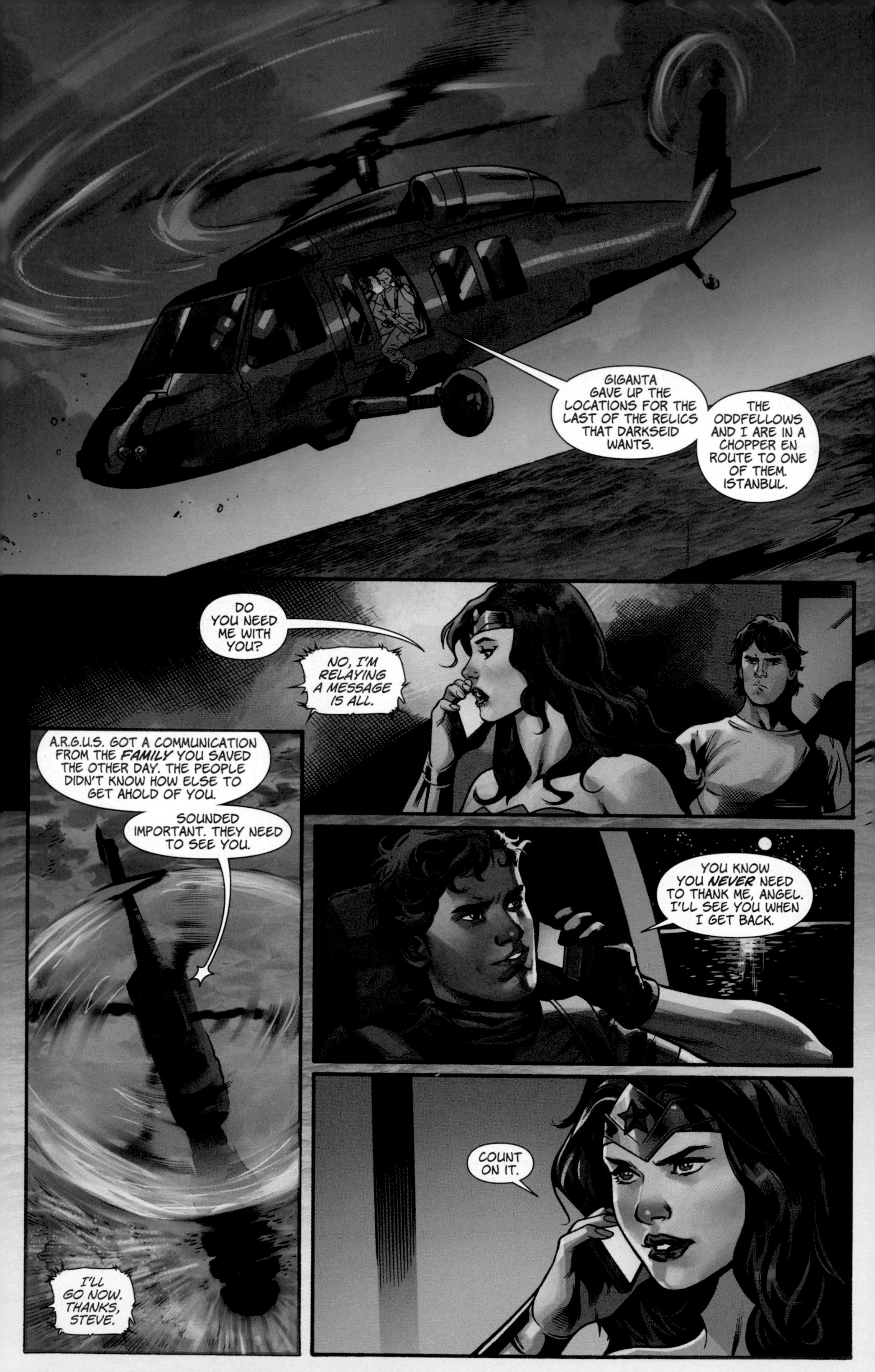
GIGANTA GAVE UP THE LOCATIONS FOR THE LAST OF THE RELICS THAT DARKSEID WANTS.
THE ODDFELLOWS AND I ARE IN A CHOPPER EN ROUTE TO ONE OF THEM. ISTANBUL.
DO YOU NEED ME WITH YOU?
NO, I'M RELAYING A MESSAGE IS ALL.
A.R.G.U.S. GOT A COMMUNICATION FROM THE FAMILY YOU SAVED THE OTHER DAY. THE PEOPLE DIDN'T KNOW HOW ELSE TO GET AHOLD OF YOU.
SOUNDED IMPORTANT. THEY NEED TO SEE YOU.
YOU KNOW YOU NEVER NEED TO THANK ME, ANGEL. I'LL SEE YOU WHEN I GET BACK.
COUNT ON IT.
I'LL GO NOW. THANKS, STEVE.

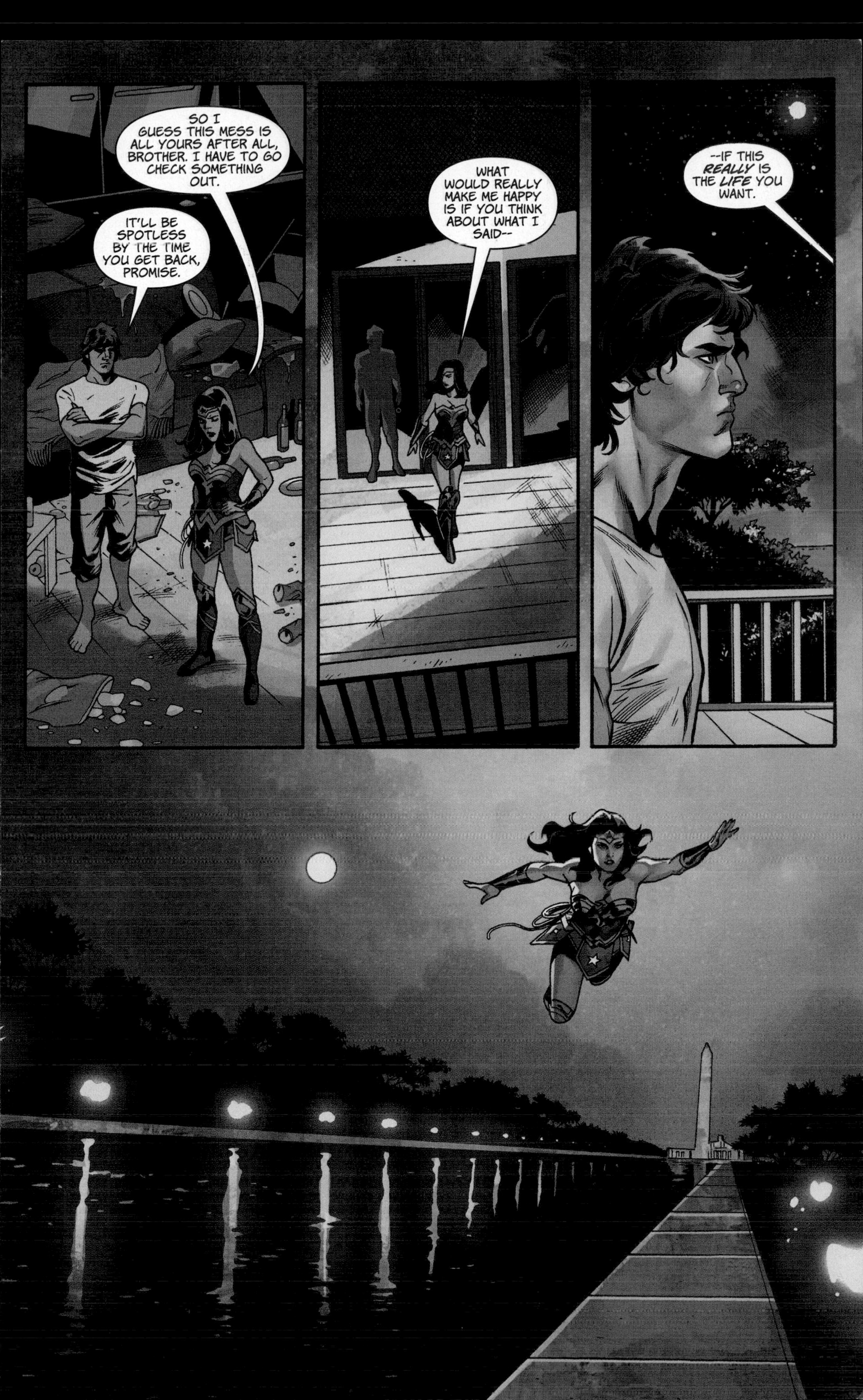
SO I GUESS THIS MESS IS ALL YOURS AFTER ALL, BROTHER. I HAVE TO GO CHECK SOMETHING OUT.
IT'LL BE SPOTLESS BY THE TIME YOU GET BACK, PROMISE.
WHAT WOULD REALLY MAKE ME HAPPY IS IF YOU THINK ABOUT WHAT I SAID--
--IF THIS REALLY IS THE LIFE YOU WANT.

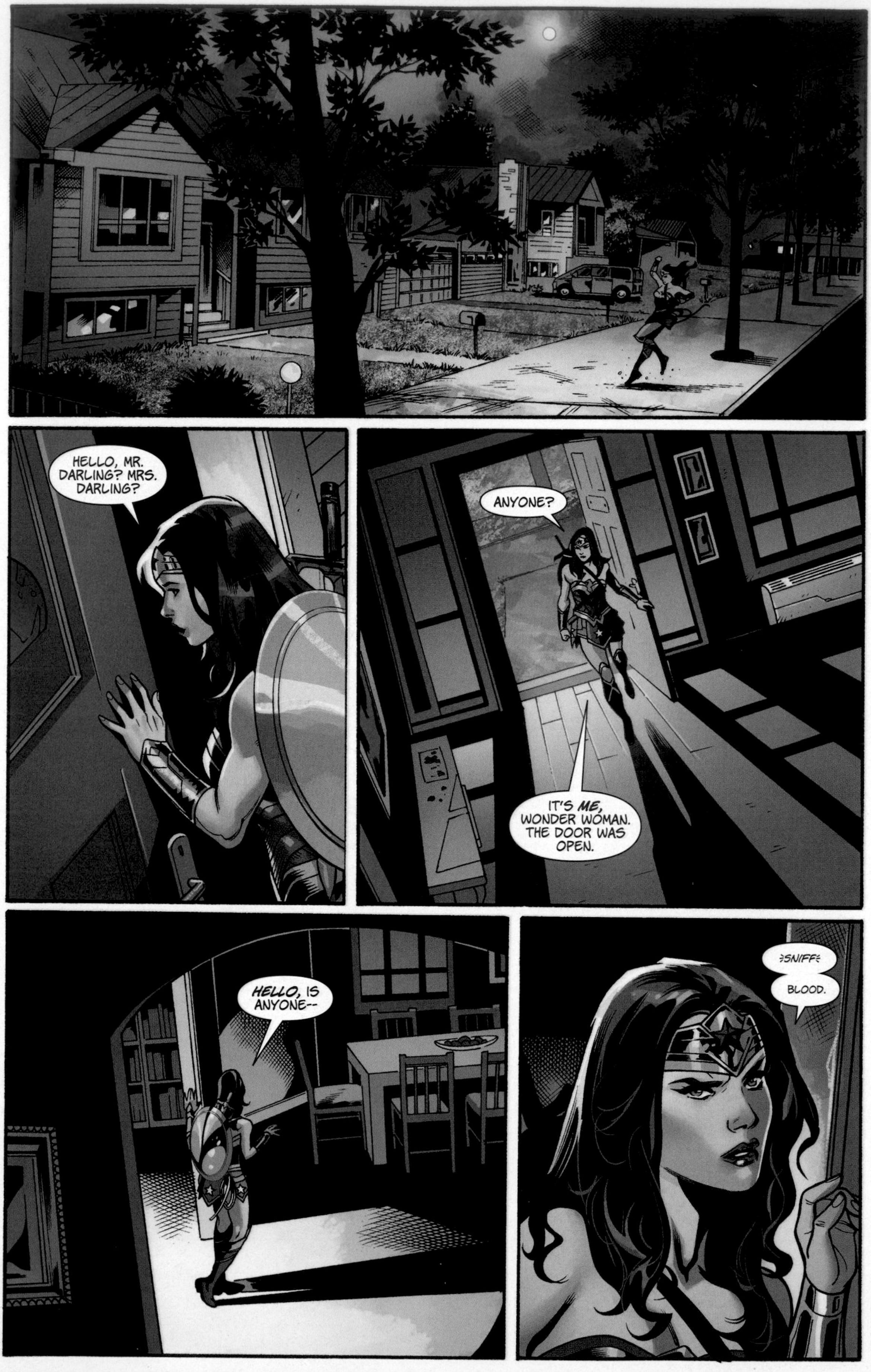
HELLO, MR. DARLING? MRS. DARLING?
ANYONE?
IT'S ME, WONDER WOMAN. THE DOOR WAS OPEN.
HELLO, IS ANYONE--
SNIFF
BLOOD.

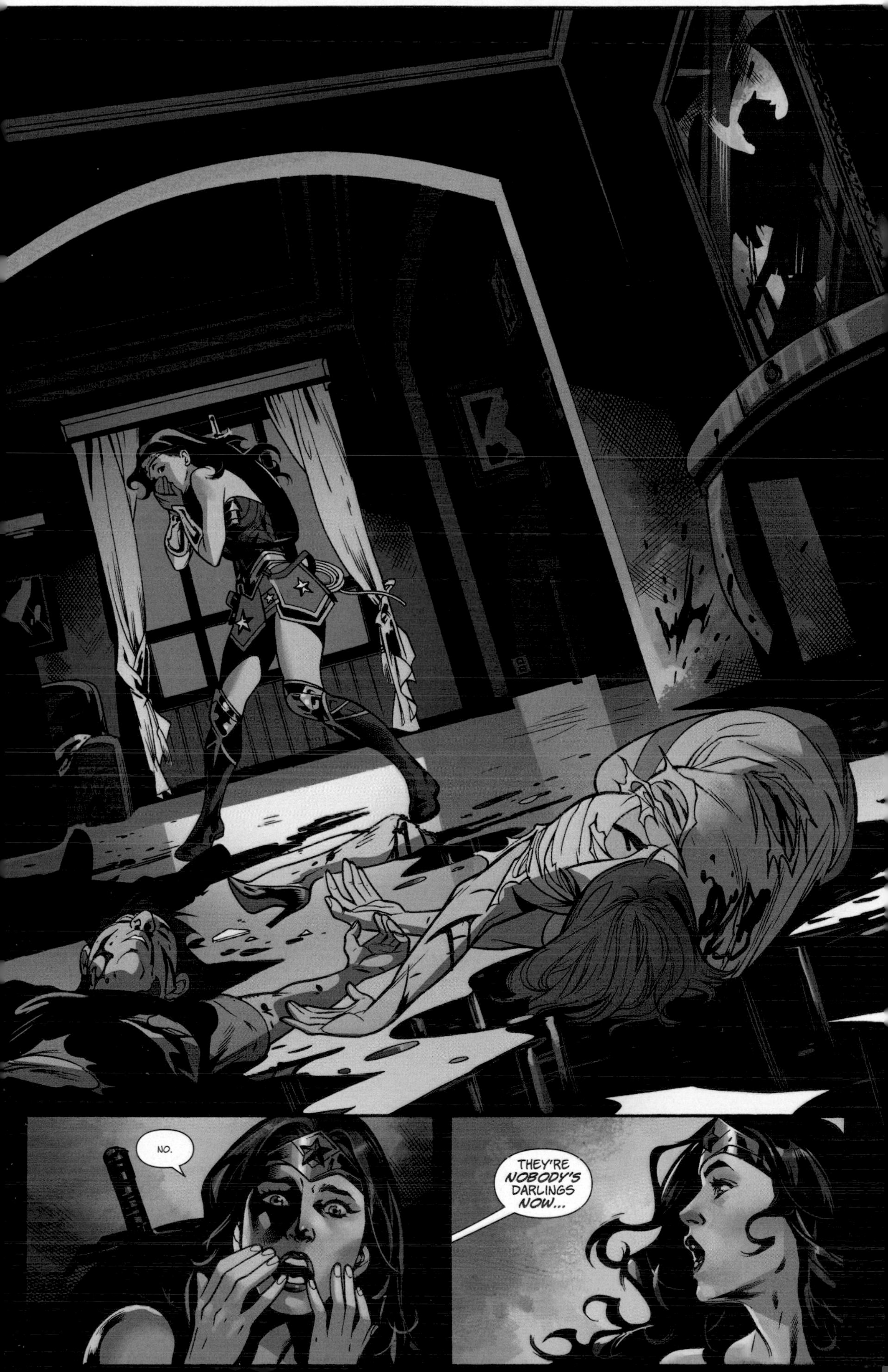
NO.
THEY'RE *NOBODY'S* DARLINGS *NOW...*

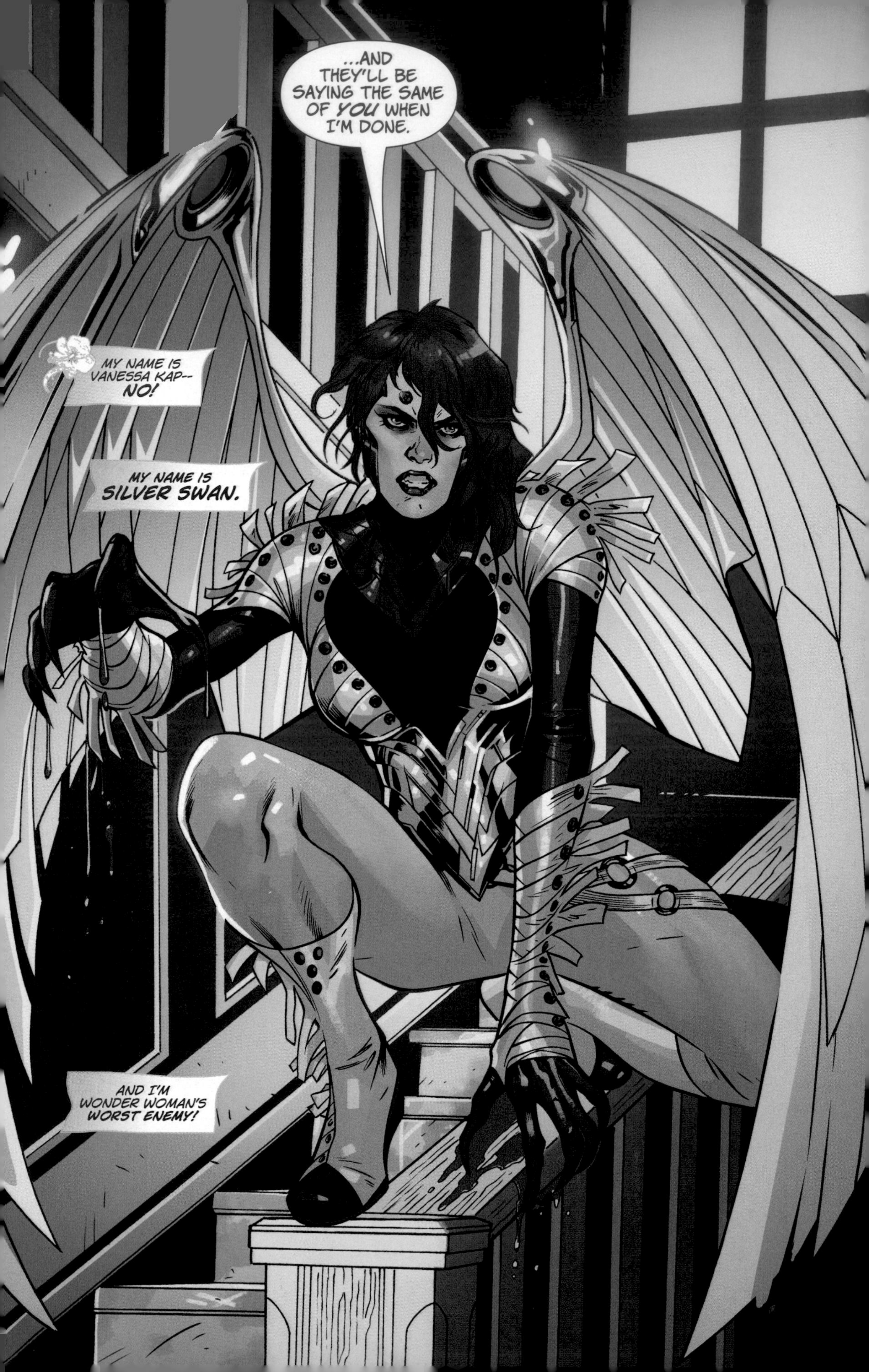
...AND THEY'LL BE SAYING THE SAME OF YOU WHEN I'M DONE.
MY NAME IS VANESSA KAP-- NO!
MY NAME IS SILVER SWAN.
AND I'M WONDER WOMAN'S WORST ENEMY!

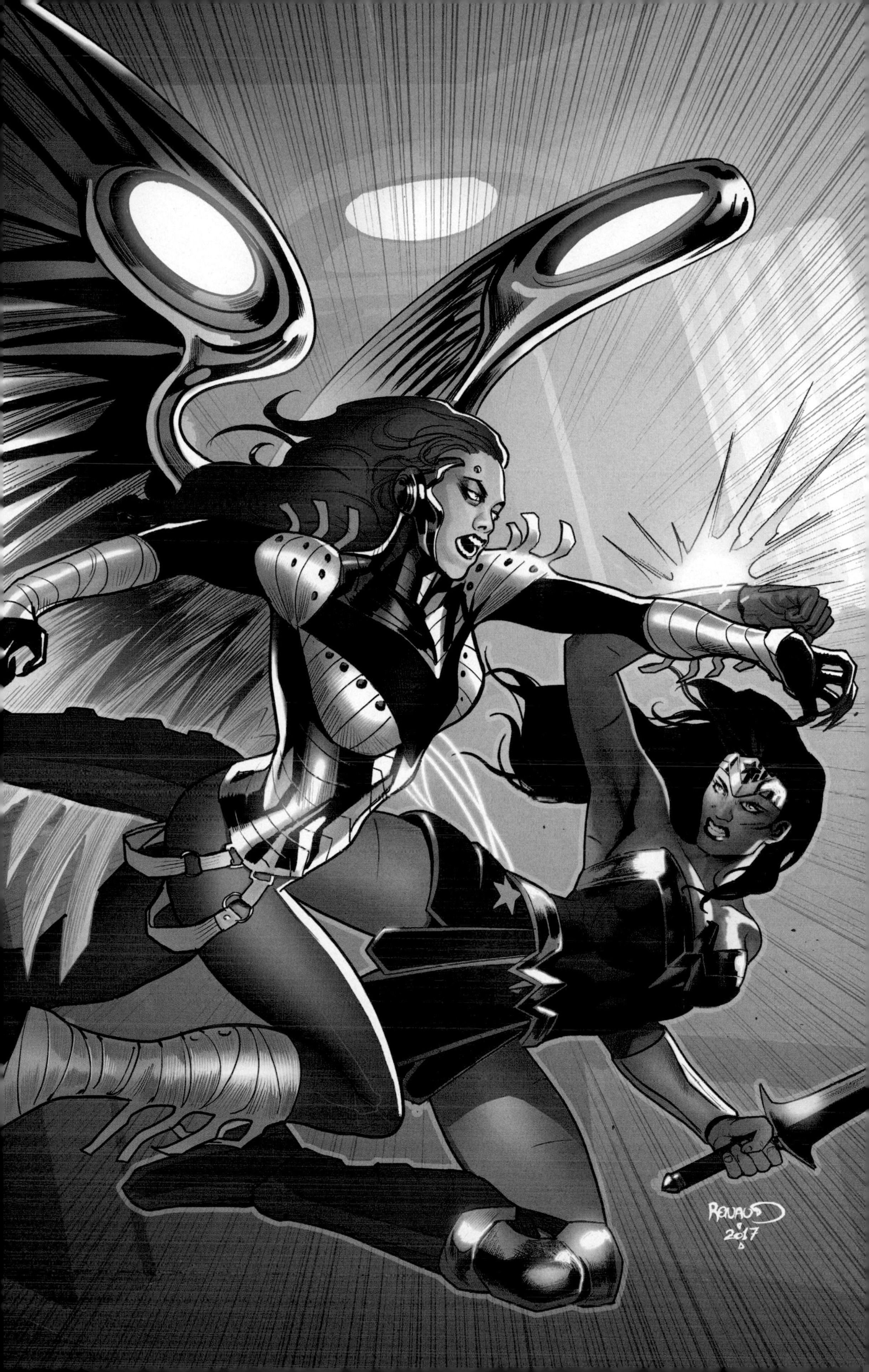

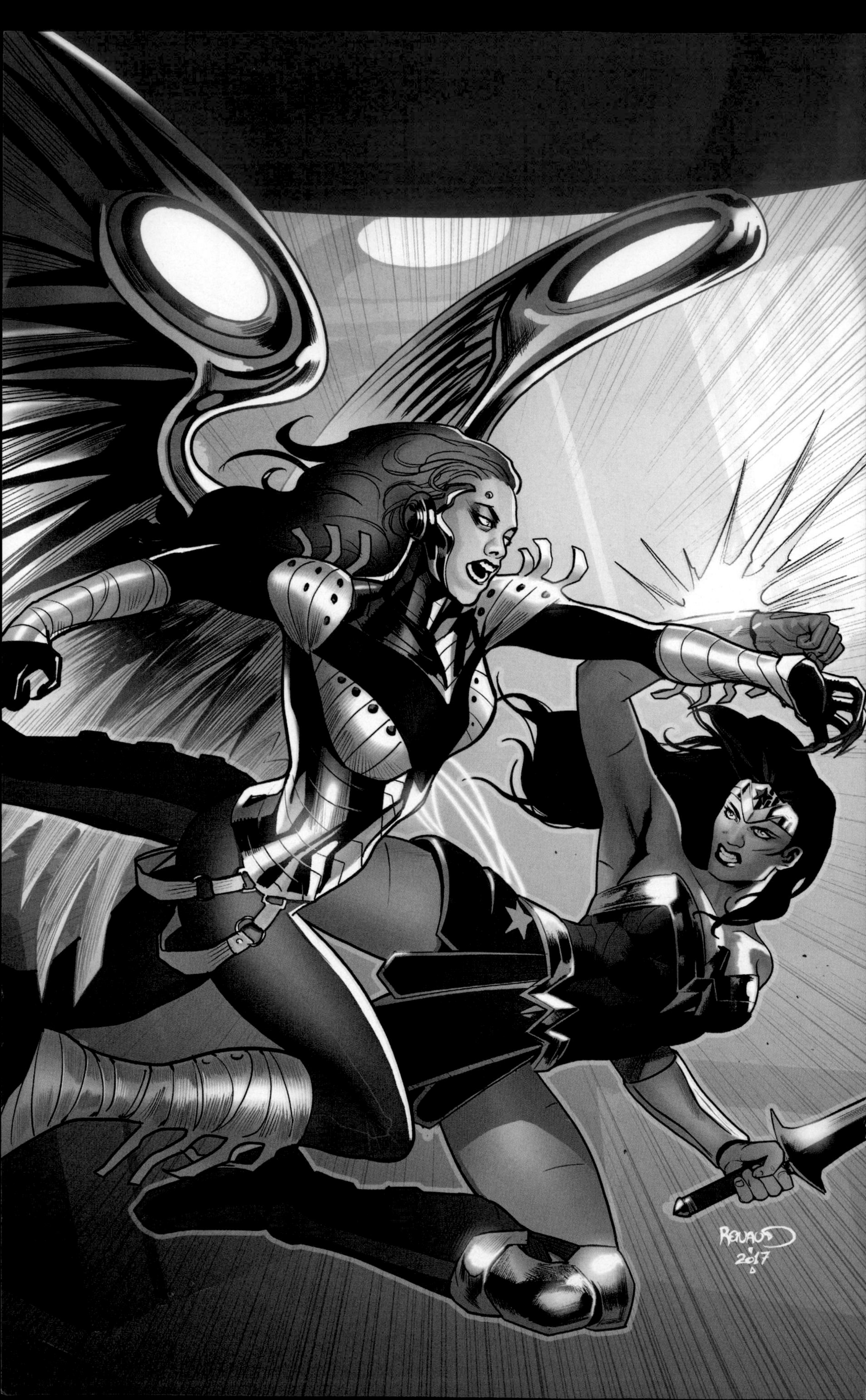

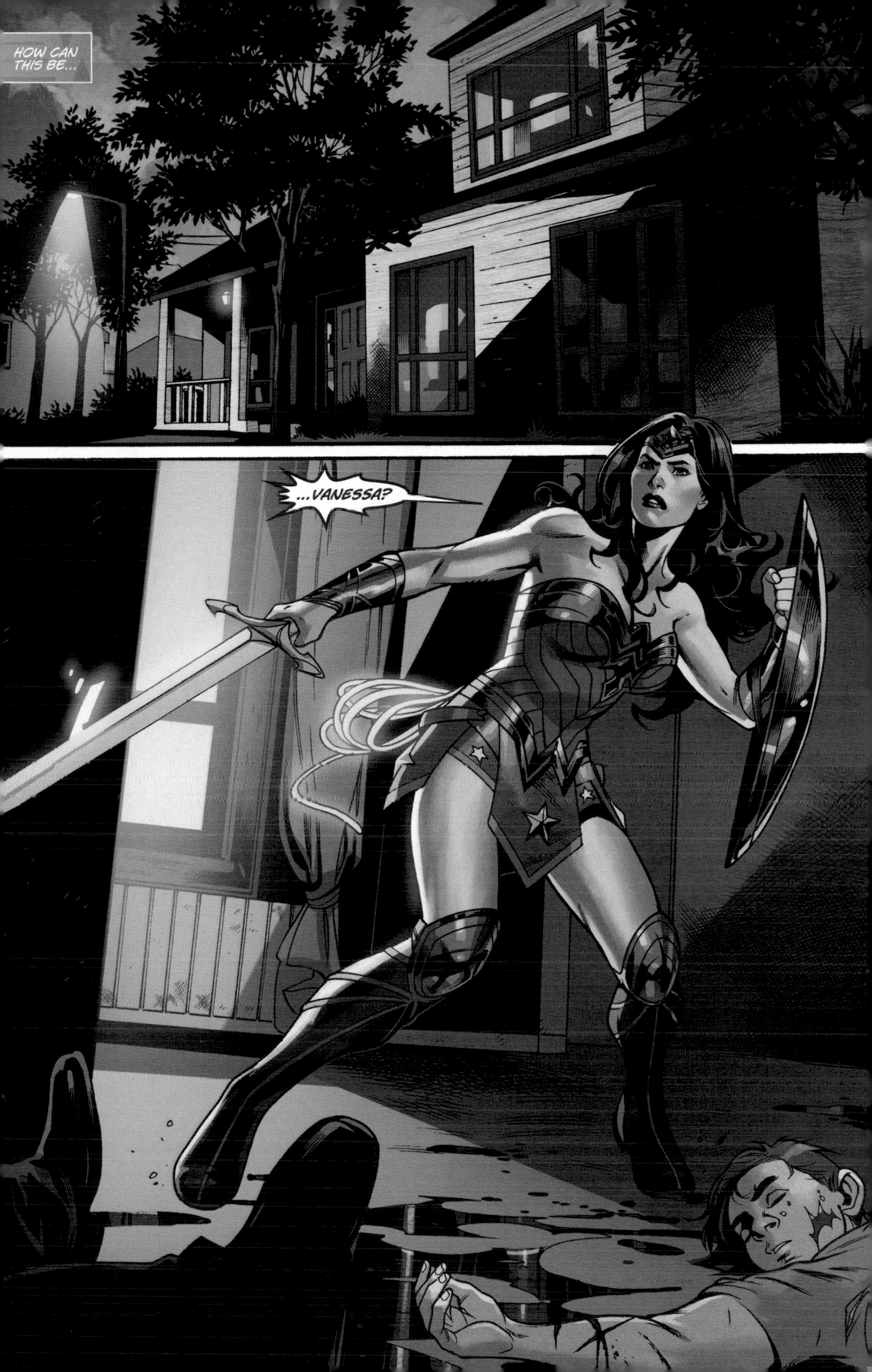
HOW CAN THIS BE...
...VANESSA?

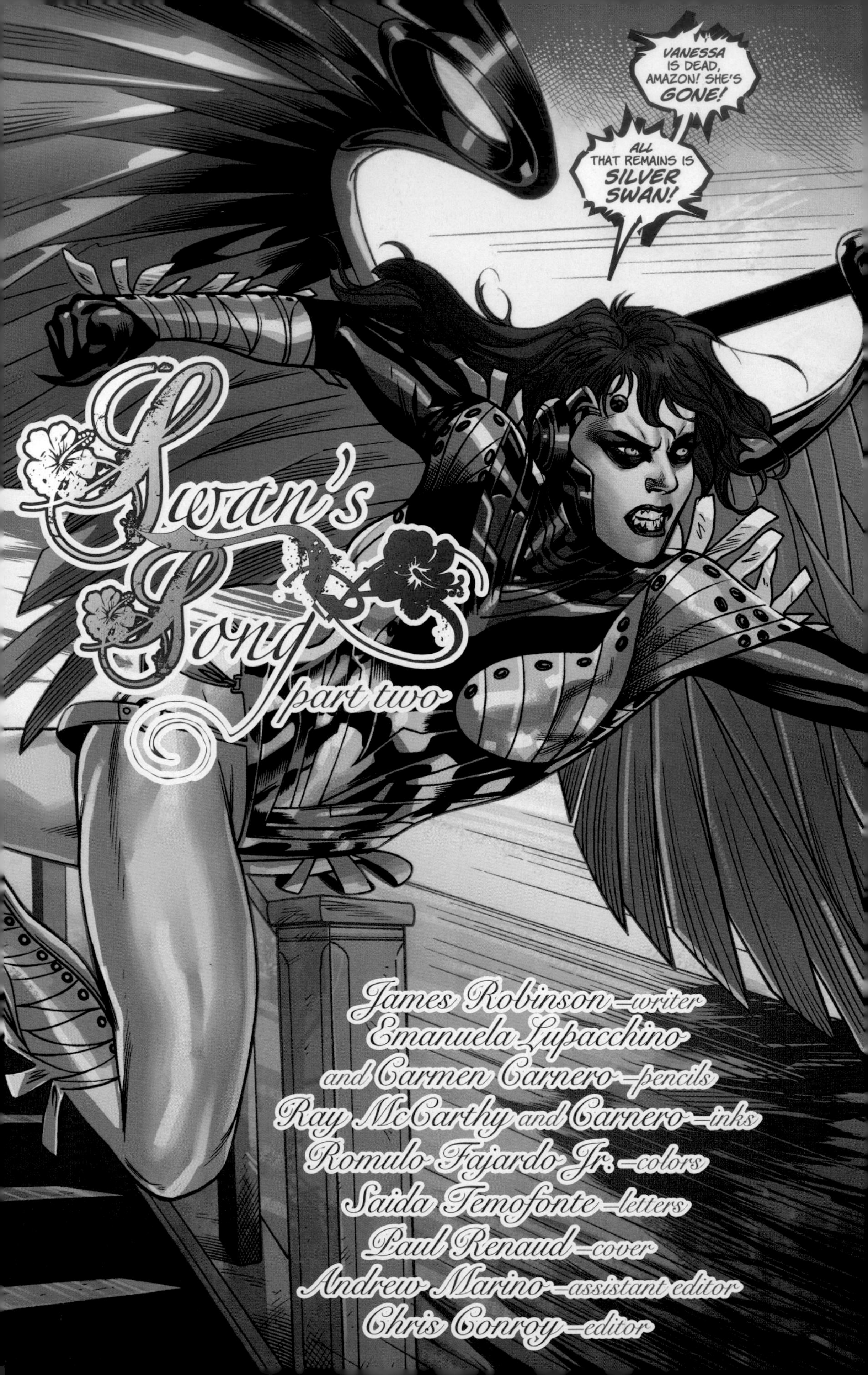
VANESSA IS DEAD, AMAZON! SHE'S GONE!
ALL THAT REMAINS IS SILVER SWAN!
Swan's Song part two
James Robinson—writer
Emanuela Lupacchino and Carmen Carnero—pencils
Ray McCarthy and Carnero—inks
Romulo Fajardo Jr.—colors
Saida Temofonte—letters
Paul Renaud—cover
Andrew Marino—assistant editor
Chris Conroy—editor

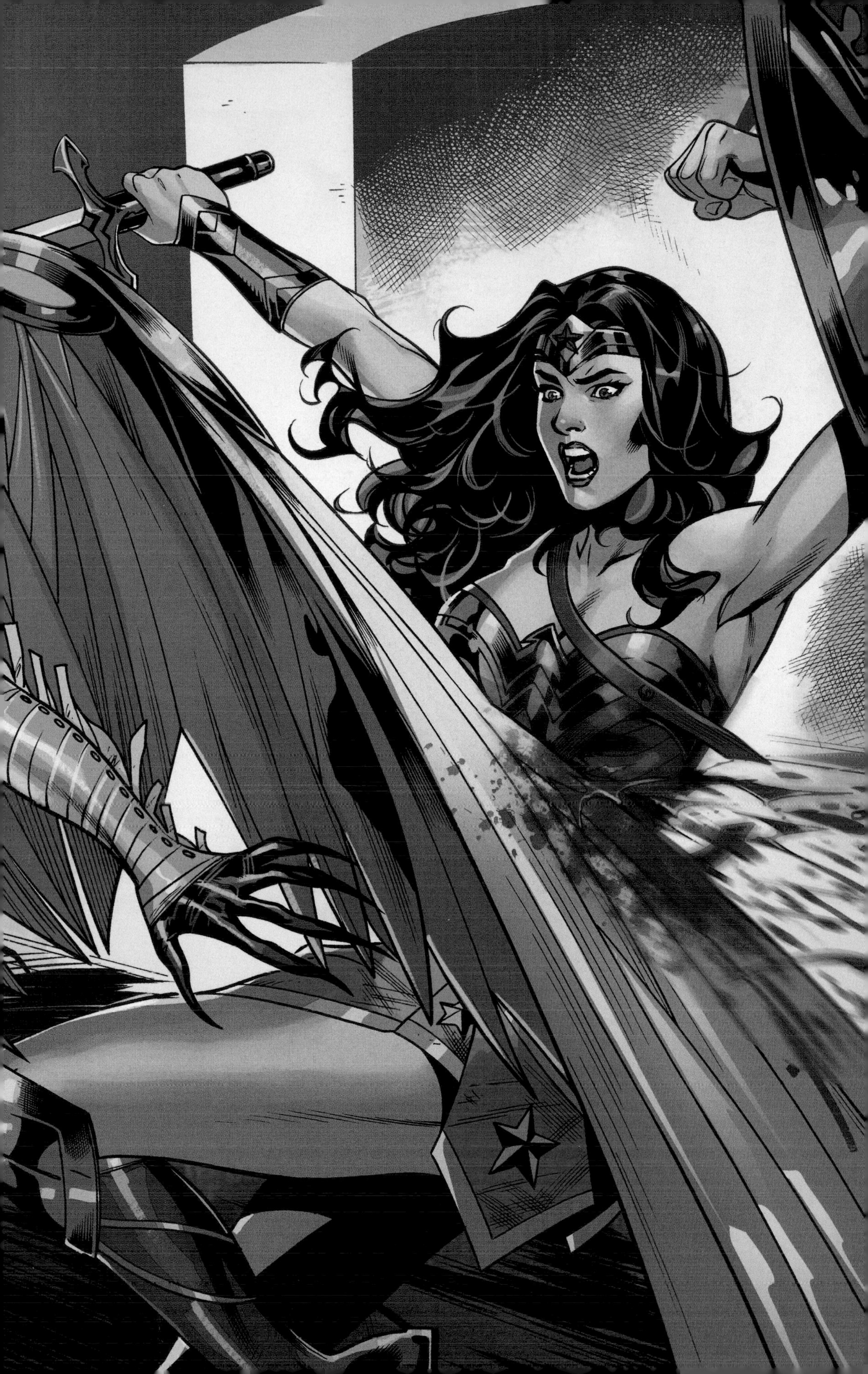

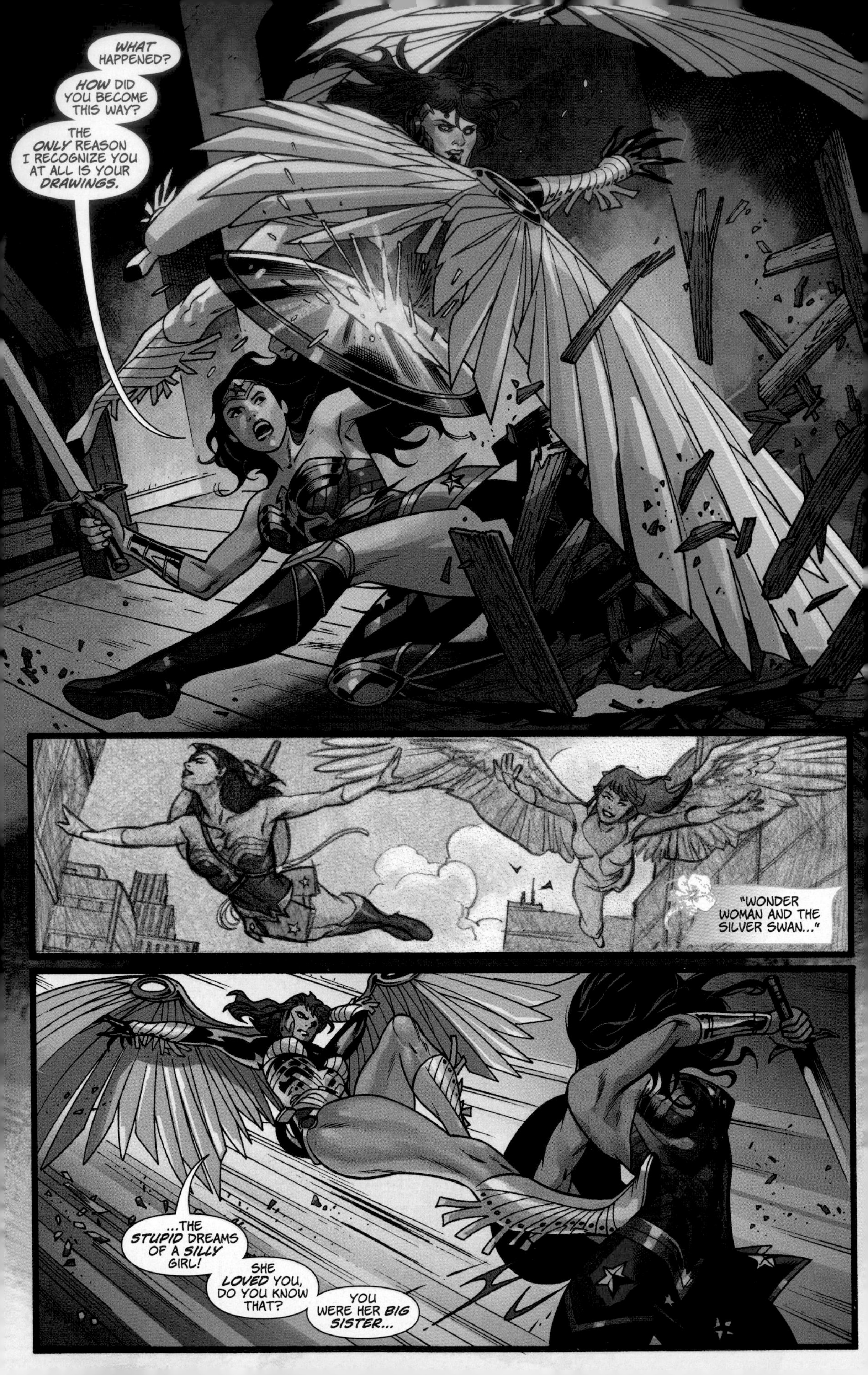
WHAT HAPPENED?
HOW DID YOU BECOME THIS WAY?
THE ONLY REASON I RECOGNIZE YOU AT ALL IS YOUR DRAWINGS.
"WONDER WOMAN AND THE SILVER SWAN..."
...THE STUPID DREAMS OF A SILLY GIRL!
SHE LOVED YOU, DO YOU KNOW THAT?
YOU WERE HER BIG SISTER...

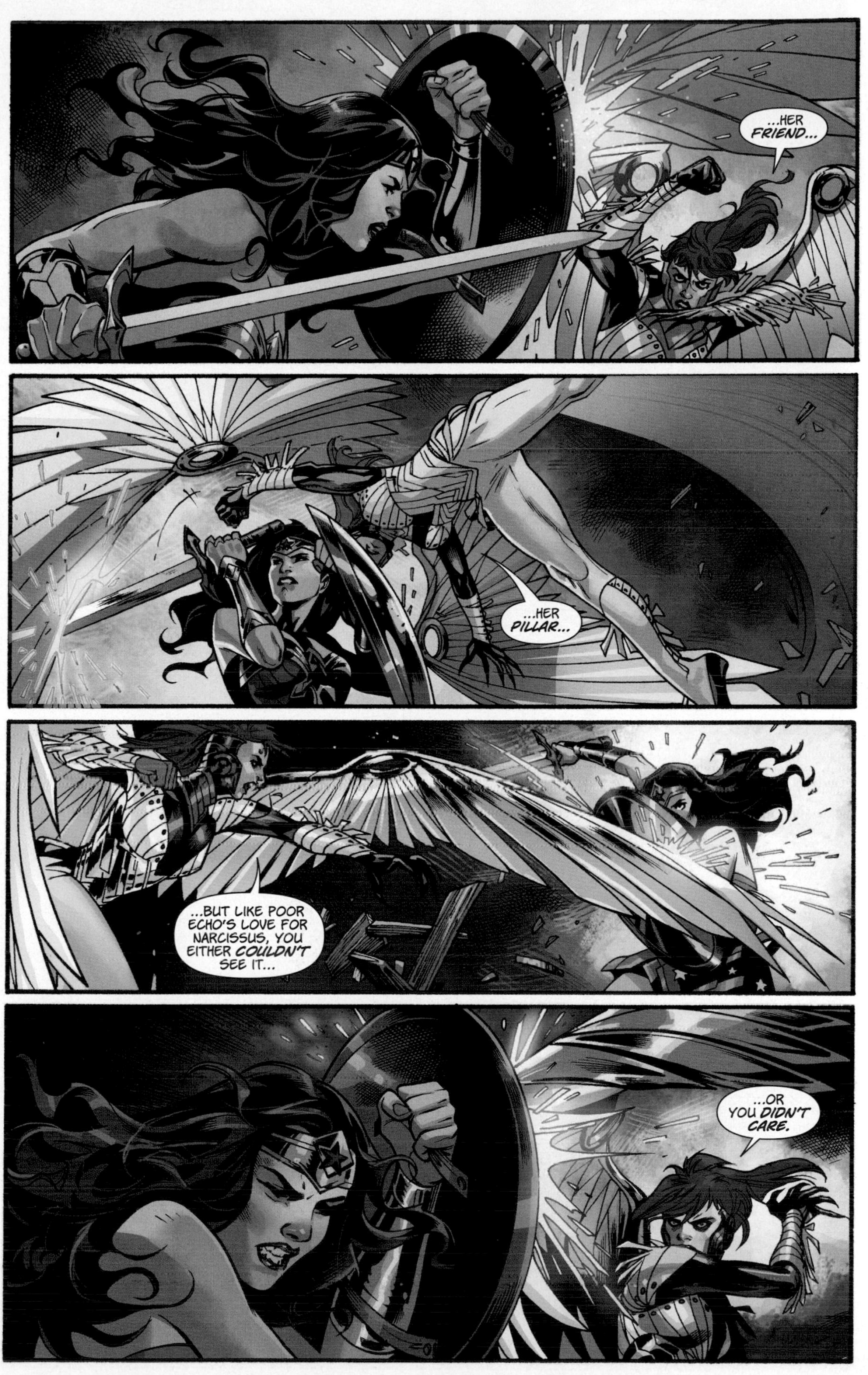
...HER FRIEND...
...HER PILLAR...
...BUT LIKE POOR ECHO'S LOVE FOR NARCISSUS, YOU EITHER COULDN'T SEE IT...
...OR YOU DIDN'T CARE.

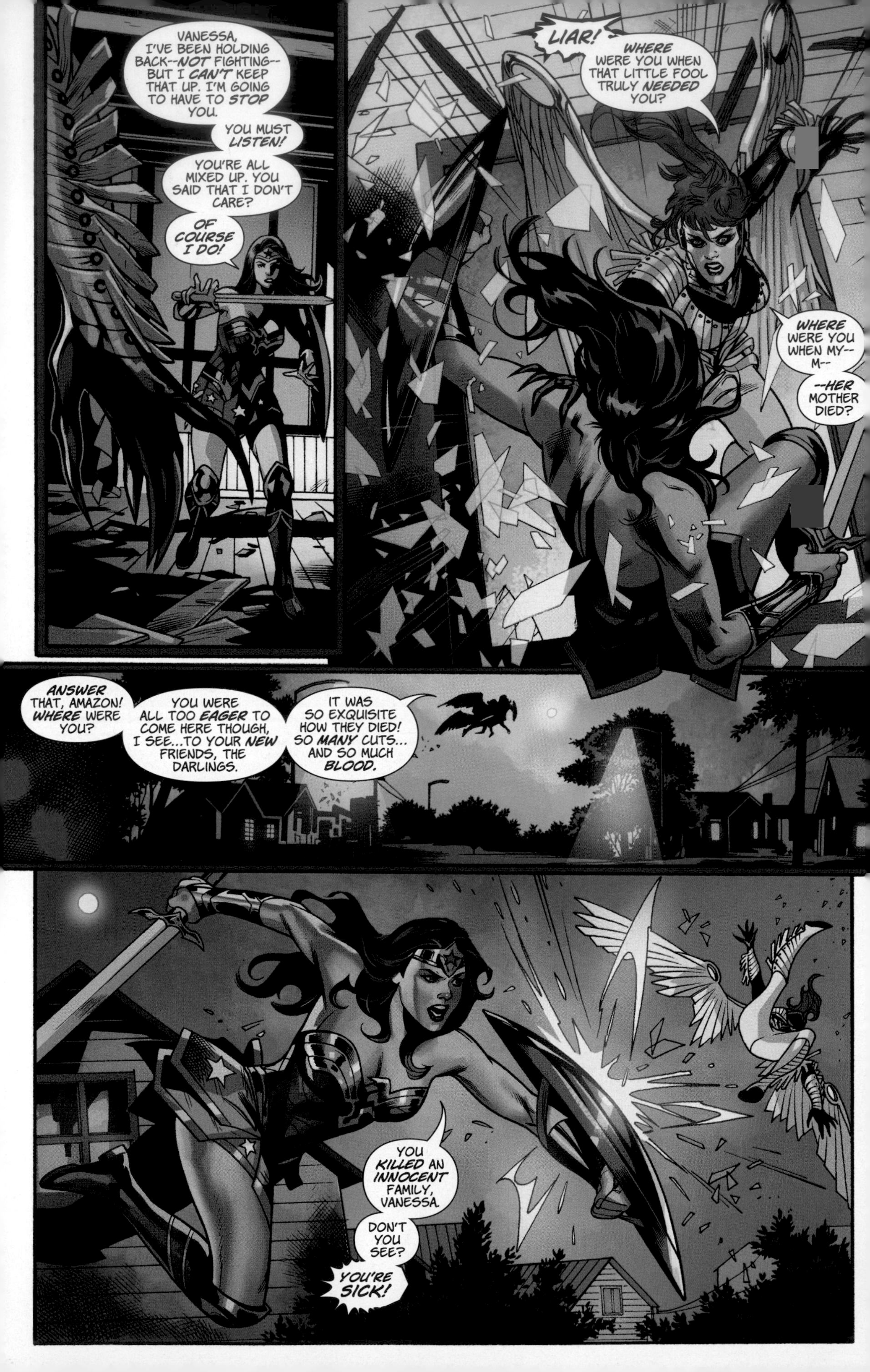
VANESSA, I'VE BEEN HOLDING BACK--NOT FIGHTING--BUT I CAN'T KEEP THAT UP. I'M GOING TO HAVE TO STOP YOU.
YOU MUST LISTEN!
YOU'RE ALL MIXED UP. YOU SAID THAT I DON'T CARE?
OF COURSE I DO!
LIAR!
WHERE WERE YOU WHEN THAT LITTLE FOOL TRULY NEEDED YOU?
WHERE WERE YOU WHEN MY--M--
--HER MOTHER DIED?
ANSWER THAT, AMAZON! WHERE WERE YOU?
YOU WERE ALL TOO EAGER TO COME HERE THOUGH, I SEE...TO YOUR NEW FRIENDS, THE DARLINGS.
IT WAS SO EXQUISITE HOW THEY DIED! SO MANY CUTS... AND SO MUCH BLOOD.
YOU KILLED AN INNOCENT FAMILY, VANESSA.
DON'T YOU SEE?
YOU'RE SICK!

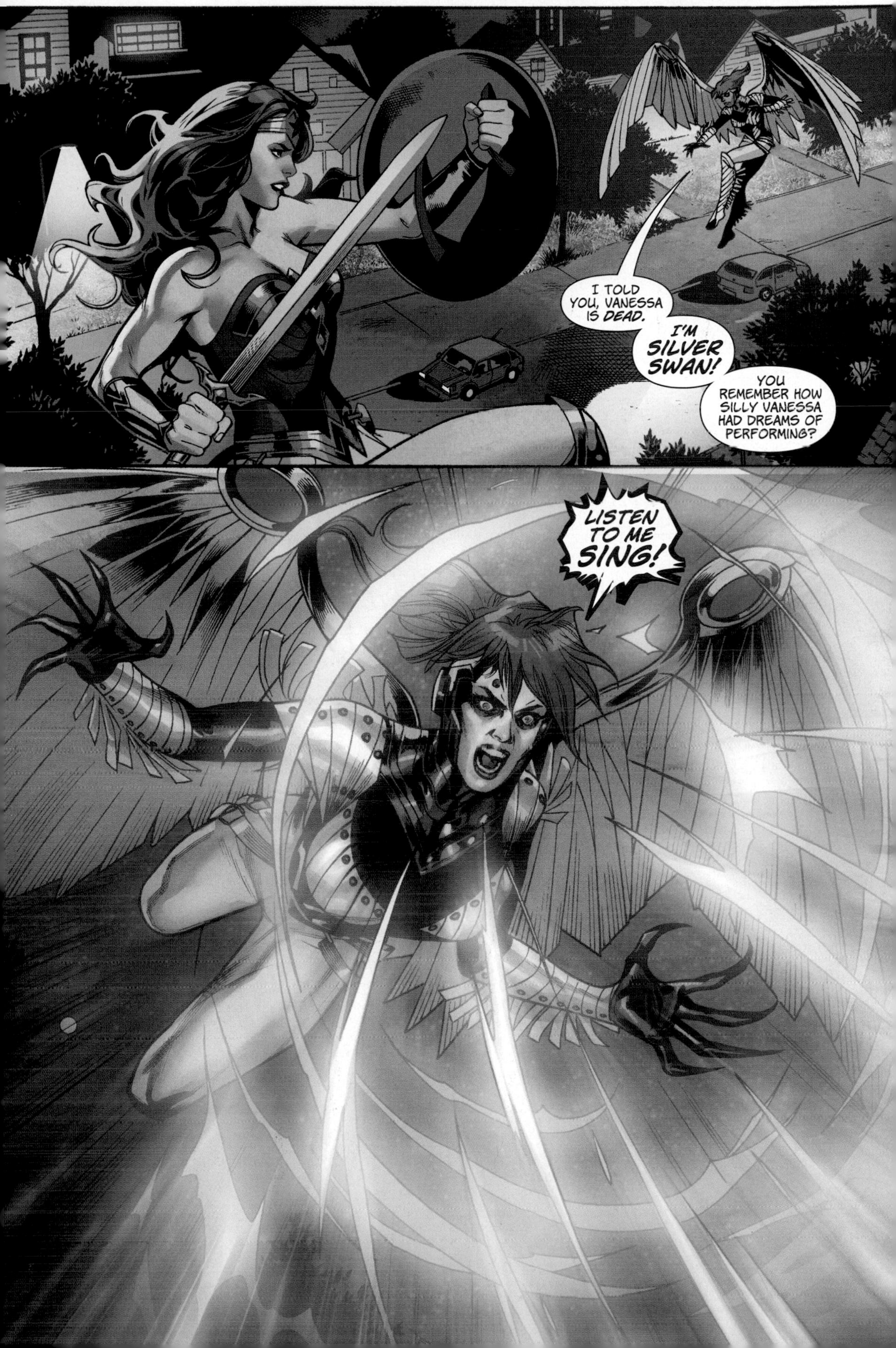
I TOLD YOU, VANESSA IS DEAD.
I'M SILVER SWAN!
YOU REMEMBER HOW SILLY VANESSA HAD DREAMS OF PERFORMING?
LISTEN TO ME SING!

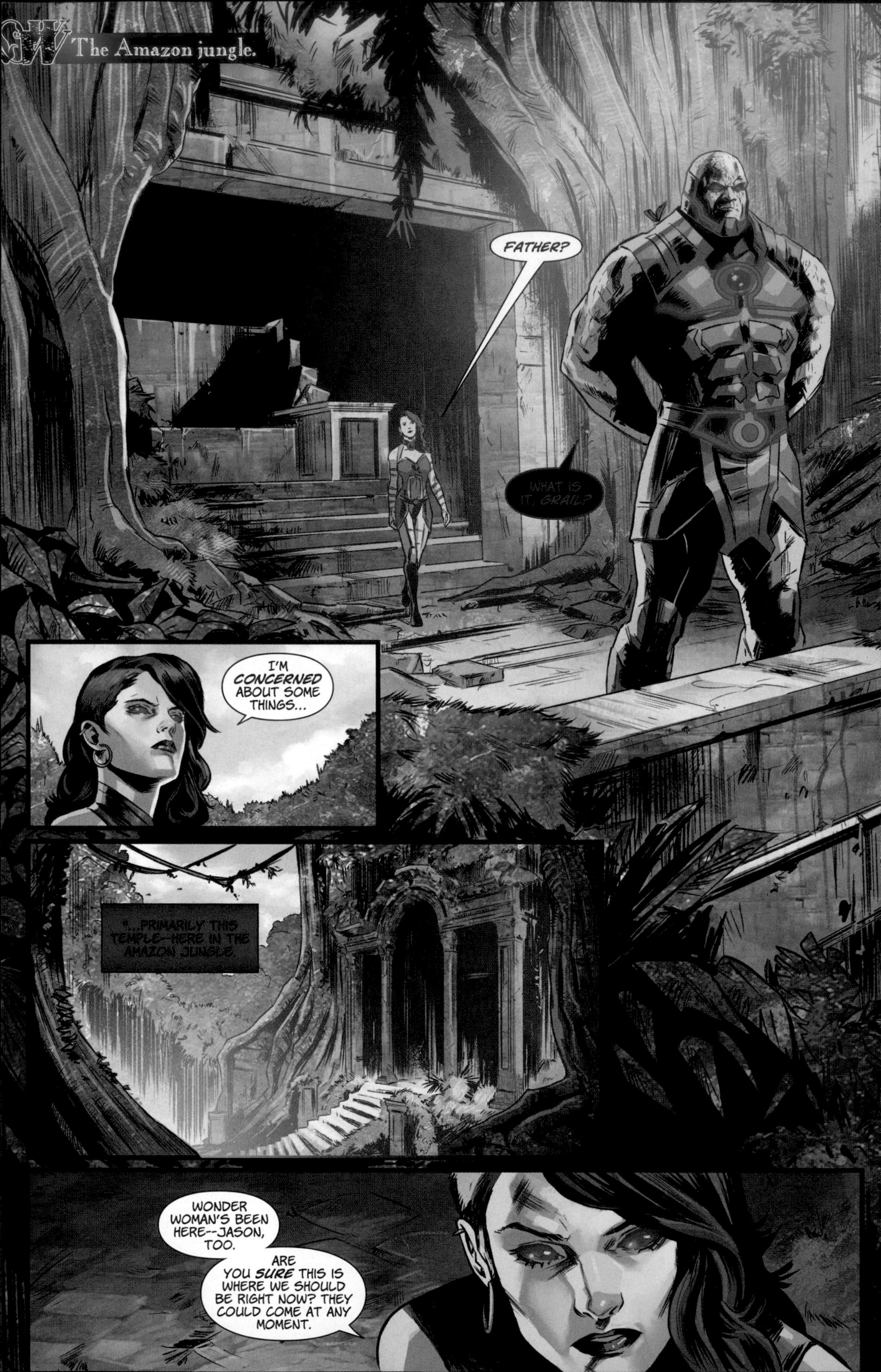

The Amazon jungle.
FATHER?
WHAT IS IT, GRAIL?
I'M CONCERNED ABOUT SOME THINGS...
"...PRIMARILY THIS TEMPLE--HERE IN THE AMAZON JUNGLE.
WONDER WOMAN'S BEEN HERE--JASON, TOO.
ARE YOU SURE THIS IS WHERE WE SHOULD BE RIGHT NOW? THEY COULD COME AT ANY MOMENT.

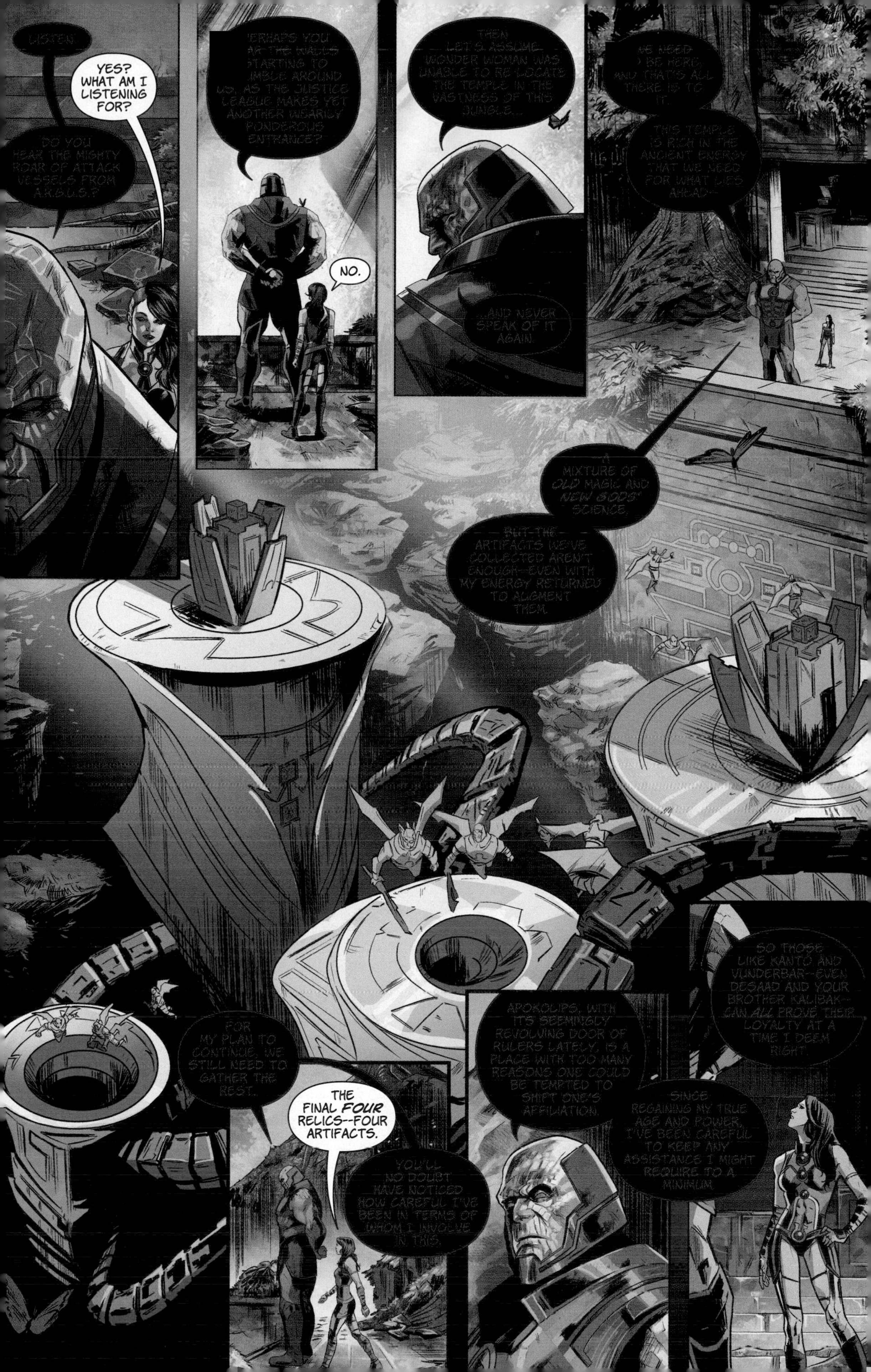
LISTEN.
YES? WHAT AM I LISTENING FOR?
DO YOU HEAR THE MIGHTY ROAR OF ATTACK VESSELS FROM A.R.G.U.S.?
ERHAPS YOU AR THE WALLS STARTING TO IMBLE AROUND US, AS THE JUSTICE LEAGUE MAKES YET ANOTHER WEARILY PONDEROUS ENTRANCE?
NO.
THEN LET'S ASSUME WONDER WOMAN WAS UNABLE TO RE-LOCATE THE TEMPLE IN THE VASTNESS OF THIS JUNGLE...
...AND NEVER SPEAK OF IT AGAIN.
E NEED BE HERE, AND THAT'S ALL THERE IS TO IT.
THIS TEMPLE IS RICH IN THE ANCIENT ENERGY THAT WE NEED FOR WHAT LIES AHEAD--
A MIXTURE OF OLD MAGIC AND NEW GODS' SCIENCE.
BUT THE ARTIFACTS WE'VE COLLECTED AREN'T ENOUGH--EVEN WITH MY ENERGY RETURNED TO AUGMENT THEM.
FOR MY PLAN TO CONTINUE, WE STILL NEED TO GATHER THE REST.
THE FINAL FOUR RELICS--FOUR ARTIFACTS.
YOU'LL NO DOUBT HAVE NOTICED HOW CAREFUL I'VE BEEN IN TERMS OF WHOM I INVOLVE IN THIS.
APOKOLIPS, WITH ITS SEEMINGLY REVOLVING DOOR OF RULERS LATELY, IS A PLACE WITH TOO MANY REASONS ONE COULD BE TEMPTED TO SHIFT ONE'S AFFILIATION.
SINCE REGAINING MY TRUE AGE AND POWER, I'VE BEEN CAREFUL TO KEEP ANY ASSISTANCE I MIGHT REQUIRE TO A MINIMUM.
SO THOSE LIKE KANTO AND VUNDERBAR--EVEN DESAAD AND YOUR BROTHER KALIBAK--CAN ALL PROVE THEIR LOYALTY AT A TIME I DEEM RIGHT.

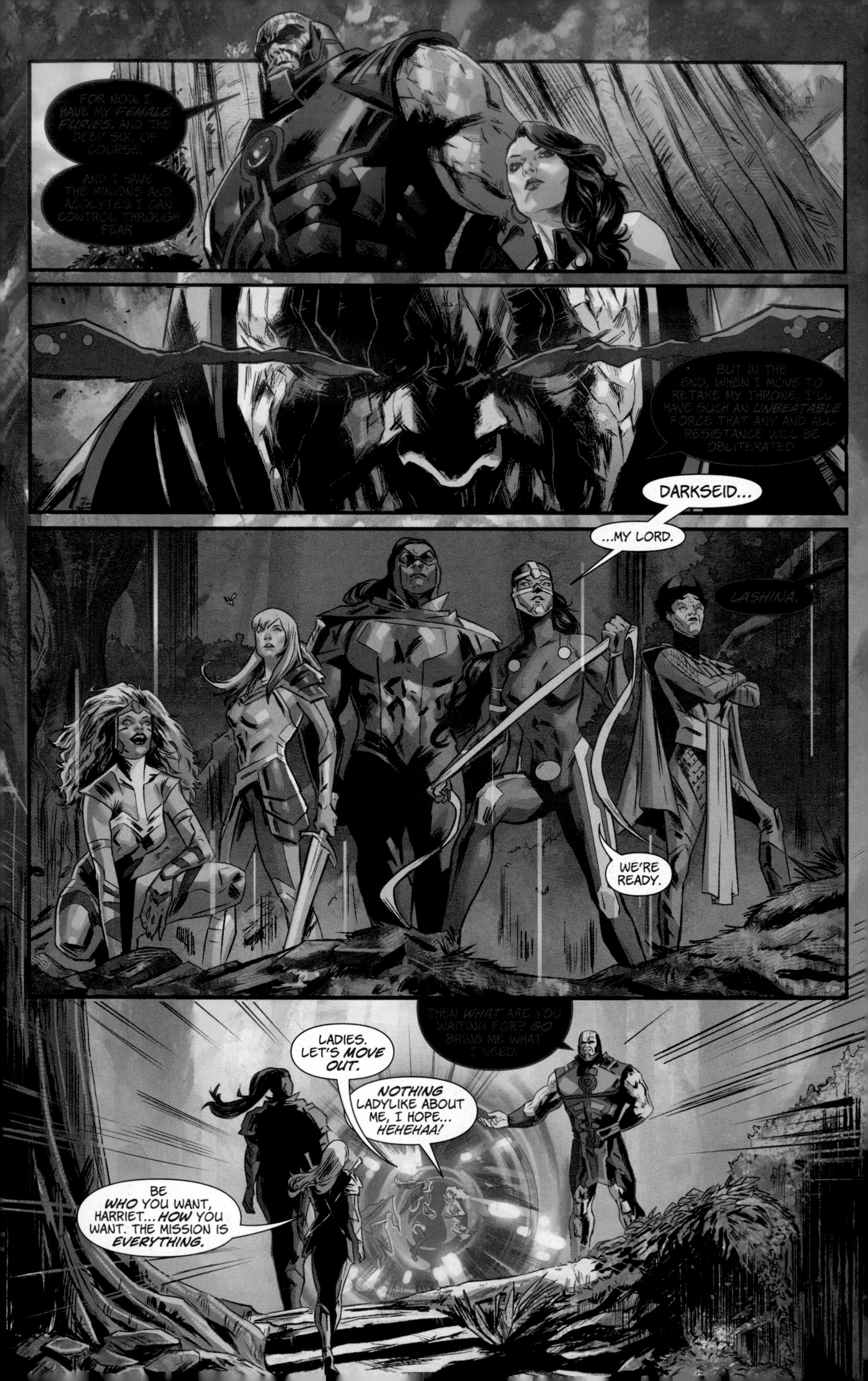

FOR NOW I HAVE MY FEMALE FURIES, AND THE DEEP SIX, OF COURSE.
AND I HAVE THE MINIONS AND ACOLYTES I CAN CONTROL THROUGH FEAR
BUT IN THE END, WHEN I MOVE TO RETAKE MY THRONE, I'LL HAVE SUCH AN UNBEATABLE FORCE THAT ANY AND ALL RESISTANCE WILL BE OBLITERATED.
DARKSEID...
...MY LORD.
LASHINA.
WE'RE READY.
THEN WHAT ARE YOU WAITING FOR? GO BRING ME WHAT I NEED.
LADIES. LET'S MOVE OUT.
NOTHING LADYLIKE ABOUT ME, I HOPE... HEHEHAA!
BE WHO YOU WANT, HARRIET... HOW YOU WANT. THE MISSION IS EVERYTHING.

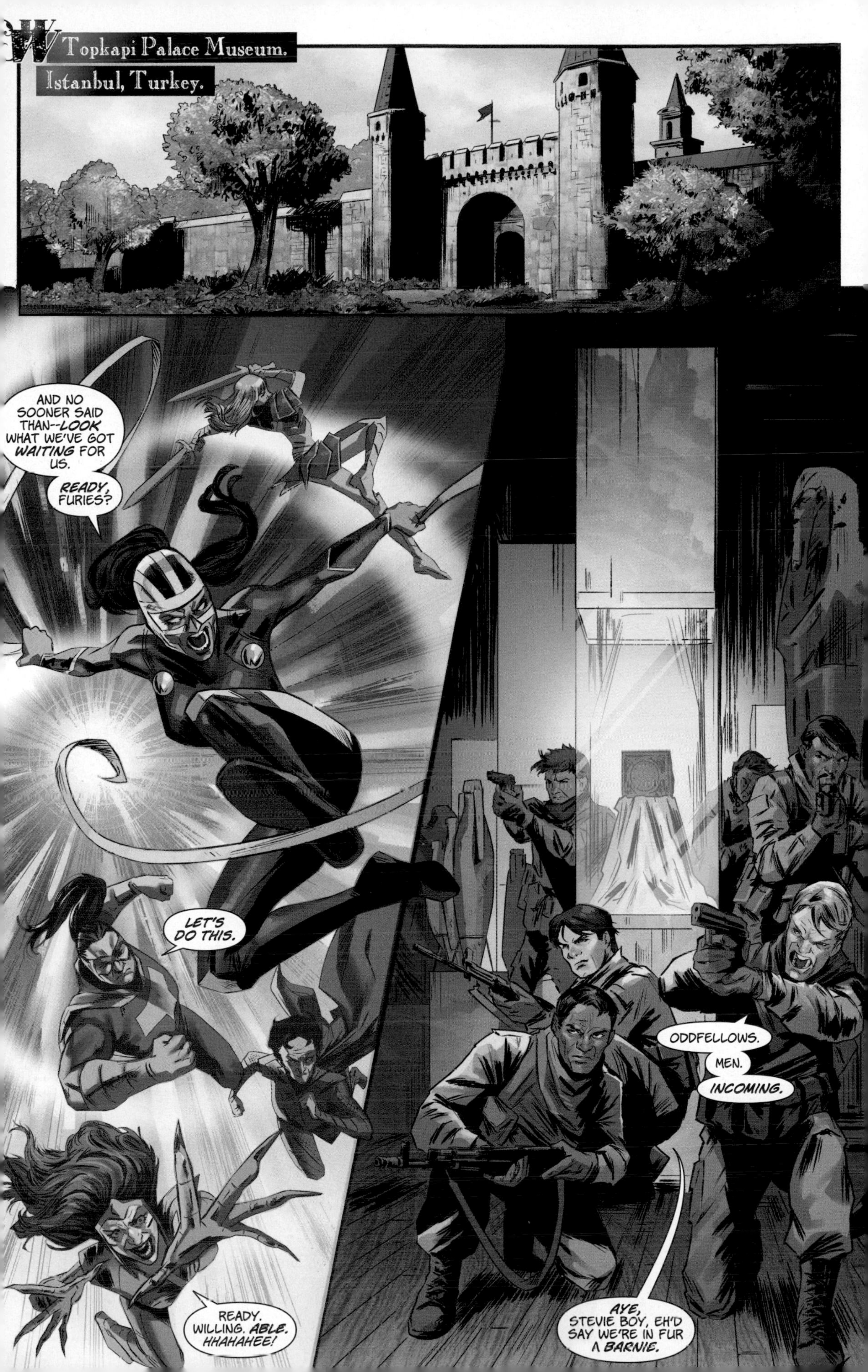
Topkapi Palace Museum.
Istanbul, Turkey.
AND NO SOONER SAID THAN--*LOOK* WHAT WE'VE GOT *WAITING* FOR US.
READY, FURIES?
LET'S DO THIS.
READY. WILLING. *ABLE.* *HHAHAHEE!*
ODDFELLOWS.
MEN.
INCOMING.
AYE, STEVIE BOY, EH'D SAY WE'RE IN FUR A *BARNIE*.

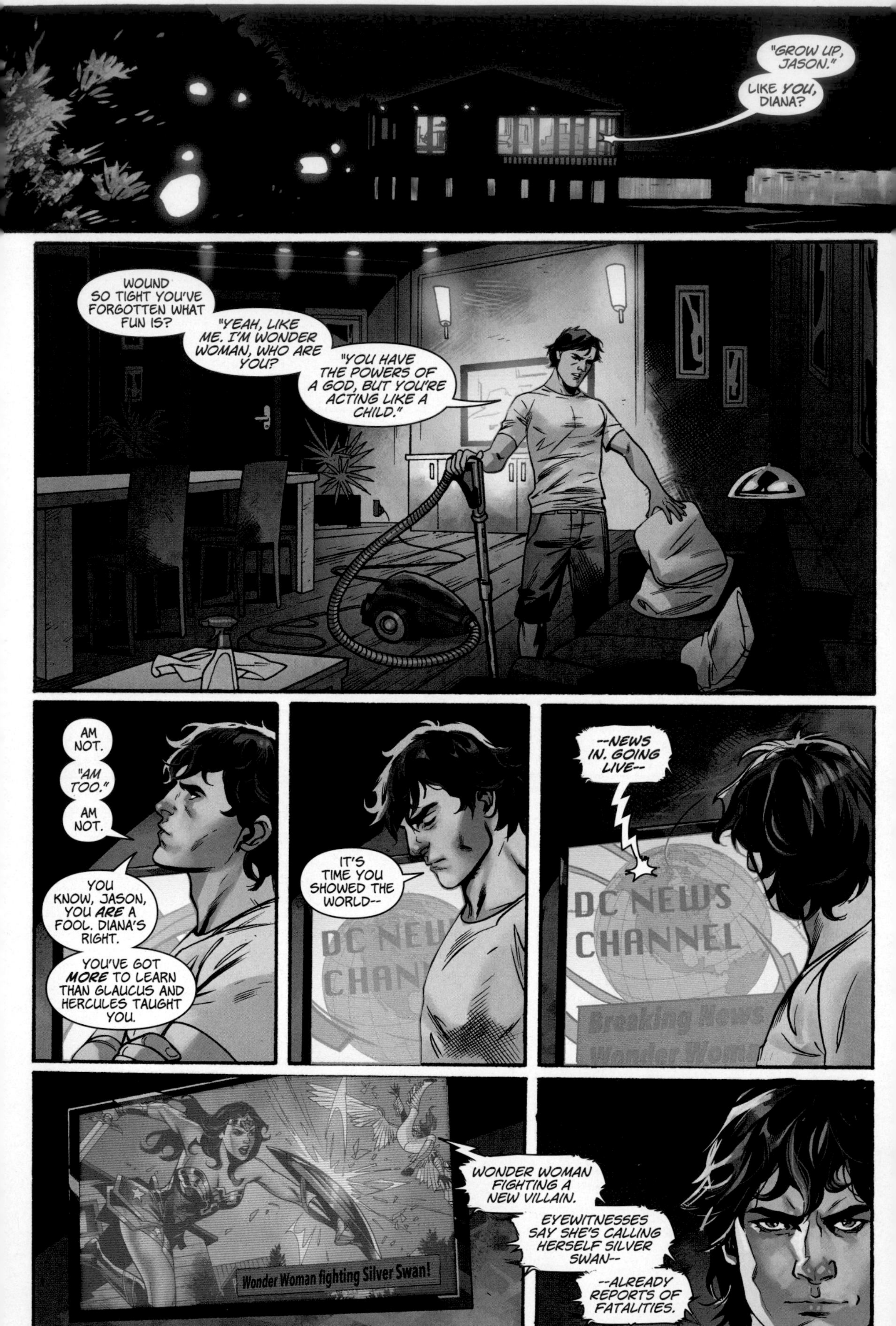
"GROW UP, JASON."
LIKE YOU, DIANA?
WOUND SO TIGHT YOU'VE FORGOTTEN WHAT FUN IS?
"YEAH, LIKE ME. I'M WONDER WOMAN, WHO ARE YOU?
"YOU HAVE THE POWERS OF A GOD, BUT YOU'RE ACTING LIKE A CHILD."
AM NOT.
"AM TOO."
AM NOT.
YOU KNOW, JASON, YOU ARE A FOOL. DIANA'S RIGHT.
YOU'VE GOT MORE TO LEARN THAN GLAUCUS AND HERCULES TAUGHT YOU.
IT'S TIME YOU SHOWED THE WORLD--
--NEWS IN. GOING LIVE--
DC NEWS CHANNEL
Breaking News
WONDER WOMAN FIGHTING A NEW VILLAIN.
EYEWITNESSES SAY SHE'S CALLING HERSELF SILVER SWAN--
--ALREADY REPORTS OF FATALITIES.
Wonder Woman fighting Silver Swan!

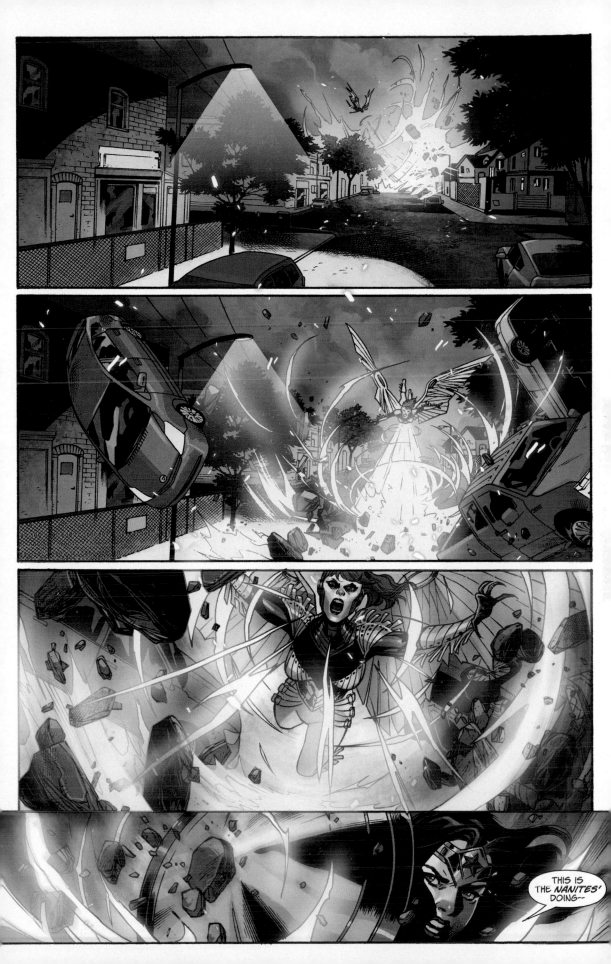

THIS IS THE *NANITES'* DOING--

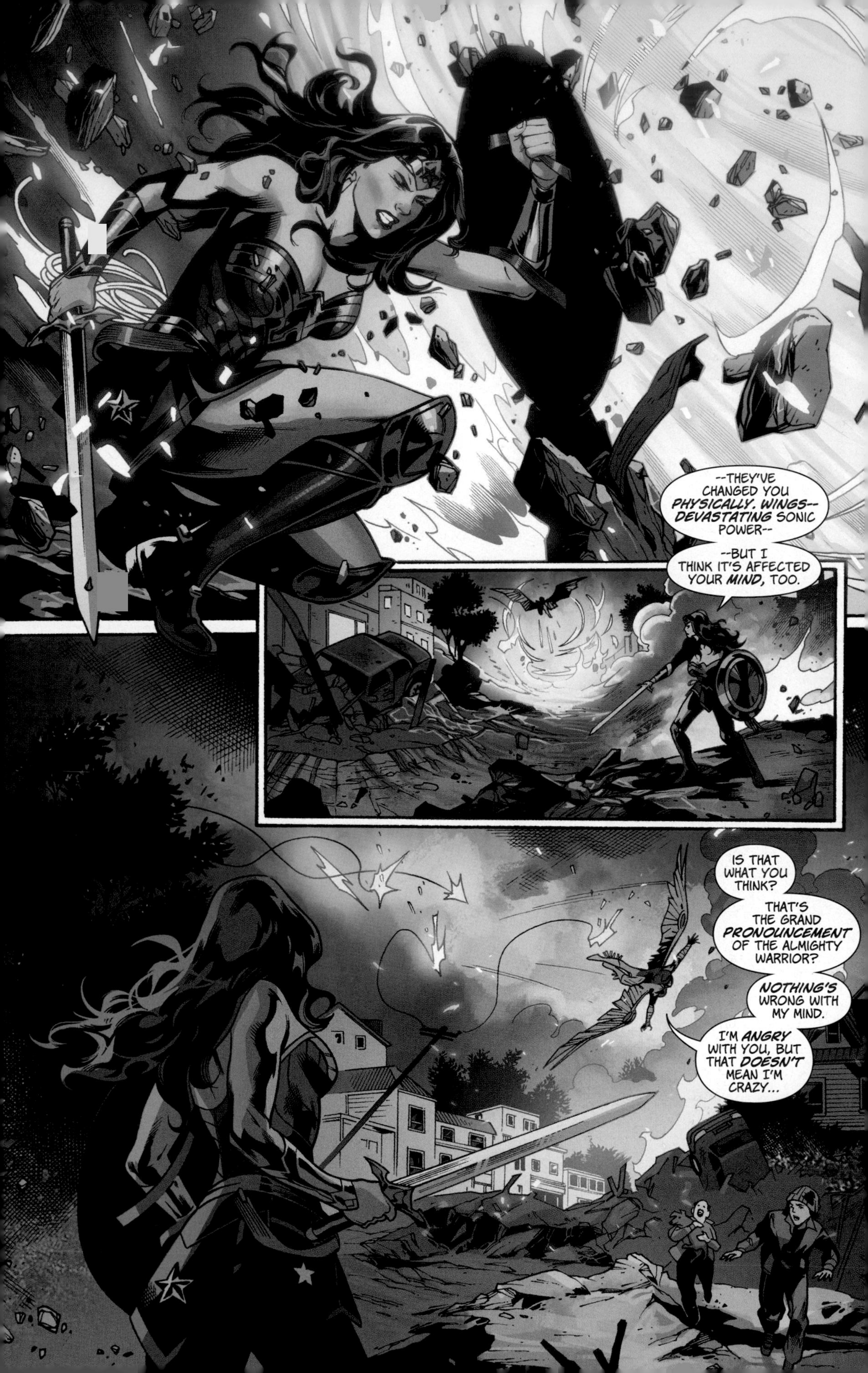
--THEY'VE CHANGED YOU PHYSICALLY. WINGS--DEVASTATING SONIC POWER--
--BUT I THINK IT'S AFFECTED YOUR MIND, TOO.
IS THAT WHAT YOU THINK?
THAT'S THE GRAND PRONOUNCEMENT OF THE ALMIGHTY WARRIOR?
NOTHING'S WRONG WITH MY MIND.
I'M ANGRY WITH YOU, BUT THAT DOESN'T MEAN I'M CRAZY...

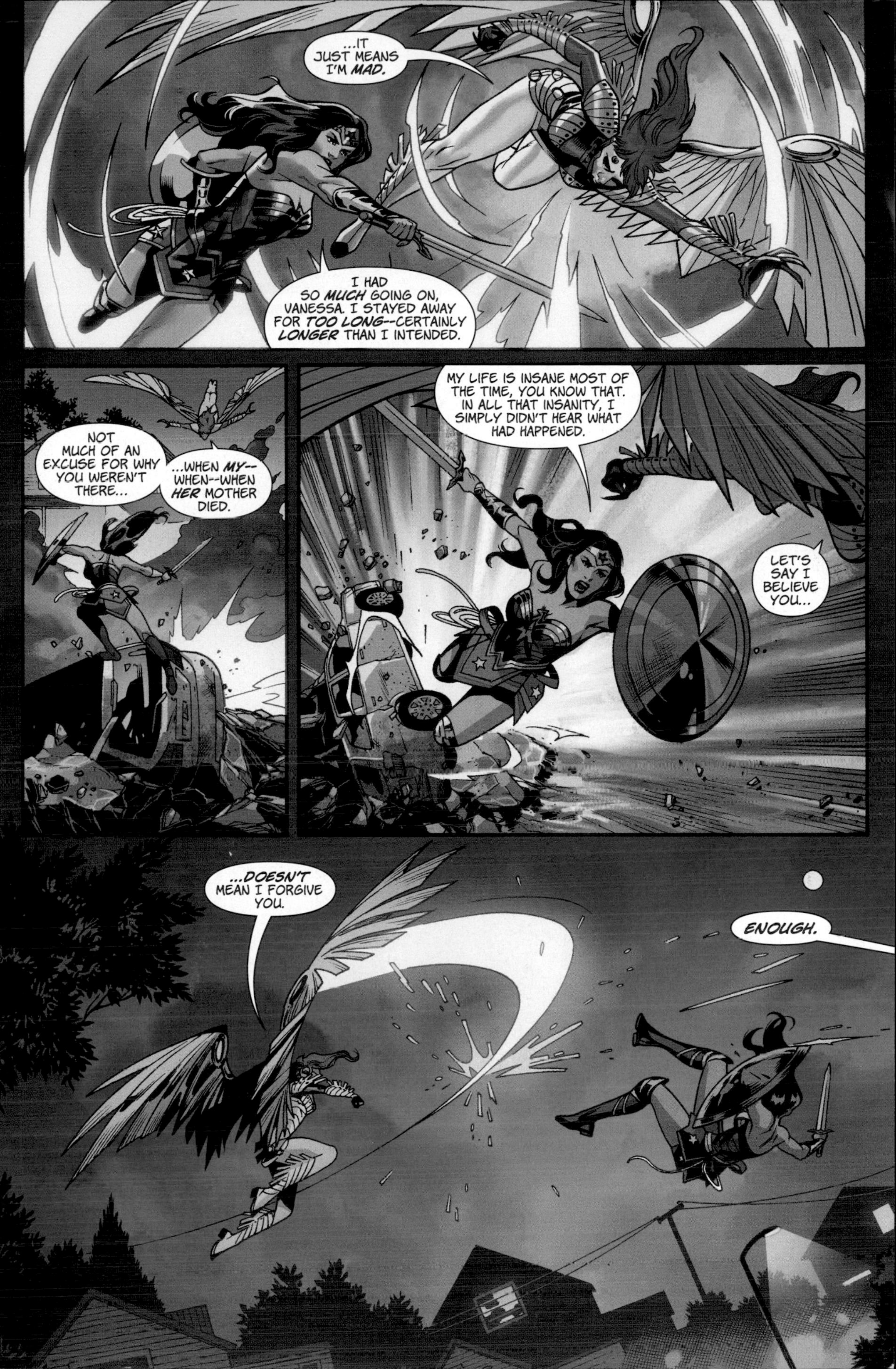
...IT JUST MEANS I'M MAD.
I HAD SO MUCH GOING ON, VANESSA. I STAYED AWAY FOR TOO LONG--CERTAINLY LONGER THAN I INTENDED.
NOT MUCH OF AN EXCUSE FOR WHY YOU WEREN'T THERE...
...WHEN MY-- WHEN--WHEN HER MOTHER DIED.
MY LIFE IS INSANE MOST OF THE TIME, YOU KNOW THAT. IN ALL THAT INSANITY, I SIMPLY DIDN'T HEAR WHAT HAD HAPPENED.
LET'S SAY I BELIEVE YOU...
...DOESN'T MEAN I FORGIVE YOU.
ENOUGH.

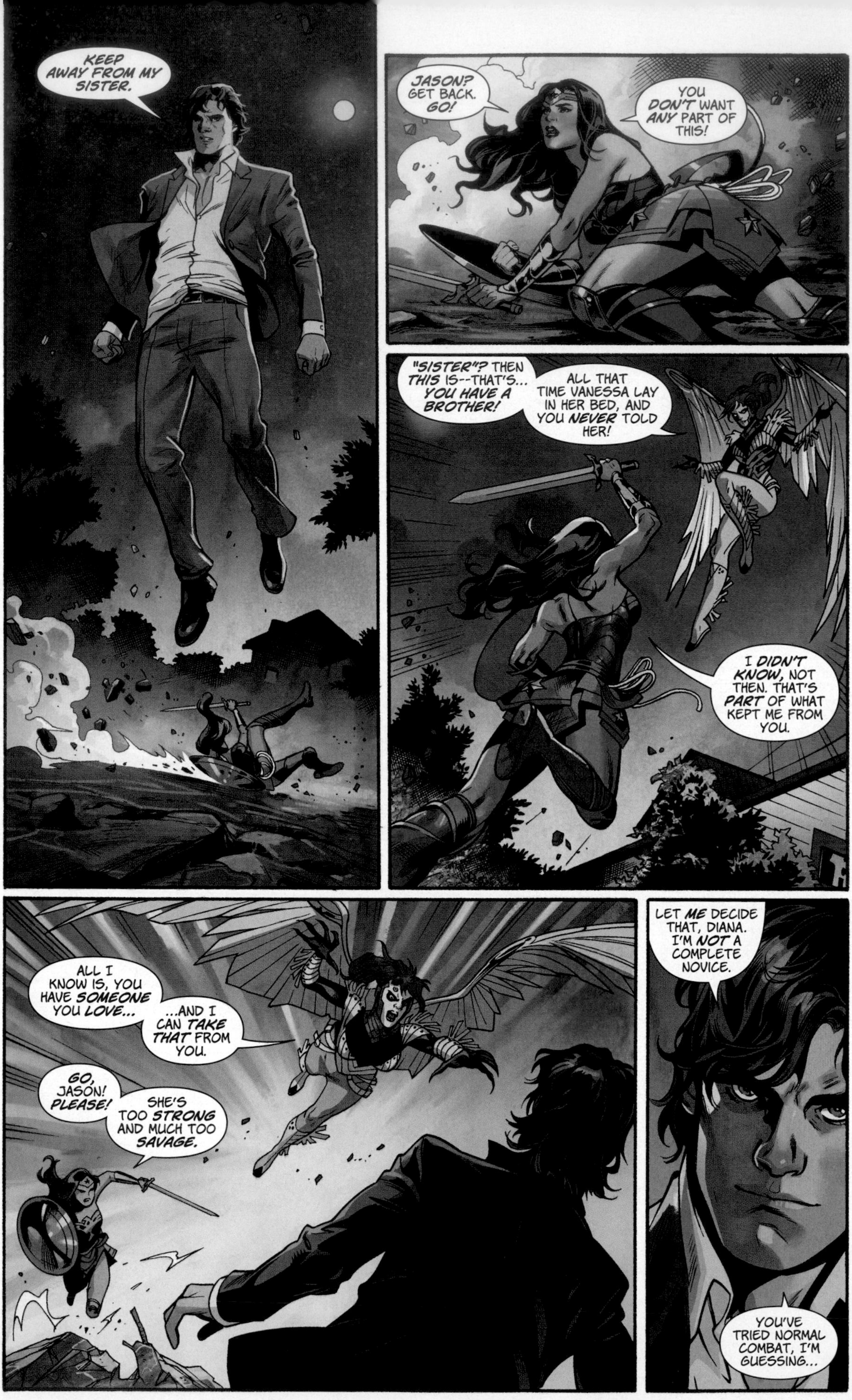
KEEP AWAY FROM MY SISTER.
JASON? GET BACK. GO!
YOU DON'T WANT ANY PART OF THIS!
"SISTER"? THEN THIS IS--THAT'S... YOU HAVE A BROTHER!
ALL THAT TIME VANESSA LAY IN HER BED, AND YOU NEVER TOLD HER!
I DIDN'T KNOW, NOT THEN. THAT'S PART OF WHAT KEPT ME FROM YOU.
ALL I KNOW IS, YOU HAVE SOMEONE YOU LOVE...
...AND I CAN TAKE THAT FROM YOU.
GO, JASON! PLEASE!
SHE'S TOO STRONG AND MUCH TOO SAVAGE.
LET ME DECIDE THAT, DIANA. I'M NOT A COMPLETE NOVICE.
YOU'VE TRIED NORMAL COMBAT, I'M GUESSING...

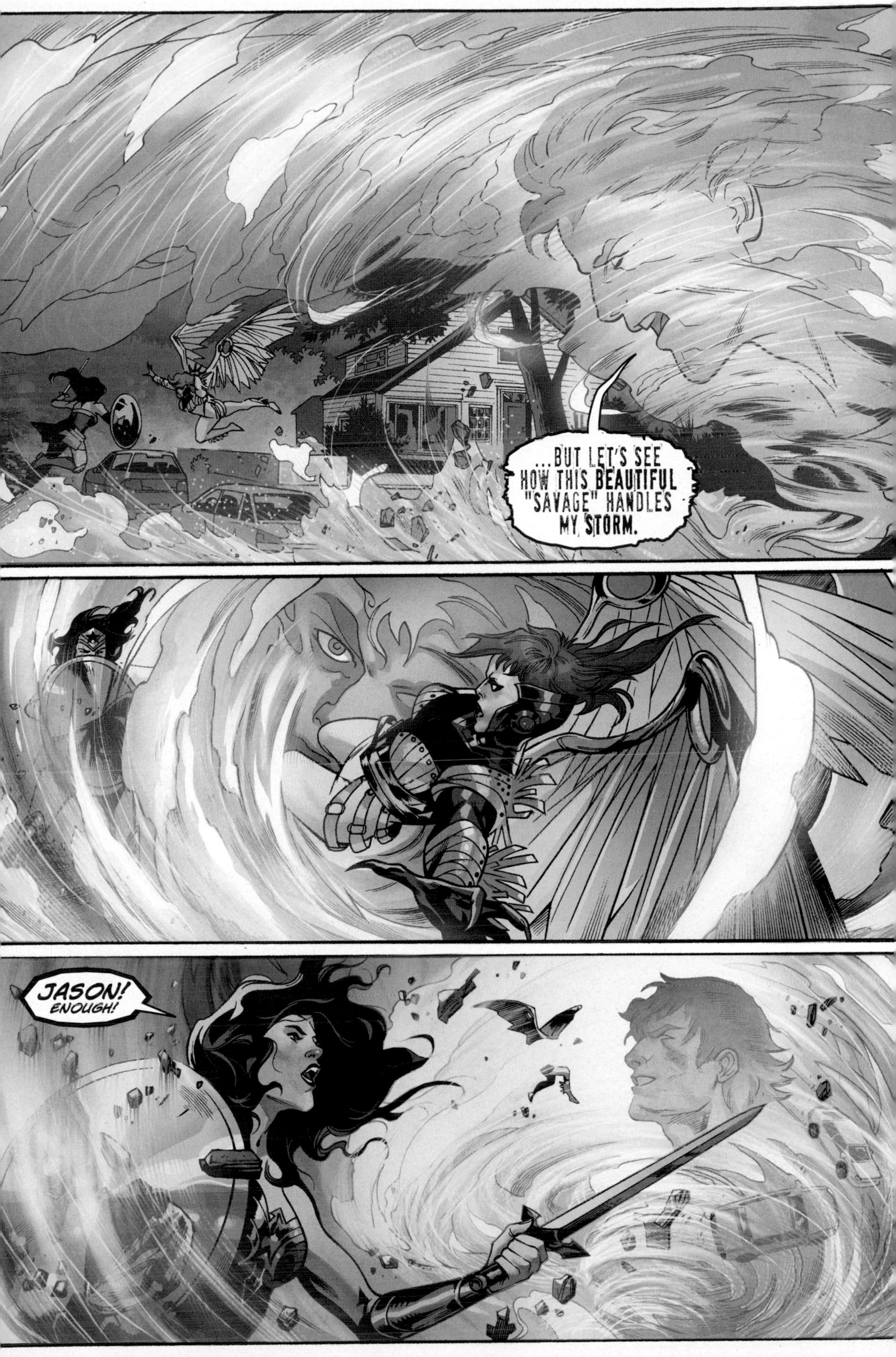
...BUT LET'S SEE HOW THIS BEAUTIFUL "SAVAGE" HANDLES MY STORM.
JASON! ENOUGH!

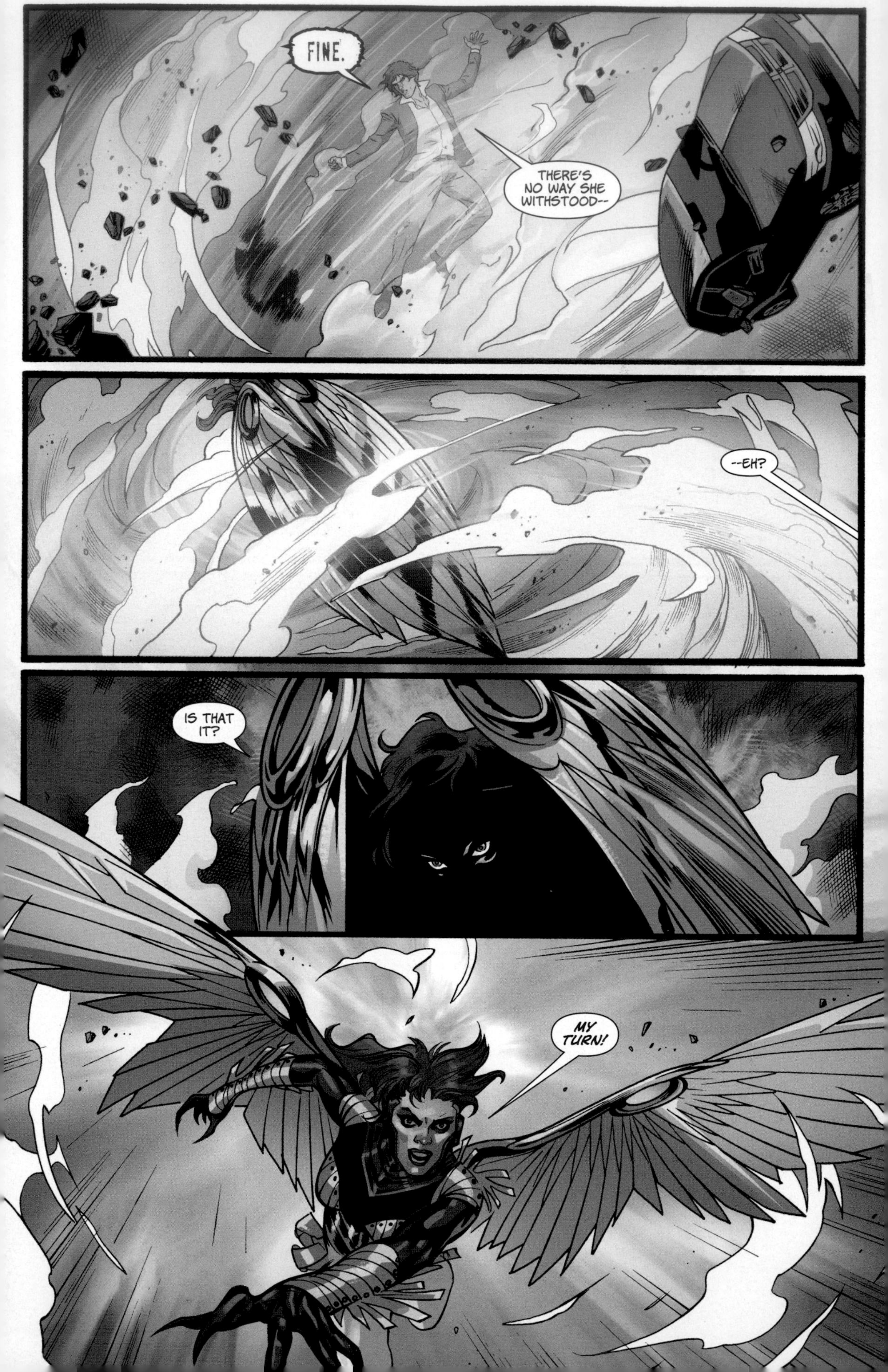
FINE.
THERE'S NO WAY SHE WITHSTOOD--
--EH?
IS THAT IT?
MY TURN!

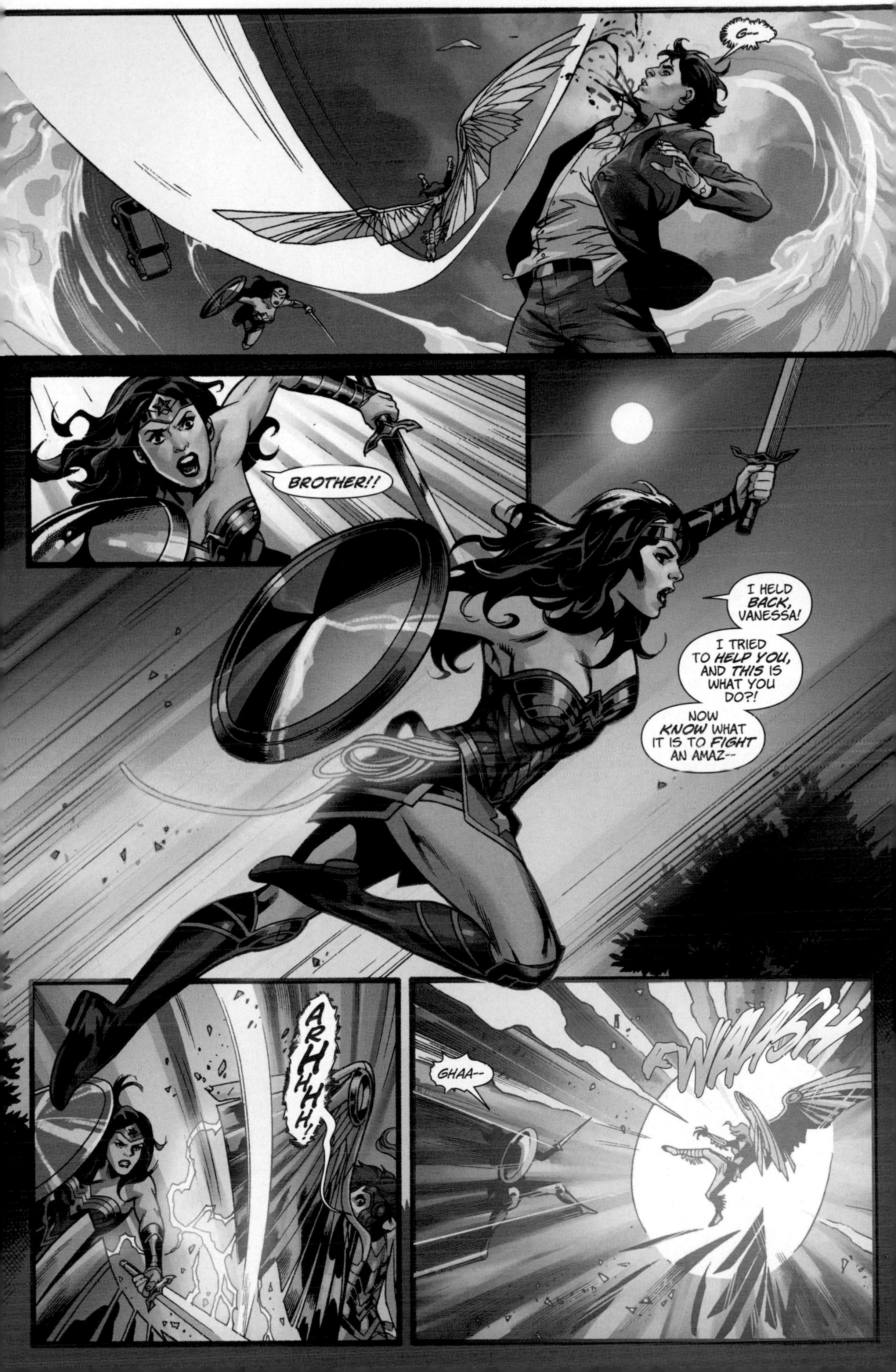
G--
BROTHER!!
I HELD BACK, VANESSA!
I TRIED TO HELP YOU, AND THIS IS WHAT YOU DO?!
NOW KNOW WHAT IT IS TO FIGHT AN AMAZ--
ARHHHH!
GHAA--
FWAASH

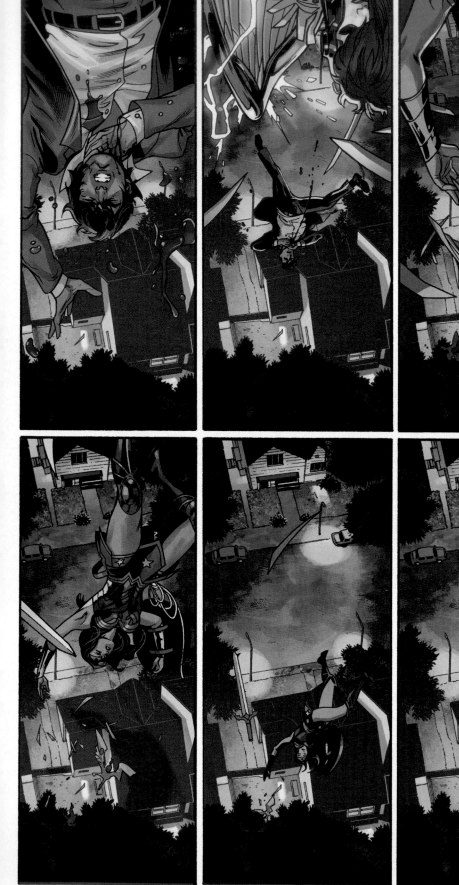

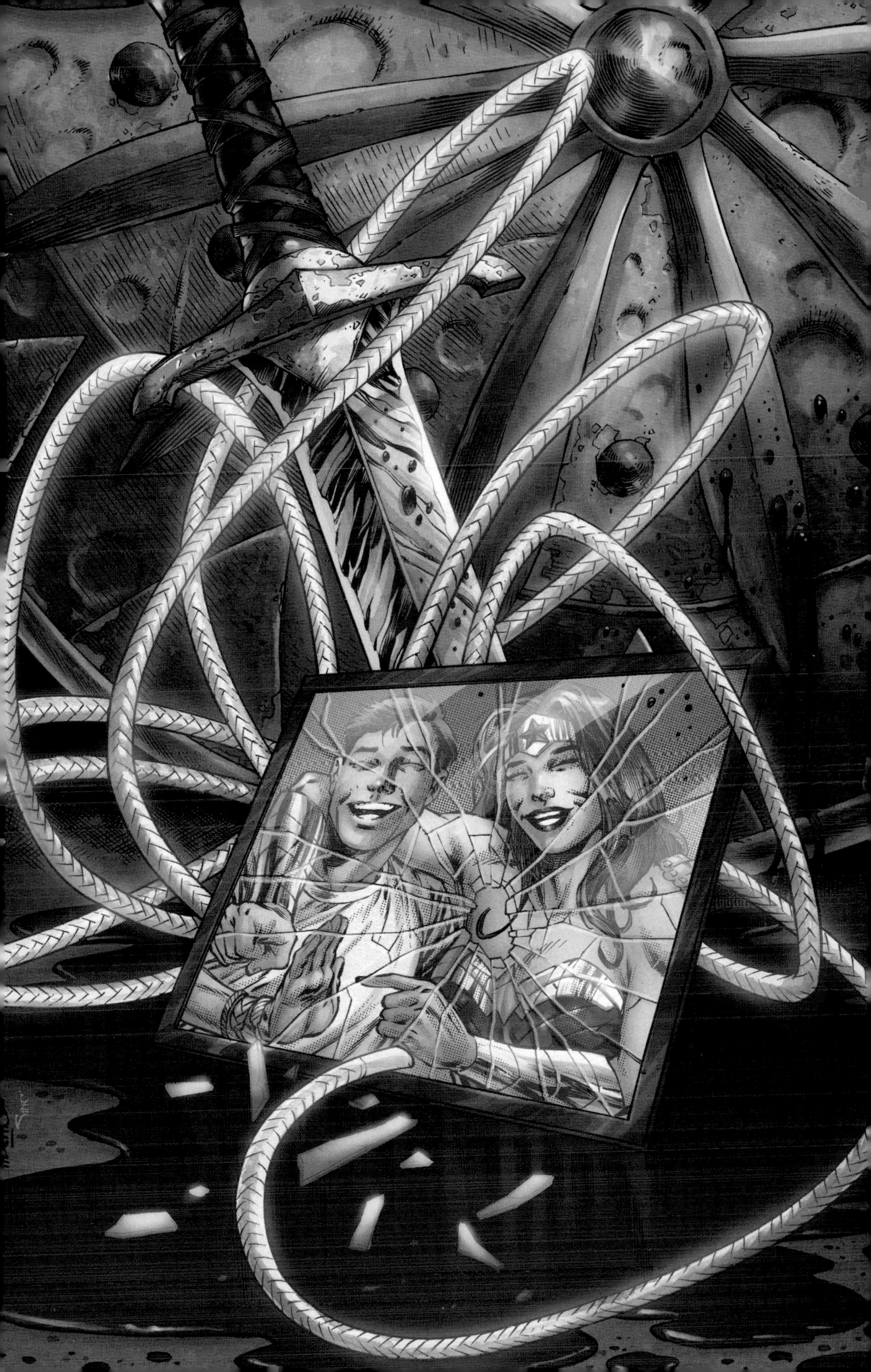

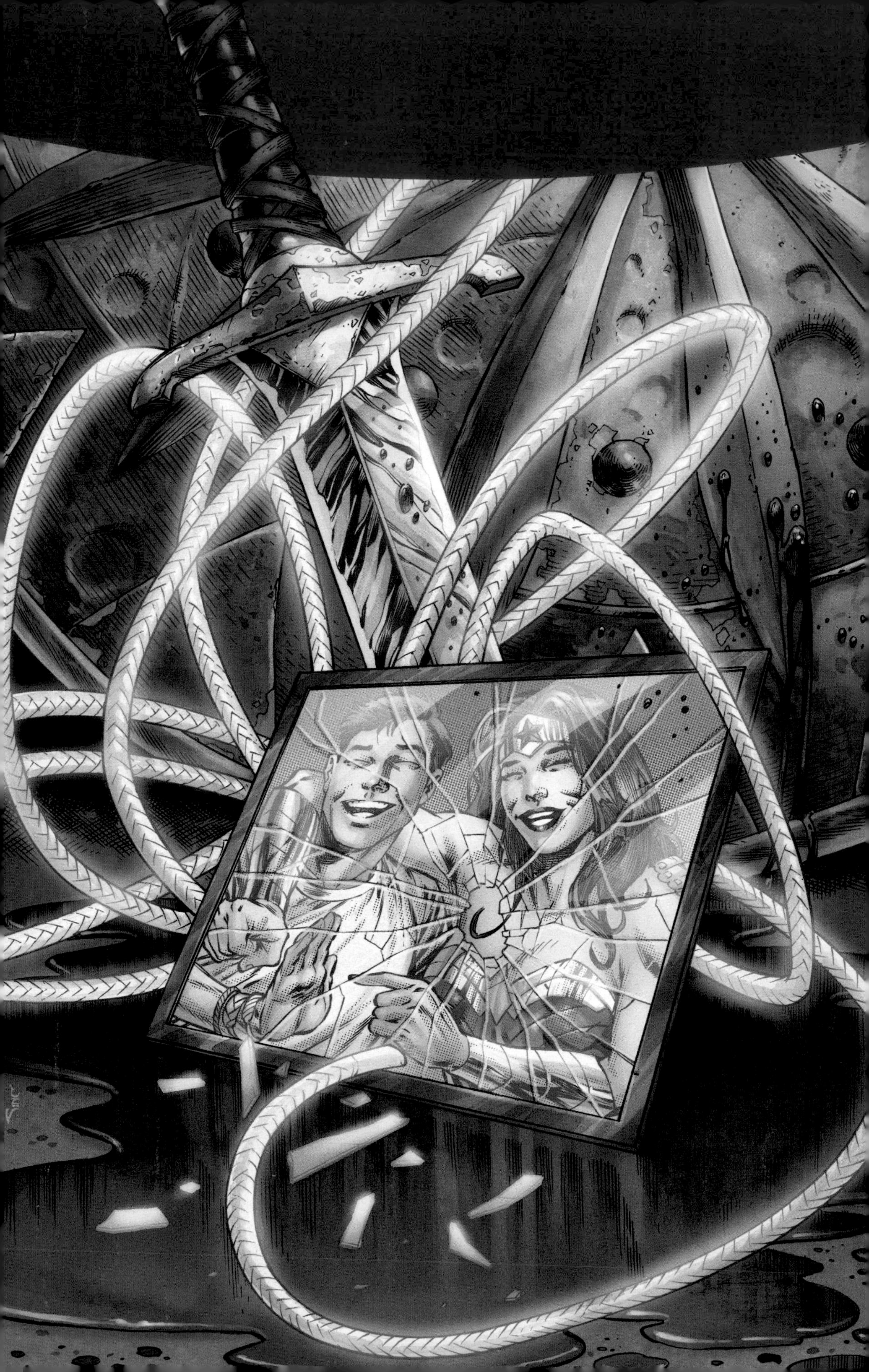

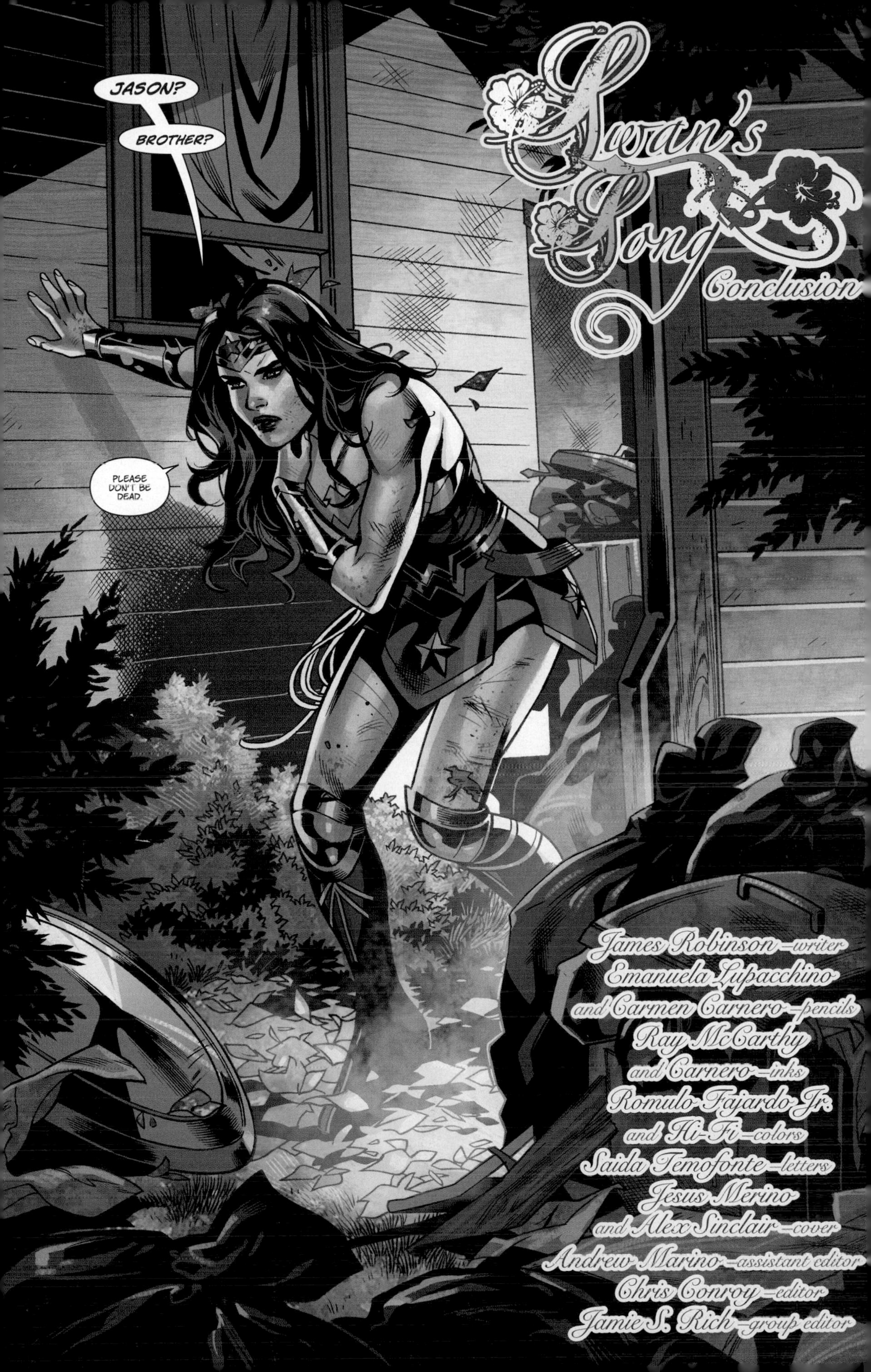

JASON?
BROTHER?
PLEASE DON'T BE DEAD.
Swan's Song
Conclusion
James Robinson—writer
Emanuela Lupacchino and Carmen Carnero—pencils
Ray McCarthy and Carnero—inks
Romulo Fajardo Jr. and Hi-Fi—colors
Saida Temofonte—letters
Jesus Merino and Alex Sinclair—cover
Andrew Marino—assistant editor
Chris Conroy—editor
Jamie S. Rich—group editor

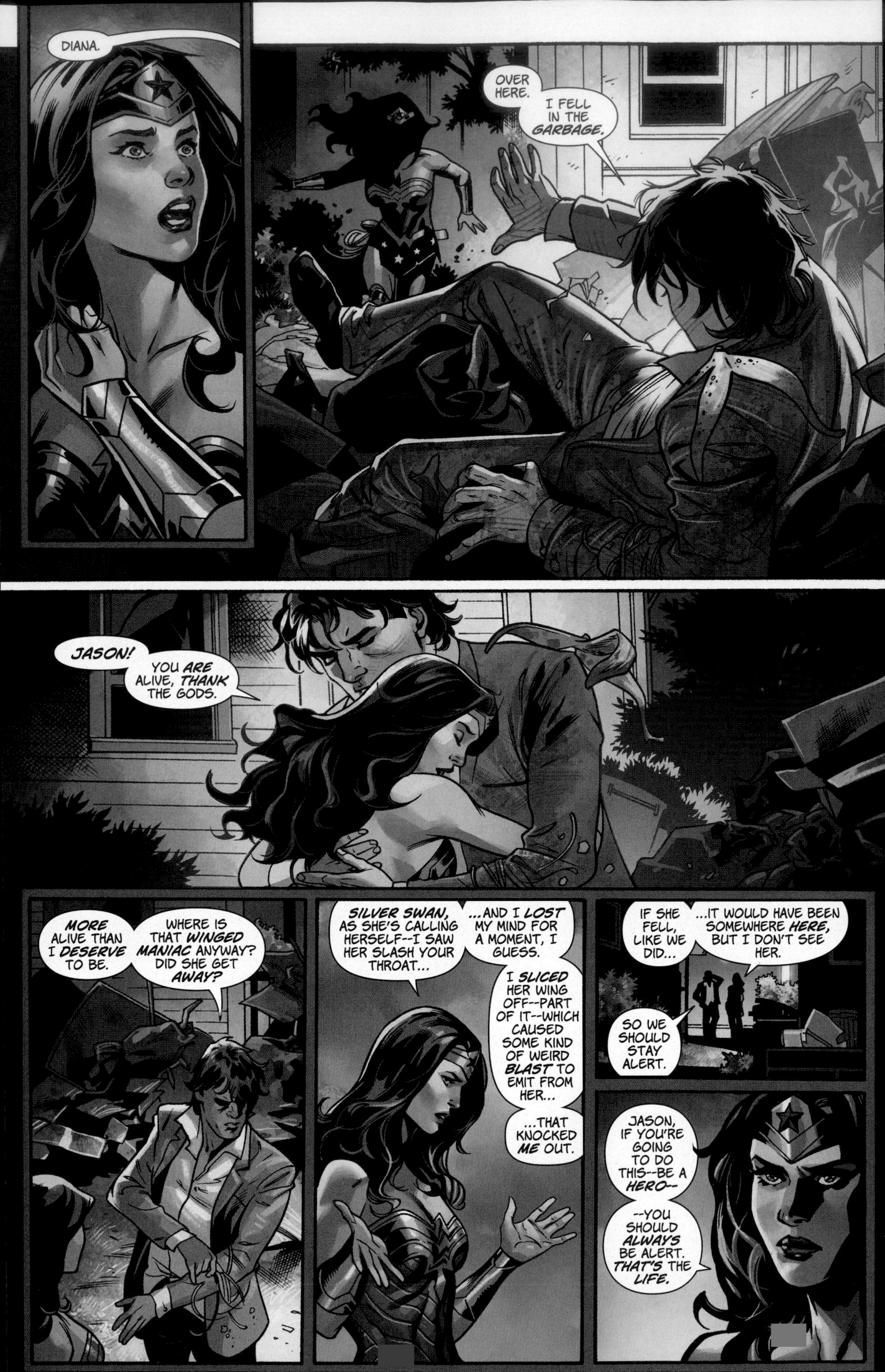
DIANA.
OVER HERE.
I FELL IN THE GARBAGE.
JASON!
YOU ARE ALIVE, THANK THE GODS.
MORE ALIVE THAN I DESERVE TO BE.
WHERE IS THAT WINGED MANIAC ANYWAY? DID SHE GET AWAY?
SILVER SWAN, AS SHE'S CALLING HERSELF--I SAW HER SLASH YOUR THROAT...
...AND I LOST MY MIND FOR A MOMENT, I GUESS.
I SLICED HER WING OFF--PART OF IT--WHICH CAUSED SOME KIND OF WEIRD BLAST TO EMIT FROM HER...
...THAT KNOCKED ME OUT.
IF SHE FELL, LIKE WE DID...
...IT WOULD HAVE BEEN SOMEWHERE HERE, BUT I DON'T SEE HER.
SO WE SHOULD STAY ALERT.
JASON, IF YOU'RE GOING TO DO THIS--BE A HERO--
--YOU SHOULD ALWAYS BE ALERT. THAT'S THE LIFE.

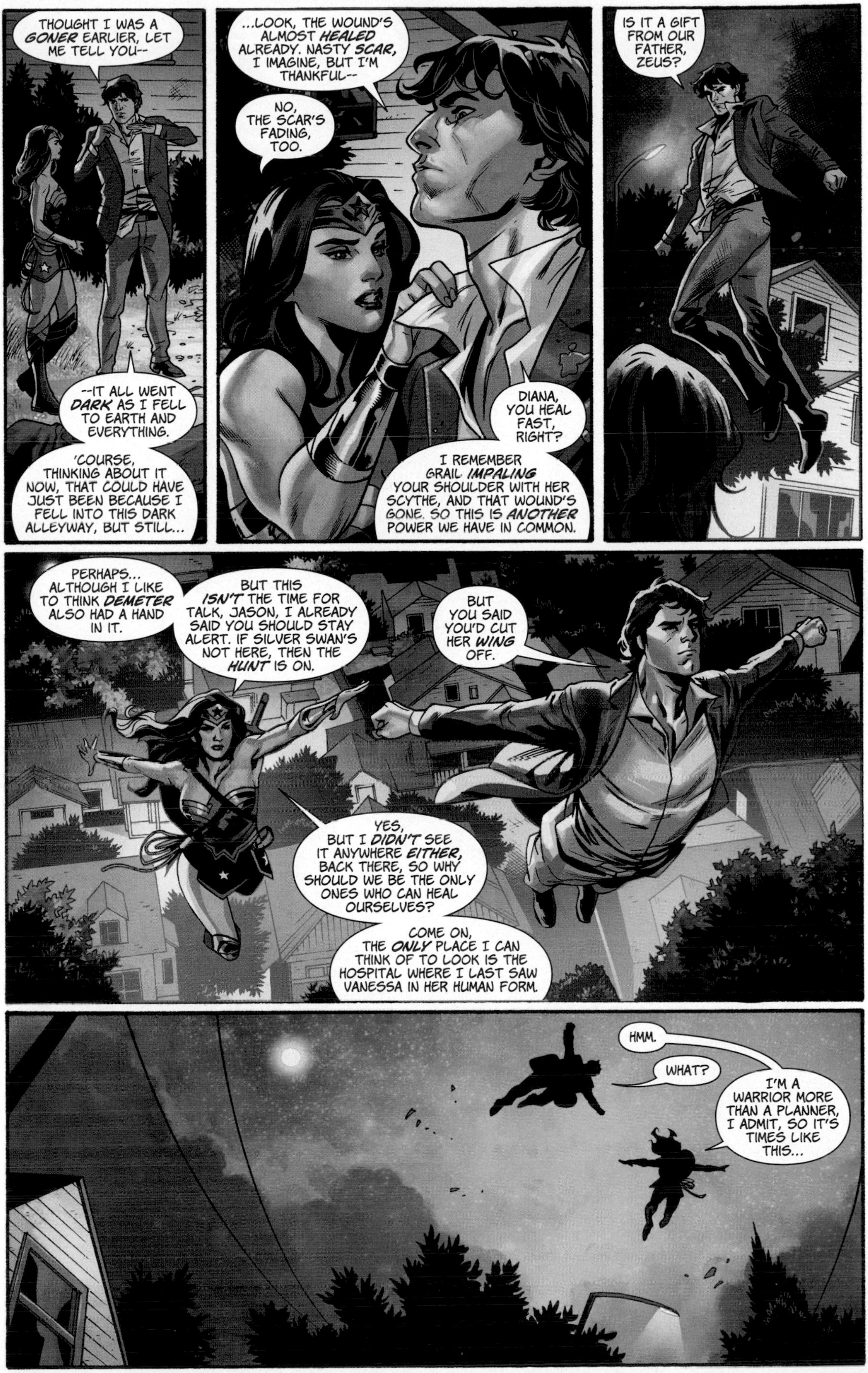
THOUGHT I WAS A GONER EARLIER, LET ME TELL YOU--
--IT ALL WENT DARK AS I FELL TO EARTH AND EVERYTHING.
'COURSE, THINKING ABOUT IT NOW, THAT COULD HAVE JUST BEEN BECAUSE I FELL INTO THIS DARK ALLEYWAY, BUT STILL...
...LOOK, THE WOUND'S ALMOST HEALED ALREADY. NASTY SCAR, I IMAGINE, BUT I'M THANKFUL--
NO, THE SCAR'S FADING, TOO.
DIANA, YOU HEAL FAST, RIGHT?
I REMEMBER GRAIL IMPALING YOUR SHOULDER WITH HER SCYTHE, AND THAT WOUND'S GONE. SO THIS IS ANOTHER POWER WE HAVE IN COMMON.
IS IT A GIFT FROM OUR FATHER, ZEUS?
PERHAPS... ALTHOUGH I LIKE TO THINK DEMETER ALSO HAD A HAND IN IT.
BUT THIS ISN'T THE TIME FOR TALK, JASON, I ALREADY SAID YOU SHOULD STAY ALERT. IF SILVER SWAN'S NOT HERE, THEN THE HUNT IS ON.
BUT YOU SAID YOU'D CUT HER WING OFF.
YES, BUT I DIDN'T SEE IT ANYWHERE EITHER, BACK THERE, SO WHY SHOULD WE BE THE ONLY ONES WHO CAN HEAL OURSELVES?
COME ON, THE ONLY PLACE I CAN THINK OF TO LOOK IS THE HOSPITAL WHERE I LAST SAW VANESSA IN HER HUMAN FORM.
HMM.
WHAT?
I'M A WARRIOR MORE THAN A PLANNER, I ADMIT, SO IT'S TIMES LIKE THIS...

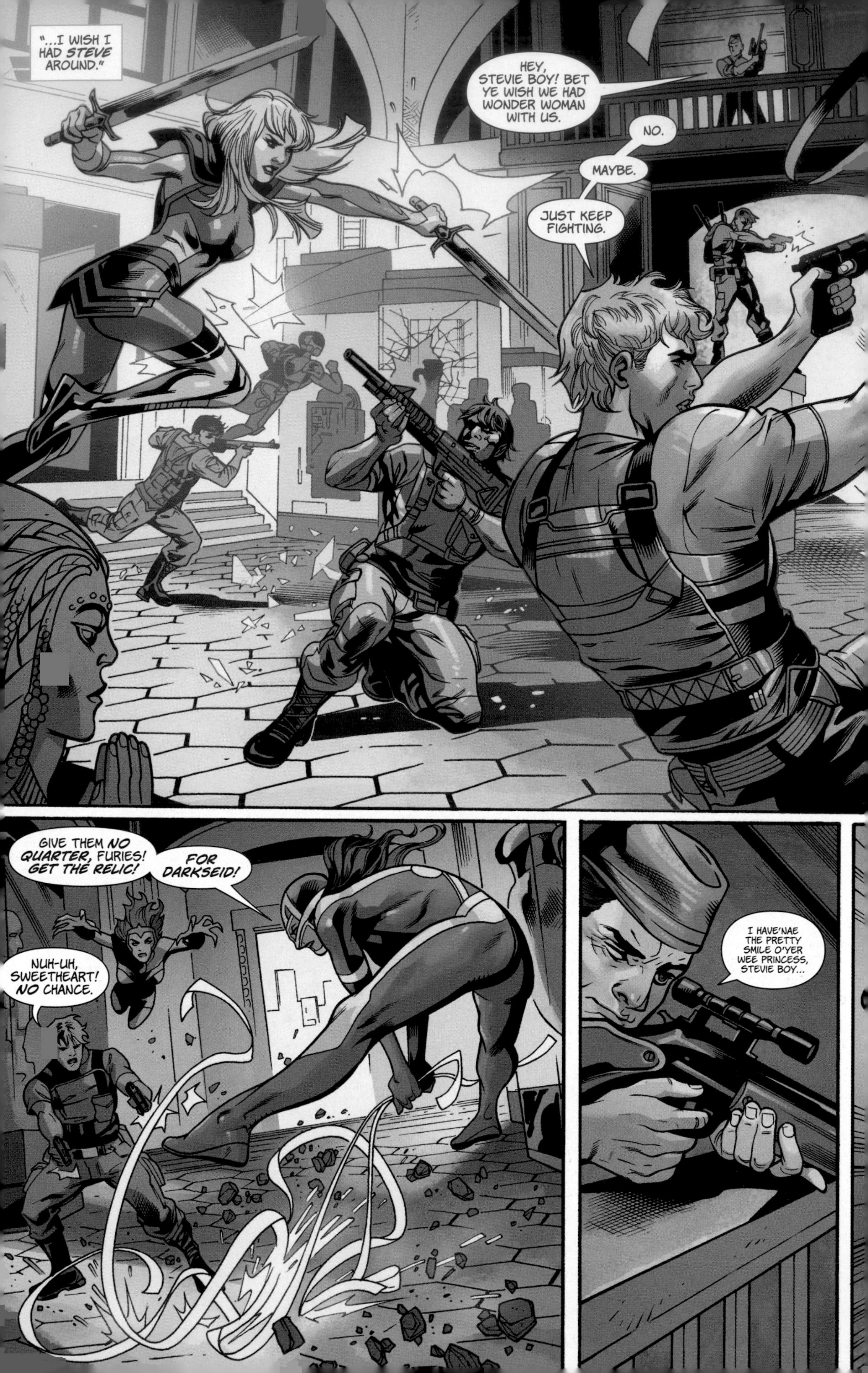
"...I WISH I HAD STEVE AROUND."
HEY, STEVIE BOY! BET YE WISH WE HAD WONDER WOMAN WITH US.
NO.
MAYBE.
JUST KEEP FIGHTING.
GIVE THEM NO QUARTER, FURIES! GET THE RELIC!
FOR DARKSEID!
NUH-UH, SWEETHEART! NO CHANCE.
I HAVE'NAE THE PRETTY SMILE O'YER WEE PRINCESS, STEVIE BOY...

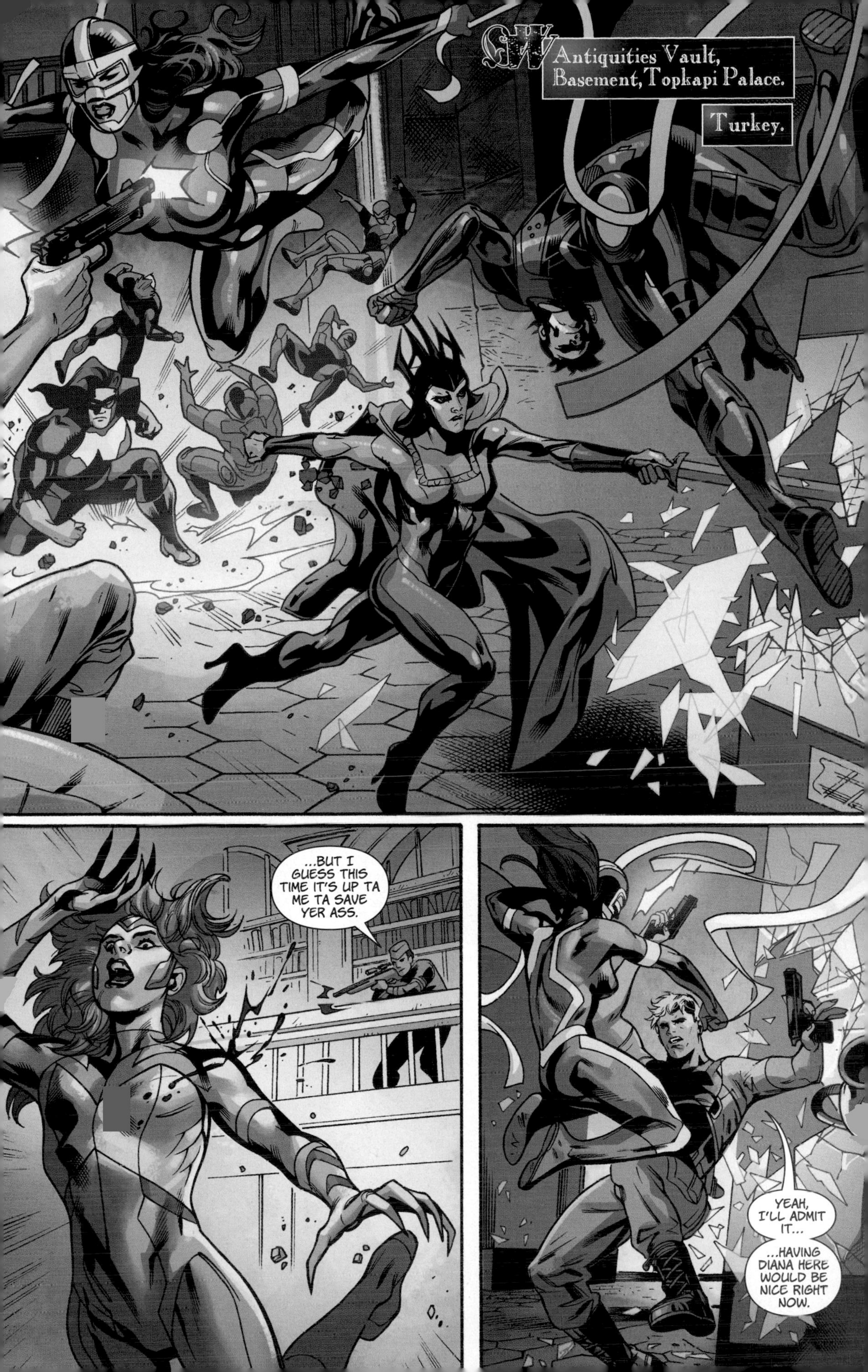

Antiquities Vault, Basement, Topkapi Palace.
Turkey.
...BUT I GUESS THIS TIME IT'S UP TA ME TA SAVE YER ASS.
YEAH, I'LL ADMIT IT...
...HAVING DIANA HERE WOULD BE NICE RIGHT NOW.

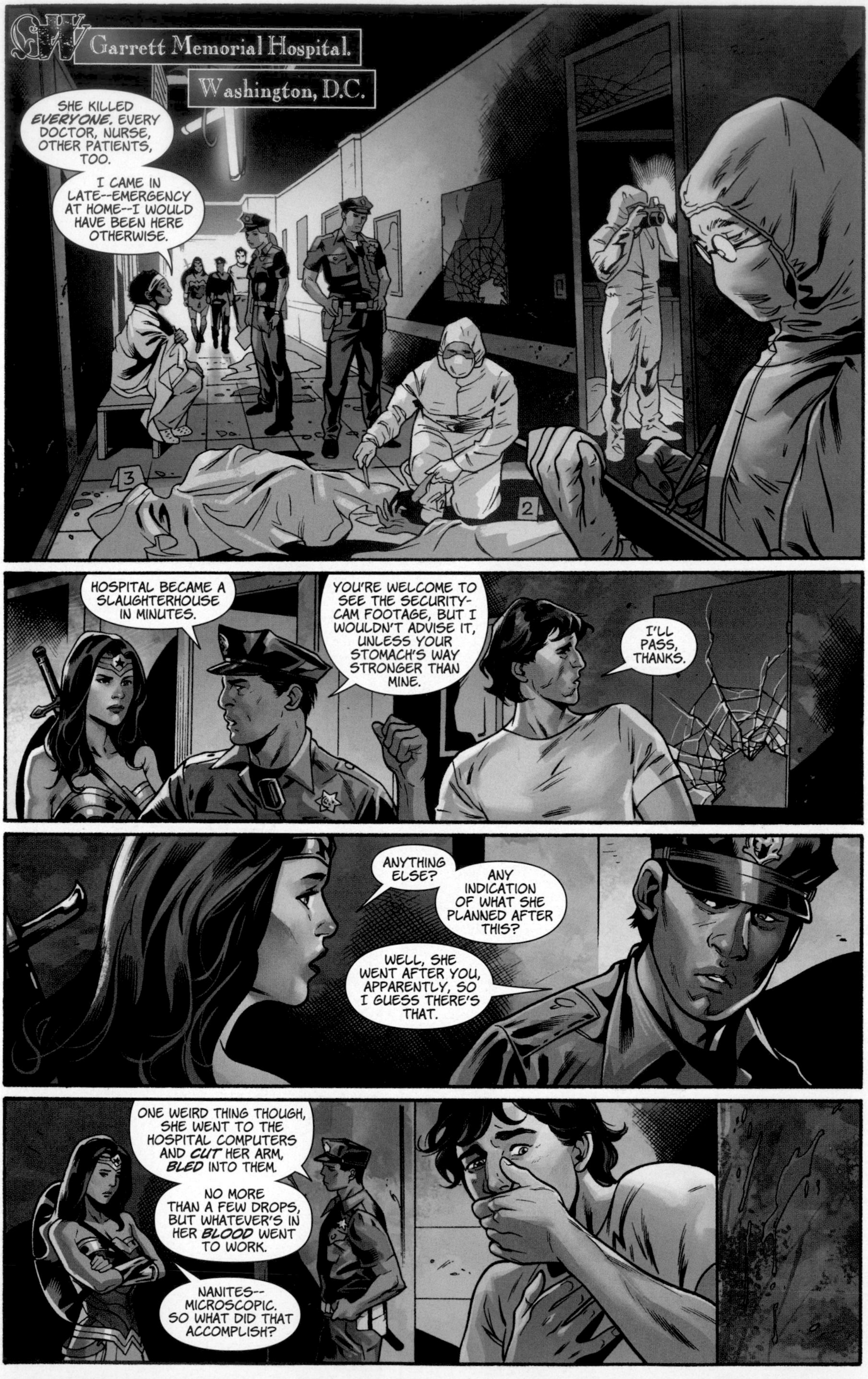
Garrett Memorial Hospital.
Washington, D.C.
SHE KILLED EVERYONE. EVERY DOCTOR, NURSE, OTHER PATIENTS, TOO.
I CAME IN LATE--EMERGENCY AT HOME--I WOULD HAVE BEEN HERE OTHERWISE.
HOSPITAL BECAME A SLAUGHTERHOUSE IN MINUTES.
YOU'RE WELCOME TO SEE THE SECURITY-CAM FOOTAGE, BUT I WOULDN'T ADVISE IT, UNLESS YOUR STOMACH'S WAY STRONGER THAN MINE.
I'LL PASS, THANKS.
ANYTHING ELSE?
ANY INDICATION OF WHAT SHE PLANNED AFTER THIS?
WELL, SHE WENT AFTER YOU, APPARENTLY, SO I GUESS THERE'S THAT.
ONE WEIRD THING THOUGH, SHE WENT TO THE HOSPITAL COMPUTERS AND CUT HER ARM, BLED INTO THEM.
NO MORE THAN A FEW DROPS, BUT WHATEVER'S IN HER BLOOD WENT TO WORK.
NANITES--MICROSCOPIC. SO WHAT DID THAT ACCOMPLISH?

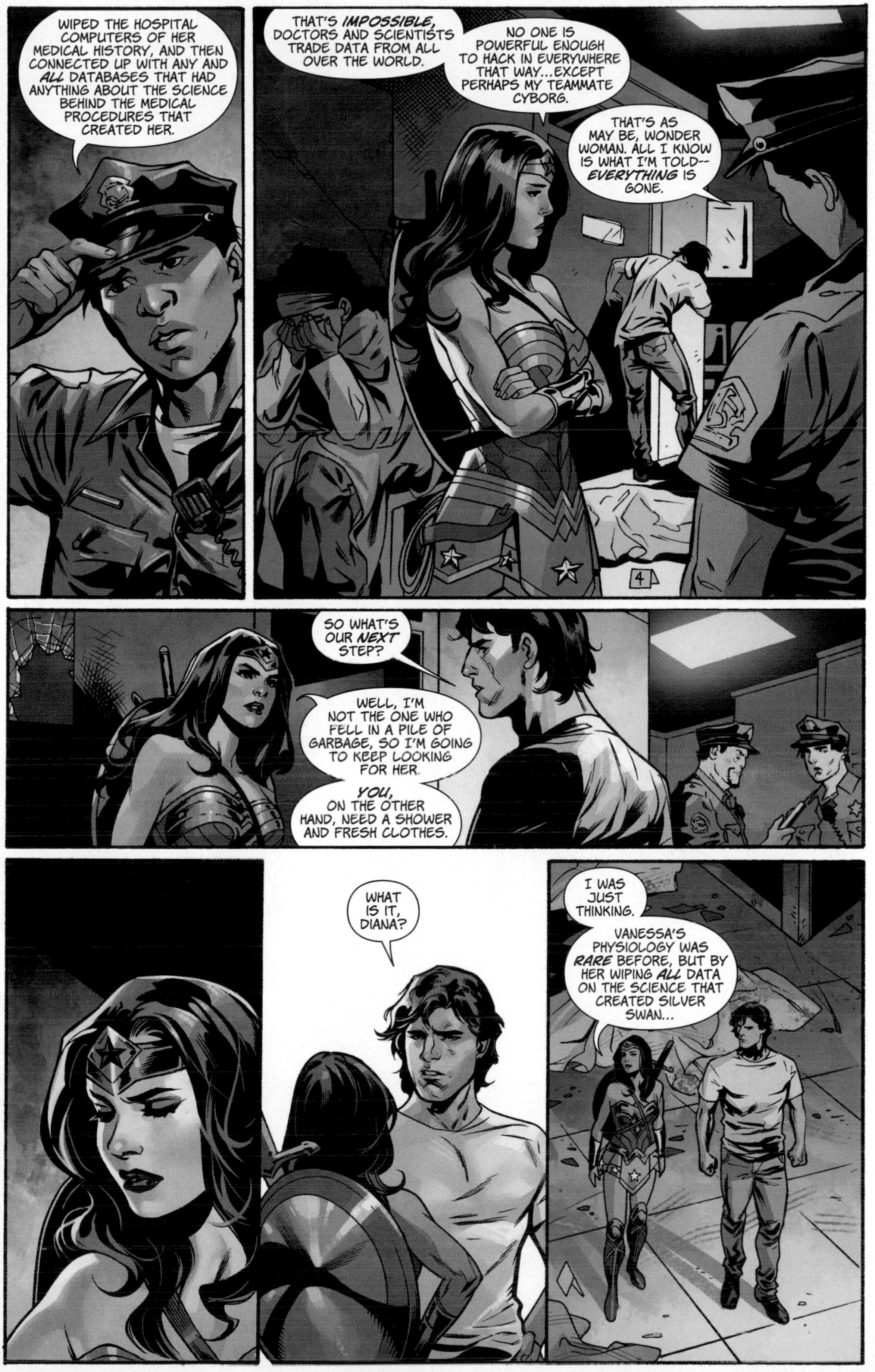
WIPED THE HOSPITAL COMPUTERS OF HER MEDICAL HISTORY, AND THEN CONNECTED UP WITH ANY AND ALL DATABASES THAT HAD ANYTHING ABOUT THE SCIENCE BEHIND THE MEDICAL PROCEDURES THAT CREATED HER.
THAT'S IMPOSSIBLE, DOCTORS AND SCIENTISTS TRADE DATA FROM ALL OVER THE WORLD.
NO ONE IS POWERFUL ENOUGH TO HACK IN EVERYWHERE THAT WAY...EXCEPT PERHAPS MY TEAMMATE CYBORG.
THAT'S AS MAY BE, WONDER WOMAN. ALL I KNOW IS WHAT I'M TOLD--EVERYTHING IS GONE.
4
SO WHAT'S OUR NEXT STEP?
WELL, I'M NOT THE ONE WHO FELL IN A PILE OF GARBAGE, SO I'M GOING TO KEEP LOOKING FOR HER.
YOU, ON THE OTHER HAND, NEED A SHOWER AND FRESH CLOTHES.
WHAT IS IT, DIANA?
I WAS JUST THINKING.
VANESSA'S PHYSIOLOGY WAS RARE BEFORE, BUT BY HER WIPING ALL DATA ON THE SCIENCE THAT CREATED SILVER SWAN...

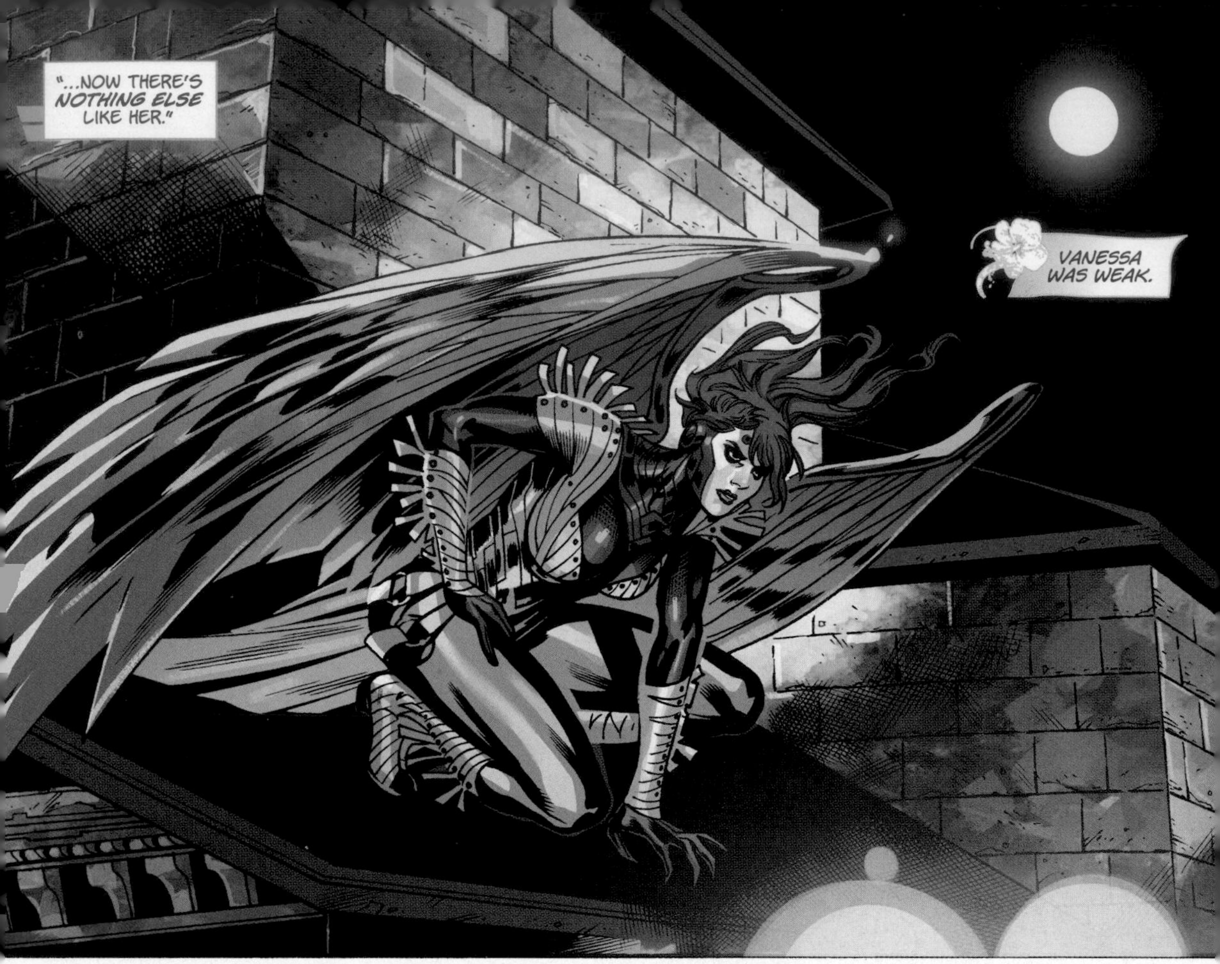
"...NOW THERE'S NOTHING ELSE LIKE HER."
VANESSA WAS WEAK.

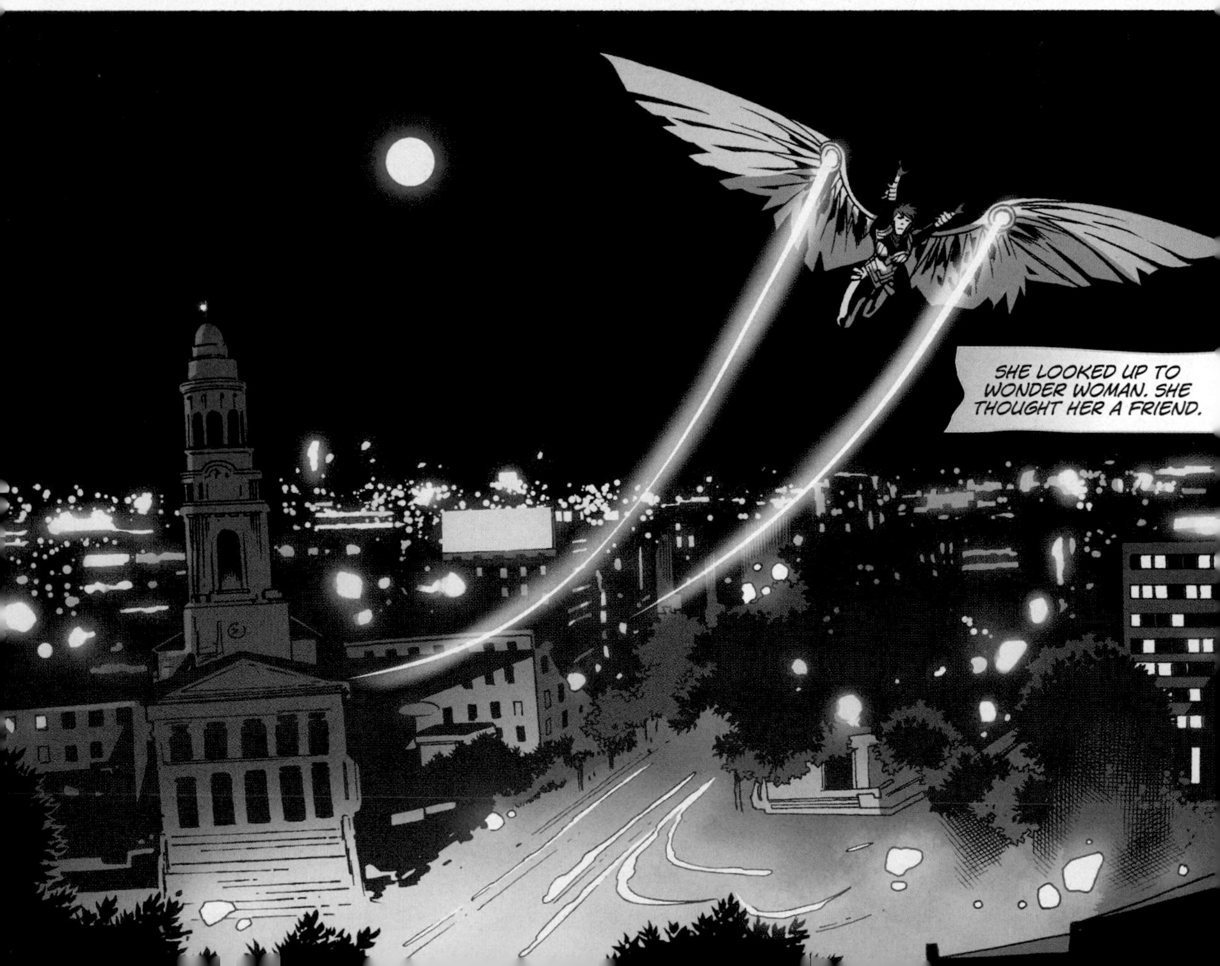
SHE LOOKED UP TO WONDER WOMAN. SHE THOUGHT HER A FRIEND.

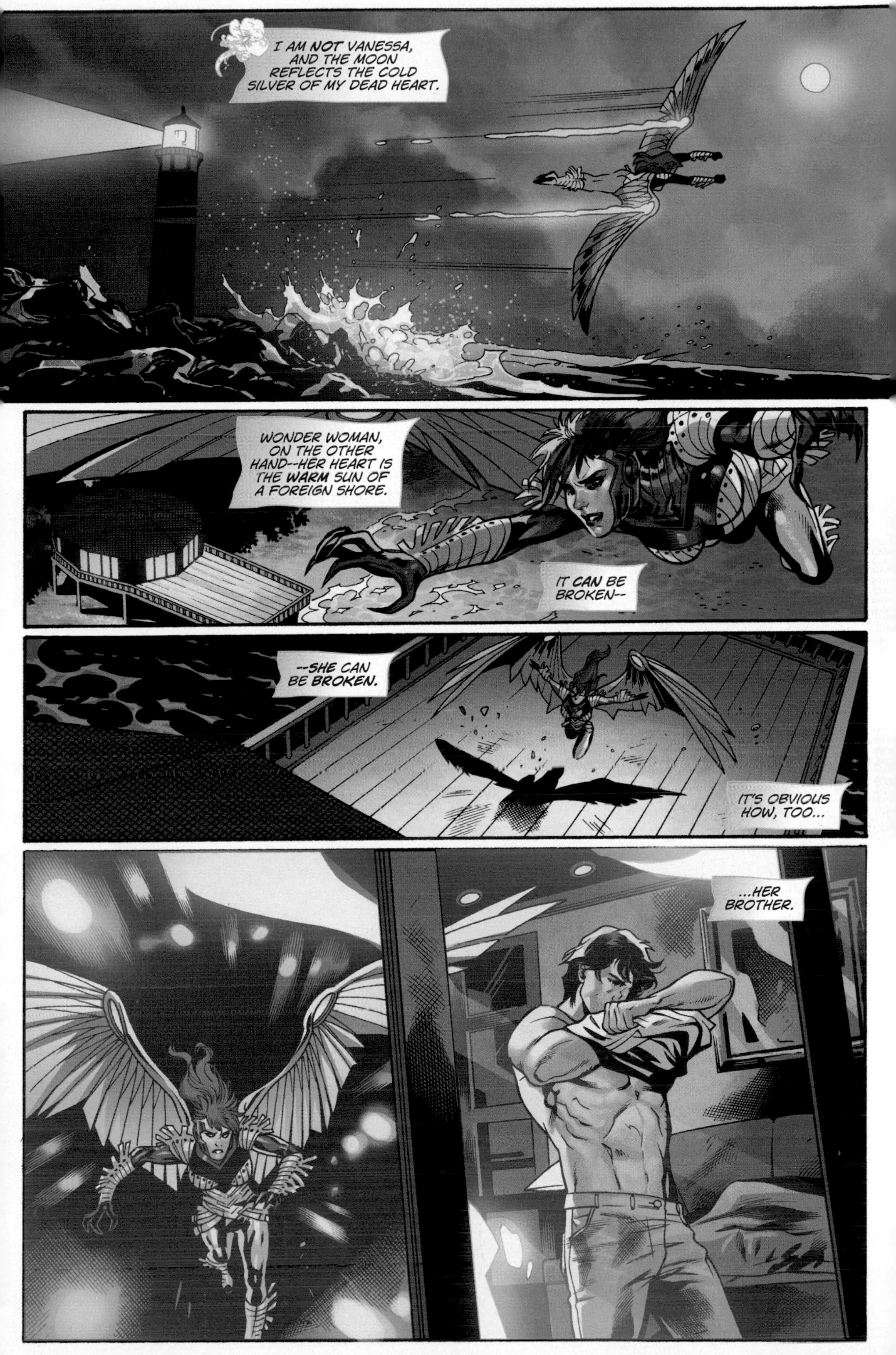
I AM NOT VANESSA, AND THE MOON REFLECTS THE COLD SILVER OF MY DEAD HEART.
WONDER WOMAN, ON THE OTHER HAND--HER HEART IS THE WARM SUN OF A FOREIGN SHORE.
IT CAN BE BROKEN--
--SHE CAN BE BROKEN.
IT'S OBVIOUS HOW, TOO...
...HER BROTHER.

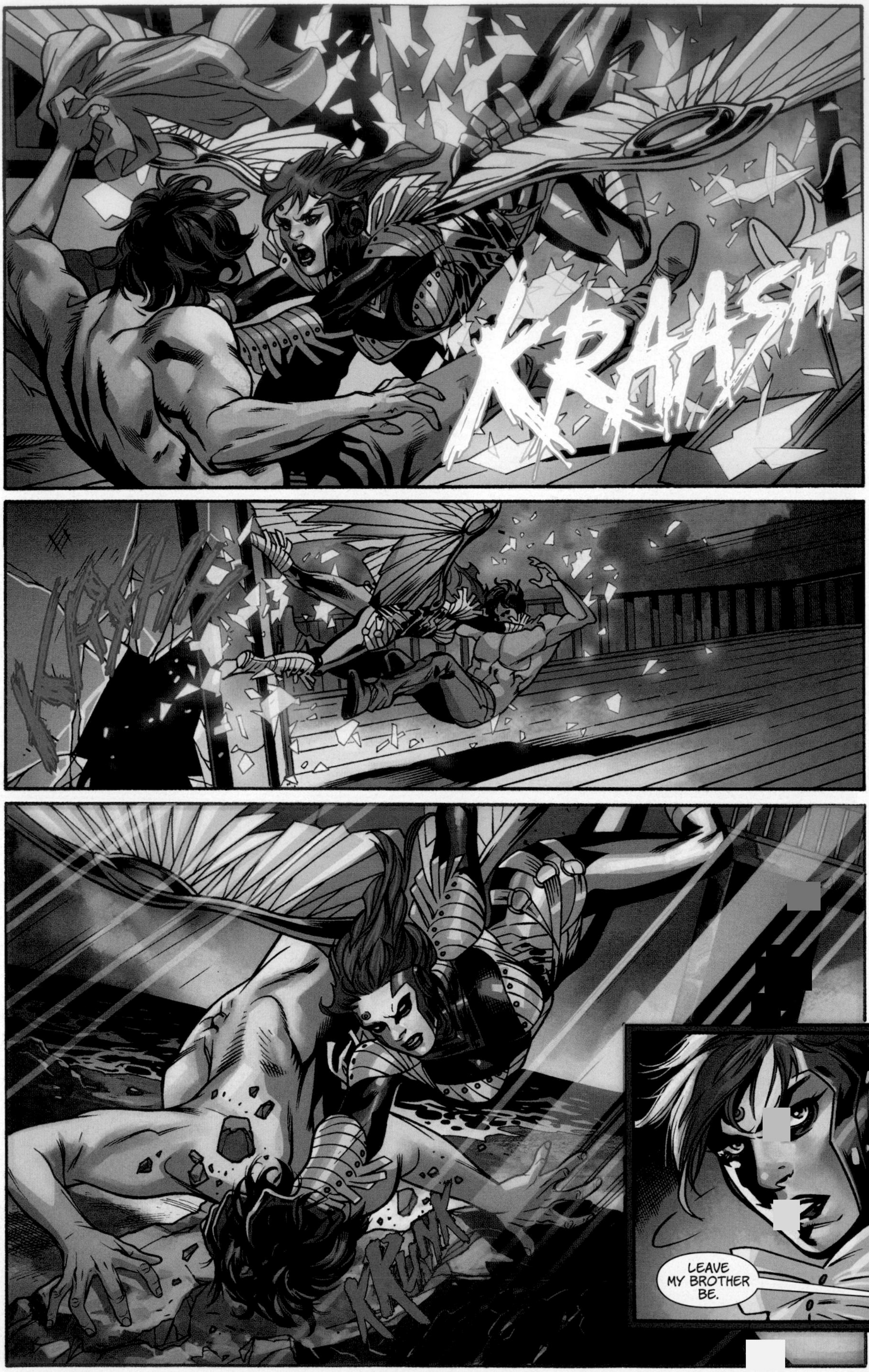
KRAASH
LEAVE MY BROTHER BE.

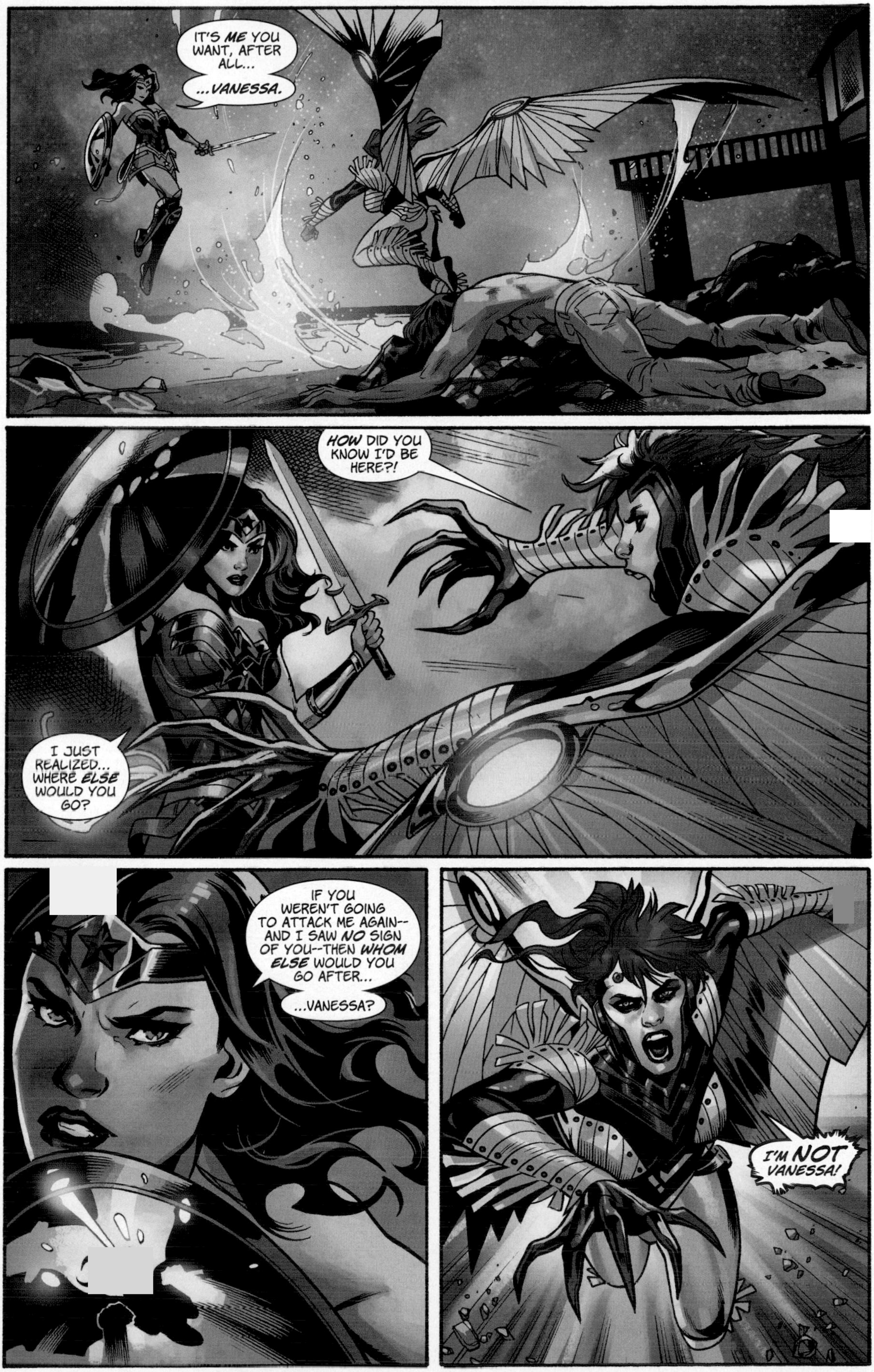
IT'S *ME* YOU WANT, AFTER ALL...
...*VANESSA.*
HOW DID YOU KNOW I'D BE HERE?!
I JUST REALIZED... WHERE *ELSE* WOULD YOU GO?
IF YOU WEREN'T GOING TO ATTACK ME AGAIN--AND I SAW *NO* SIGN OF YOU--THEN *WHOM ELSE* WOULD YOU GO AFTER...
...VANESSA?
I'M NOT VANESSA!

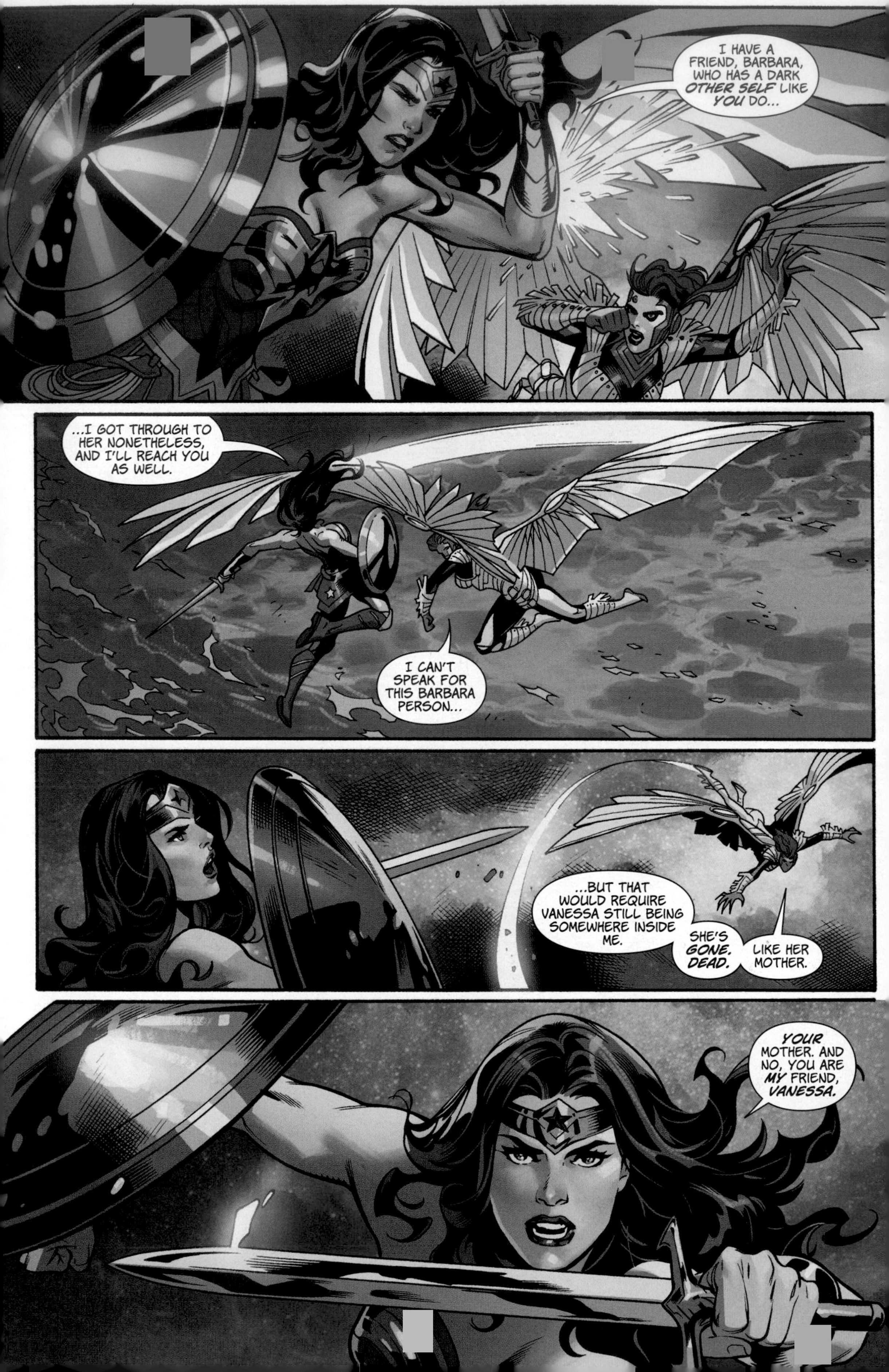
I HAVE A FRIEND, BARBARA, WHO HAS A DARK *OTHER SELF* LIKE *YOU* DO...
...I GOT THROUGH TO HER NONETHELESS, AND I'LL REACH YOU AS WELL.
I CAN'T SPEAK FOR THIS BARBARA PERSON...
...BUT THAT WOULD REQUIRE VANESSA STILL BEING SOMEWHERE INSIDE ME.
SHE'S *GONE. DEAD.*
LIKE HER MOTHER.
YOUR MOTHER. AND NO, YOU ARE *MY* FRIEND, *VANESSA.*

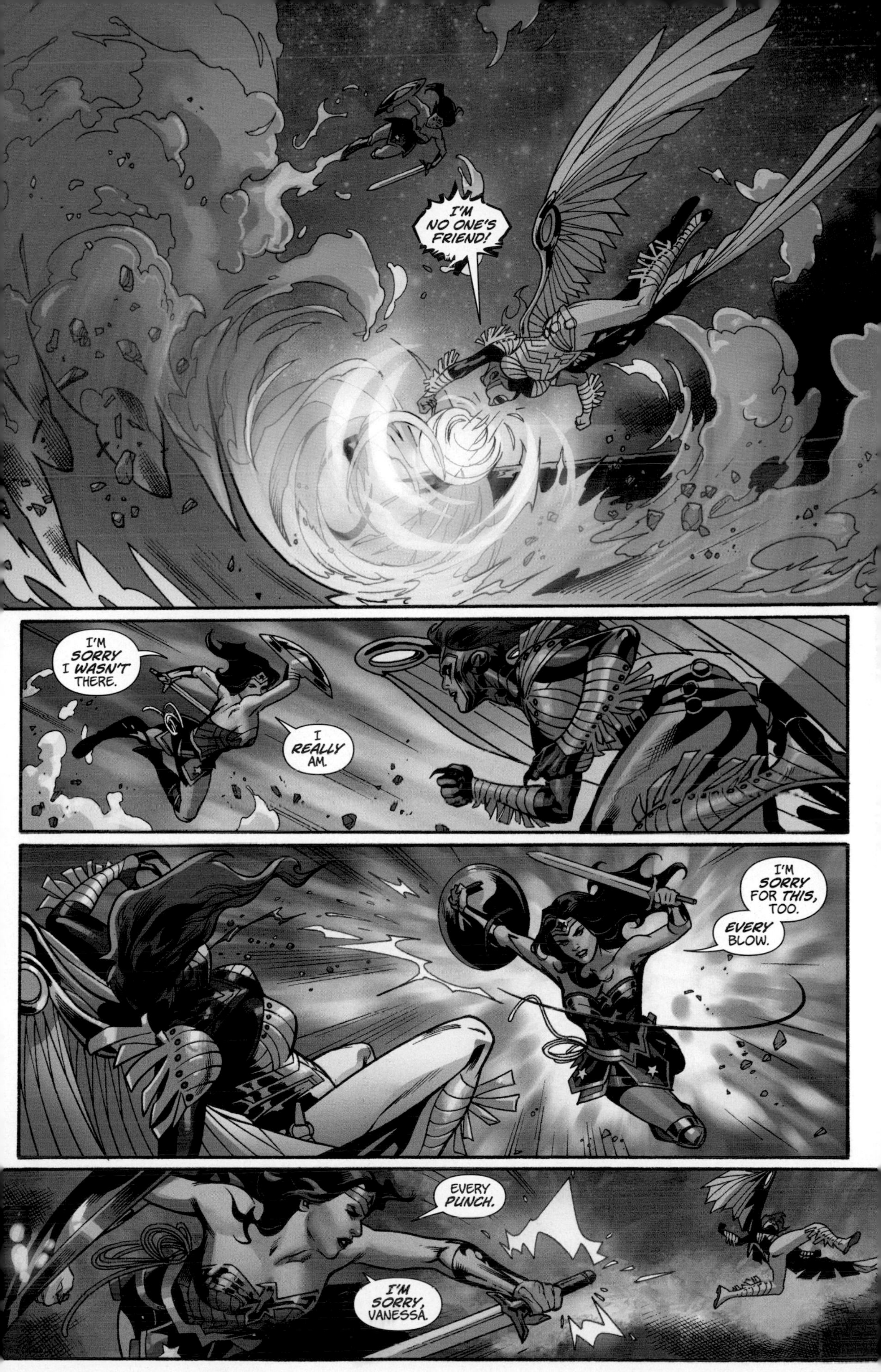
I'M NO ONE'S FRIEND!
I'M SORRY I WASN'T THERE.
I REALLY AM.
I'M SORRY FOR THIS, TOO.
EVERY BLOW.
EVERY PUNCH.
I'M SORRY, VANESSA.

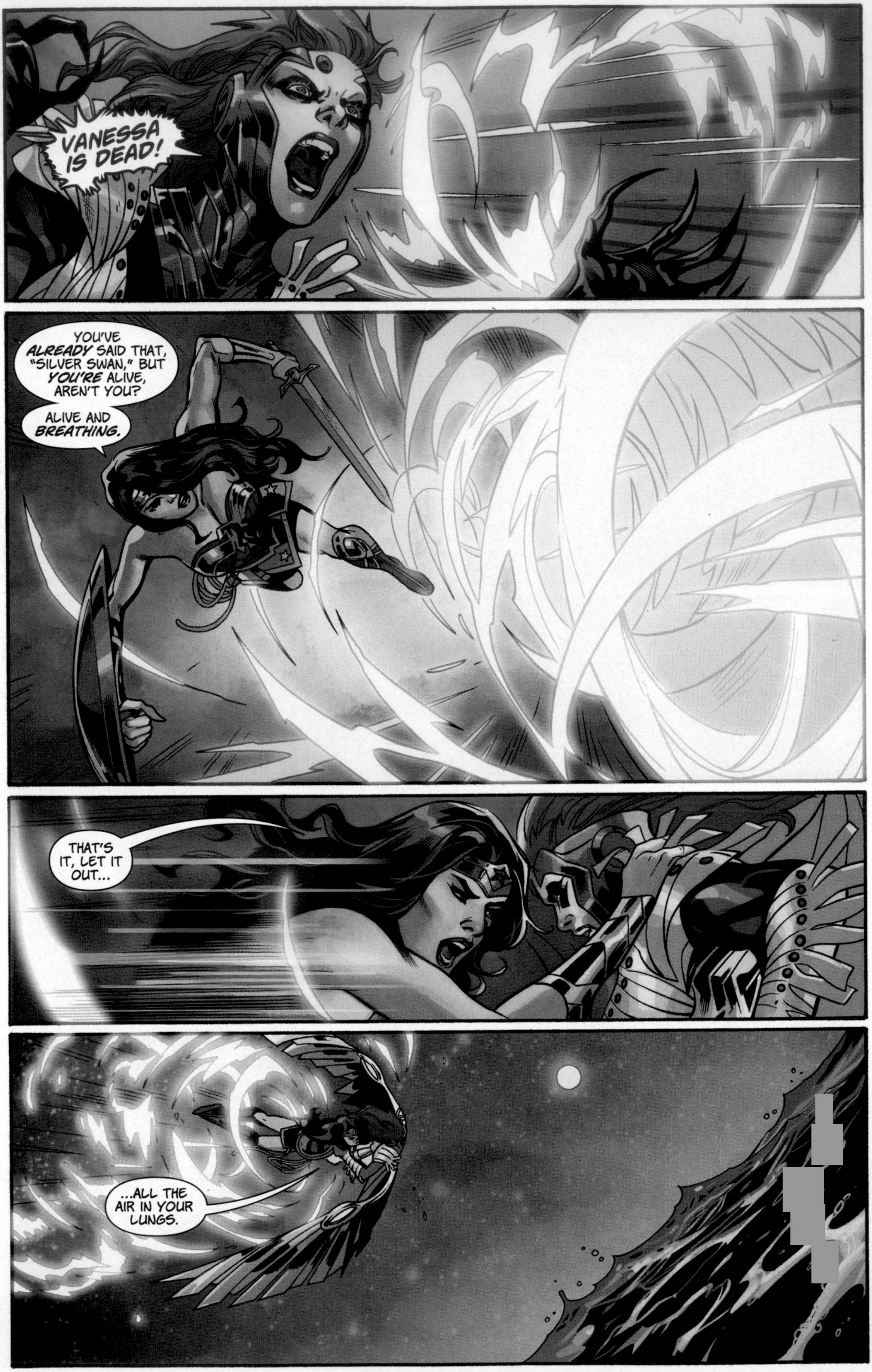
VANESSA IS DEAD!
YOU'VE ALREADY SAID THAT, "SILVER SWAN," BUT YOU'RE ALIVE, AREN'T YOU?
ALIVE AND BREATHING.
THAT'S IT, LET IT OUT...
...ALL THE AIR IN YOUR LUNGS.

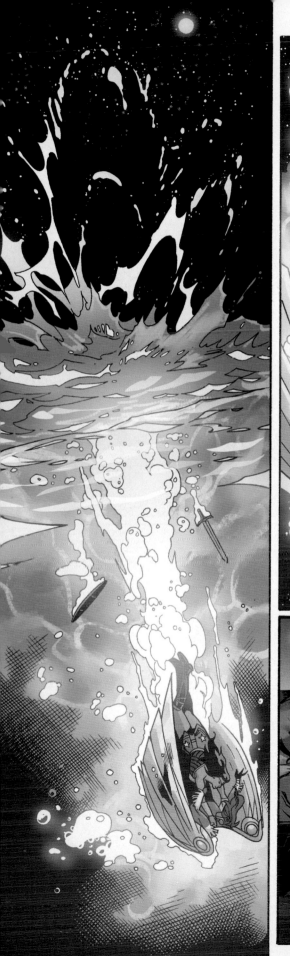
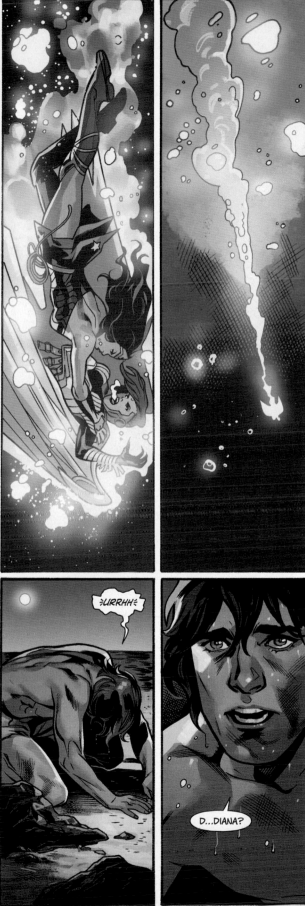

≥URRHH≤

D...DIANA?

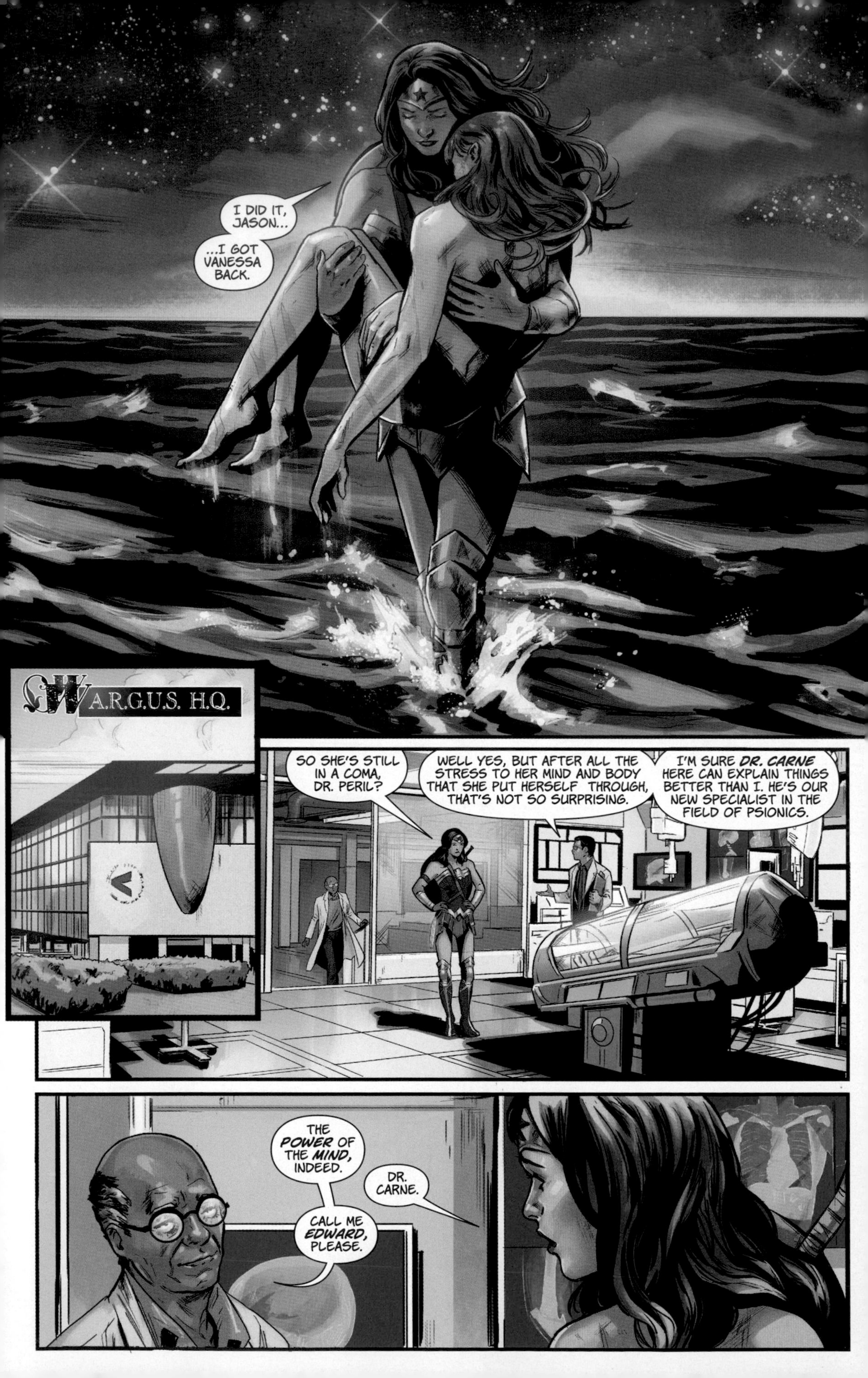
I DID IT, JASON...
...I GOT VANESSA BACK.
A.R.G.U.S. H.Q.
SO SHE'S STILL IN A COMA, DR. PERIL?
WELL YES, BUT AFTER ALL THE STRESS TO HER MIND AND BODY THAT SHE PUT HERSELF THROUGH, THAT'S NOT SO SURPRISING.
I'M SURE DR. CARNE HERE CAN EXPLAIN THINGS BETTER THAN I. HE'S OUR NEW SPECIALIST IN THE FIELD OF PSIONICS.
THE POWER OF THE MIND, INDEED.
DR. CARNE.
CALL ME EDWARD, PLEASE.

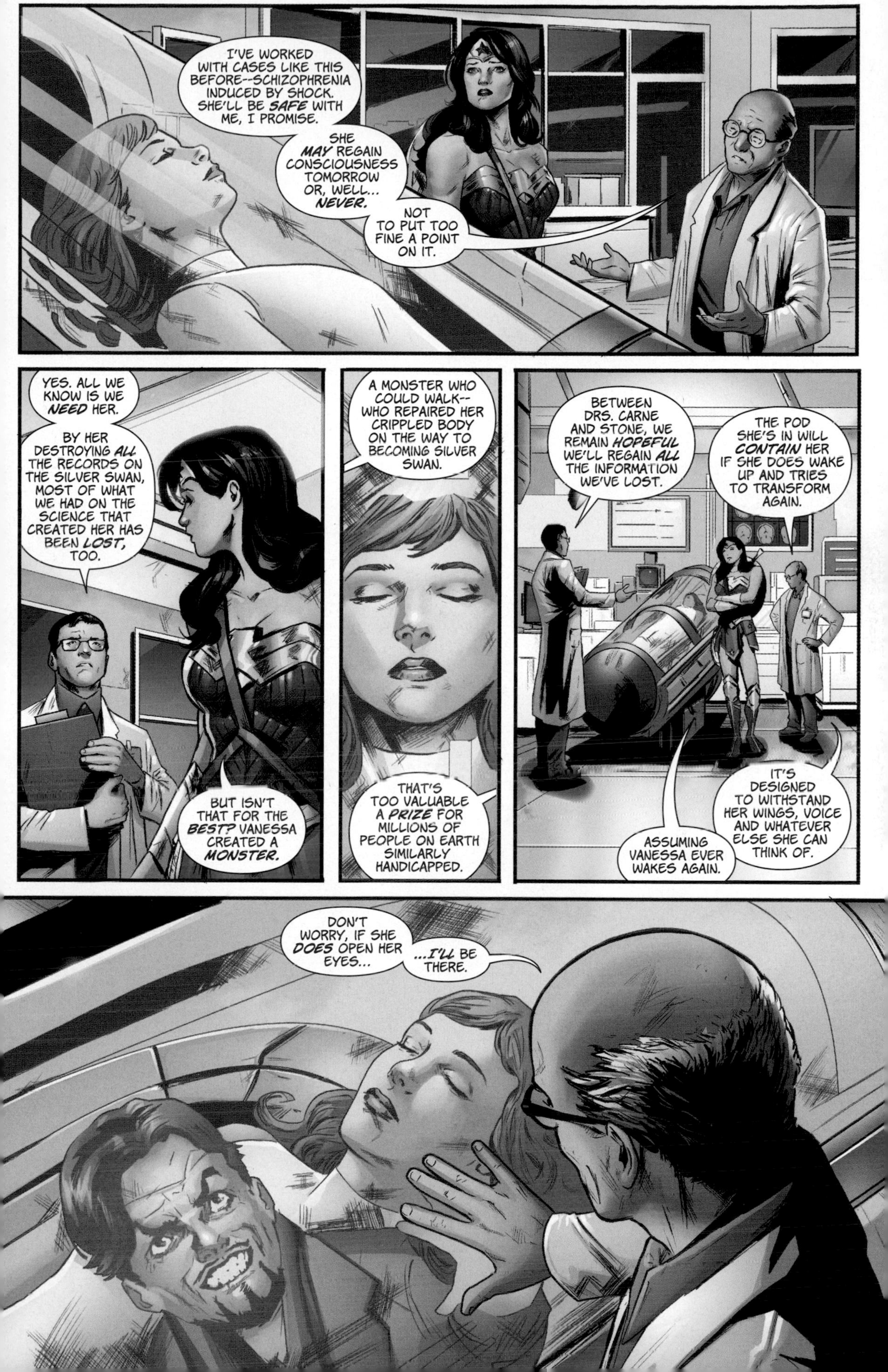

I'VE WORKED WITH CASES LIKE THIS BEFORE--SCHIZOPHRENIA INDUCED BY SHOCK. SHE'LL BE SAFE WITH ME, I PROMISE.
SHE MAY REGAIN CONSCIOUSNESS TOMORROW OR, WELL... NEVER.
NOT TO PUT TOO FINE A POINT ON IT.
YES. ALL WE KNOW IS WE NEED HER.
BY HER DESTROYING ALL THE RECORDS ON THE SILVER SWAN, MOST OF WHAT WE HAD ON THE SCIENCE THAT CREATED HER HAS BEEN LOST, TOO.
BUT ISN'T THAT FOR THE BEST? VANESSA CREATED A MONSTER.
A MONSTER WHO COULD WALK-- WHO REPAIRED HER CRIPPLED BODY ON THE WAY TO BECOMING SILVER SWAN.
THAT'S TOO VALUABLE A PRIZE FOR MILLIONS OF PEOPLE ON EARTH SIMILARLY HANDICAPPED.
BETWEEN DRS. CARNE AND STONE, WE REMAIN HOPEFUL WE'LL REGAIN ALL THE INFORMATION WE'VE LOST.
THE POD SHE'S IN WILL CONTAIN HER IF SHE DOES WAKE UP AND TRIES TO TRANSFORM AGAIN.
IT'S DESIGNED TO WITHSTAND HER WINGS, VOICE AND WHATEVER ELSE SHE CAN THINK OF.
ASSUMING VANESSA EVER WAKES AGAIN.
DON'T WORRY, IF SHE DOES OPEN HER EYES...
...I'LL BE THERE.

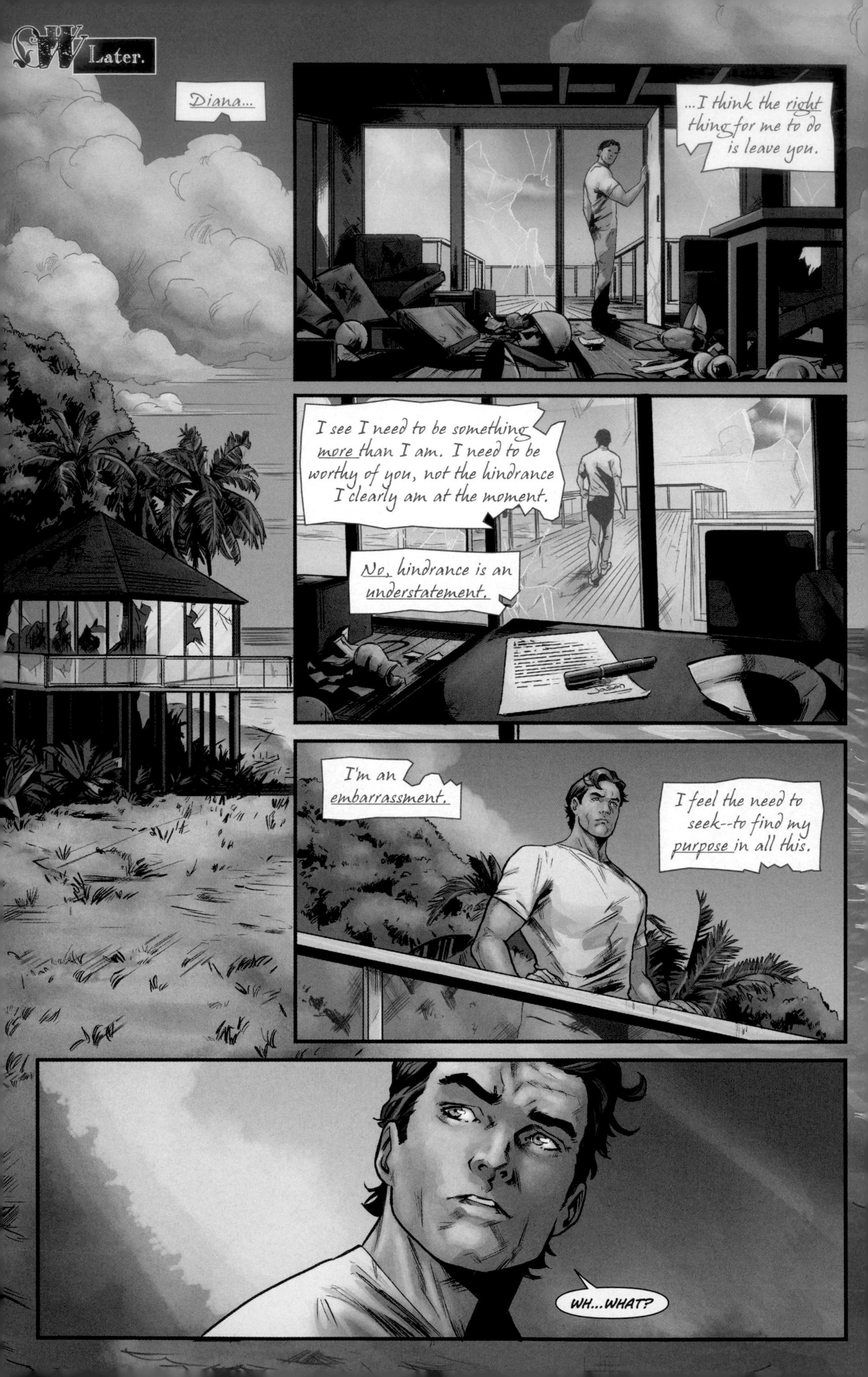
Later.
Diana...
...I think the right thing for me to do is leave you.
I see I need to be something more than I am. I need to be worthy of you, not the hindrance I clearly am at the moment.
No, hindrance is an understatement.
I'm an embarrassment.
I feel the need to seek--to find my purpose in all this.
WH...WHAT?

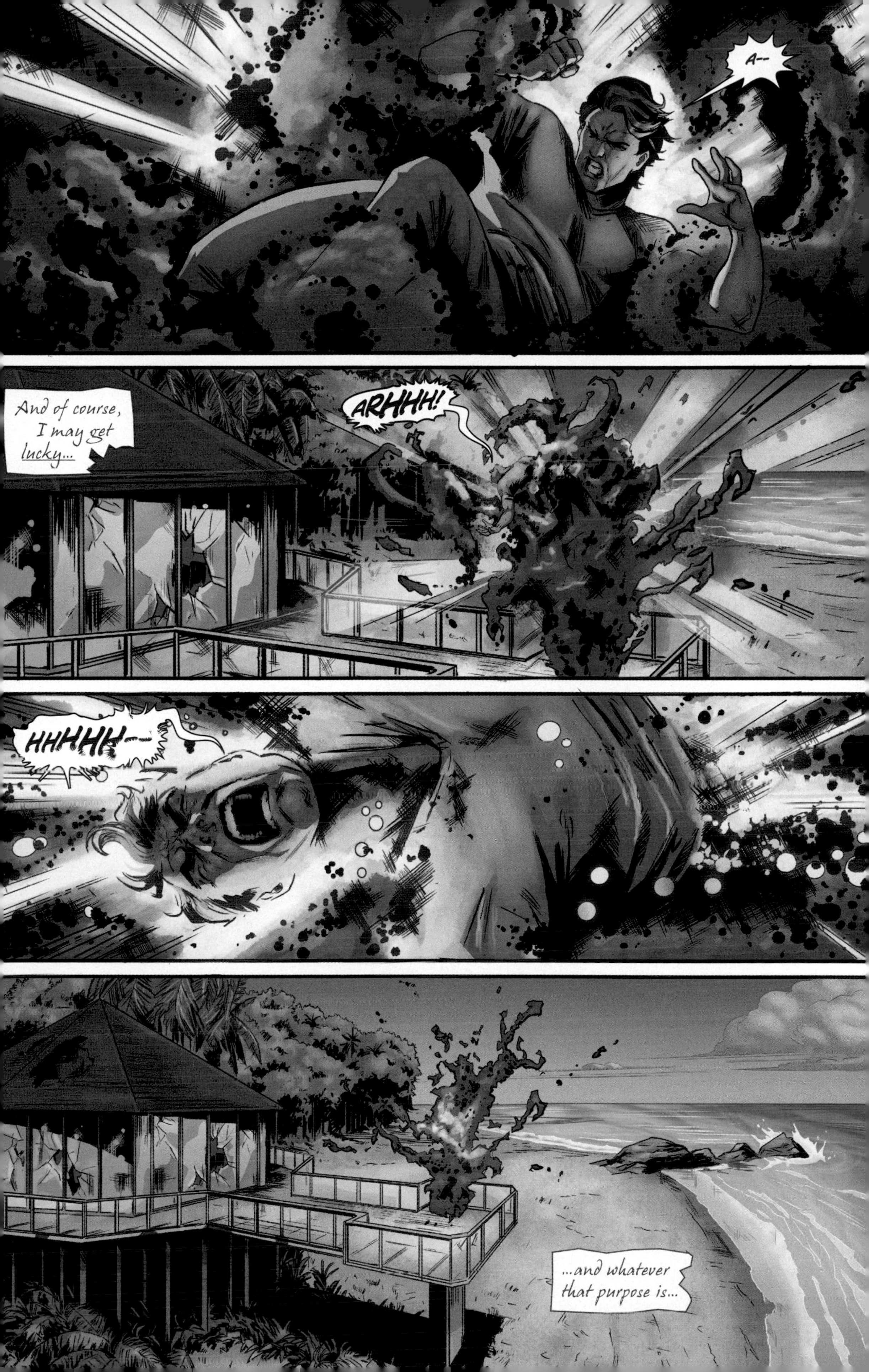
A--
And of course, I may get lucky...
ARHHH!
HHHHH--
...and whatever that purpose is...

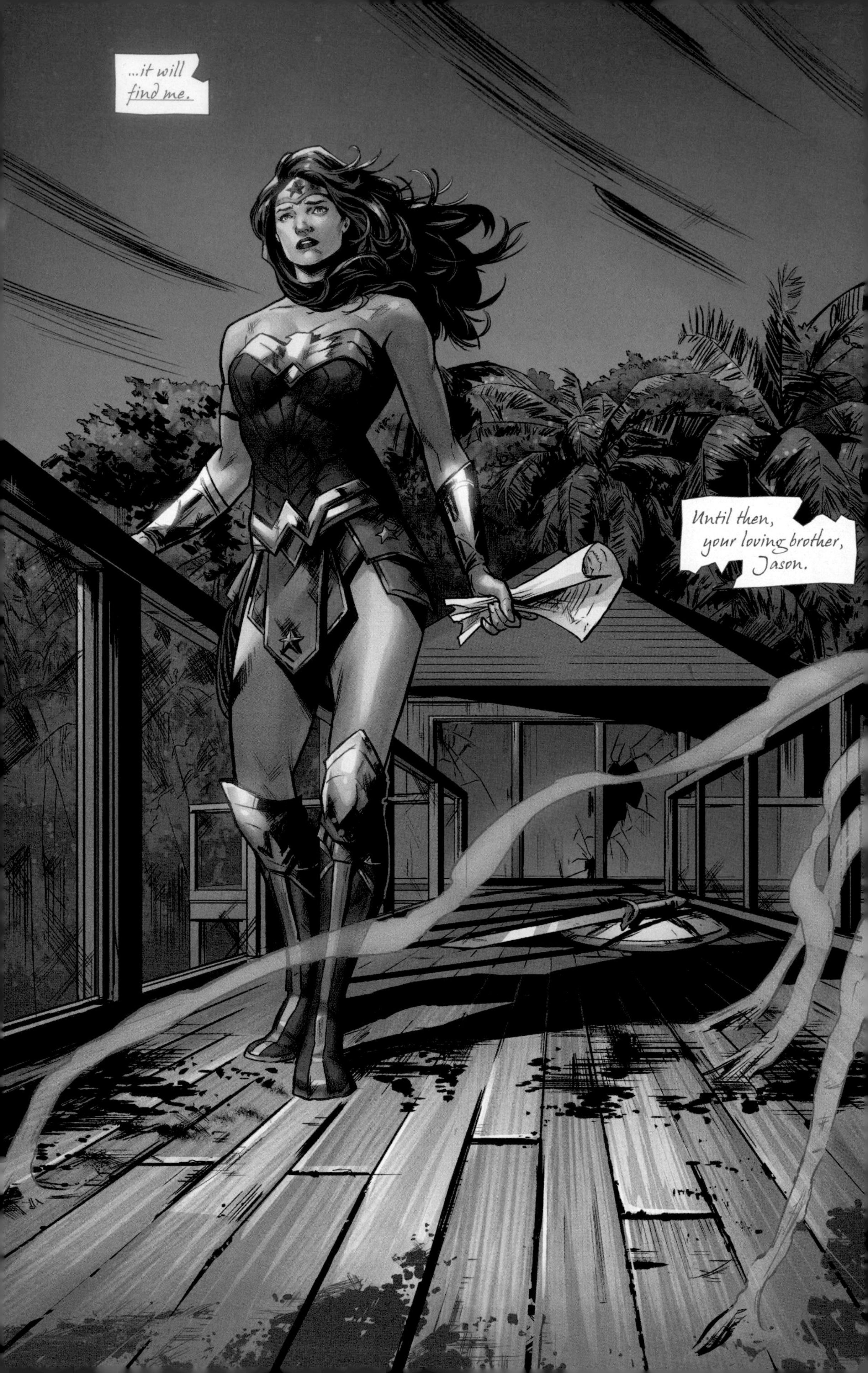
...it will find me.
Until then, your loving brother, Jason.

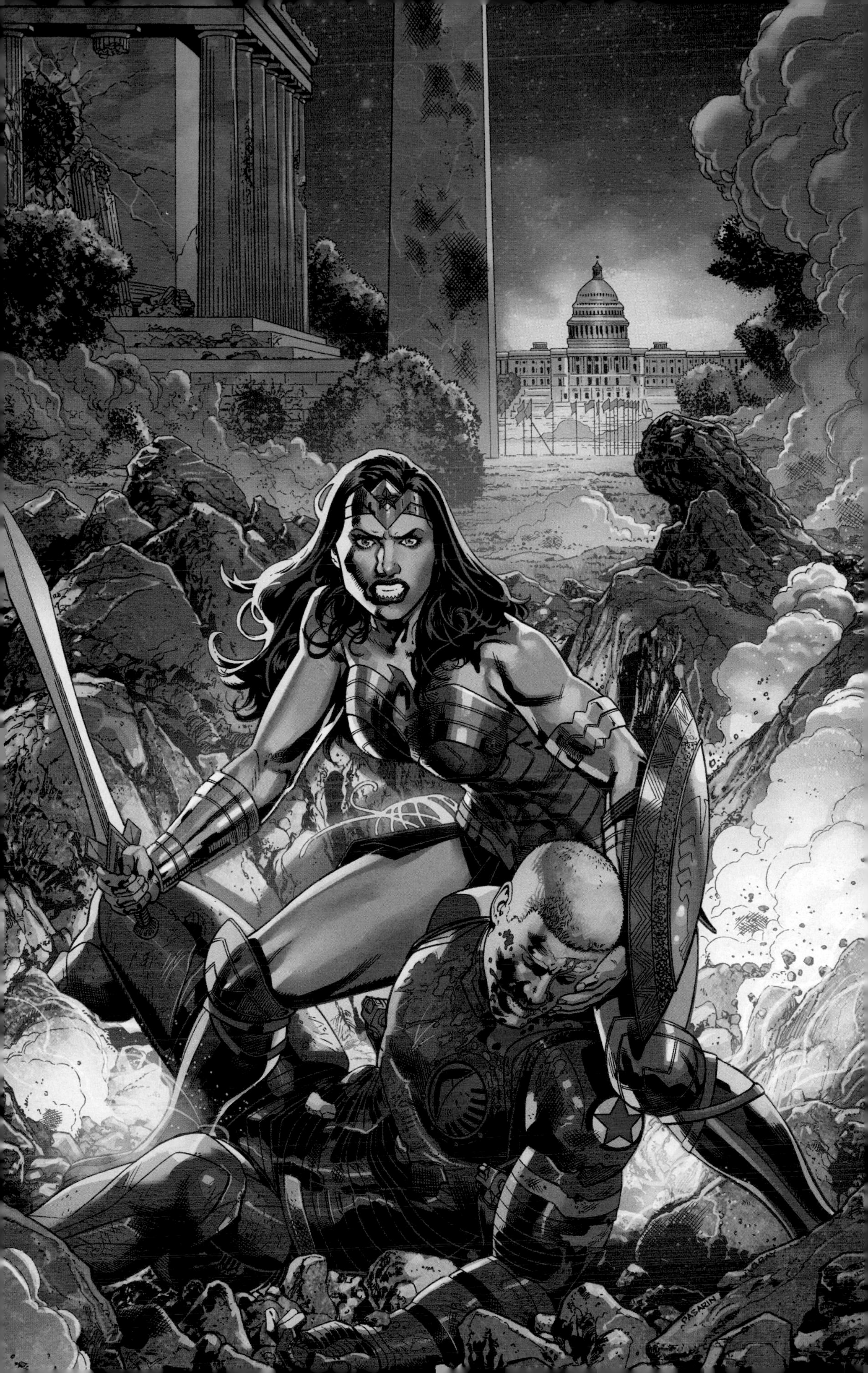
PASARIN

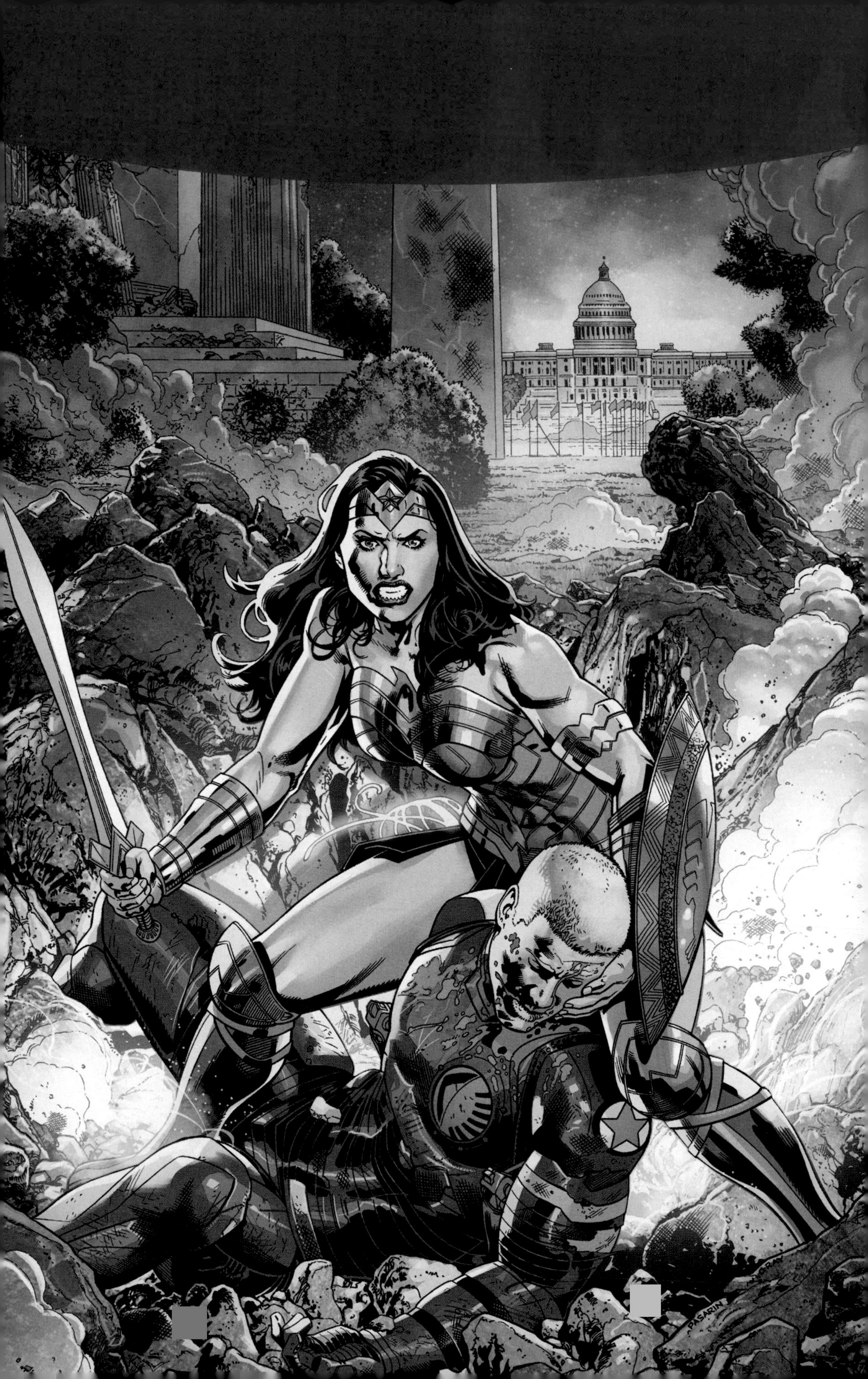
PASARIN

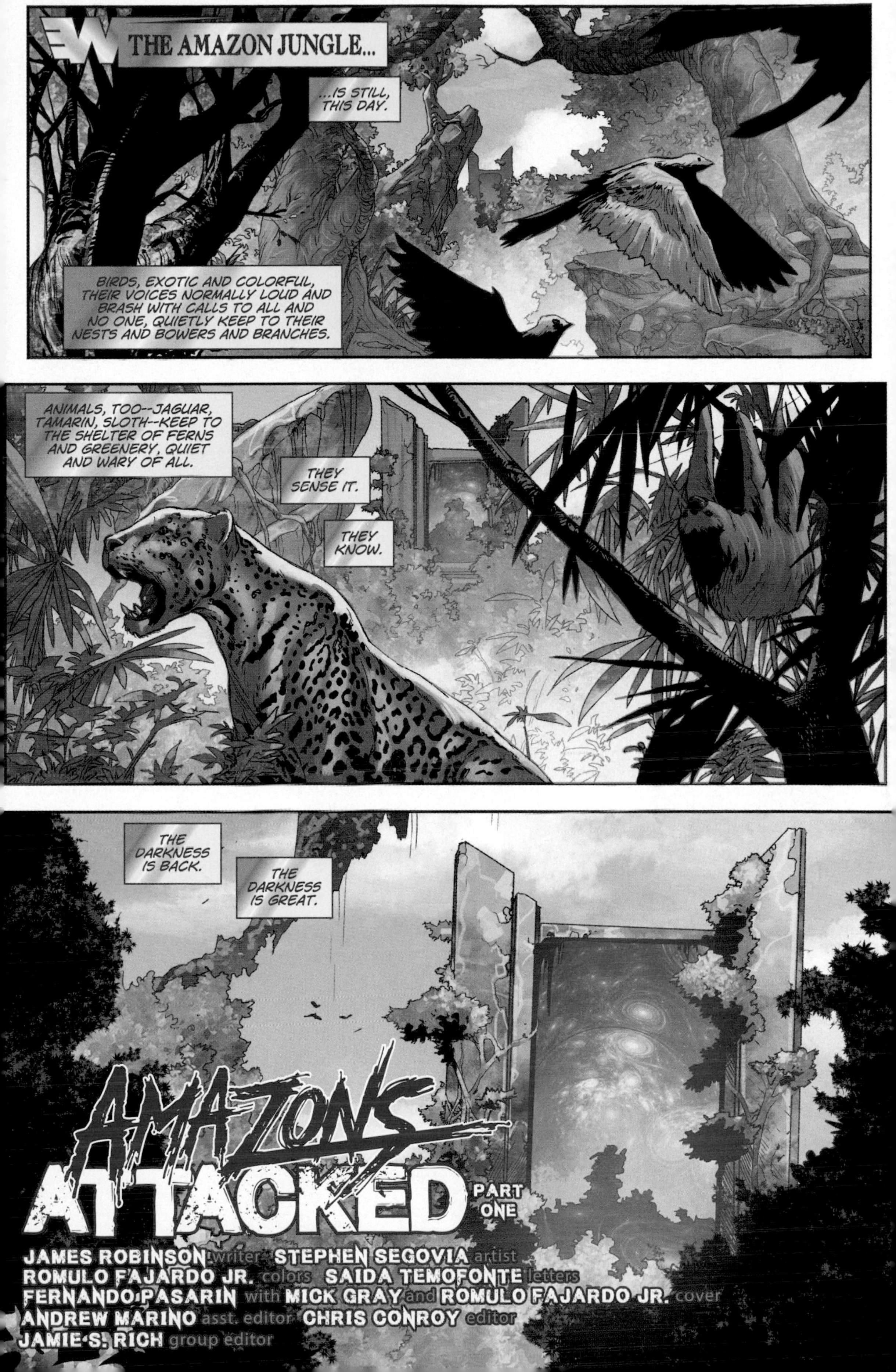
THE AMAZON JUNGLE...
...IS STILL, THIS DAY.
BIRDS, EXOTIC AND COLORFUL, THEIR VOICES NORMALLY LOUD AND BRASH WITH CALLS TO ALL AND NO ONE, QUIETLY KEEP TO THEIR NESTS AND BOWERS AND BRANCHES.
ANIMALS, TOO--JAGUAR, TAMARIN, SLOTH--KEEP TO THE SHELTER OF FERNS AND GREENERY, QUIET AND WARY OF ALL.
THEY SENSE IT.
THEY KNOW.
THE DARKNESS IS BACK.
THE DARKNESS IS GREAT.
AMAZONS ATTACKED PART ONE
JAMES ROBINSON writer STEPHEN SEGOVIA artist
ROMULO FAJARDO JR. colors SAIDA TEMOFONTE letters
FERNANDO PASARIN with MICK GRAY and ROMULO FAJARDO JR. cover
ANDREW MARINO asst. editor CHRIS CONROY editor
JAMIE S. RICH group editor

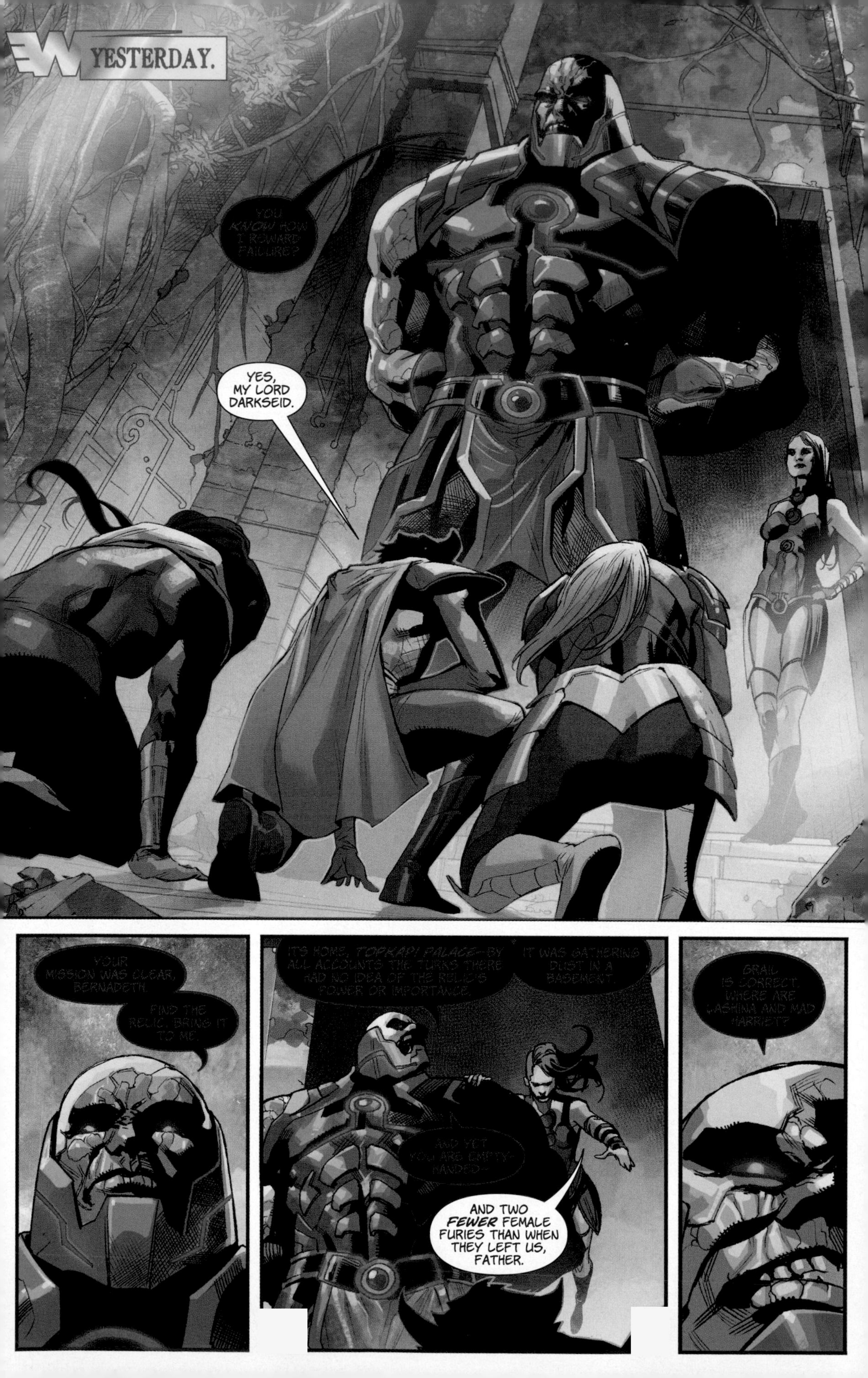
YESTERDAY.
YOU KNOW HOW I REWARD FAILURE?
YES, MY LORD DARKSEID.
YOUR MISSION WAS CLEAR, BERNADETH.
FIND THE RELIC. BRING IT TO ME.
ITS HOME, TOPKAPI PALACE—BY ALL ACCOUNTS THE TURKS THERE HAD NO IDEA OF THE RELIC'S POWER OR IMPORTANCE.
IT WAS GATHERING DUST IN A BASEMENT.
AND YET YOU ARE EMPTY-HANDED—
AND TWO *FEWER* FEMALE FURIES THAN WHEN THEY LEFT US, FATHER.
GRAIL IS CORRECT. WHERE ARE LASHINA AND MAD HARRIET?

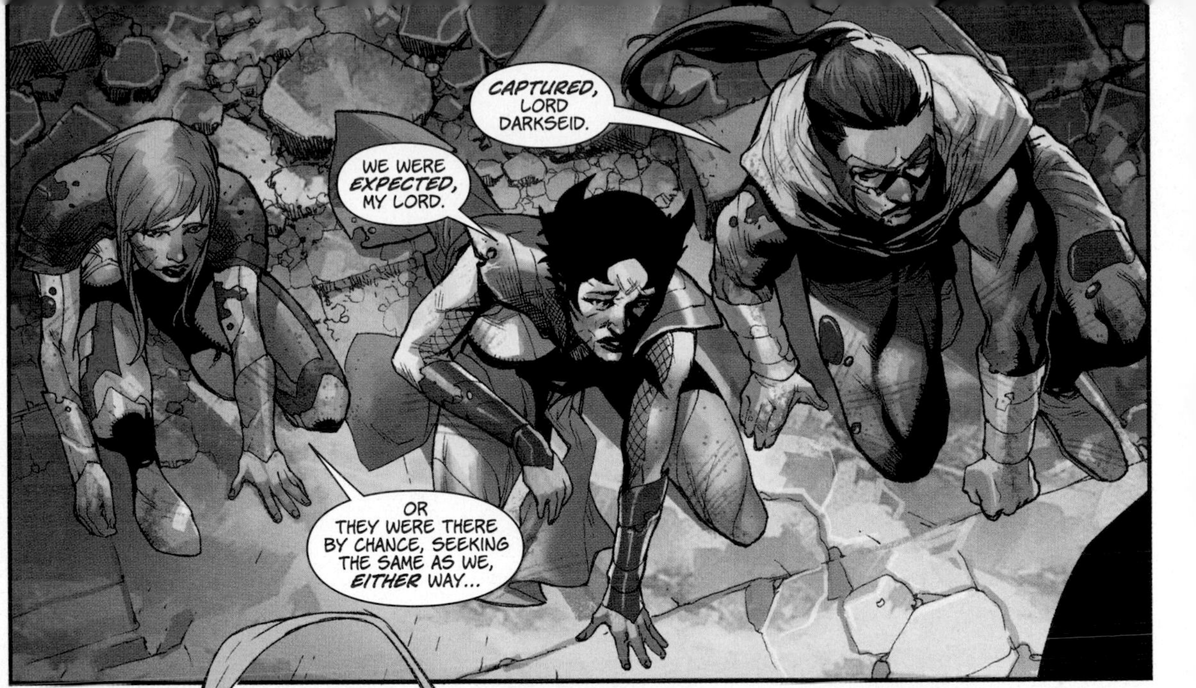
CAPTURED, LORD DARKSEID.
WE WERE EXPECTED, MY LORD.
OR THEY WERE THERE BY CHANCE, SEEKING THE SAME AS WE, EITHER WAY...
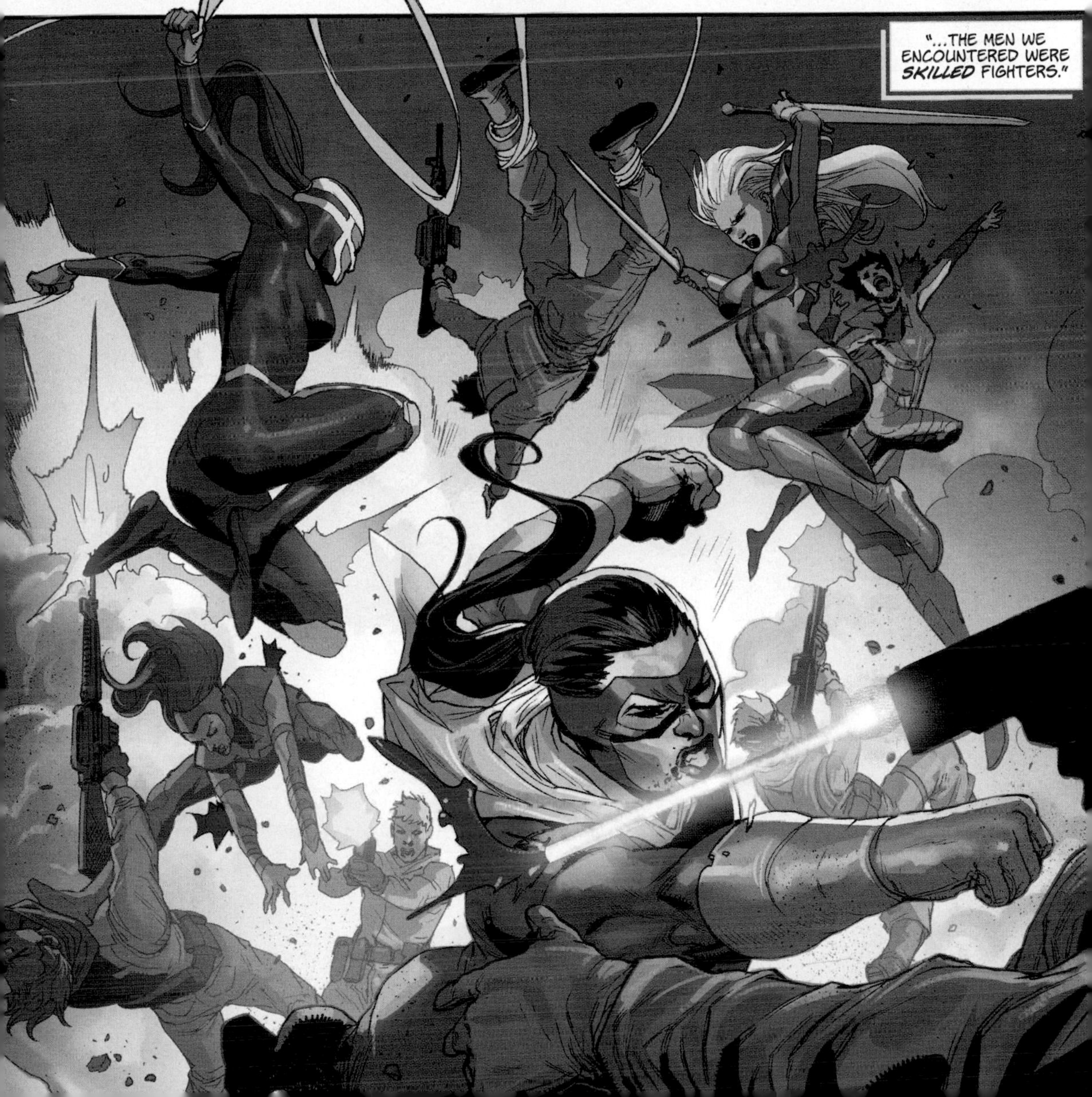
"...THE MEN WE ENCOUNTERED WERE SKILLED FIGHTERS."

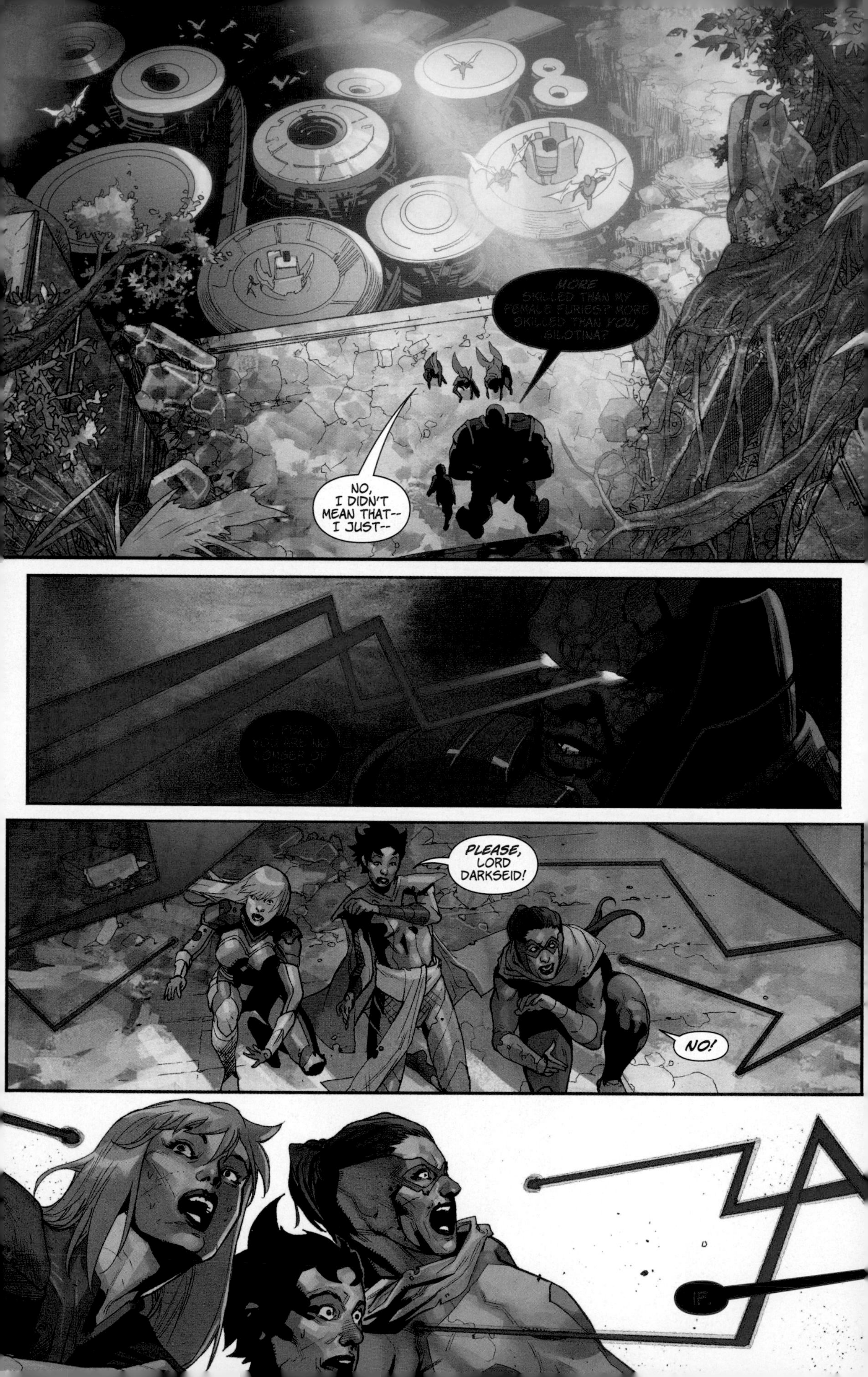
MORE SKILLED THAN MY FEMALE FURIES? MORE SKILLED THAN YOU, GILOTINA?
NO, I DIDN'T MEAN THAT-- I JUST--
I FEAR YOU ARE NO LONGER OF USE TO ME.
PLEASE, LORD DARKSEID!
NO!

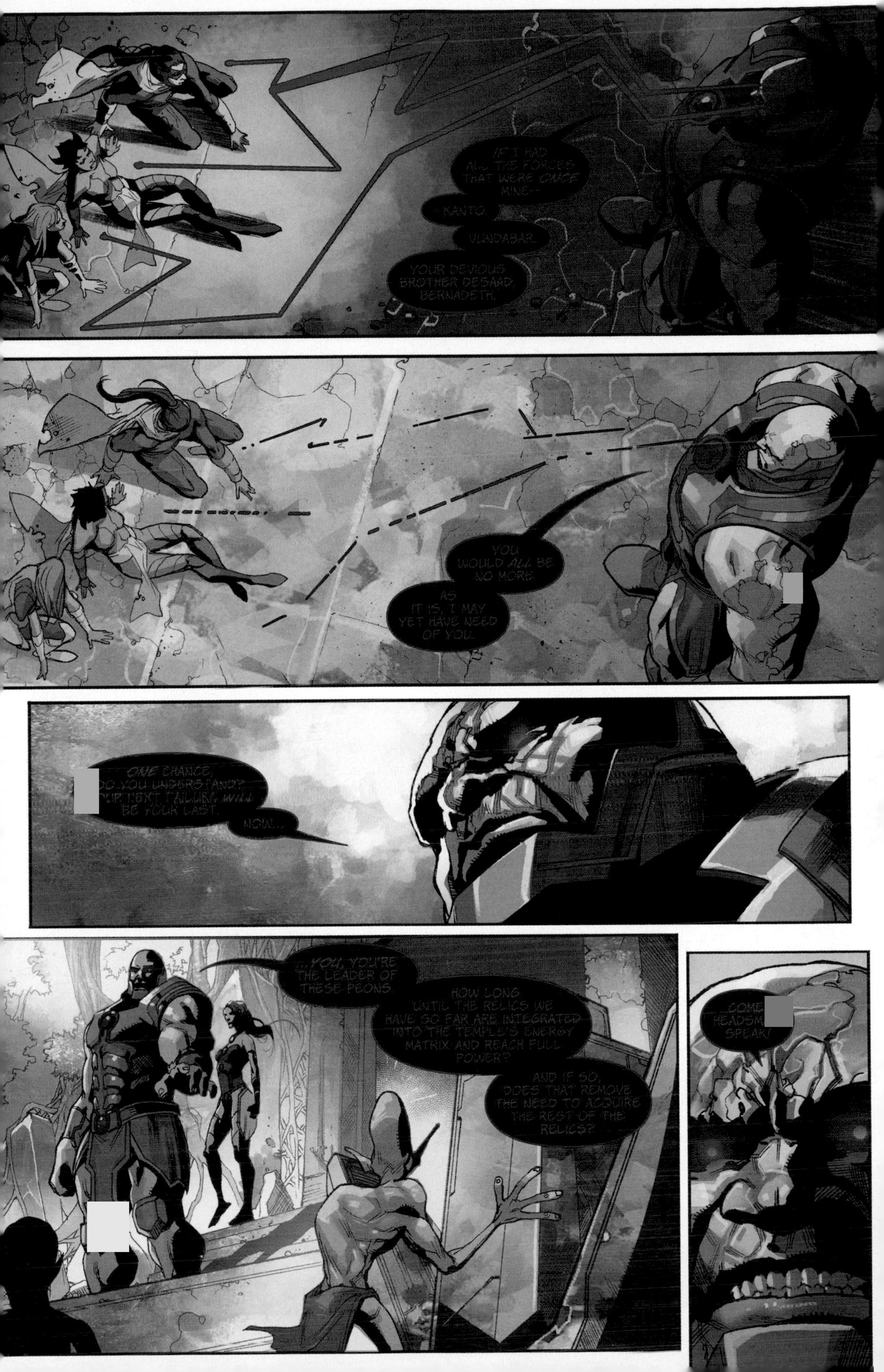

IF I HAD ALL THE FORCES THAT WERE ONCE MINE--
--KANTO.
VUNDABAR.
YOUR DEVIOUS BROTHER DESAAD, BERNADETH.
YOU WOULD ALL BE NO MORE.
AS IT IS, I MAY YET HAVE NEED OF YOU.
ONE CHANCE, DO YOU UNDERSTAND? OUR NEXT FAILURE WILL BE YOUR LAST.
NOW...
...YOU. YOU'RE THE LEADER OF THESE PEONS.
HOW LONG UNTIL THE RELICS WE HAVE SO FAR ARE INTEGRATED INTO THE TEMPLE'S ENERGY MATRIX AND REACH FULL POWER?
AND IF SO, DOES THAT REMOVE THE NEED TO ACQUIRE THE REST OF THE RELICS?
COME HEADSM SPEAK!

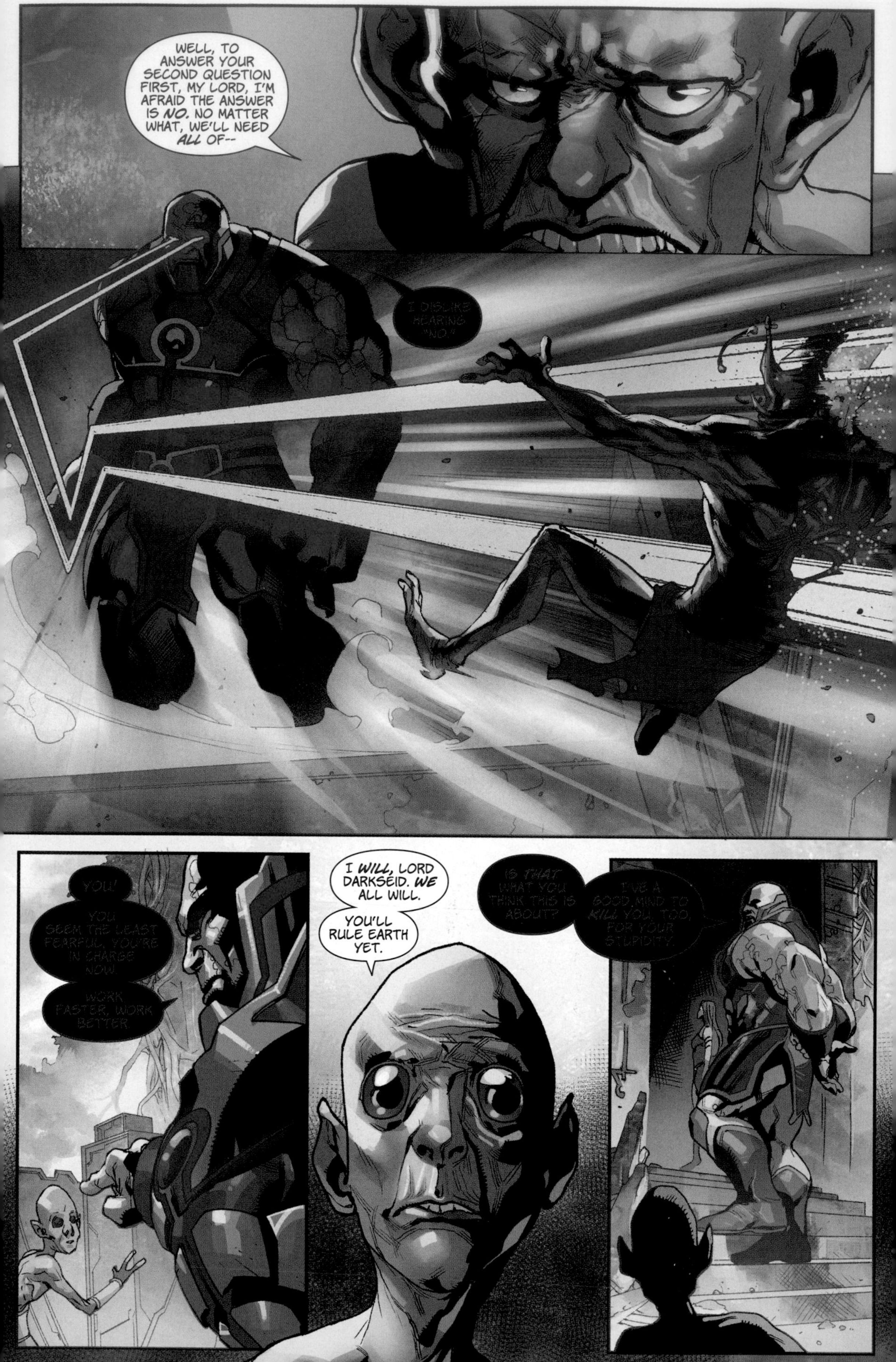

WELL, TO ANSWER YOUR SECOND QUESTION FIRST, MY LORD, I'M AFRAID THE ANSWER IS *NO.* NO MATTER WHAT, WE'LL NEED *ALL* OF--
I DISLIKE HEARING "NO."
YOU!
YOU SEEM THE LEAST FEARFUL. YOU'RE IN CHARGE NOW.
WORK FASTER, WORK BETTER.
I *WILL,* LORD DARKSEID. *WE* ALL WILL.
YOU'LL RULE EARTH YET.
IS *THAT* WHAT YOU THINK THIS IS ABOUT?
I'VE A GOOD MIND TO *KILL* YOU, TOO, FOR YOUR STUPIDITY.

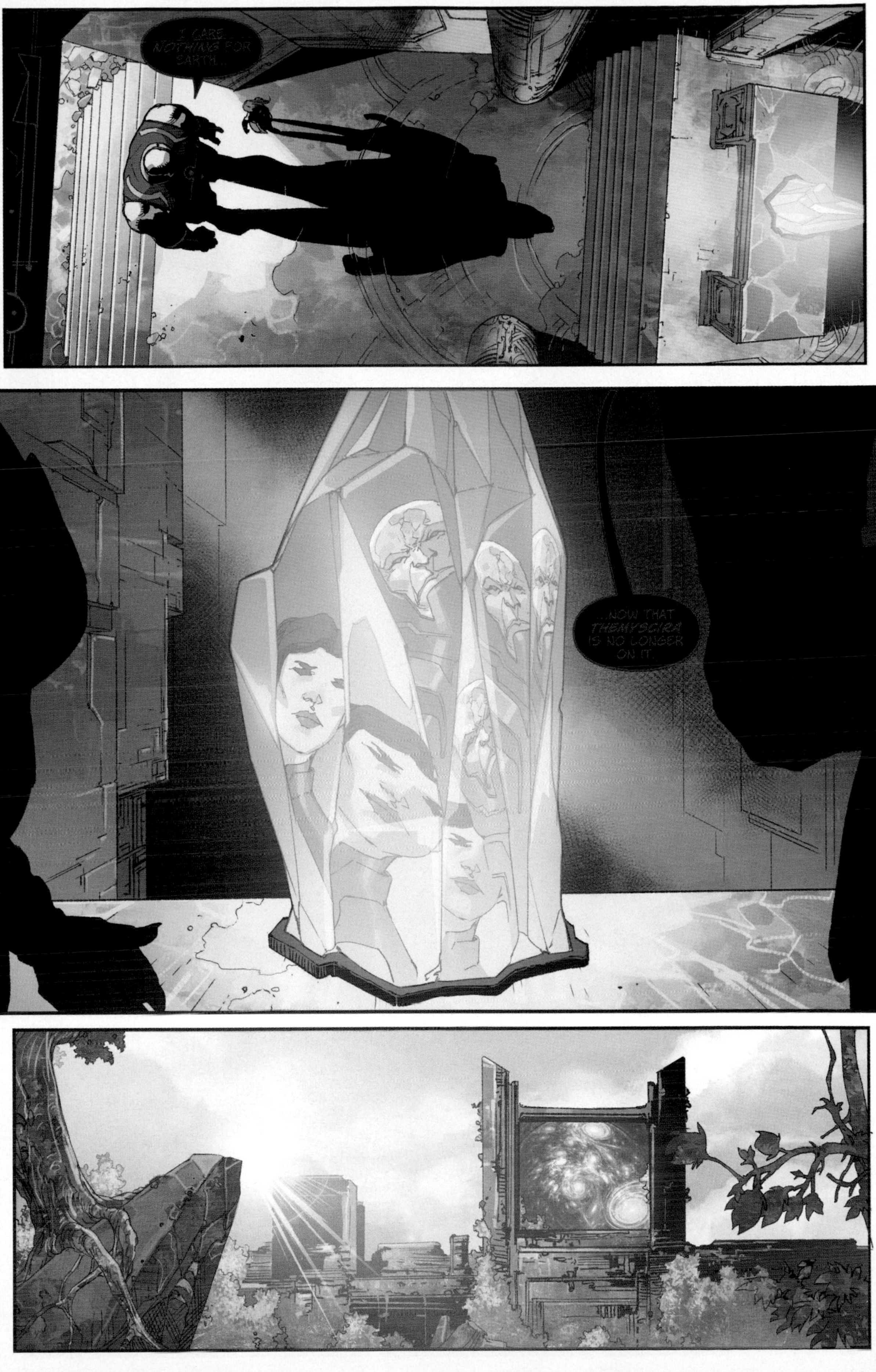
I CARE NOTHING FOR EARTH...
...NOW THAT THEMYSCIRA IS NO LONGER ON IT.

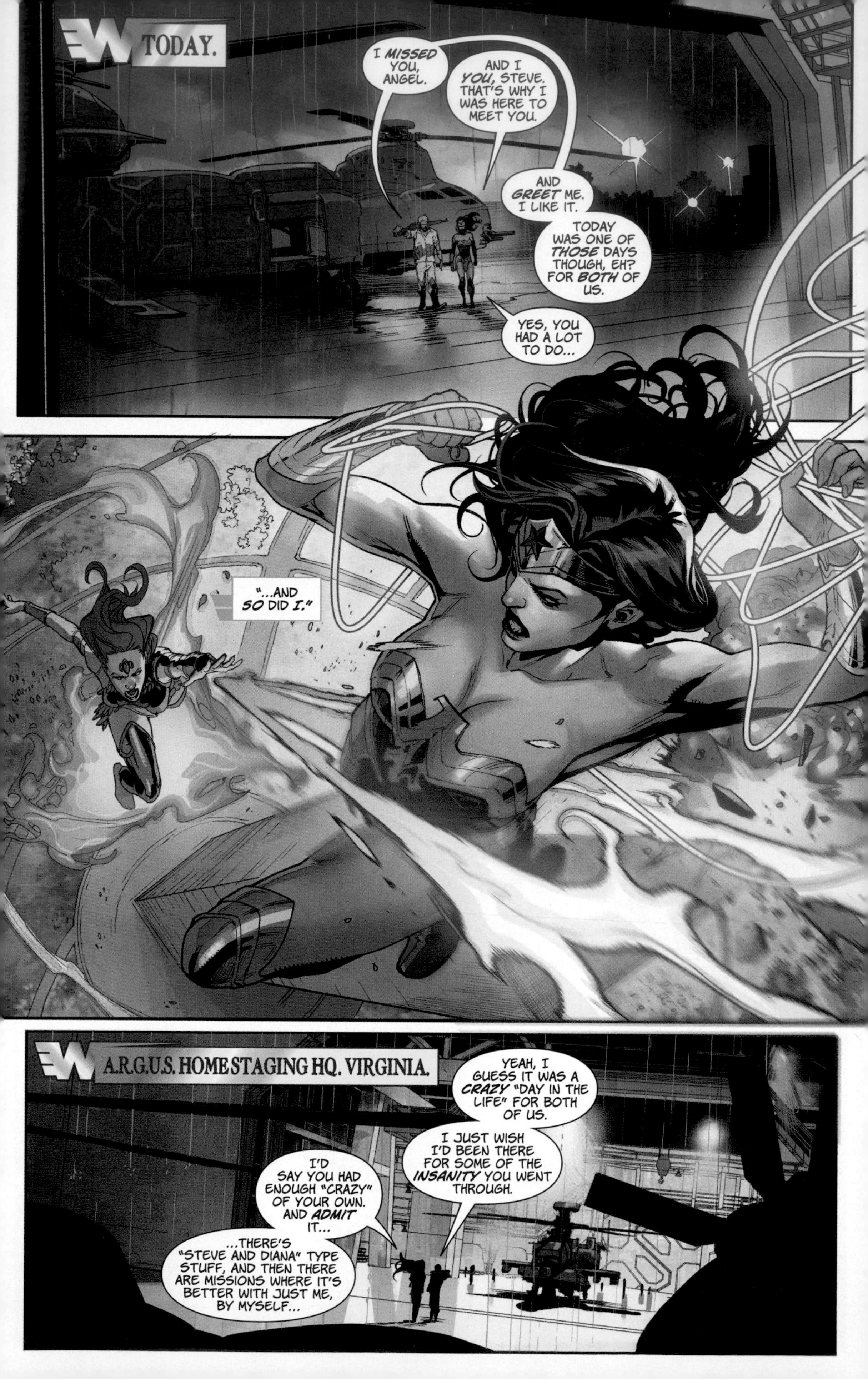
TODAY.
I MISSED YOU, ANGEL.
AND I YOU, STEVE. THAT'S WHY I WAS HERE TO MEET YOU.
AND GREET ME. I LIKE IT.
TODAY WAS ONE OF THOSE DAYS THOUGH, EH? FOR BOTH OF US.
YES, YOU HAD A LOT TO DO...
"...AND SO DID I."
A.R.G.U.S. HOME STAGING HQ. VIRGINIA.
YEAH, I GUESS IT WAS A CRAZY "DAY IN THE LIFE" FOR BOTH OF US.
I JUST WISH I'D BEEN THERE FOR SOME OF THE INSANITY YOU WENT THROUGH.
I'D SAY YOU HAD ENOUGH "CRAZY" OF YOUR OWN. AND ADMIT IT...
...THERE'S "STEVE AND DIANA" TYPE STUFF, AND THEN THERE ARE MISSIONS WHERE IT'S BETTER WITH JUST ME, BY MYSELF...

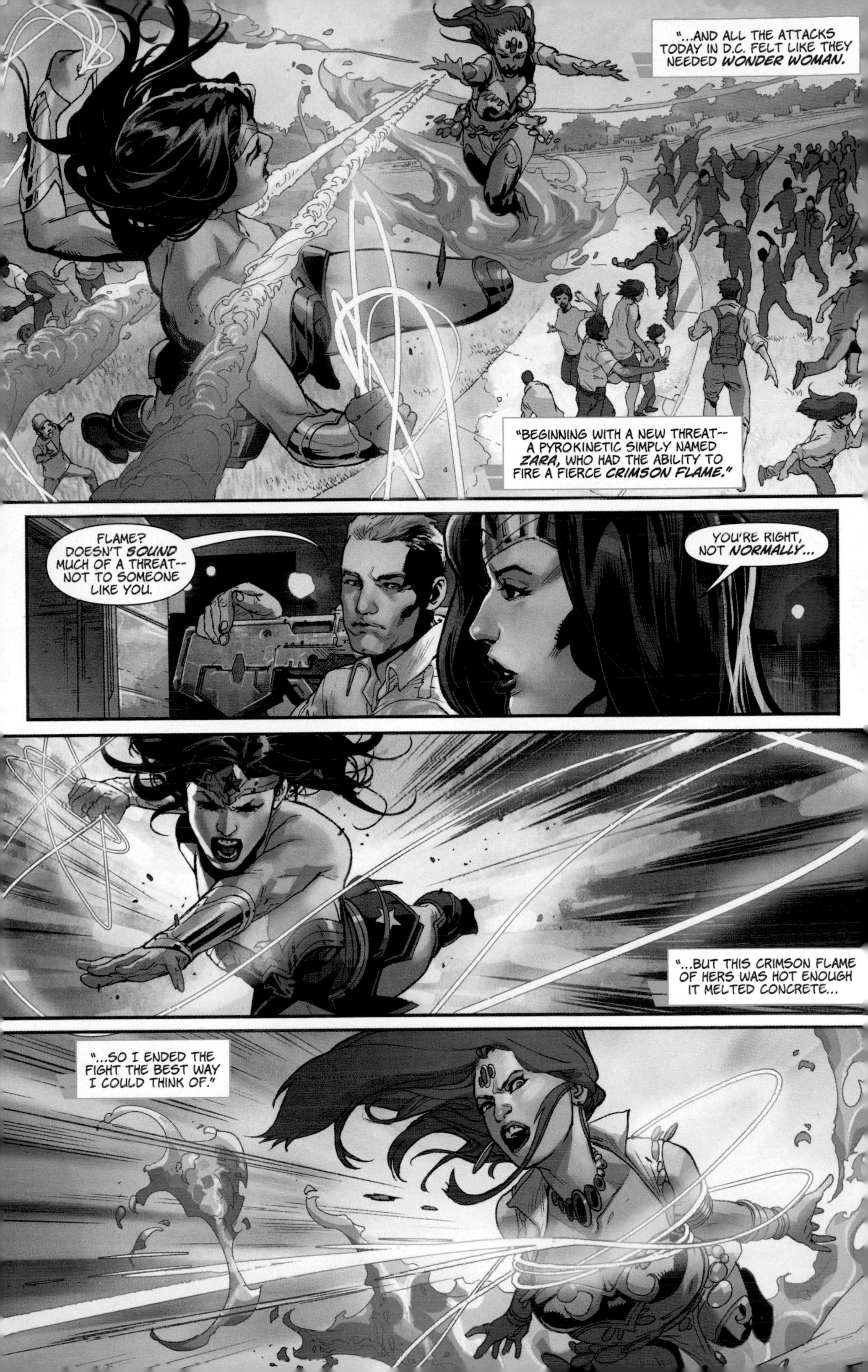
"...AND ALL THE ATTACKS TODAY IN D.C. FELT LIKE THEY NEEDED WONDER WOMAN.
"BEGINNING WITH A NEW THREAT-- A PYROKINETIC SIMPLY NAMED ZARA, WHO HAD THE ABILITY TO FIRE A FIERCE CRIMSON FLAME."
FLAME? DOESN'T SOUND MUCH OF A THREAT-- NOT TO SOMEONE LIKE YOU.
YOU'RE RIGHT, NOT NORMALLY...
"...BUT THIS CRIMSON FLAME OF HERS WAS HOT ENOUGH IT MELTED CONCRETE...
"...SO I ENDED THE FIGHT THE BEST WAY I COULD THINK OF."

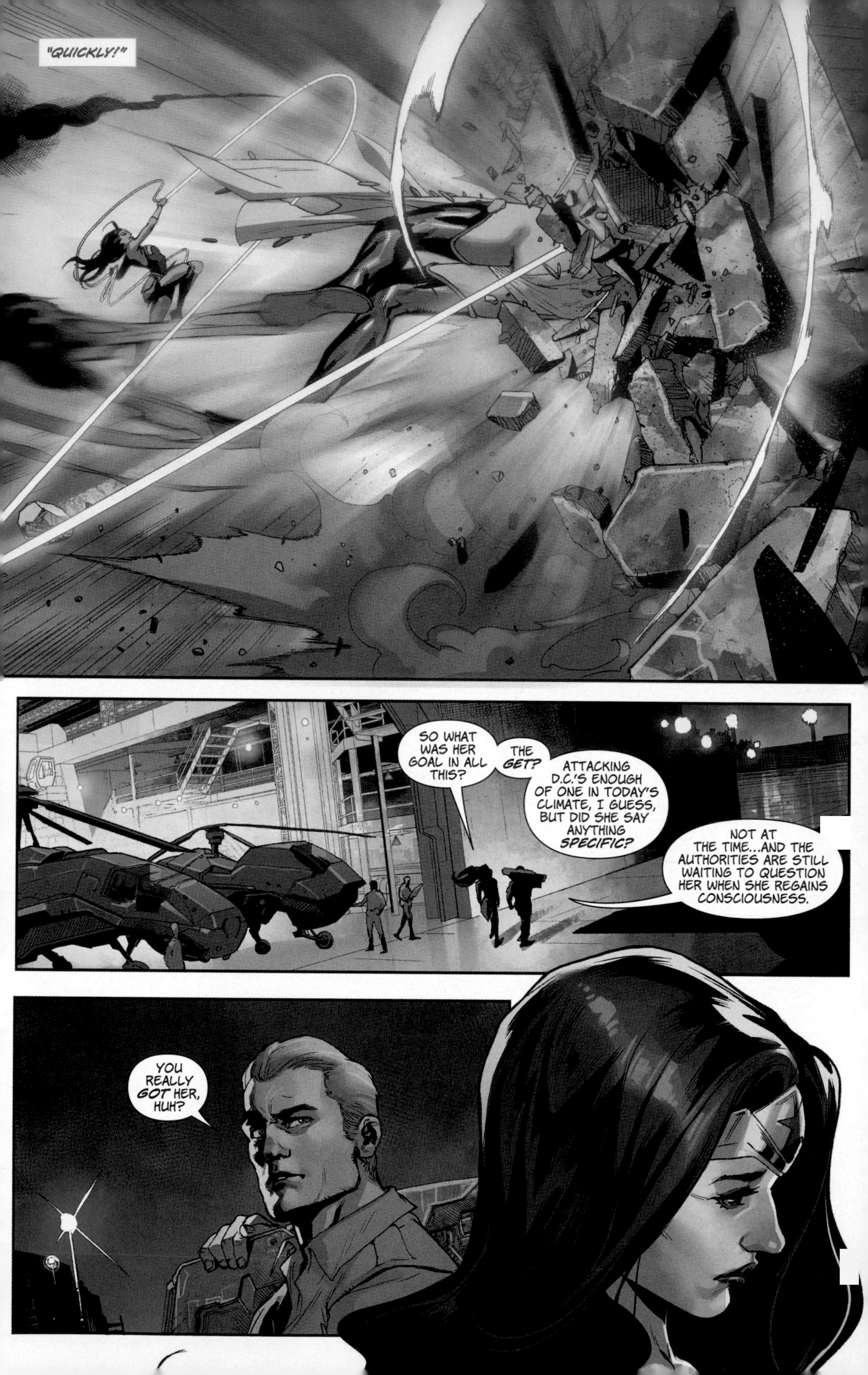
"QUICKLY!"
SO WHAT WAS HER GOAL IN ALL THIS?
THE GET?
ATTACKING D.C.'S ENOUGH OF ONE IN TODAY'S CLIMATE, I GUESS, BUT DID SHE SAY ANYTHING SPECIFIC?
NOT AT THE TIME...AND THE AUTHORITIES ARE STILL WAITING TO QUESTION HER WHEN SHE REGAINS CONSCIOUSNESS.
YOU REALLY GOT HER, HUH?

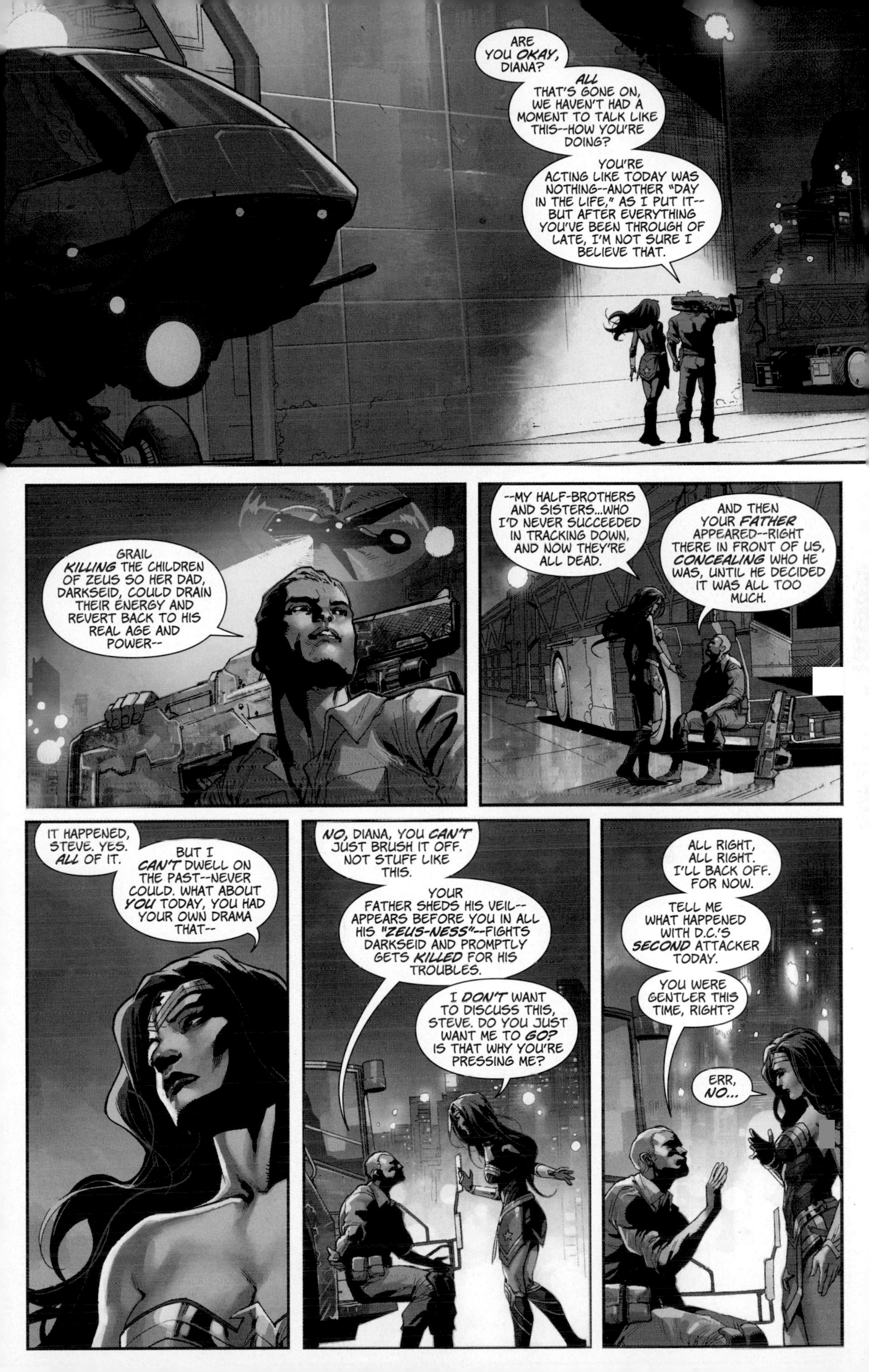
ARE YOU *OKAY,* DIANA?
ALL THAT'S GONE ON, WE HAVEN'T HAD A MOMENT TO TALK LIKE THIS--HOW YOU'RE DOING?
YOU'RE ACTING LIKE TODAY WAS NOTHING--ANOTHER "DAY IN THE LIFE," AS I PUT IT--BUT AFTER EVERYTHING YOU'VE BEEN THROUGH OF LATE, I'M NOT SURE I BELIEVE THAT.
GRAIL *KILLING* THE CHILDREN OF ZEUS SO HER DAD, DARKSEID, COULD DRAIN THEIR ENERGY AND REVERT BACK TO HIS REAL AGE AND POWER--
--MY HALF-BROTHERS AND SISTERS...WHO I'D NEVER SUCCEEDED IN TRACKING DOWN, AND NOW THEY'RE ALL DEAD.
AND THEN YOUR *FATHER* APPEARED--RIGHT THERE IN FRONT OF US, *CONCEALING* WHO HE WAS, UNTIL HE DECIDED IT WAS ALL TOO MUCH.
IT HAPPENED, STEVE. YES. *ALL* OF IT.
BUT I *CAN'T* DWELL ON THE PAST--NEVER COULD. WHAT ABOUT *YOU* TODAY, YOU HAD YOUR OWN DRAMA THAT--
NO, DIANA, YOU *CAN'T* JUST BRUSH IT OFF. NOT STUFF LIKE THIS.
YOUR FATHER SHEDS HIS VEIL--APPEARS BEFORE YOU IN ALL HIS *"ZEUS-NESS"*--FIGHTS DARKSEID AND PROMPTLY GETS *KILLED* FOR HIS TROUBLES.
I *DON'T* WANT TO DISCUSS THIS, STEVE. DO YOU JUST WANT ME TO *GO?* IS THAT WHY YOU'RE PRESSING ME?
ALL RIGHT, ALL RIGHT. I'LL BACK OFF. FOR NOW.
TELL ME WHAT HAPPENED WITH D.C.'S *SECOND* ATTACKER TODAY.
YOU WERE GENTLER THIS TIME, RIGHT?
ERR, *NO...*

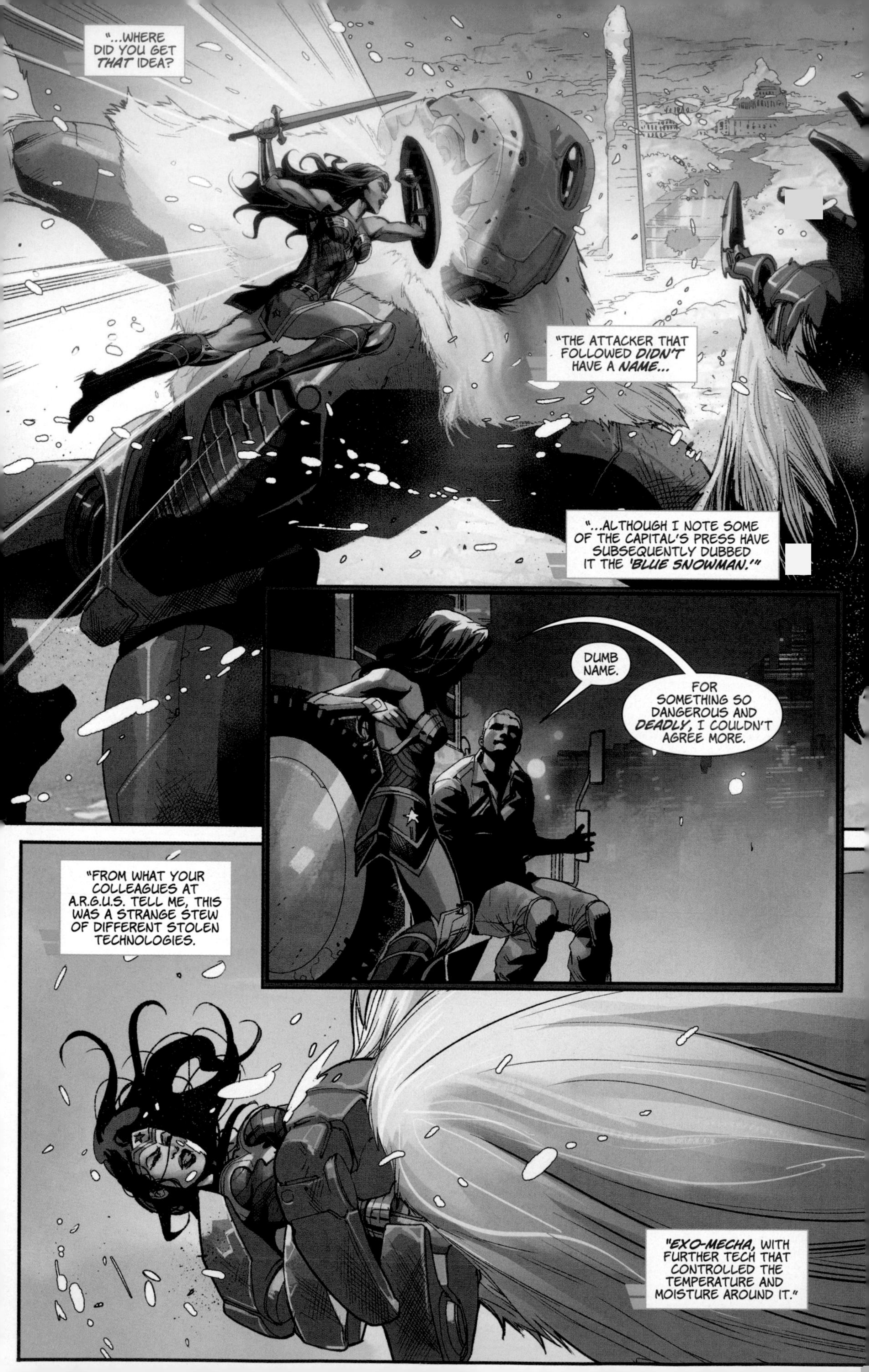
"...WHERE DID YOU GET *THAT* IDEA?
"THE ATTACKER THAT FOLLOWED *DIDN'T* HAVE A *NAME*...
"...ALTHOUGH I NOTE SOME OF THE CAPITAL'S PRESS HAVE SUBSEQUENTLY DUBBED IT THE *'BLUE SNOWMAN.'*"
DUMB NAME.
FOR SOMETHING SO DANGEROUS AND *DEADLY*, I COULDN'T AGREE MORE.
"FROM WHAT YOUR COLLEAGUES AT A.R.G.U.S. TELL ME, THIS WAS A STRANGE STEW OF DIFFERENT STOLEN TECHNOLOGIES.
"EXO-MECHA, WITH FURTHER TECH THAT CONTROLLED THE TEMPERATURE AND MOISTURE AROUND IT."

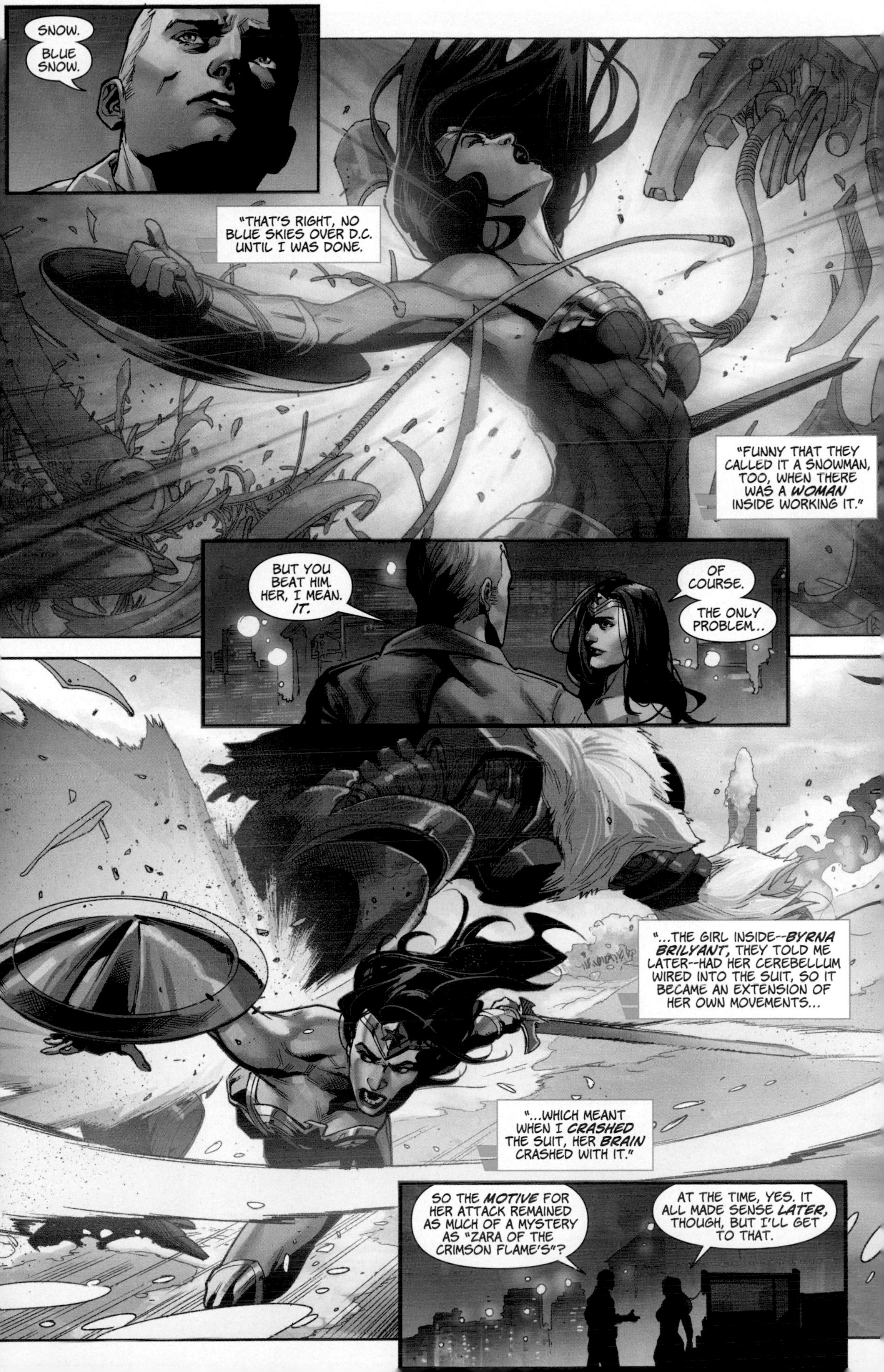
SNOW. BLUE SNOW.
"THAT'S RIGHT, NO BLUE SKIES OVER D.C. UNTIL I WAS DONE.
"FUNNY THAT THEY CALLED IT A SNOWMAN, TOO, WHEN THERE WAS A *WOMAN* INSIDE WORKING IT."
BUT YOU BEAT HIM. HER, I MEAN. *IT.*
OF COURSE.
THE ONLY PROBLEM...
"...THE GIRL INSIDE--*BYRNA BRILYANT*, THEY TOLD ME LATER--HAD HER CEREBELLUM WIRED INTO THE SUIT, SO IT BECAME AN EXTENSION OF HER OWN MOVEMENTS...
"...WHICH MEANT WHEN I *CRASHED* THE SUIT, HER *BRAIN* CRASHED WITH IT."
SO THE *MOTIVE* FOR HER ATTACK REMAINED AS MUCH OF A MYSTERY AS "ZARA OF THE CRIMSON FLAME'S"?
AT THE TIME, YES. IT ALL MADE SENSE *LATER,* THOUGH, BUT I'LL GET TO THAT.

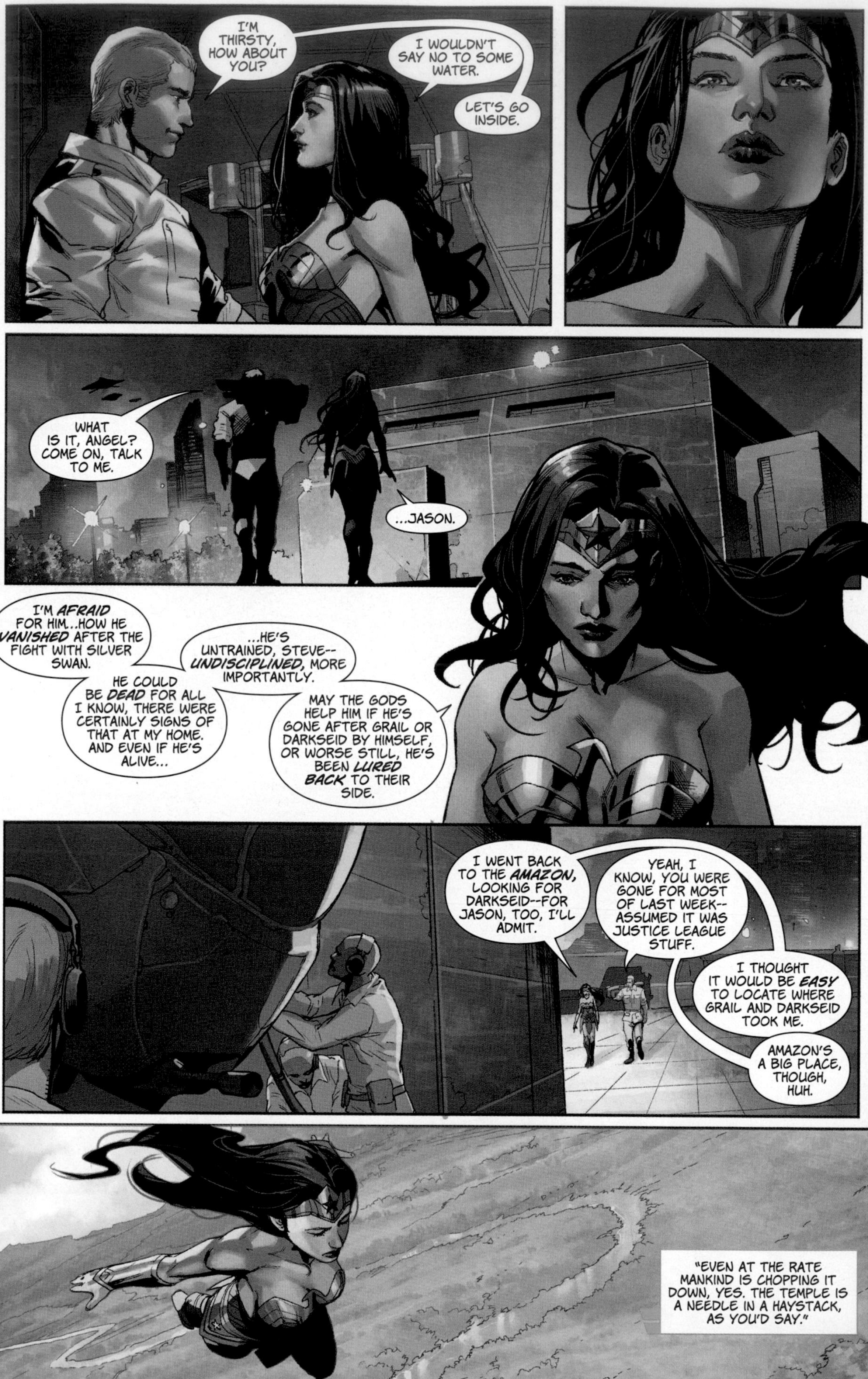
I'M THIRSTY, HOW ABOUT YOU?
I WOULDN'T SAY NO TO SOME WATER.
LET'S GO INSIDE.
WHAT IS IT, ANGEL? COME ON, TALK TO ME.
...JASON.
I'M AFRAID FOR HIM...HOW HE VANISHED AFTER THE FIGHT WITH SILVER SWAN.
HE COULD BE DEAD FOR ALL I KNOW, THERE WERE CERTAINLY SIGNS OF THAT AT MY HOME. AND EVEN IF HE'S ALIVE...
...HE'S UNTRAINED, STEVE--UNDISCIPLINED, MORE IMPORTANTLY.
MAY THE GODS HELP HIM IF HE'S GONE AFTER GRAIL OR DARKSEID BY HIMSELF, OR WORSE STILL, HE'S BEEN LURED BACK TO THEIR SIDE.
I WENT BACK TO THE AMAZON, LOOKING FOR DARKSEID--FOR JASON, TOO, I'LL ADMIT.
YEAH, I KNOW, YOU WERE GONE FOR MOST OF LAST WEEK--ASSUMED IT WAS JUSTICE LEAGUE STUFF.
I THOUGHT IT WOULD BE EASY TO LOCATE WHERE GRAIL AND DARKSEID TOOK ME.
AMAZON'S A BIG PLACE, THOUGH, HUH.
"EVEN AT THE RATE MANKIND IS CHOPPING IT DOWN, YES. THE TEMPLE IS A NEEDLE IN A HAYSTACK, AS YOU'D SAY."

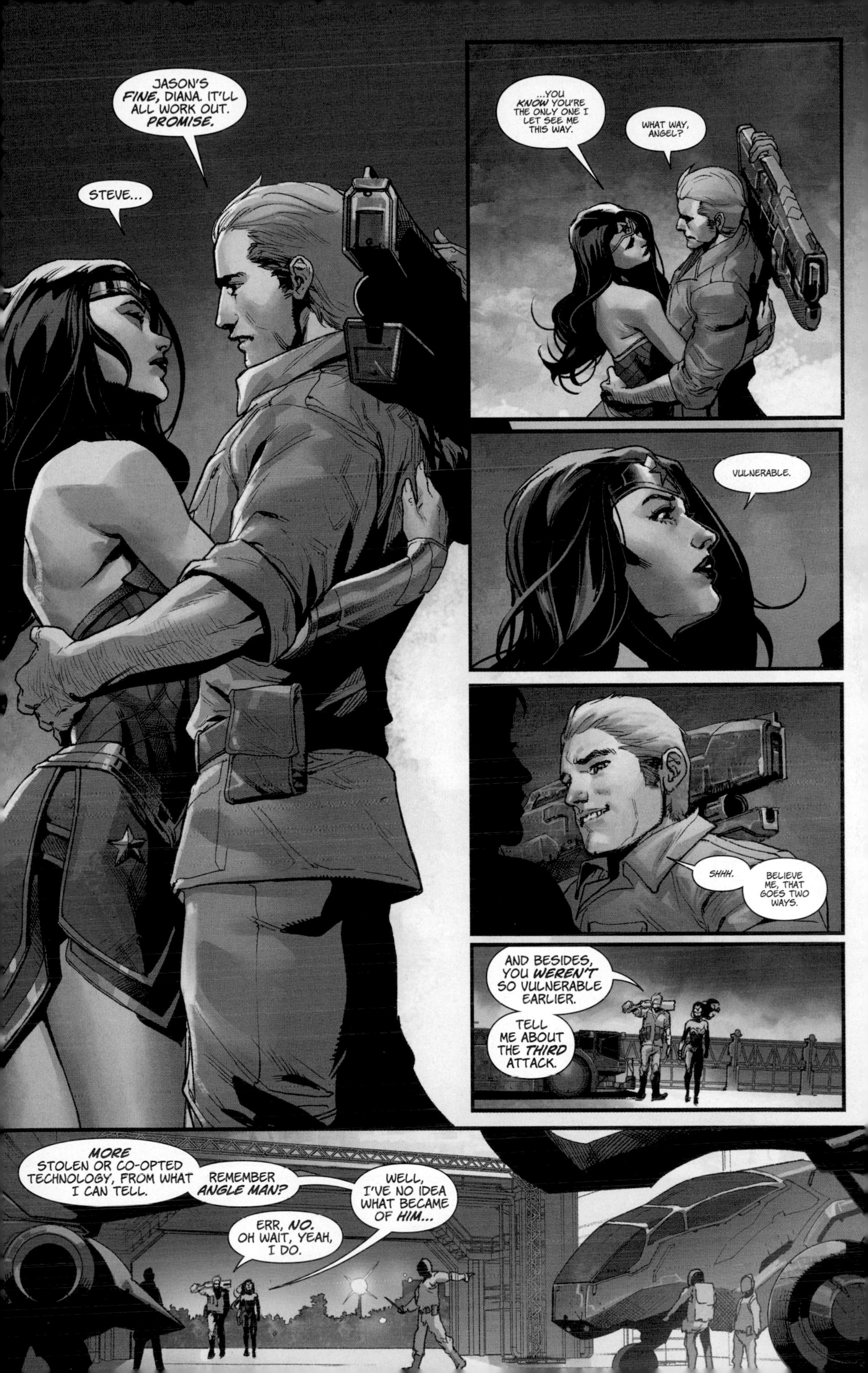
STEVE...
JASON'S FINE, DIANA. IT'LL ALL WORK OUT. PROMISE.
...YOU KNOW YOU'RE THE ONLY ONE I LET SEE ME THIS WAY.
WHAT WAY, ANGEL?
VULNERABLE.
SHHH.
BELIEVE ME, THAT GOES TWO WAYS.
AND BESIDES, YOU WEREN'T SO VULNERABLE EARLIER.
TELL ME ABOUT THE THIRD ATTACK.
MORE STOLEN OR CO-OPTED TECHNOLOGY, FROM WHAT I CAN TELL.
REMEMBER ANGLE MAN?
ERR, NO. OH WAIT, YEAH, I DO.
WELL, I'VE NO IDEA WHAT BECAME OF HIM...

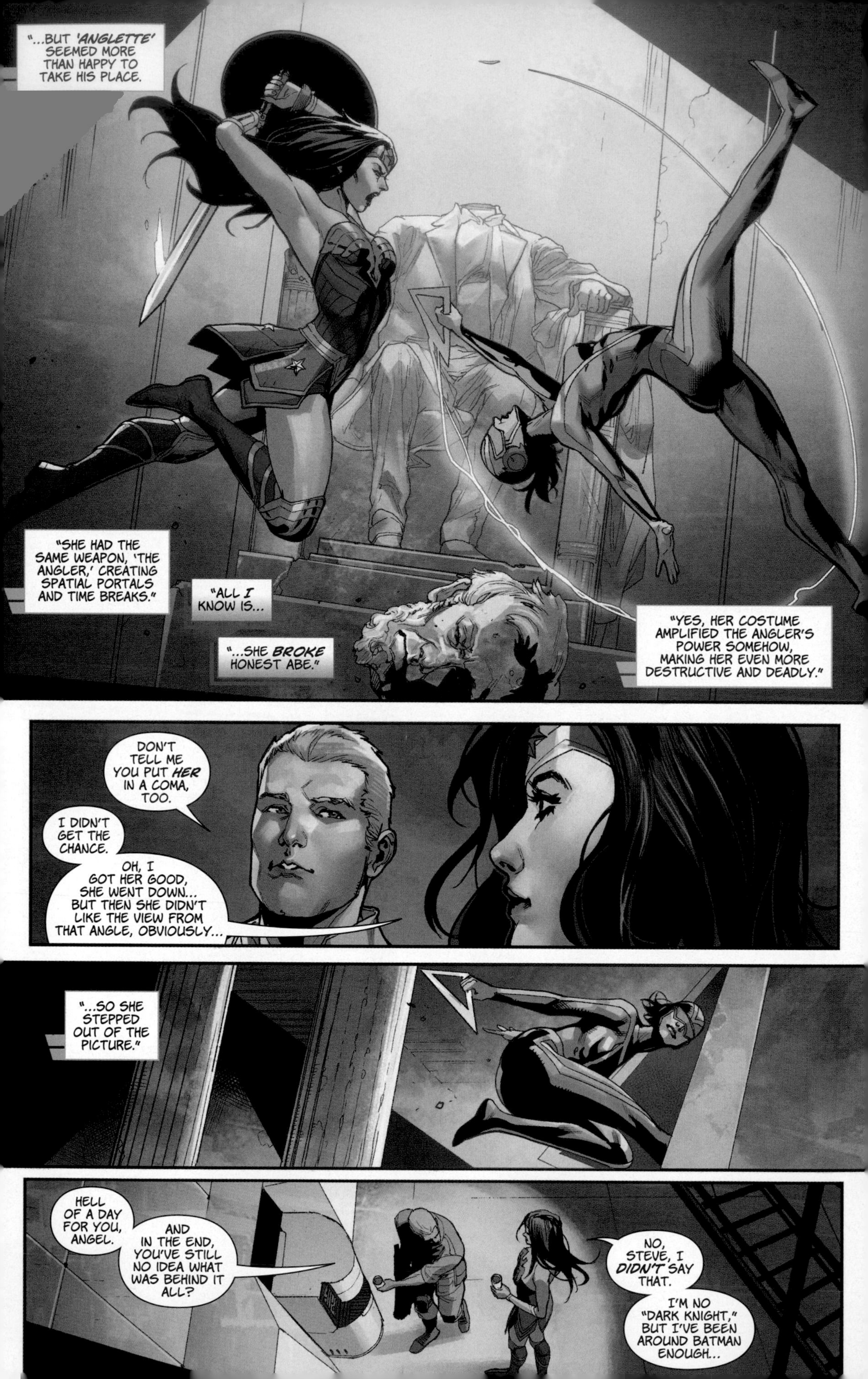
"...BUT 'ANGLETTE' SEEMED MORE THAN HAPPY TO TAKE HIS PLACE.
"SHE HAD THE SAME WEAPON, 'THE ANGLER,' CREATING SPATIAL PORTALS AND TIME BREAKS."
"ALL I KNOW IS...
"...SHE BROKE HONEST ABE."
"YES, HER COSTUME AMPLIFIED THE ANGLER'S POWER SOMEHOW, MAKING HER EVEN MORE DESTRUCTIVE AND DEADLY."
DON'T TELL ME YOU PUT HER IN A COMA, TOO.
I DIDN'T GET THE CHANCE.
OH, I GOT HER GOOD, SHE WENT DOWN... BUT THEN SHE DIDN'T LIKE THE VIEW FROM THAT ANGLE, OBVIOUSLY...
"...SO SHE STEPPED OUT OF THE PICTURE."
HELL OF A DAY FOR YOU, ANGEL.
AND IN THE END, YOU'VE STILL NO IDEA WHAT WAS BEHIND IT ALL?
NO, STEVE, I DIDN'T SAY THAT.
I'M NO "DARK KNIGHT," BUT I'VE BEEN AROUND BATMAN ENOUGH...

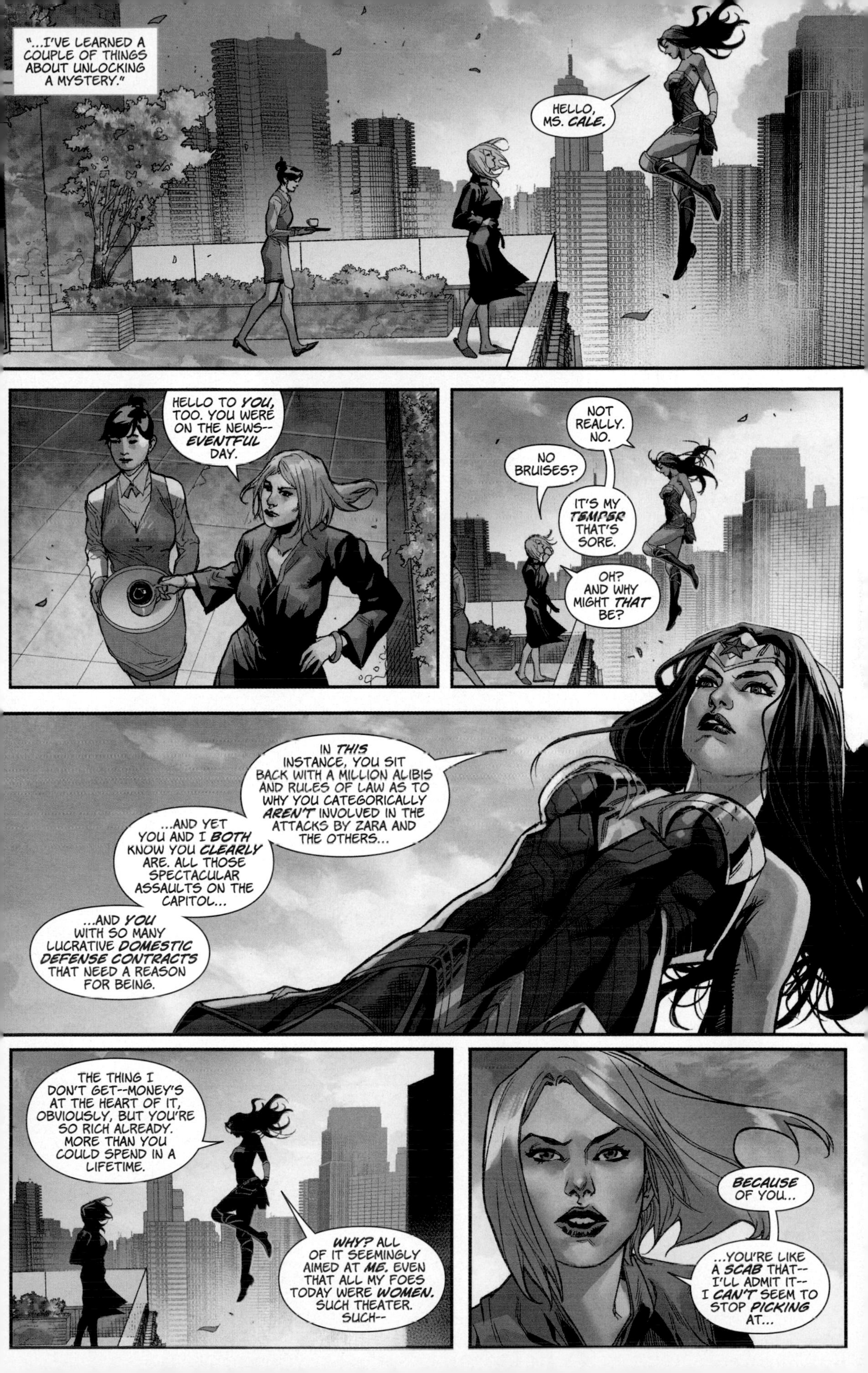

"...I'VE LEARNED A COUPLE OF THINGS ABOUT UNLOCKING A MYSTERY."
HELLO, MS. CALE.
HELLO TO YOU, TOO. YOU WERE ON THE NEWS--EVENTFUL DAY.
NO BRUISES?
NOT REALLY. NO.
IT'S MY TEMPER THAT'S SORE.
OH? AND WHY MIGHT THAT BE?
IN THIS INSTANCE, YOU SIT BACK WITH A MILLION ALIBIS AND RULES OF LAW AS TO WHY YOU CATEGORICALLY AREN'T INVOLVED IN THE ATTACKS BY ZARA AND THE OTHERS...
...AND YET YOU AND I BOTH KNOW YOU CLEARLY ARE. ALL THOSE SPECTACULAR ASSAULTS ON THE CAPITOL...
...AND YOU WITH SO MANY LUCRATIVE DOMESTIC DEFENSE CONTRACTS THAT NEED A REASON FOR BEING.
THE THING I DON'T GET--MONEY'S AT THE HEART OF IT, OBVIOUSLY, BUT YOU'RE SO RICH ALREADY. MORE THAN YOU COULD SPEND IN A LIFETIME.
WHY? ALL OF IT SEEMINGLY AIMED AT ME. EVEN THAT ALL MY FOES TODAY WERE WOMEN. SUCH THEATER. SUCH--
BECAUSE OF YOU...
...YOU'RE LIKE A SCAB THAT--I'LL ADMIT IT--I CAN'T SEEM TO STOP PICKING AT...

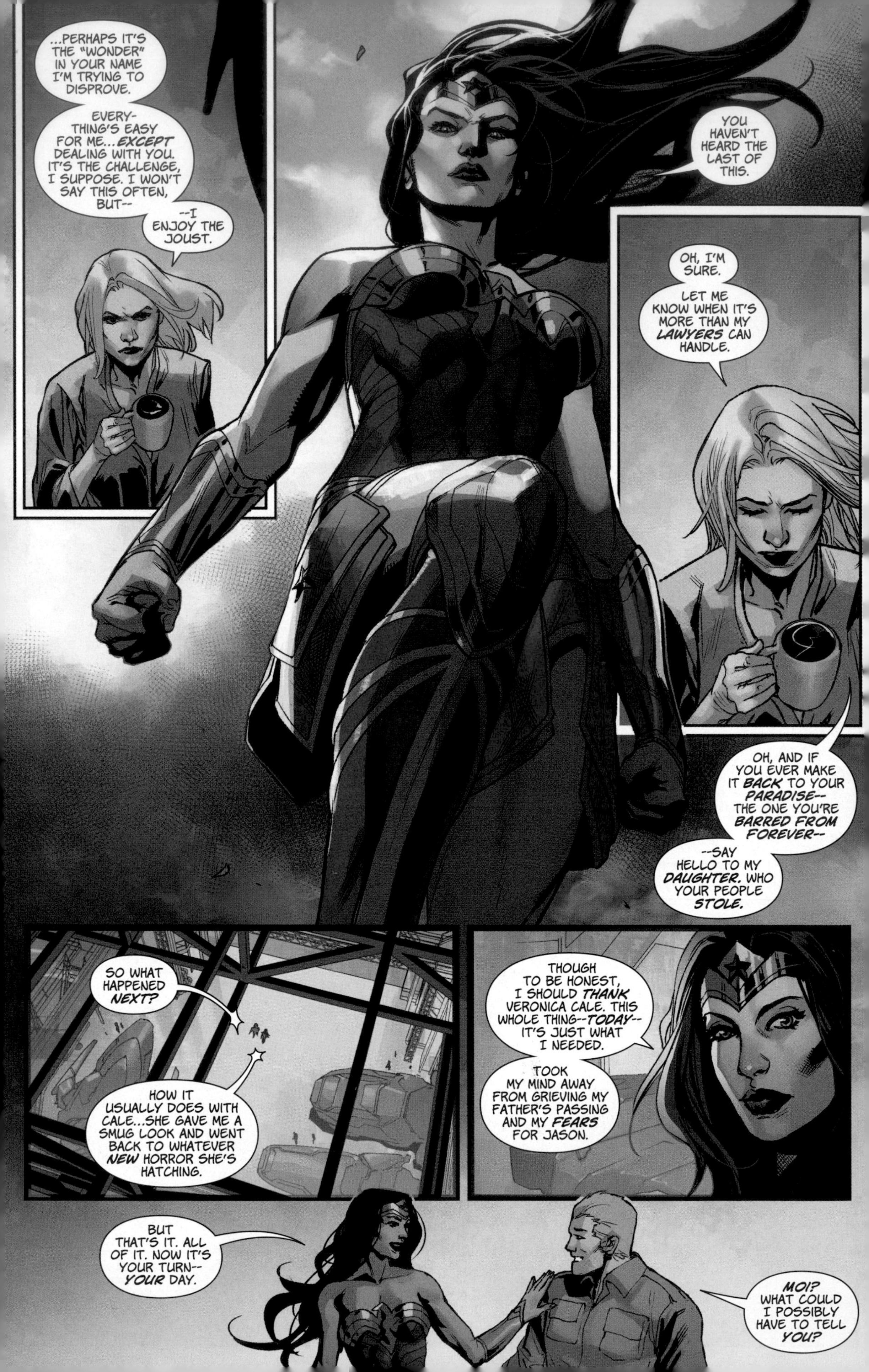
...PERHAPS IT'S THE "WONDER" IN YOUR NAME I'M TRYING TO DISPROVE.
EVERY-THING'S EASY FOR ME...EXCEPT DEALING WITH YOU. IT'S THE CHALLENGE, I SUPPOSE. I WON'T SAY THIS OFTEN, BUT--
--I ENJOY THE JOUST.
YOU HAVEN'T HEARD THE LAST OF THIS.
OH, I'M SURE.
LET ME KNOW WHEN IT'S MORE THAN MY LAWYERS CAN HANDLE.
OH, AND IF YOU EVER MAKE IT BACK TO YOUR PARADISE-- THE ONE YOU'RE BARRED FROM FOREVER--
--SAY HELLO TO MY DAUGHTER. WHO YOUR PEOPLE STOLE.
SO WHAT HAPPENED NEXT?
HOW IT USUALLY DOES WITH CALE...SHE GAVE ME A SMUG LOOK AND WENT BACK TO WHATEVER NEW HORROR SHE'S HATCHING.
THOUGH TO BE HONEST, I SHOULD THANK VERONICA CALE. THIS WHOLE THING--TODAY-- IT'S JUST WHAT I NEEDED.
TOOK MY MIND AWAY FROM GRIEVING MY FATHER'S PASSING AND MY FEARS FOR JASON.
BUT THAT'S IT. ALL OF IT. NOW IT'S YOUR TURN-- YOUR DAY.
MOI? WHAT COULD I POSSIBLY HAVE TO TELL YOU?

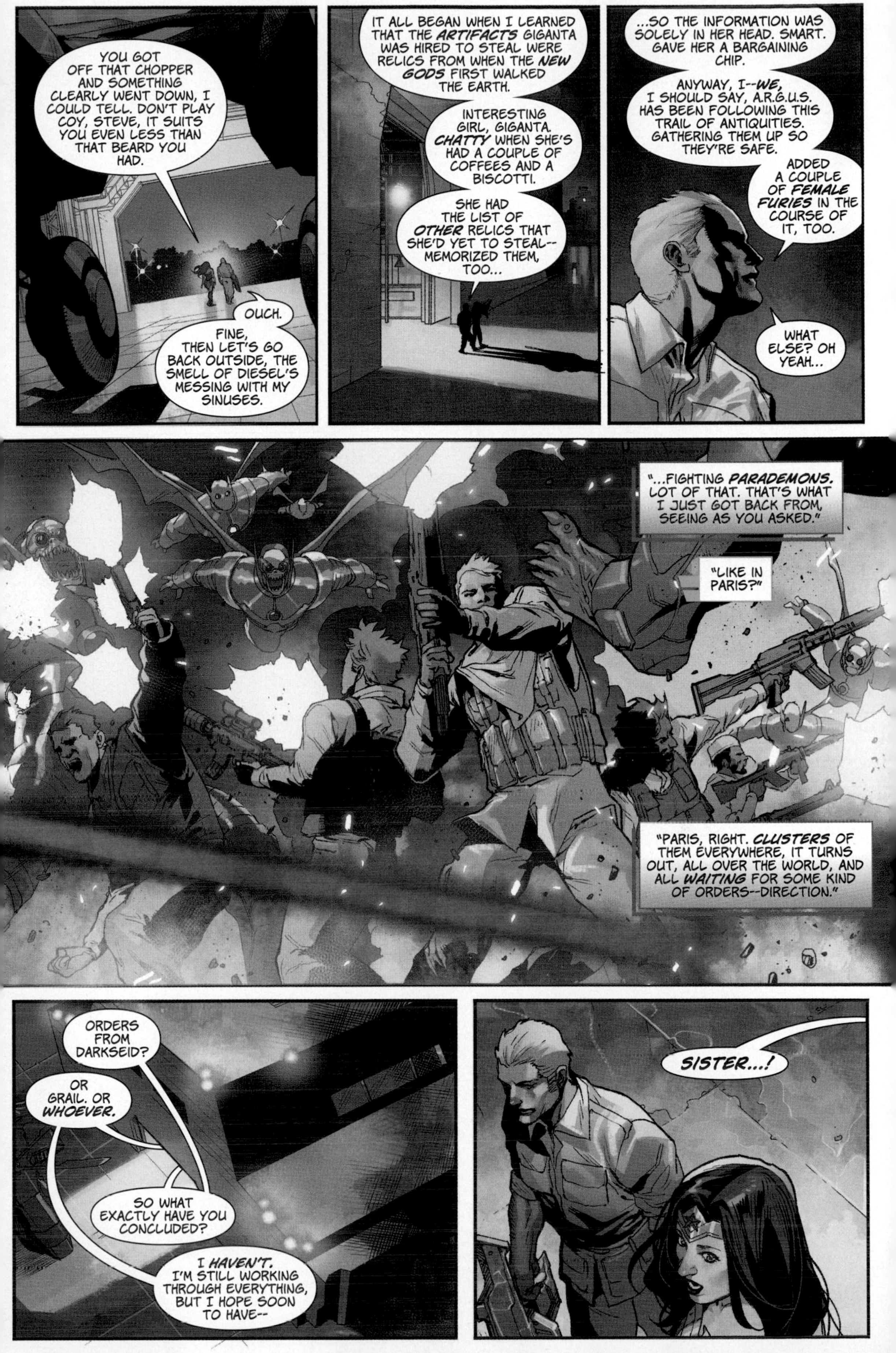
YOU GOT OFF THAT CHOPPER AND SOMETHING CLEARLY WENT DOWN, I COULD TELL. DON'T PLAY COY, STEVE, IT SUITS YOU EVEN LESS THAN THAT BEARD YOU HAD.
OUCH.
FINE, THEN LET'S GO BACK OUTSIDE, THE SMELL OF DIESEL'S MESSING WITH MY SINUSES.
IT ALL BEGAN WHEN I LEARNED THAT THE ARTIFACTS GIGANTA WAS HIRED TO STEAL WERE RELICS FROM WHEN THE NEW GODS FIRST WALKED THE EARTH.
INTERESTING GIRL, GIGANTA. CHATTY WHEN SHE'S HAD A COUPLE OF COFFEES AND A BISCOTTI.
SHE HAD THE LIST OF OTHER RELICS THAT SHE'D YET TO STEAL--MEMORIZED THEM, TOO...
...SO THE INFORMATION WAS SOLELY IN HER HEAD. SMART. GAVE HER A BARGAINING CHIP.
ANYWAY, I--WE, I SHOULD SAY, A.R.G.U.S. HAS BEEN FOLLOWING THIS TRAIL OF ANTIQUITIES. GATHERING THEM UP SO THEY'RE SAFE.
ADDED A COUPLE OF FEMALE FURIES IN THE COURSE OF IT, TOO.
WHAT ELSE? OH YEAH...
"...FIGHTING PARADEMONS. LOT OF THAT. THAT'S WHAT I JUST GOT BACK FROM, SEEING AS YOU ASKED."
"LIKE IN PARIS?"
"PARIS, RIGHT. CLUSTERS OF THEM EVERYWHERE, IT TURNS OUT, ALL OVER THE WORLD, AND ALL WAITING FOR SOME KIND OF ORDERS--DIRECTION."
ORDERS FROM DARKSEID?
OR GRAIL. OR WHOEVER.
SO WHAT EXACTLY HAVE YOU CONCLUDED?
I HAVEN'T. I'M STILL WORKING THROUGH EVERYTHING, BUT I HOPE SOON TO HAVE--
SISTER...!

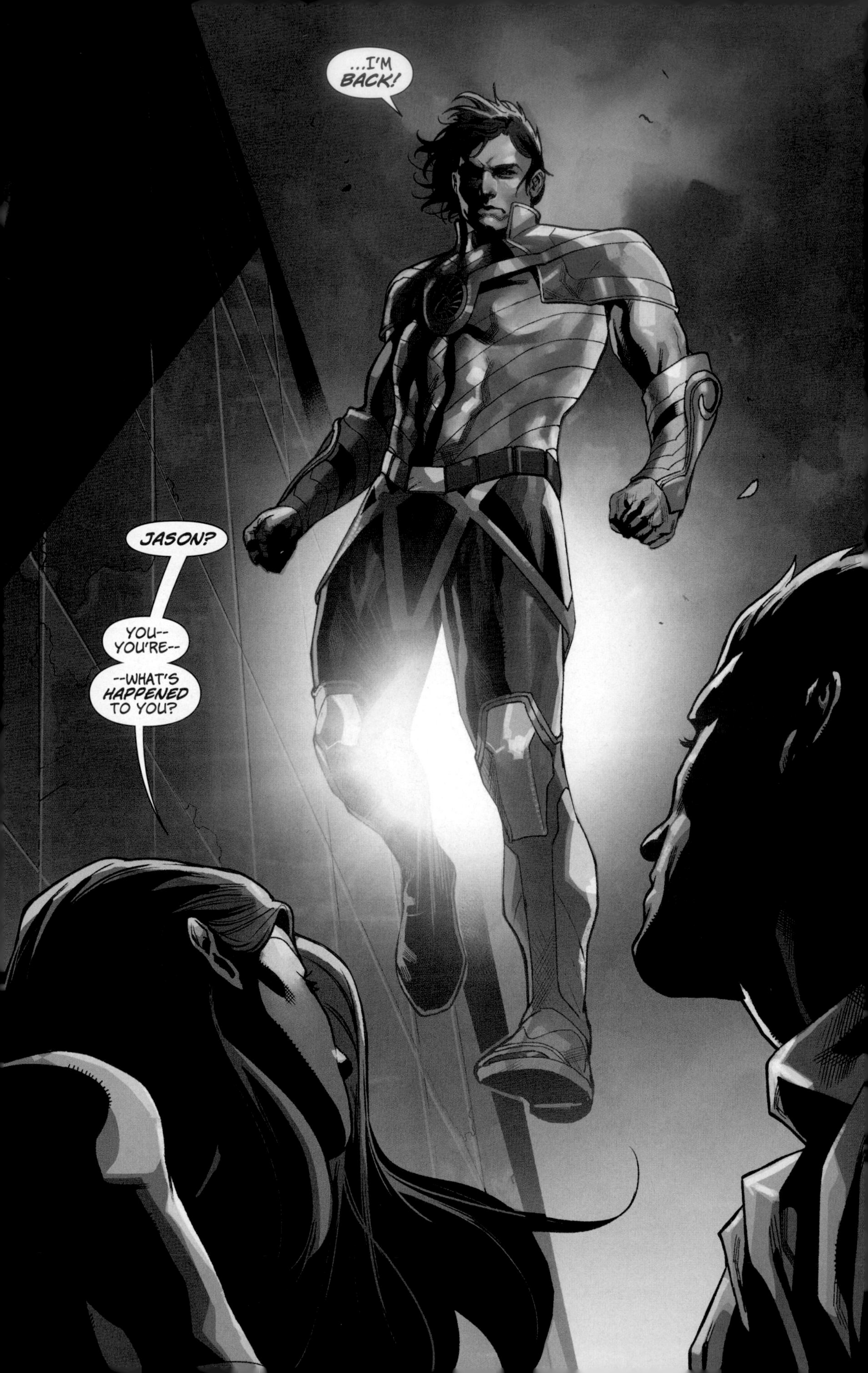
...I'M BACK!
JASON?
YOU-- YOU'RE--
--WHAT'S HAPPENED TO YOU?

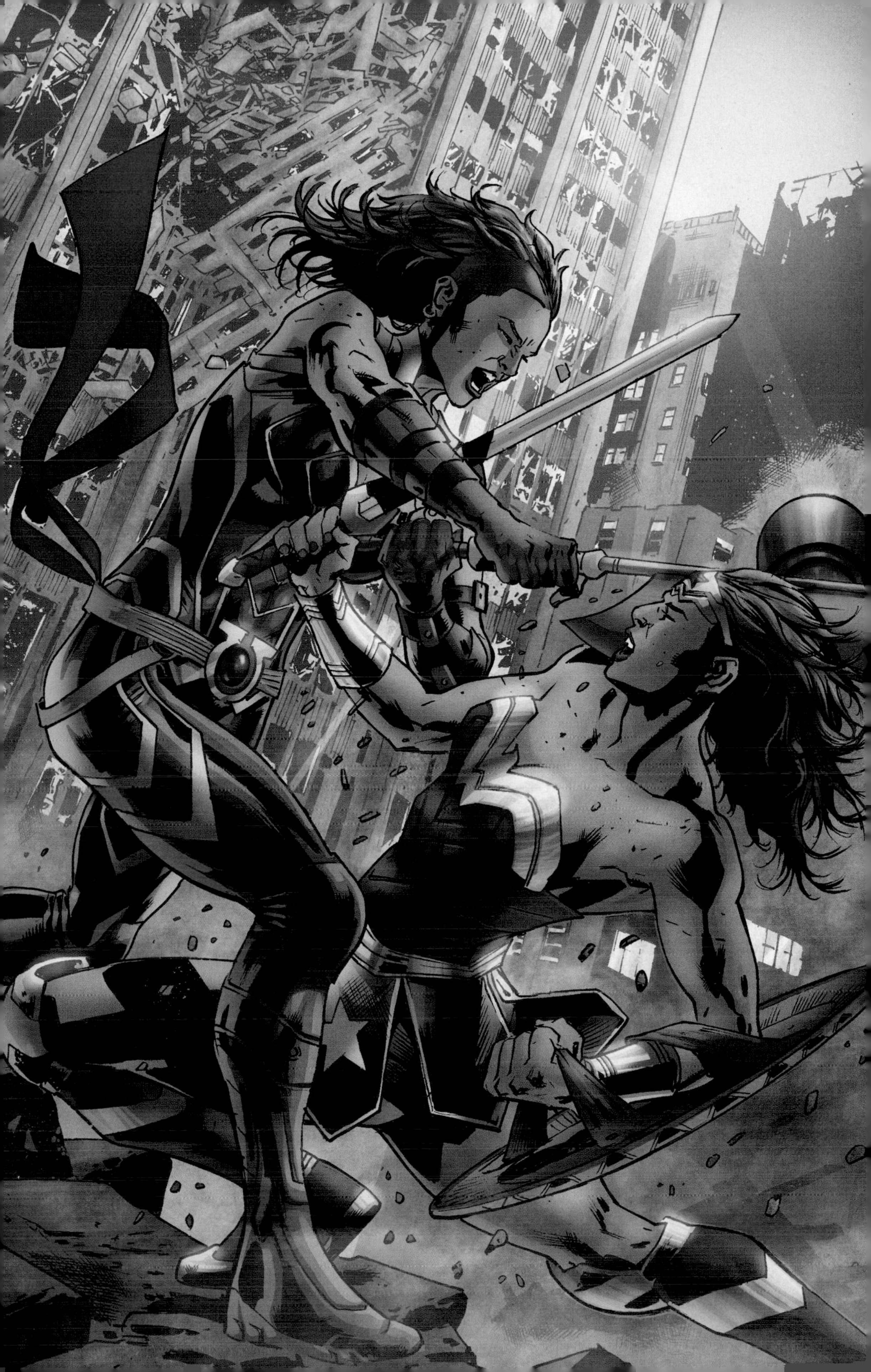

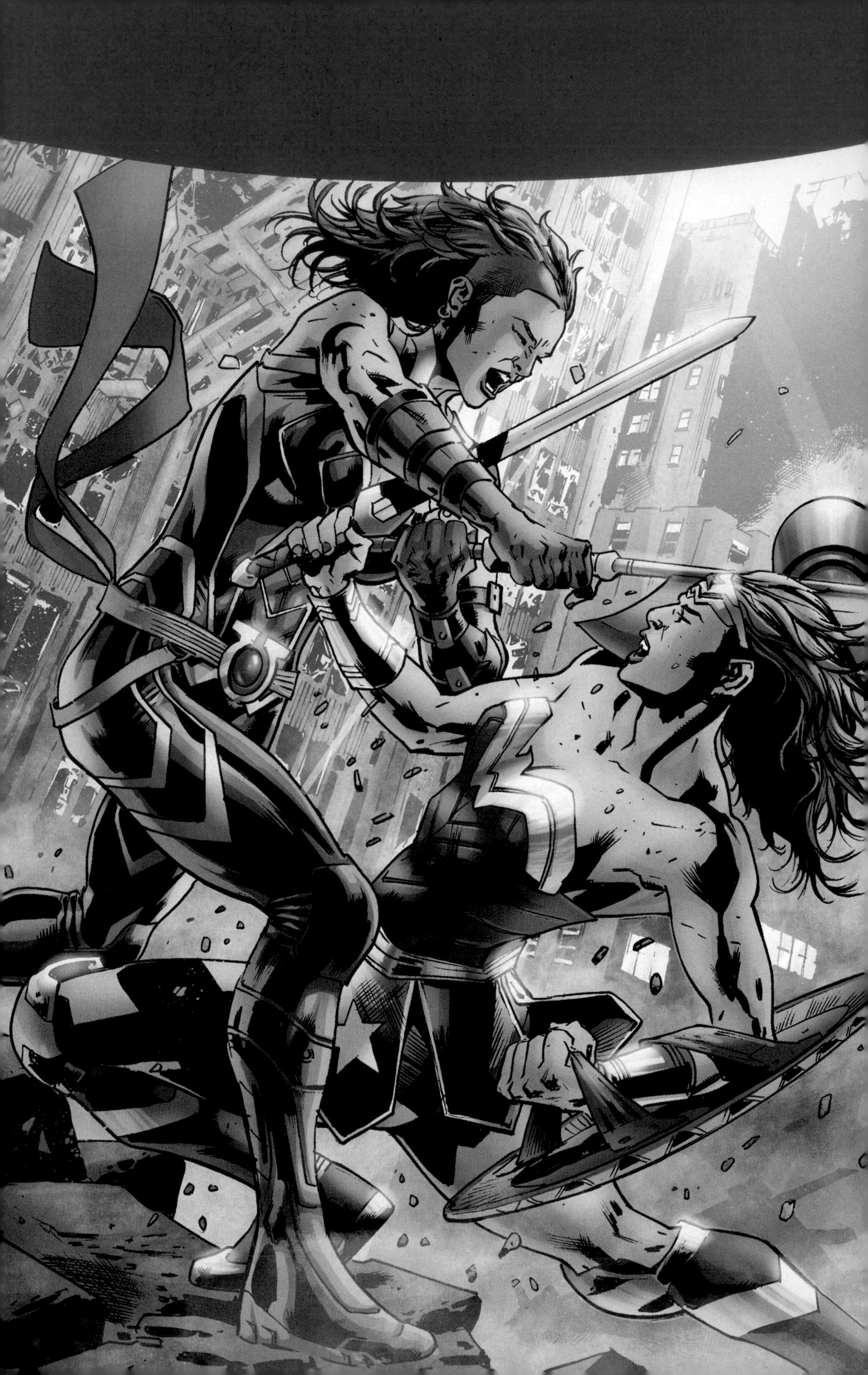

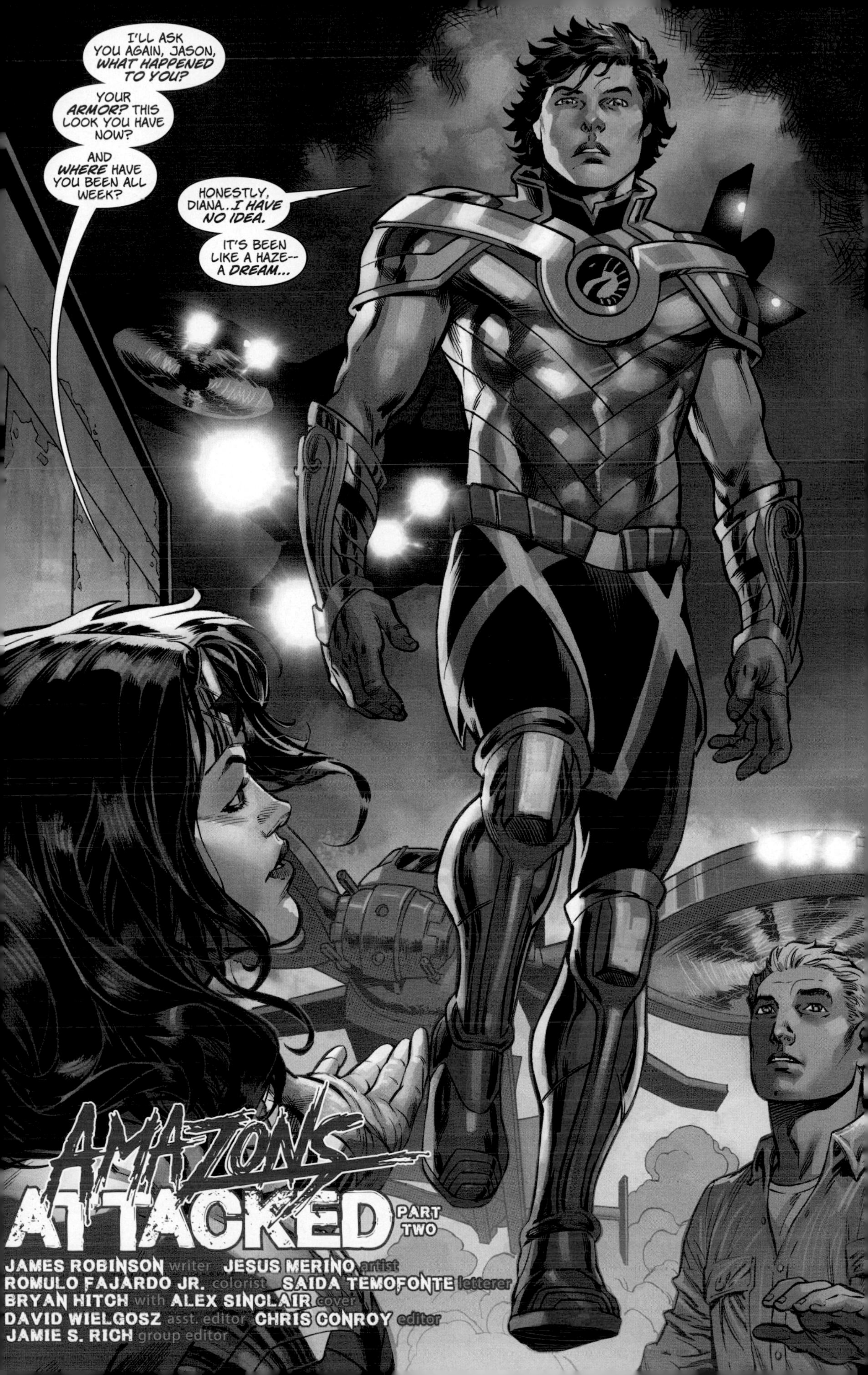
I'LL ASK YOU AGAIN, JASON, WHAT HAPPENED TO YOU?
YOUR ARMOR? THIS LOOK YOU HAVE NOW?
AND WHERE HAVE YOU BEEN ALL WEEK?
HONESTLY, DIANA...I HAVE NO IDEA.
IT'S BEEN LIKE A HAZE-- A DREAM...
AMAZONS ATTACKED PART TWO
JAMES ROBINSON writer JESUS MERINO artist
ROMULO FAJARDO JR. colorist SAIDA TEMOFONTE letterer
BRYAN HITCH with ALEX SINCLAIR cover
DAVID WIELGOSZ asst. editor CHRIS CONROY editor
JAMIE S. RICH group editor

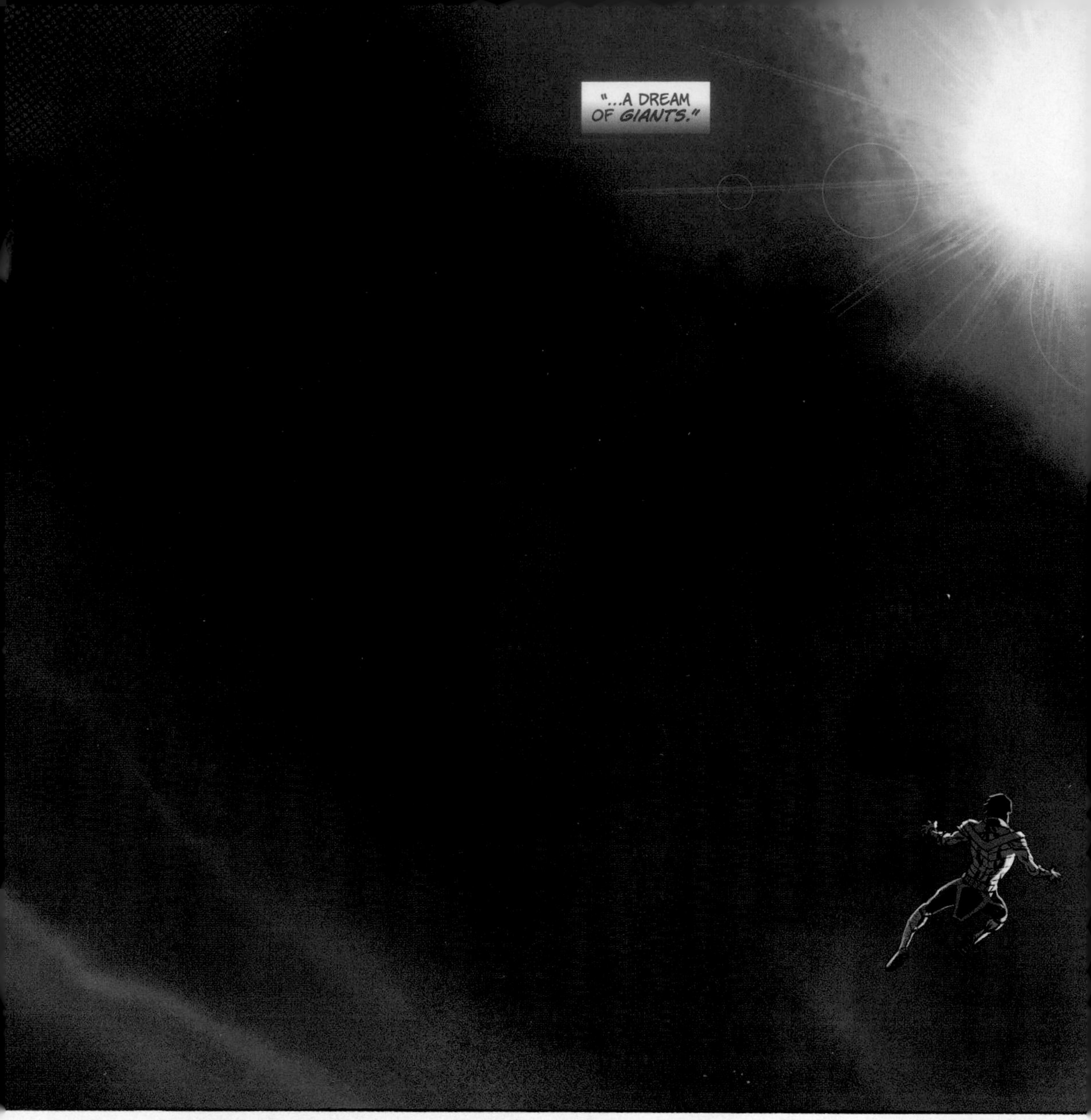
"...A DREAM OF GIANTS."

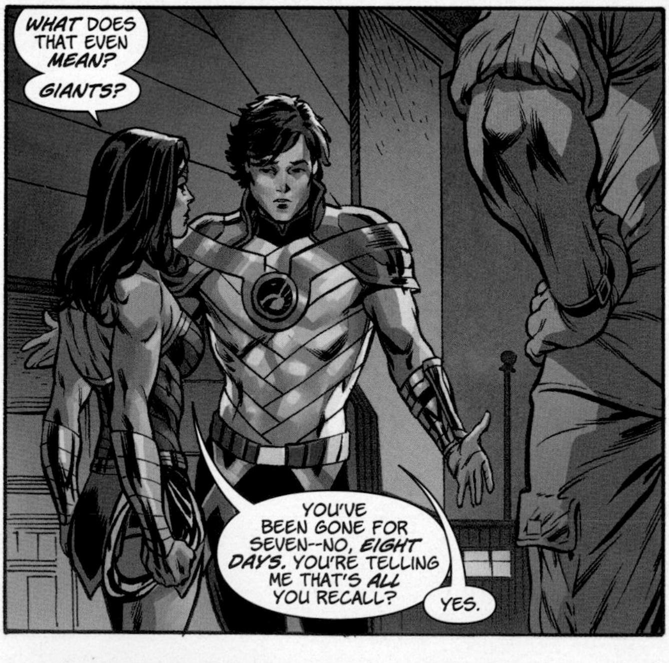
WHAT DOES THAT EVEN MEAN?
GIANTS?
YOU'VE BEEN GONE FOR SEVEN--NO, EIGHT DAYS. YOU'RE TELLING ME THAT'S ALL YOU RECALL?
YES.

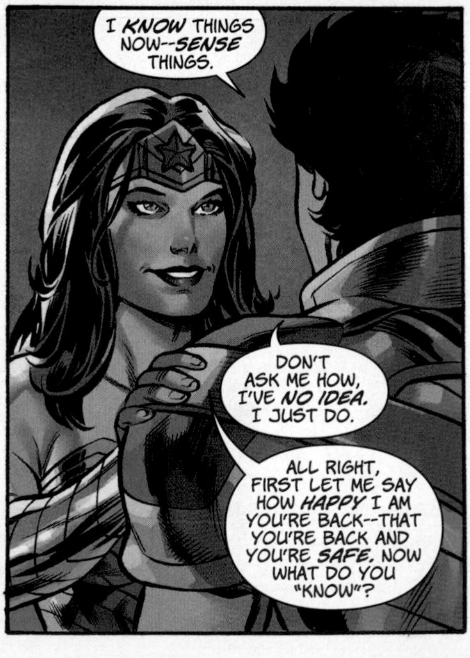
I KNOW THINGS NOW--SENSE THINGS.
DON'T ASK ME HOW, I'VE NO IDEA. I JUST DO.
ALL RIGHT, FIRST LET ME SAY HOW HAPPY I AM YOU'RE BACK--THAT YOU'RE BACK AND YOU'RE SAFE. NOW WHAT DO YOU "KNOW"?

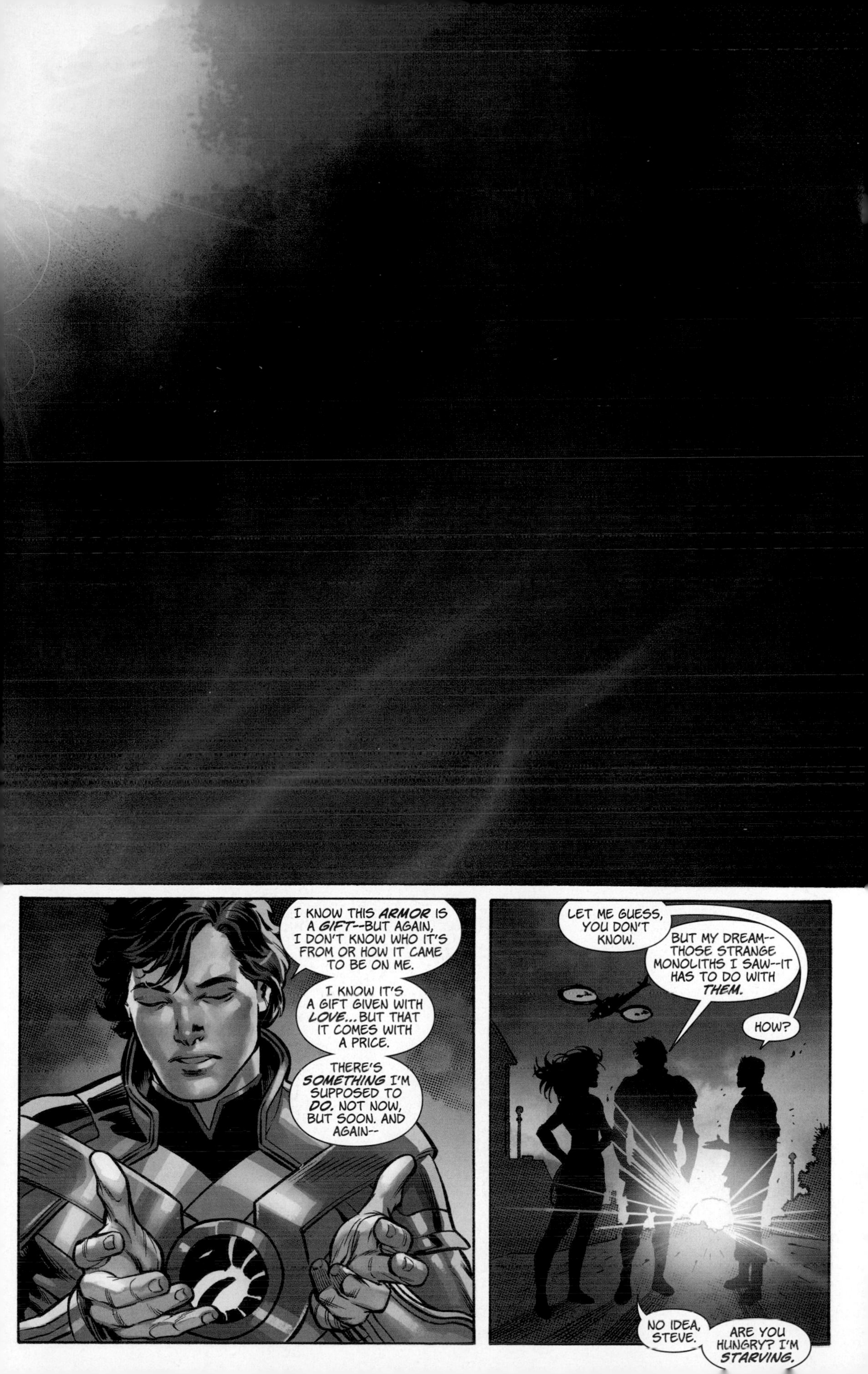
I KNOW THIS ARMOR IS A GIFT--BUT AGAIN, I DON'T KNOW WHO IT'S FROM OR HOW IT CAME TO BE ON ME.
I KNOW IT'S A GIFT GIVEN WITH LOVE... BUT THAT IT COMES WITH A PRICE.
THERE'S SOMETHING I'M SUPPOSED TO DO. NOT NOW, BUT SOON. AND AGAIN--
LET ME GUESS, YOU DON'T KNOW.
BUT MY DREAM-- THOSE STRANGE MONOLITHS I SAW--IT HAS TO DO WITH THEM.
HOW?
NO IDEA, STEVE.
ARE YOU HUNGRY? I'M STARVING.

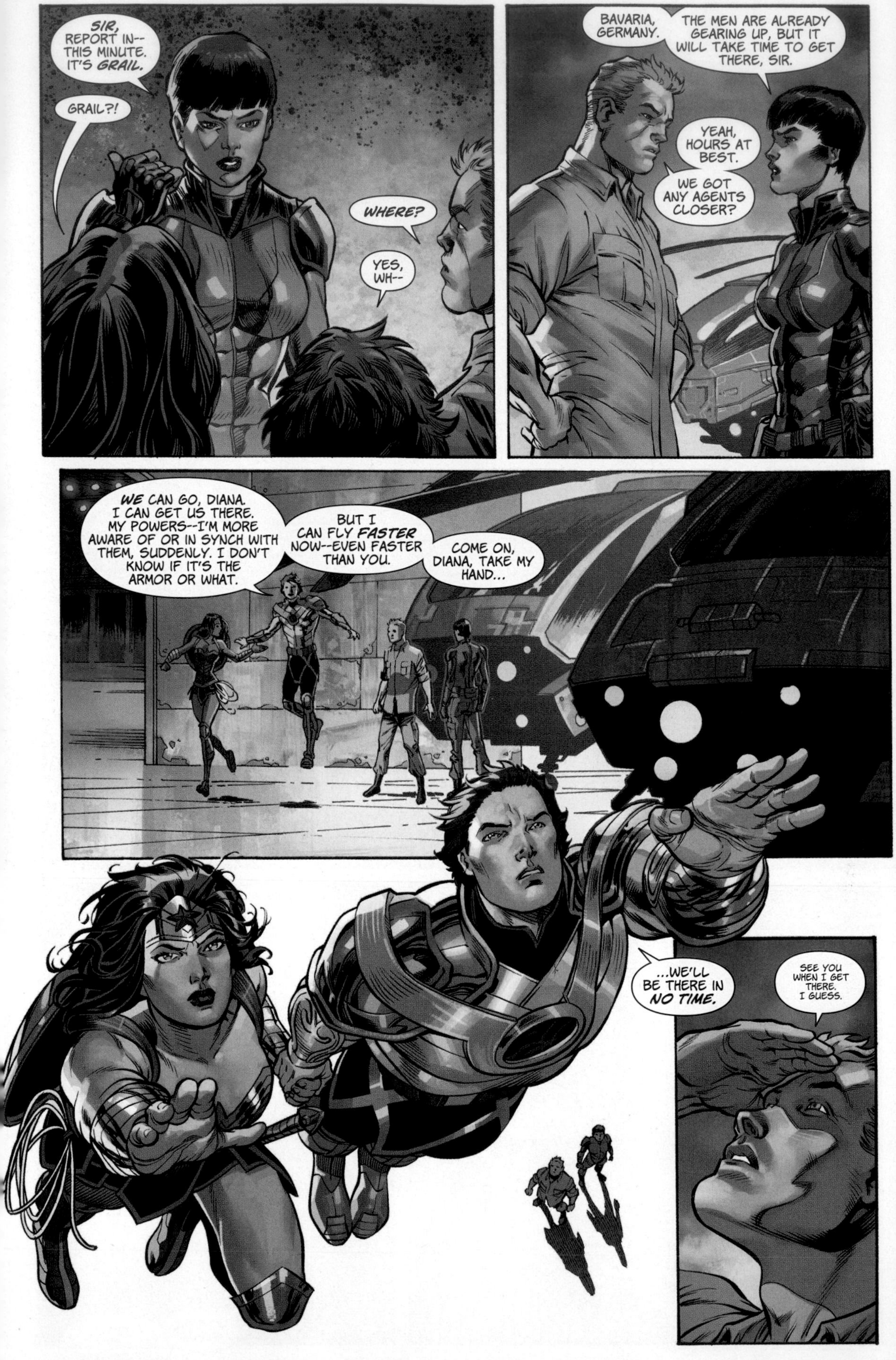

SIR, REPORT IN-- THIS MINUTE. IT'S GRAIL.
GRAIL?!
WHERE?
YES, WH--
BAVARIA, GERMANY.
THE MEN ARE ALREADY GEARING UP, BUT IT WILL TAKE TIME TO GET THERE, SIR.
YEAH, HOURS AT BEST.
WE GOT ANY AGENTS CLOSER?
WE CAN GO, DIANA. I CAN GET US THERE. MY POWERS--I'M MORE AWARE OF OR IN SYNCH WITH THEM, SUDDENLY. I DON'T KNOW IF IT'S THE ARMOR OR WHAT.
BUT I CAN FLY FASTER NOW--EVEN FASTER THAN YOU.
COME ON, DIANA, TAKE MY HAND...
...WE'LL BE THERE IN NO TIME.
SEE YOU WHEN I GET THERE. I GUESS.

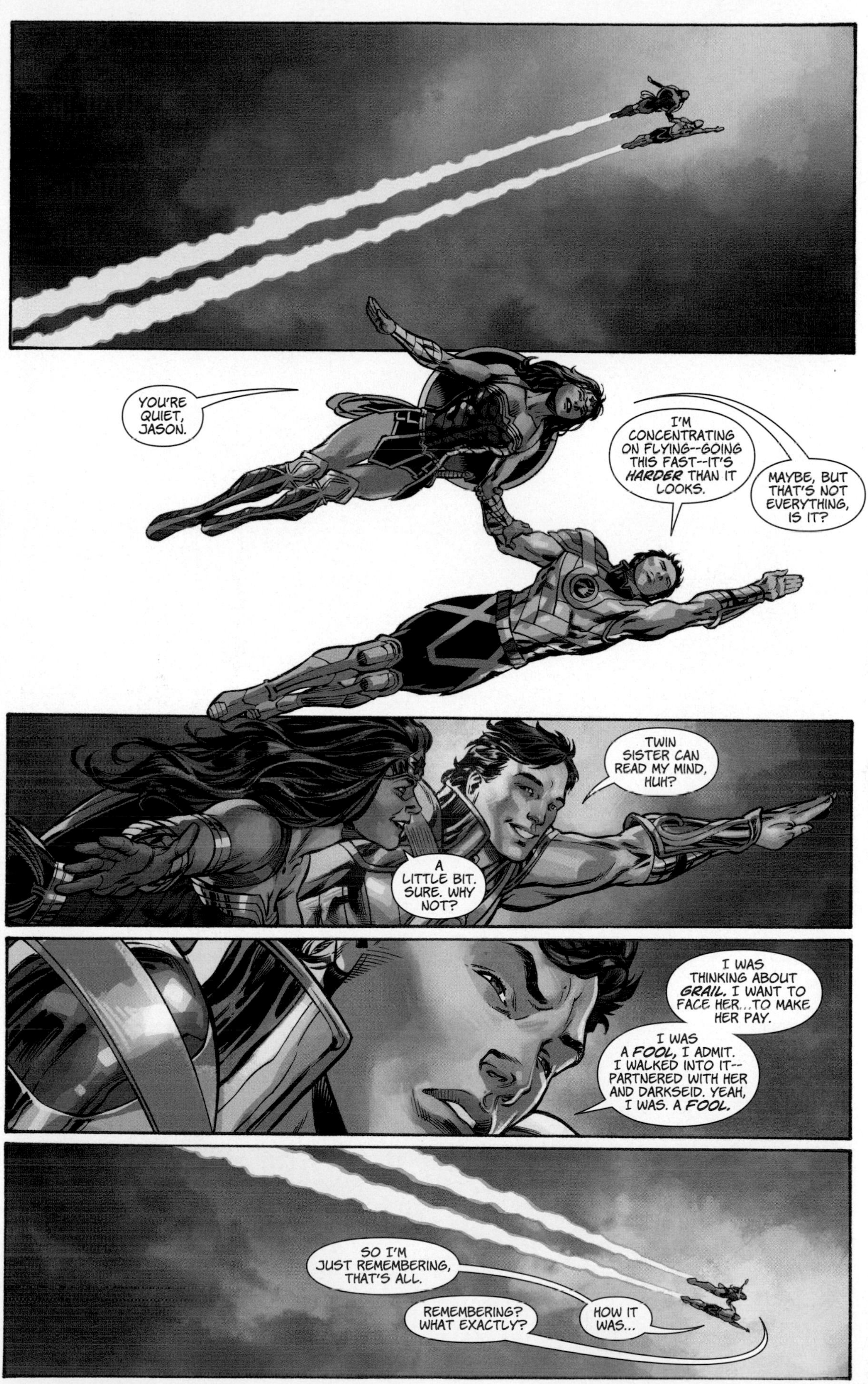
YOU'RE QUIET, JASON.
I'M CONCENTRATING ON FLYING--GOING THIS FAST--IT'S HARDER THAN IT LOOKS.
MAYBE, BUT THAT'S NOT EVERYTHING, IS IT?
TWIN SISTER CAN READ MY MIND, HUH?
A LITTLE BIT. SURE. WHY NOT?
I WAS THINKING ABOUT GRAIL. I WANT TO FACE HER...TO MAKE HER PAY.
I WAS A FOOL, I ADMIT. I WALKED INTO IT--PARTNERED WITH HER AND DARKSEID. YEAH, I WAS. A FOOL.
SO I'M JUST REMEMBERING, THAT'S ALL.
REMEMBERING? WHAT EXACTLY?
HOW IT WAS...

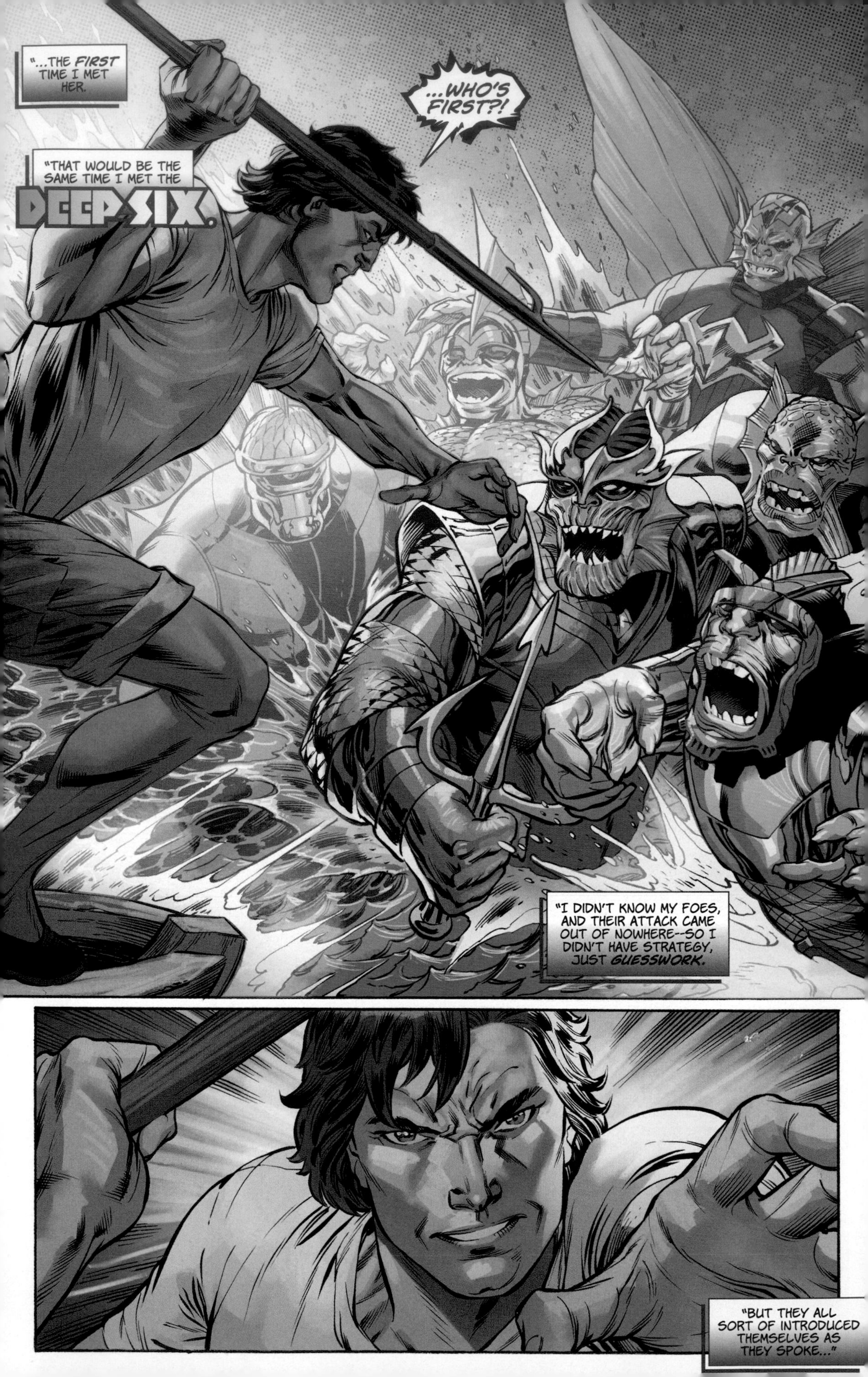

"...THE FIRST TIME I MET HER.
...WHO'S FIRST?!
"THAT WOULD BE THE SAME TIME I MET THE
DEEP SIX.
"I DIDN'T KNOW MY FOES, AND THEIR ATTACK CAME OUT OF NOWHERE--SO I DIDN'T HAVE STRATEGY, JUST GUESSWORK.
"BUT THEY ALL SORT OF INTRODUCED THEMSELVES AS THEY SPOKE..."

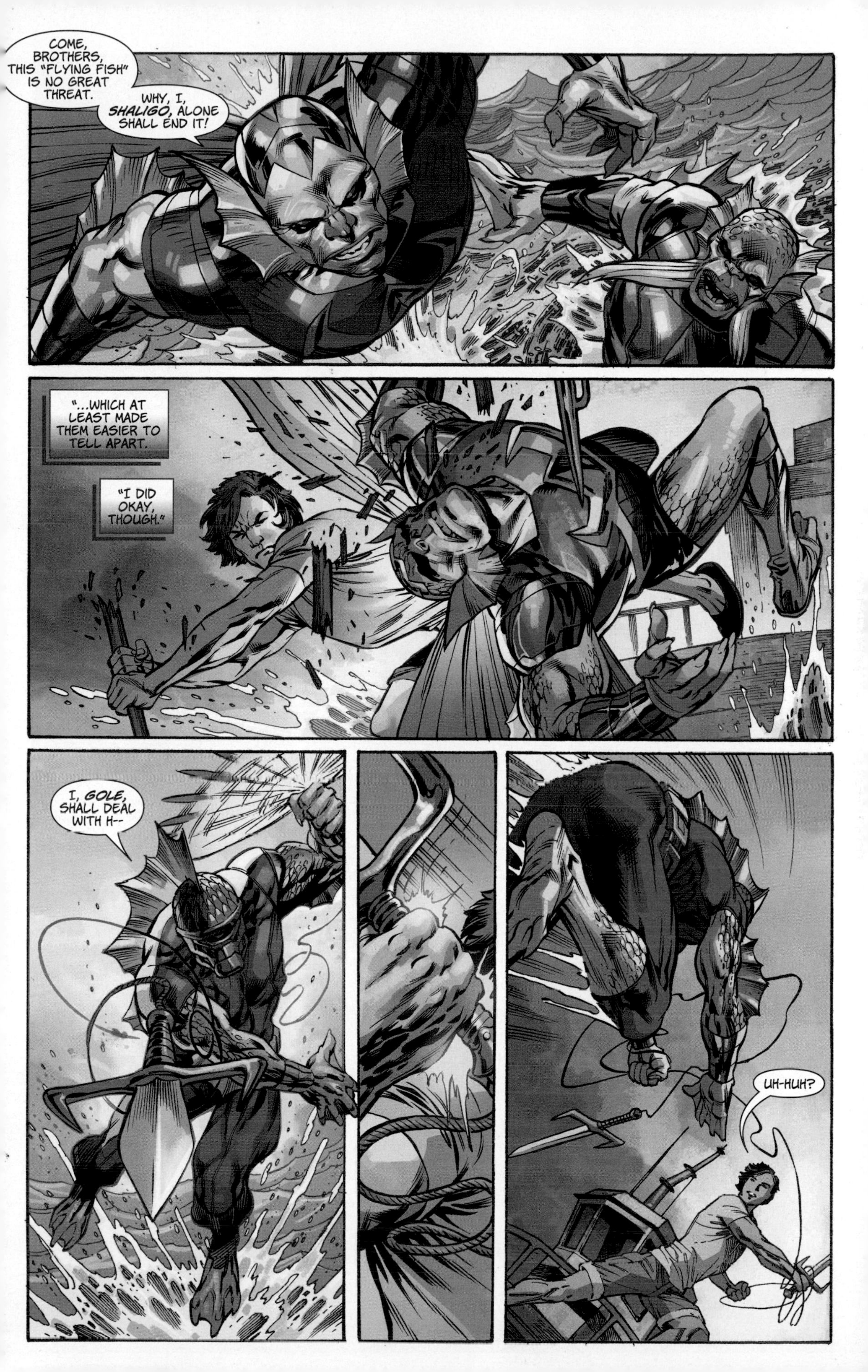
COME, BROTHERS, THIS "FLYING FISH" IS NO GREAT THREAT.
WHY, I, SHALIGO, ALONE SHALL END IT!
"...WHICH AT LEAST MADE THEM EASIER TO TELL APART.
"I DID OKAY, THOUGH."
I, GOLE, SHALL DEAL WITH H--
UH-HUH?

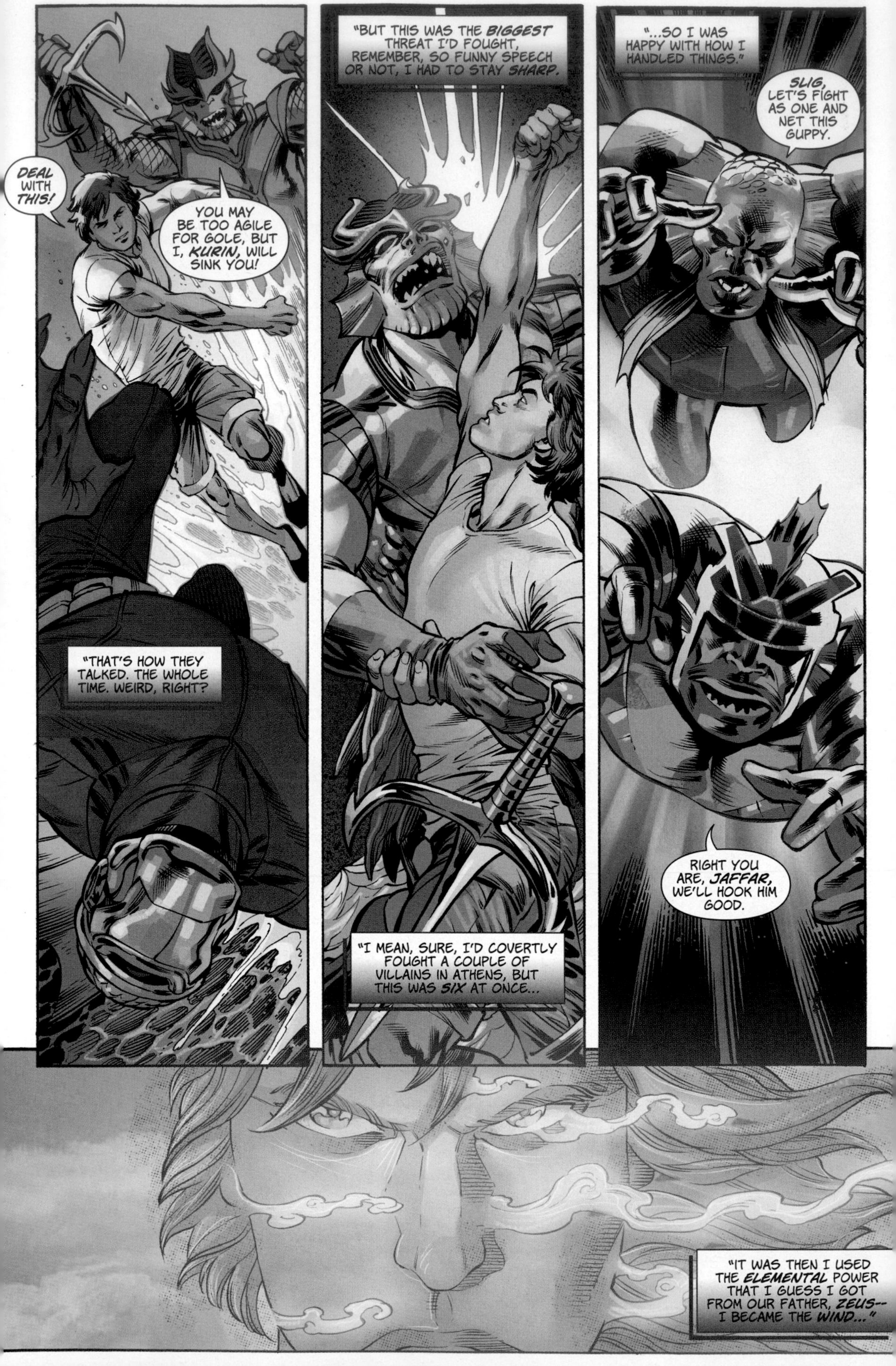
DEAL WITH THIS!
YOU MAY BE TOO AGILE FOR GOLE, BUT I, KURIN, WILL SINK YOU!
"THAT'S HOW THEY TALKED. THE WHOLE TIME. WEIRD, RIGHT?
"BUT THIS WAS THE BIGGEST THREAT I'D FOUGHT, REMEMBER, SO FUNNY SPEECH OR NOT, I HAD TO STAY SHARP.
"I MEAN, SURE, I'D COVERTLY FOUGHT A COUPLE OF VILLAINS IN ATHENS, BUT THIS WAS SIX AT ONCE...
"...SO I WAS HAPPY WITH HOW I HANDLED THINGS."
SLIG, LET'S FIGHT AS ONE AND NET THIS GUPPY.
RIGHT YOU ARE, JAFFAR, WE'LL HOOK HIM GOOD.
"IT WAS THEN I USED THE ELEMENTAL POWER THAT I GUESS I GOT FROM OUR FATHER, ZEUS-- I BECAME THE WIND..."

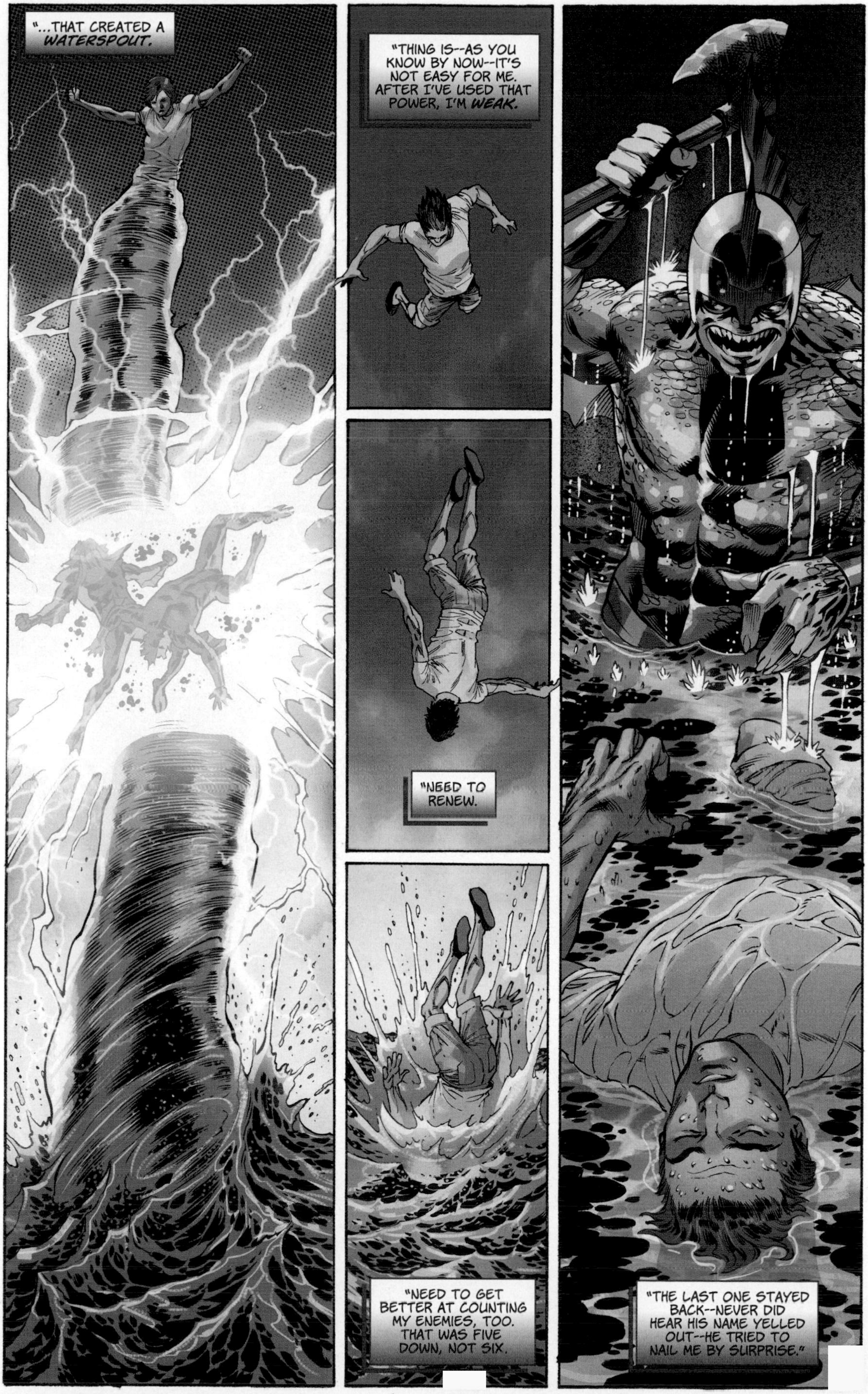
"...THAT CREATED A *WATERSPOUT*.
"THING IS--AS YOU KNOW BY NOW--IT'S NOT EASY FOR ME. AFTER I'VE USED THAT POWER, I'M *WEAK*.
"NEED TO RENEW.
"NEED TO GET BETTER AT COUNTING MY ENEMIES, TOO. THAT WAS FIVE DOWN, NOT SIX.
"THE LAST ONE STAYED BACK--NEVER DID HEAR HIS NAME YELLED OUT--HE TRIED TO NAIL ME BY SURPRISE."

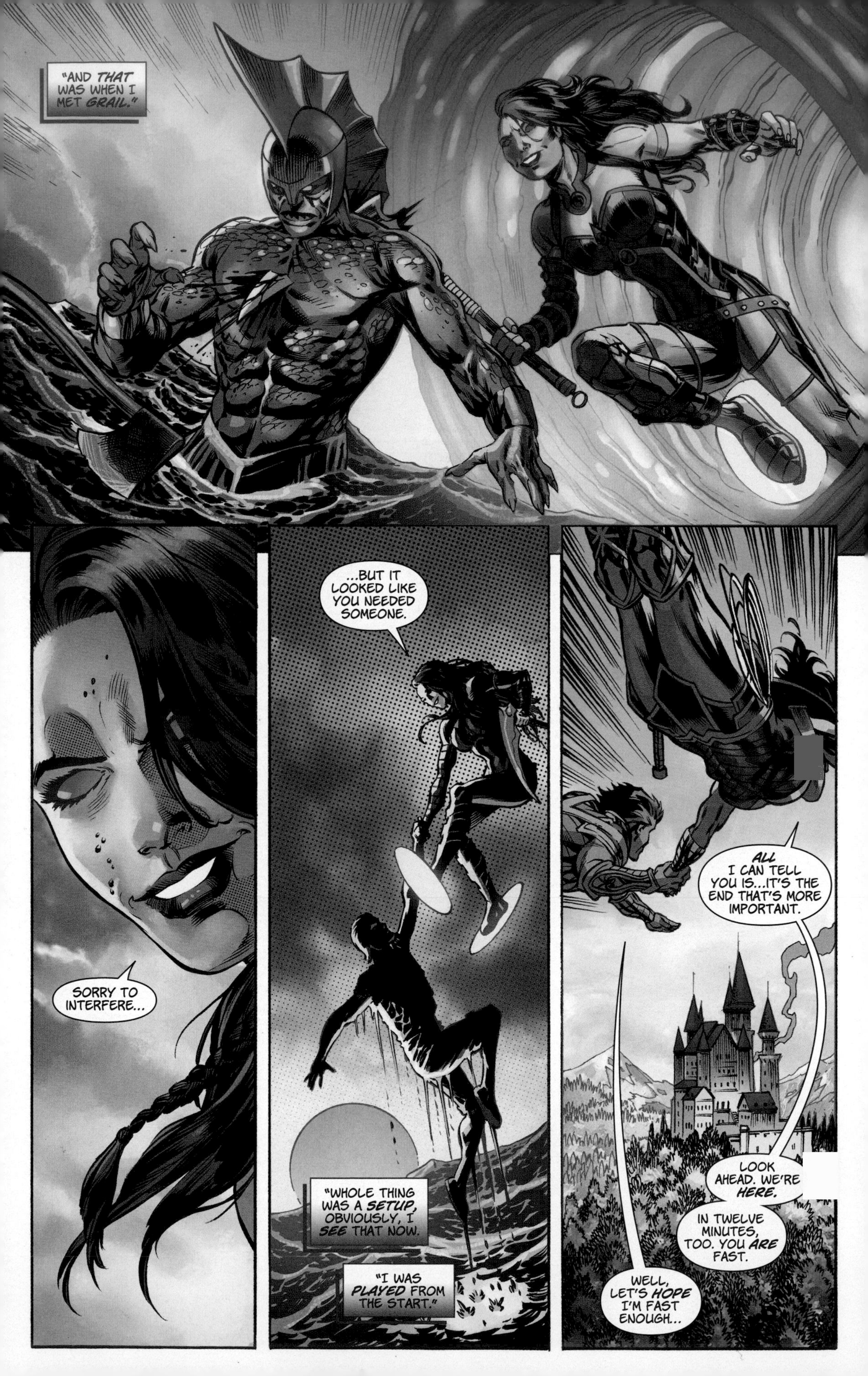
"AND THAT WAS WHEN I MET GRAIL."
SORRY TO INTERFERE...
...BUT IT LOOKED LIKE YOU NEEDED SOMEONE.
"WHOLE THING WAS A SETUP, OBVIOUSLY, I SEE THAT NOW.
"I WAS PLAYED FROM THE START."
ALL I CAN TELL YOU IS...IT'S THE END THAT'S MORE IMPORTANT.
LOOK AHEAD. WE'RE HERE.
IN TWELVE MINUTES, TOO. YOU ARE FAST.
WELL, LET'S HOPE I'M FAST ENOUGH...

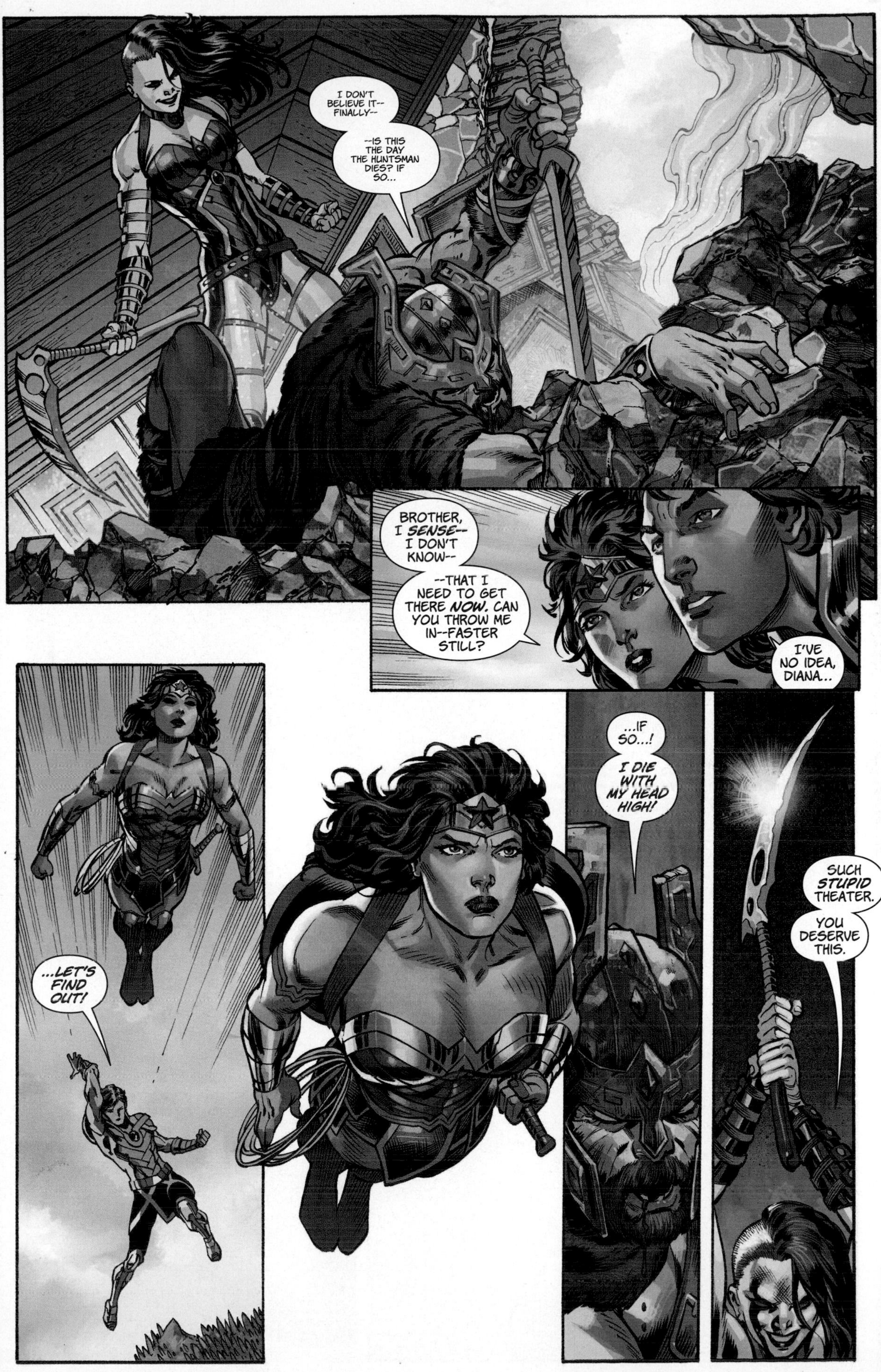
I DON'T BELIEVE IT-- FINALLY--
--IS THIS THE DAY THE HUNTSMAN DIES? IF SO...
BROTHER, I SENSE-- I DON'T KNOW--
--THAT I NEED TO GET THERE NOW. CAN YOU THROW ME IN--FASTER STILL?
I'VE NO IDEA, DIANA...
...LET'S FIND OUT!
...IF SO...!
I DIE WITH MY HEAD HIGH!
SUCH STUPID THEATER.
YOU DESERVE THIS.

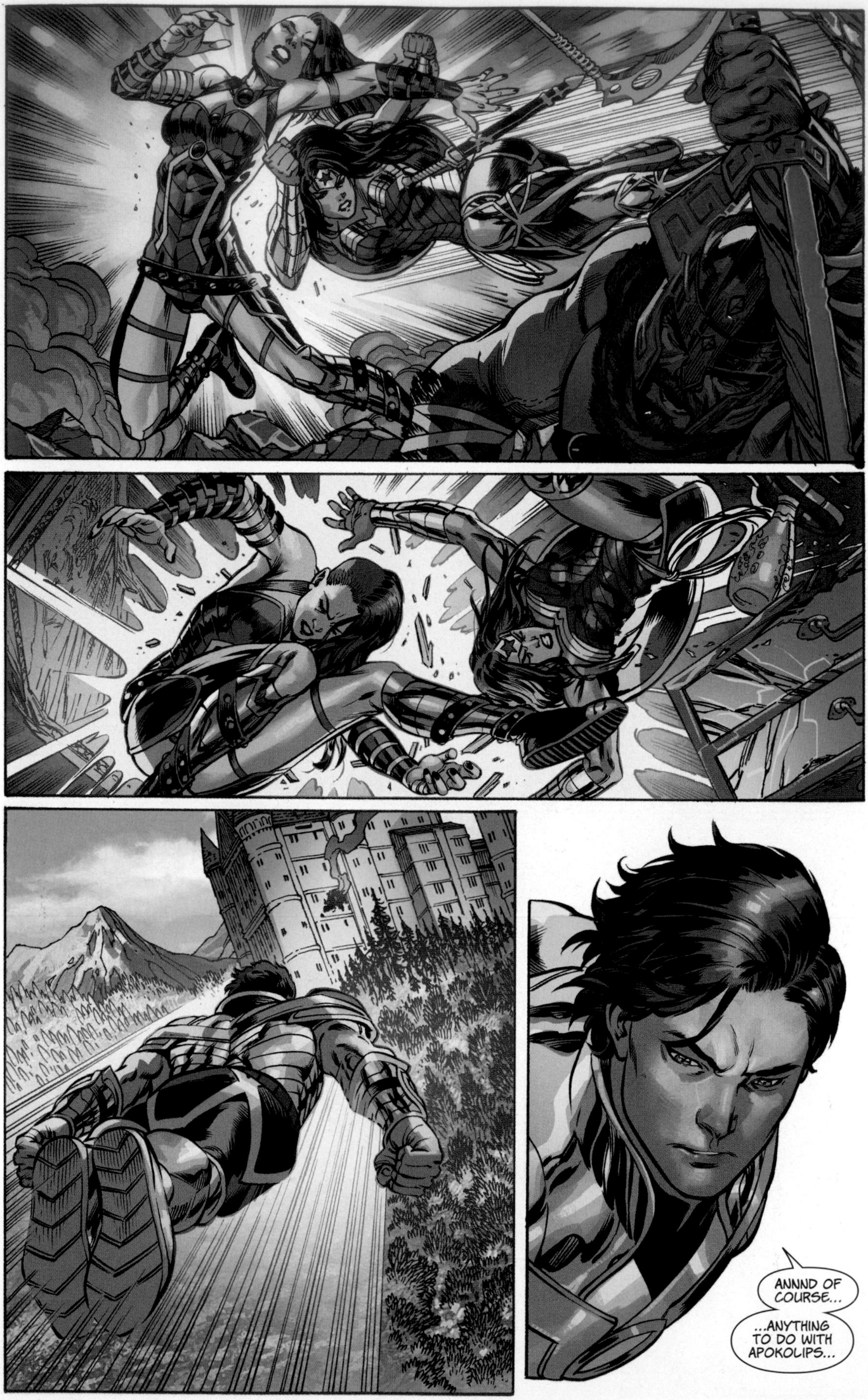
ANNND OF COURSE...
...ANYTHING TO DO WITH APOKOLIPS...

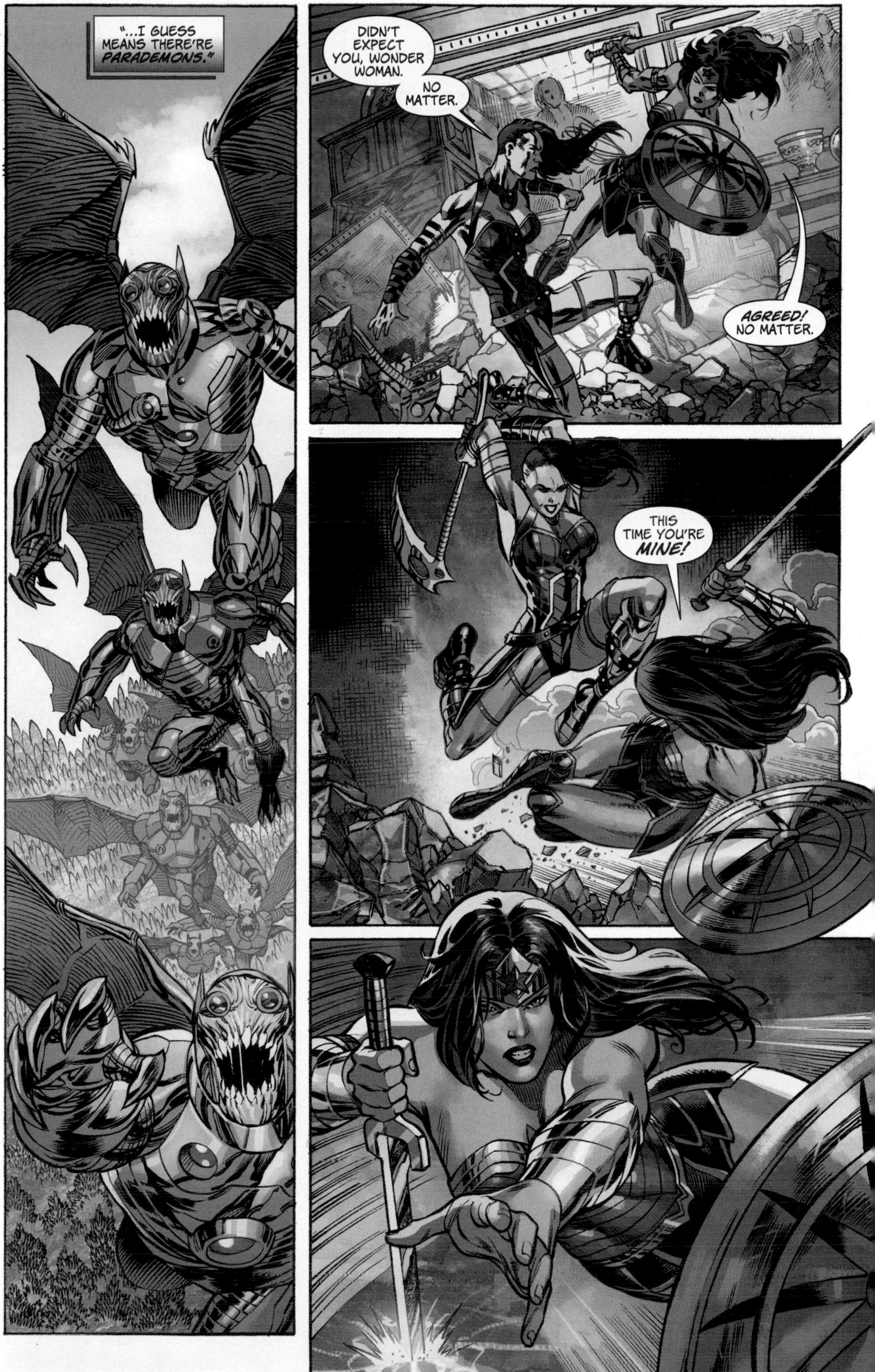
"...I GUESS MEANS THERE'RE PARADEMONS."
DIDN'T EXPECT YOU, WONDER WOMAN.
NO MATTER.
AGREED! NO MATTER.
THIS TIME YOU'RE MINE!

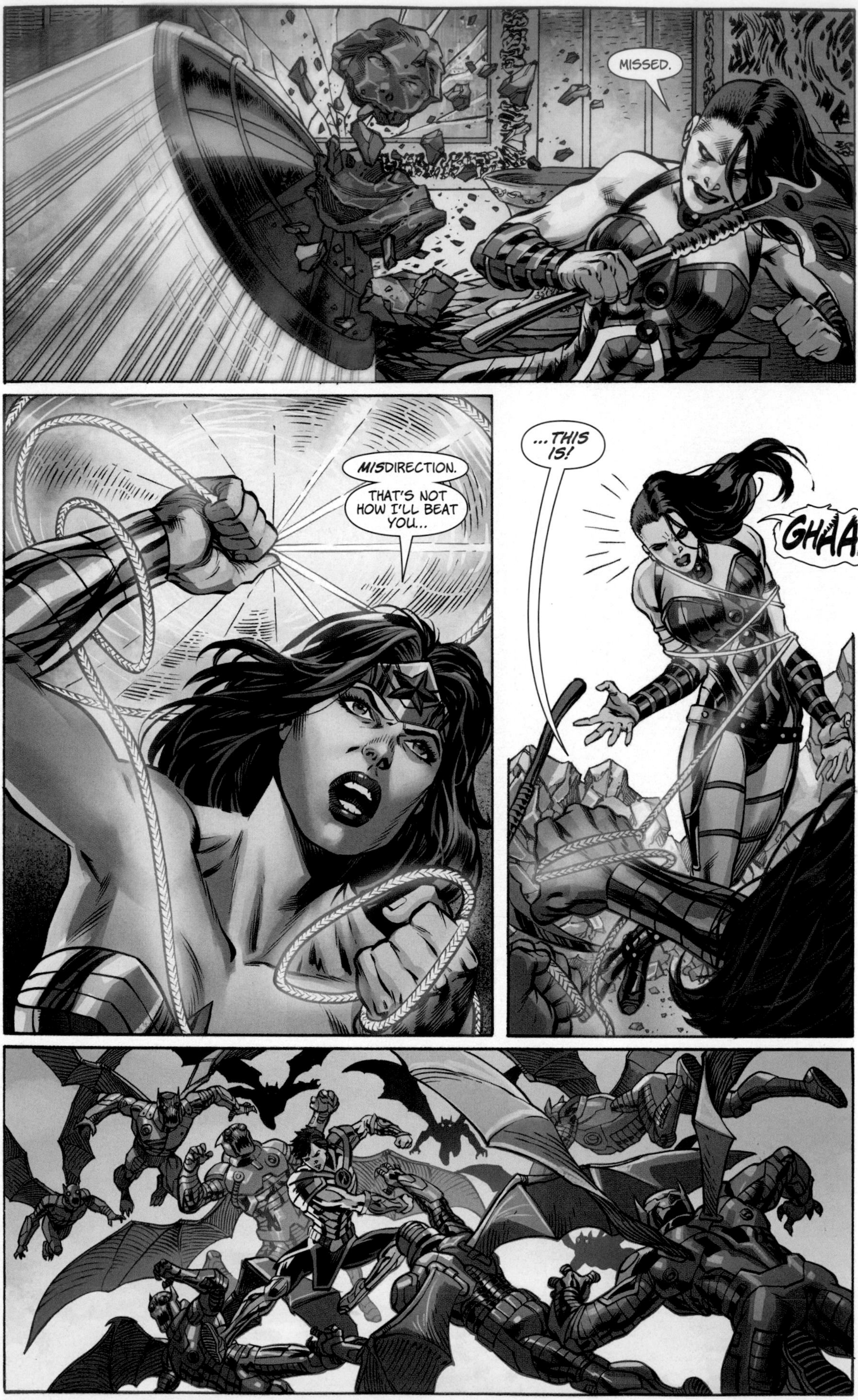
MISSED.
MISDIRECTION.
THAT'S NOT HOW I'LL BEAT YOU...
...THIS IS!
GHAA!

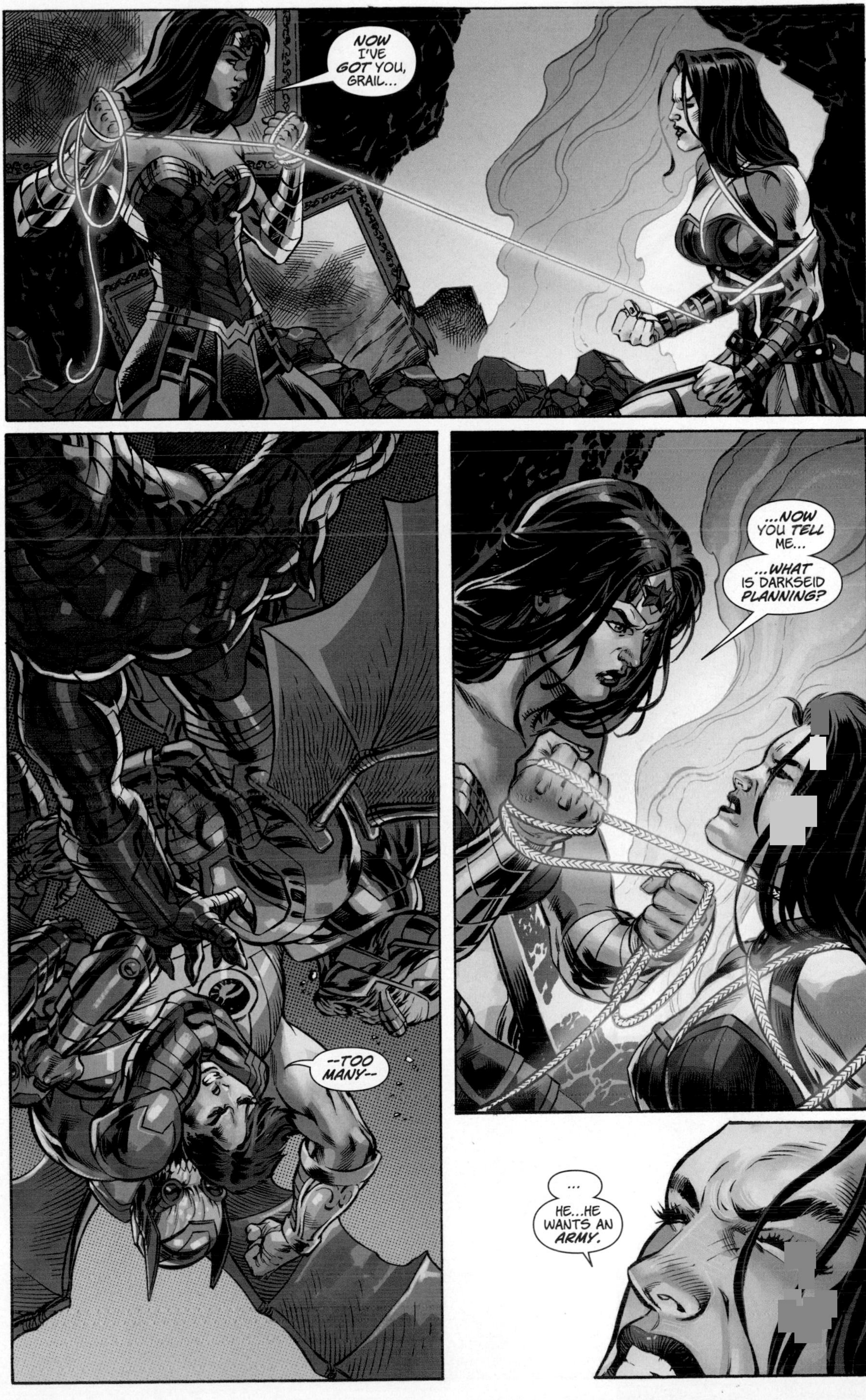
NOW I'VE GOT YOU, GRAIL...
--TOO MANY--
...NOW YOU TELL ME...
...WHAT IS DARKSEID PLANNING?
...
HE...HE WANTS AN ARMY.

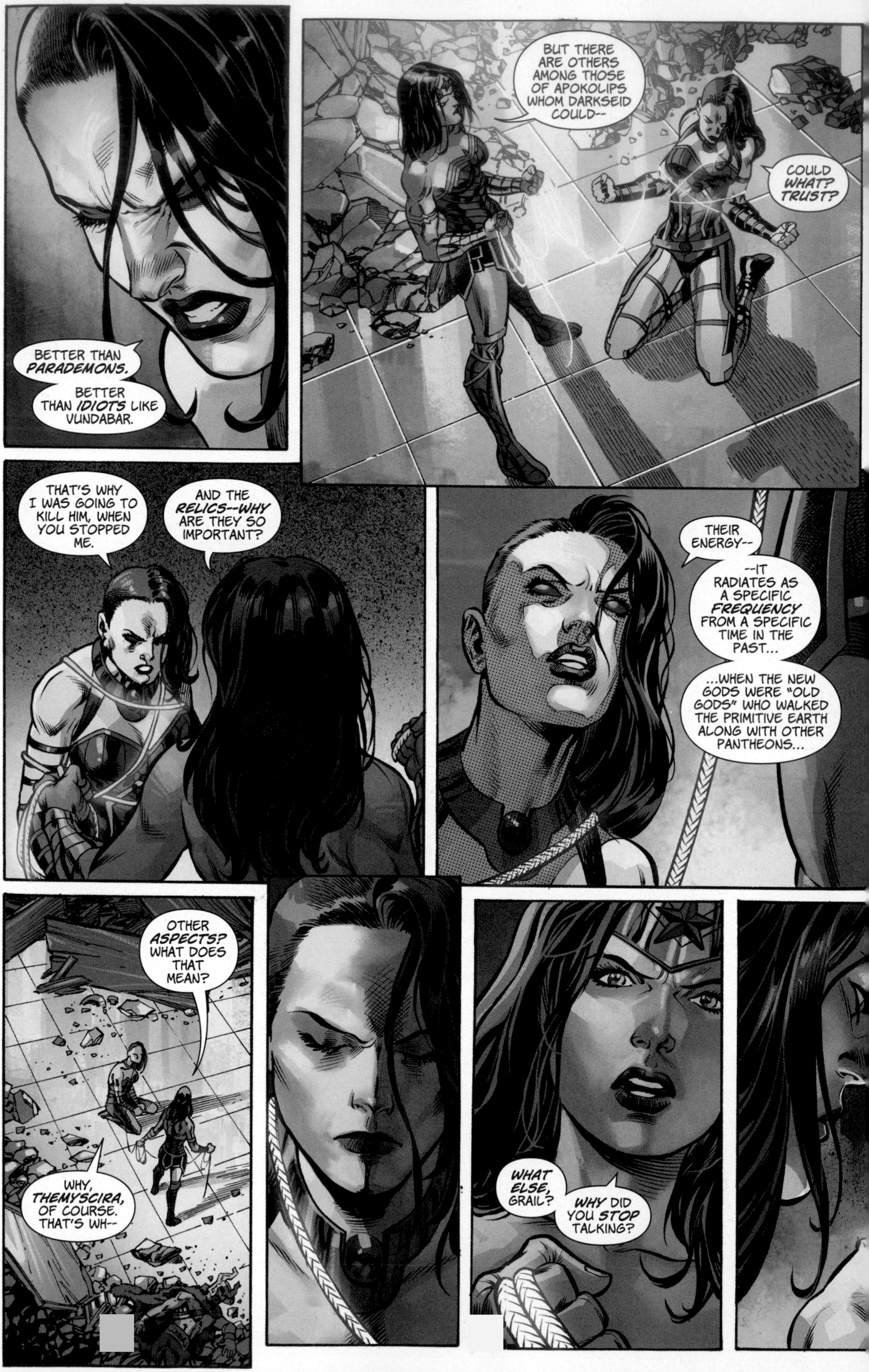
BETTER THAN PARADEMONS.
BETTER THAN IDIOTS LIKE VUNDABAR.
BUT THERE ARE OTHERS AMONG THOSE OF APOKOLIPS WHOM DARKSEID COULD--
COULD WHAT? TRUST?
THAT'S WHY I WAS GOING TO KILL HIM, WHEN YOU STOPPED ME.
AND THE RELICS--WHY ARE THEY SO IMPORTANT?
THEIR ENERGY--
--IT RADIATES AS A SPECIFIC FREQUENCY FROM A SPECIFIC TIME IN THE PAST...
...WHEN THE NEW GODS WERE "OLD GODS" WHO WALKED THE PRIMITIVE EARTH ALONG WITH OTHER PANTHEONS...
OTHER ASPECTS? WHAT DOES THAT MEAN?
WHY, THEMYSCIRA, OF COURSE. THAT'S WH--
WHAT ELSE, GRAIL?
WHY DID YOU STOP TALKING?

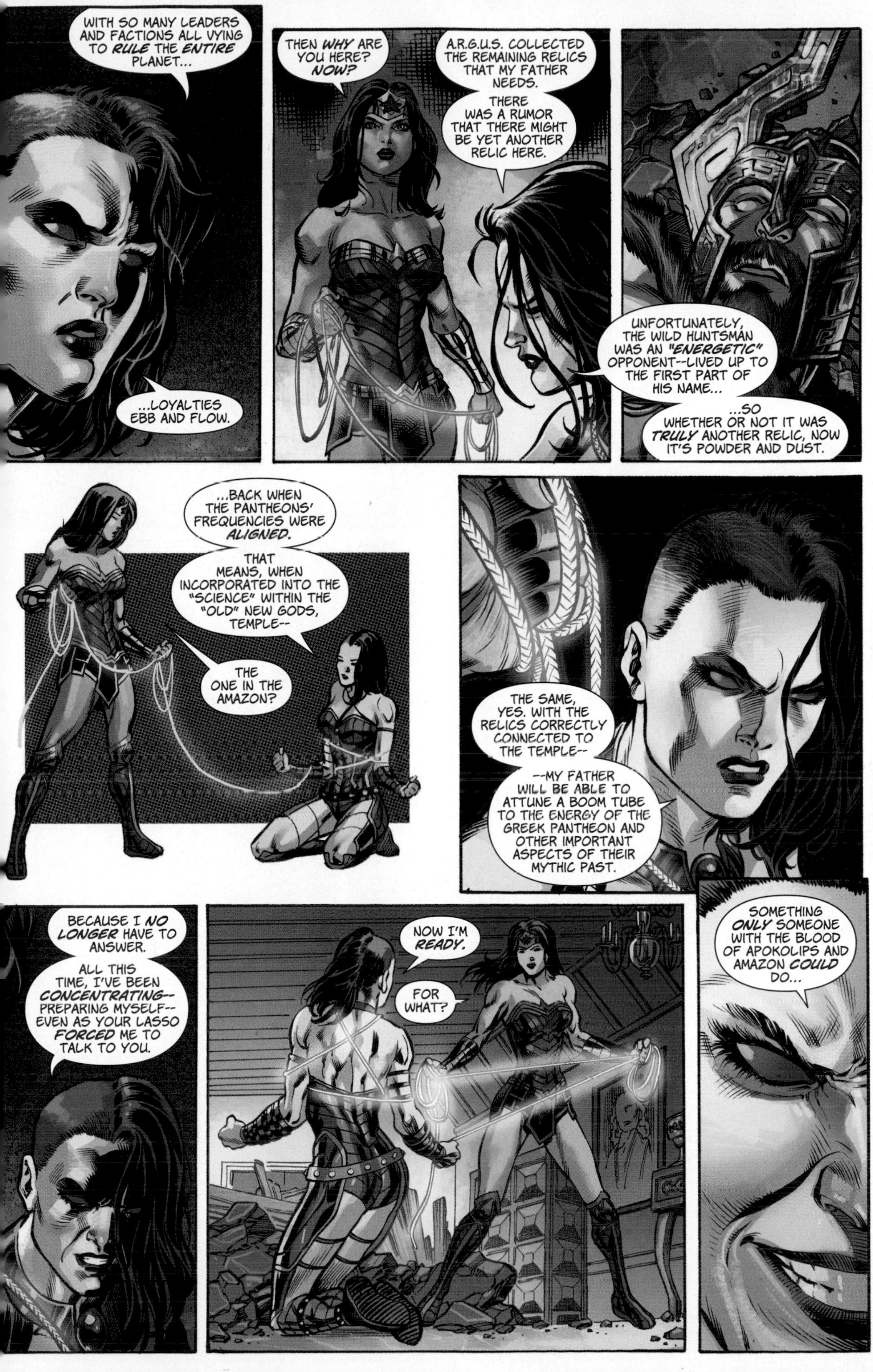
WITH SO MANY LEADERS AND FACTIONS ALL VYING TO RULE THE ENTIRE PLANET...
...LOYALTIES EBB AND FLOW.
THEN WHY ARE YOU HERE? NOW?
A.R.G.U.S. COLLECTED THE REMAINING RELICS THAT MY FATHER NEEDS.
THERE WAS A RUMOR THAT THERE MIGHT BE YET ANOTHER RELIC HERE.
UNFORTUNATELY, THE WILD HUNTSMAN WAS AN "ENERGETIC" OPPONENT--LIVED UP TO THE FIRST PART OF HIS NAME...
...SO WHETHER OR NOT IT WAS TRULY ANOTHER RELIC, NOW IT'S POWDER AND DUST.
...BACK WHEN THE PANTHEONS' FREQUENCIES WERE ALIGNED.
THAT MEANS, WHEN INCORPORATED INTO THE "SCIENCE" WITHIN THE "OLD" NEW GODS, TEMPLE--
THE ONE IN THE AMAZON?
THE SAME, YES. WITH THE RELICS CORRECTLY CONNECTED TO THE TEMPLE--
--MY FATHER WILL BE ABLE TO ATTUNE A BOOM TUBE TO THE ENERGY OF THE GREEK PANTHEON AND OTHER IMPORTANT ASPECTS OF THEIR MYTHIC PAST.
BECAUSE I NO LONGER HAVE TO ANSWER.
ALL THIS TIME, I'VE BEEN CONCENTRATING--PREPARING MYSELF--EVEN AS YOUR LASSO FORCED ME TO TALK TO YOU.
NOW I'M READY.
FOR WHAT?
SOMETHING ONLY SOMEONE WITH THE BLOOD OF APOKOLIPS AND AMAZON COULD DO...

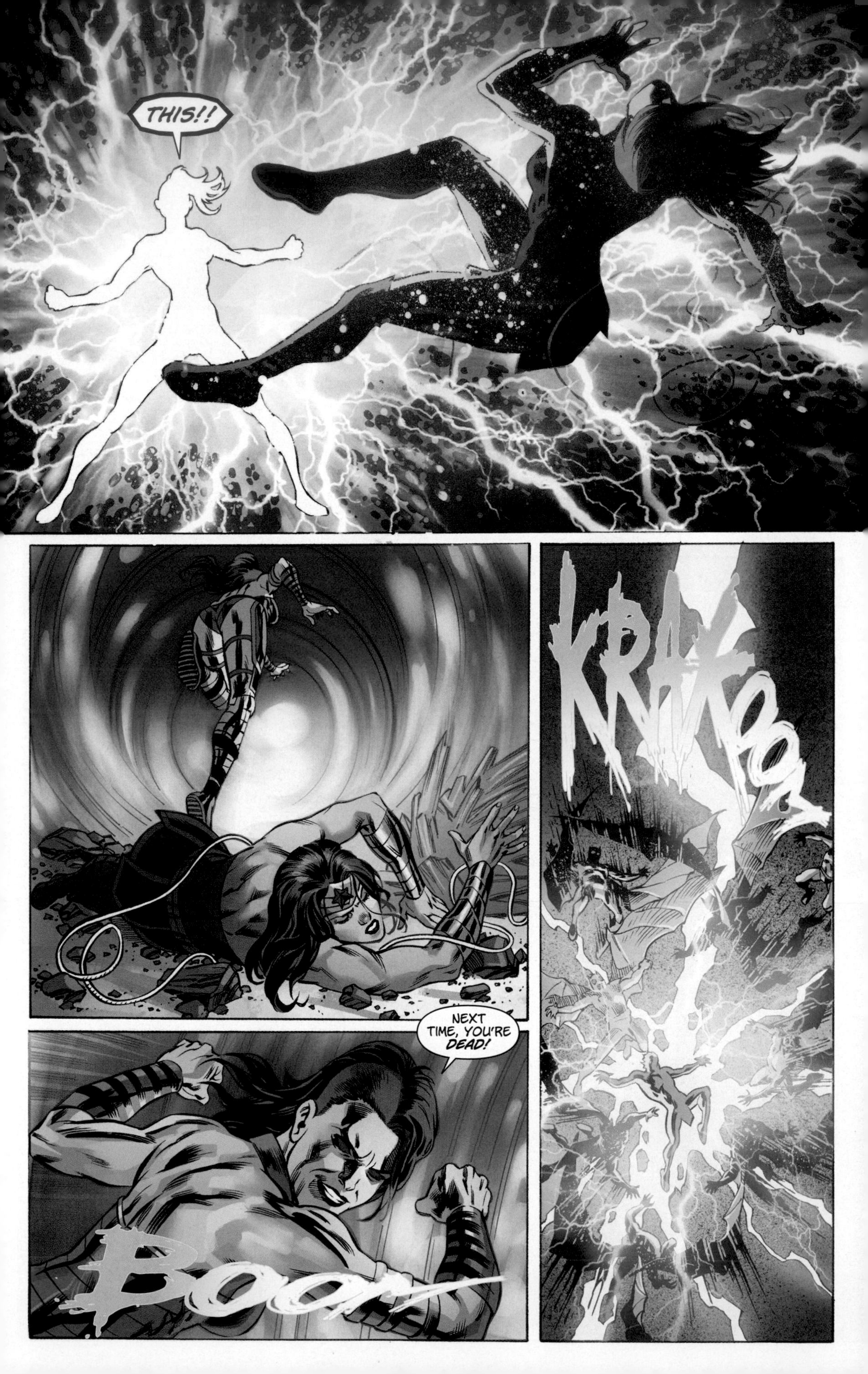
THIS!!
KRAKOOM
NEXT TIME, YOU'RE *DEAD!*
BOOM

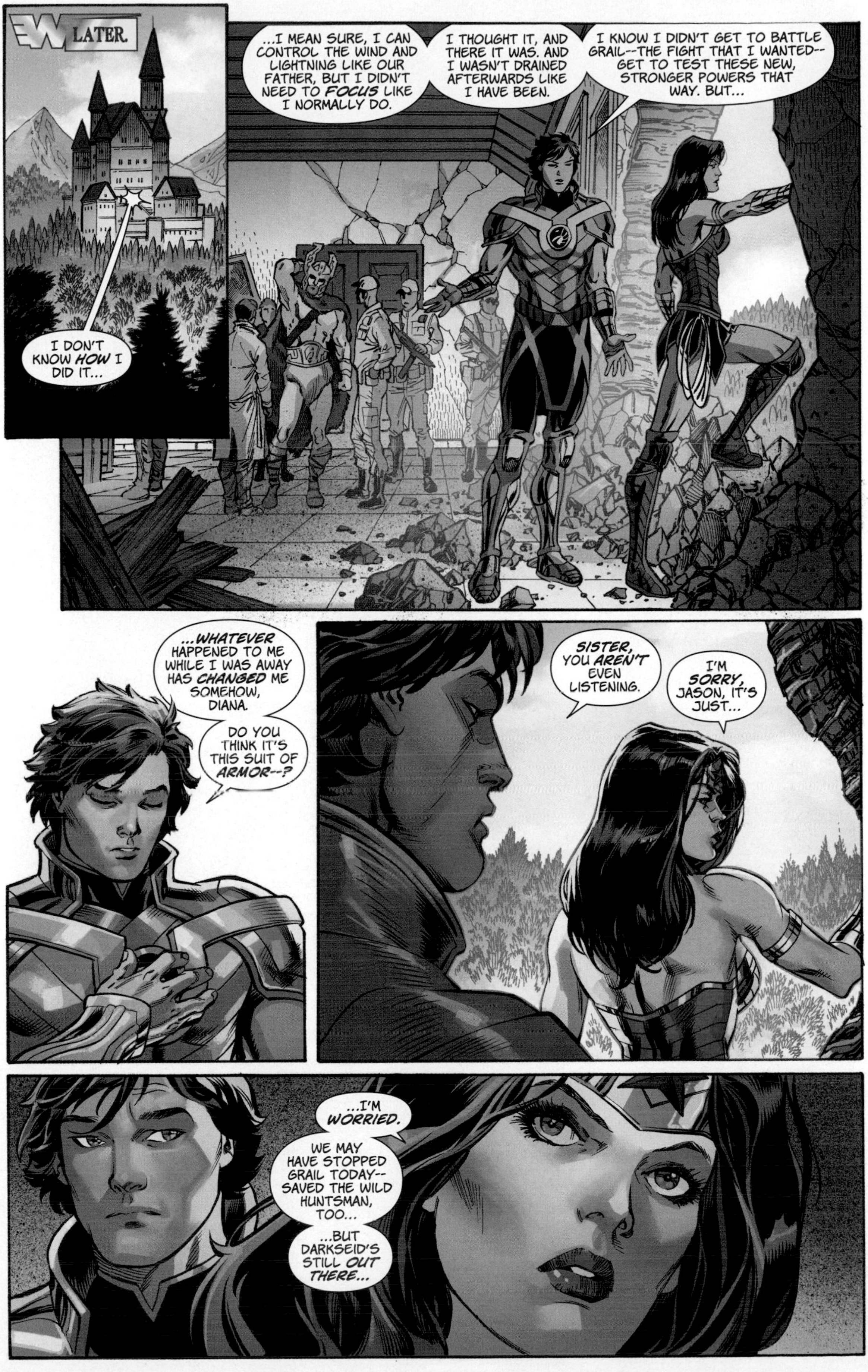
LATER.
I DON'T KNOW HOW I DID IT...
...I MEAN SURE, I CAN CONTROL THE WIND AND LIGHTNING LIKE OUR FATHER, BUT I DIDN'T NEED TO FOCUS LIKE I NORMALLY DO.
I THOUGHT IT, AND THERE IT WAS. AND I WASN'T DRAINED AFTERWARDS LIKE I HAVE BEEN.
I KNOW I DIDN'T GET TO BATTLE GRAIL--THE FIGHT THAT I WANTED--GET TO TEST THESE NEW, STRONGER POWERS THAT WAY. BUT...
...WHATEVER HAPPENED TO ME WHILE I WAS AWAY HAS CHANGED ME SOMEHOW, DIANA.
DO YOU THINK IT'S THIS SUIT OF ARMOR--?
SISTER, YOU AREN'T EVEN LISTENING.
I'M SORRY, JASON, IT'S JUST...
...I'M WORRIED.
WE MAY HAVE STOPPED GRAIL TODAY--SAVED THE WILD HUNTSMAN, TOO...
...BUT DARKSEID'S STILL OUT THERE...

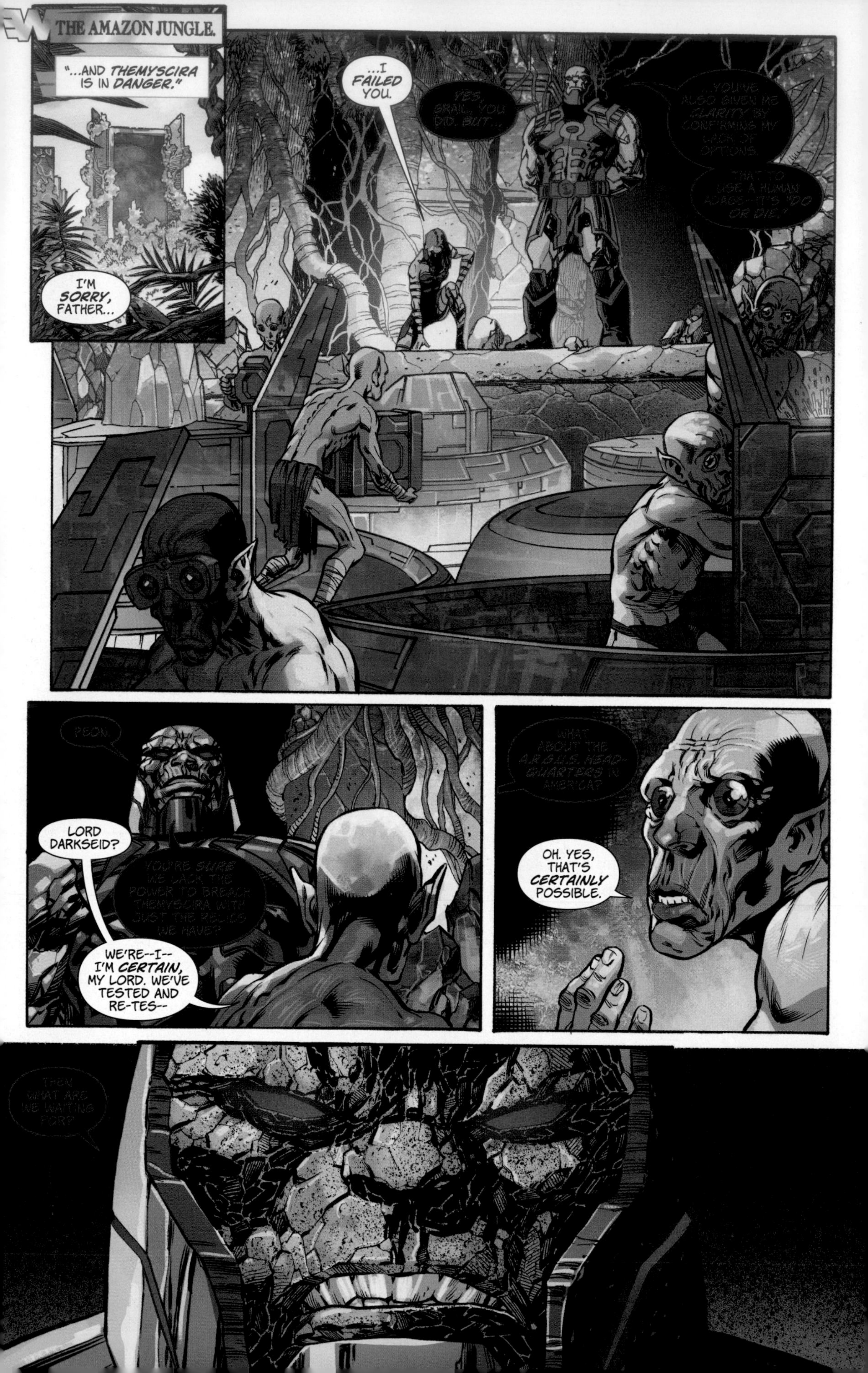
THE AMAZON JUNGLE.
"...AND THEMYSCIRA IS IN DANGER."
I'M SORRY, FATHER...
...I FAILED YOU.
YES, GRAIL, YOU DID. BUT...
...YOU'VE ALSO GIVEN ME CLARITY BY CONFIRMING MY LACK OF OPTIONS.
THAT--TO USE A HUMAN ADAGE--IT'S "DO OR DIE."
PEON.
LORD DARKSEID?
YOU'RE SURE WE LACK THE POWER TO BREACH THEMYSCIRA WITH JUST THE RELICS WE HAVE?
WE'RE--I--I'M CERTAIN, MY LORD. WE'VE TESTED AND RE-TES--
WHAT ABOUT THE A.R.G.U.S. HEAD-QUARTERS IN AMERICA?
OH. YES, THAT'S CERTAINLY POSSIBLE.
THEN WHAT ARE WE WAITING FOR?

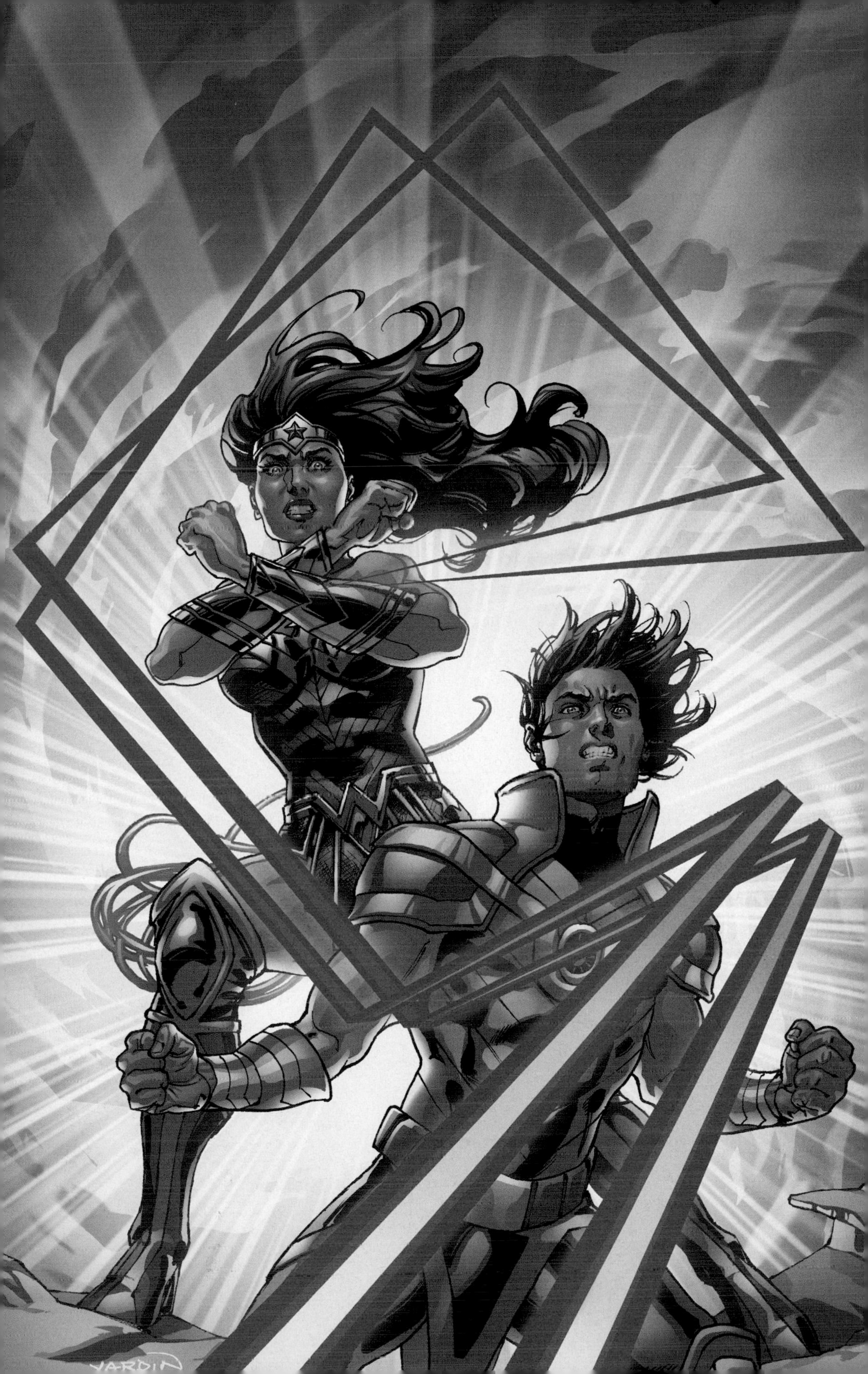
YARDIN

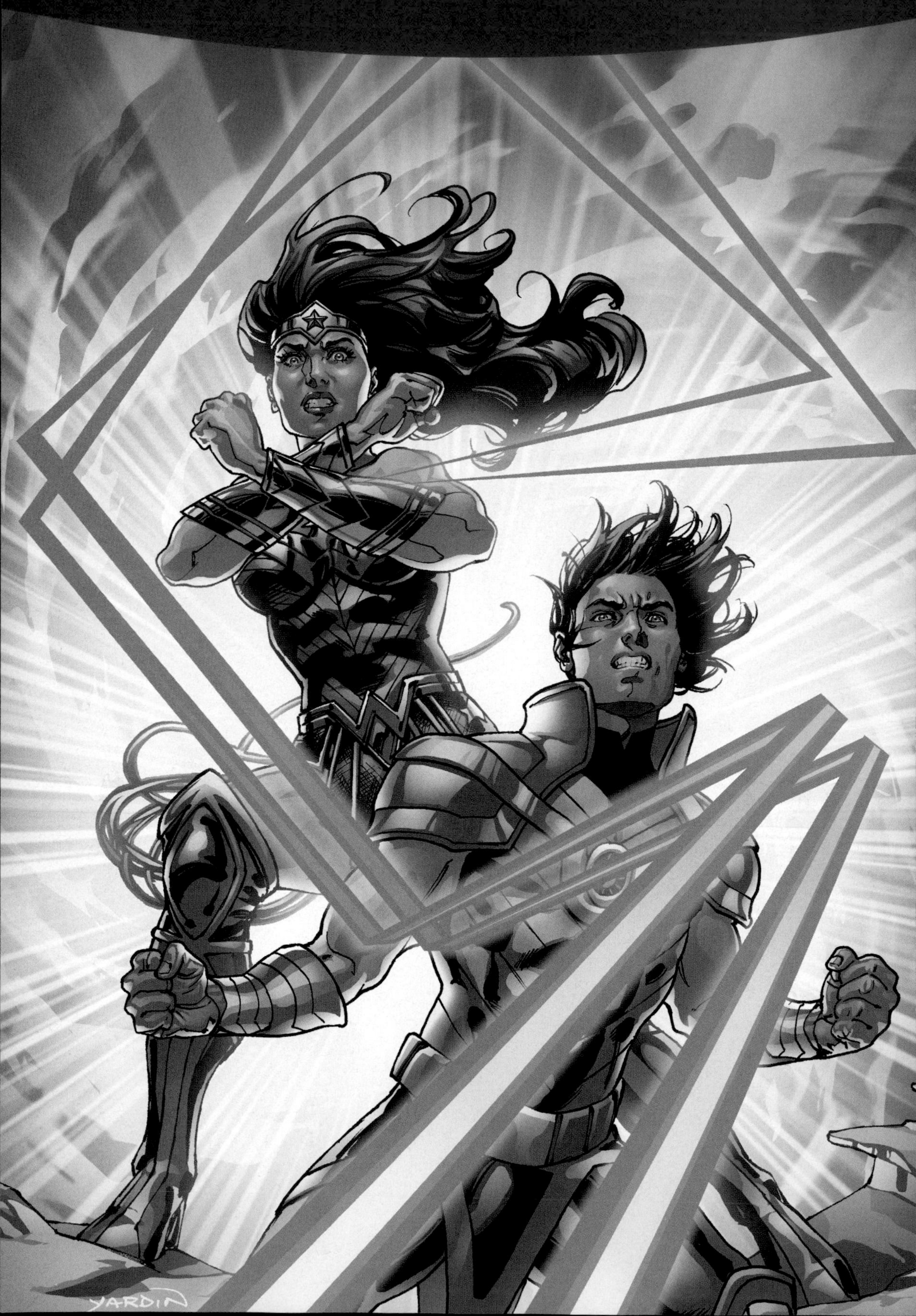
YARDIN

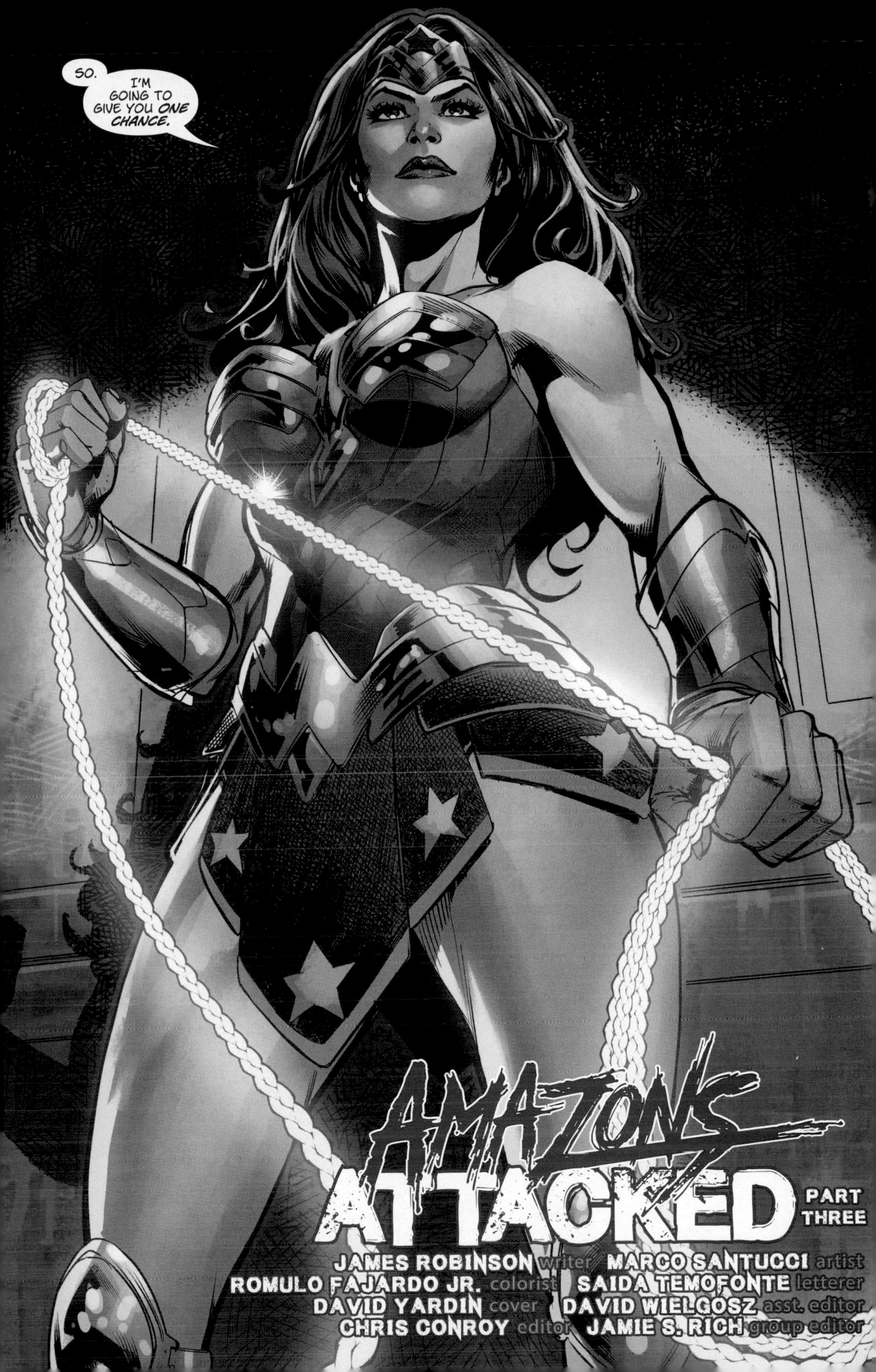

SO.
I'M GOING TO GIVE YOU ONE CHANCE.
AMAZONS ATTACKED PART THREE
JAMES ROBINSON writer MARCO SANTUCCI artist
ROMULO FAJARDO JR. colorist SAIDA TEMOFONTE letterer
DAVID YARDIN cover DAVID WIELGOSZ asst. editor
CHRIS CONROY editor JAMIE S. RICH group editor

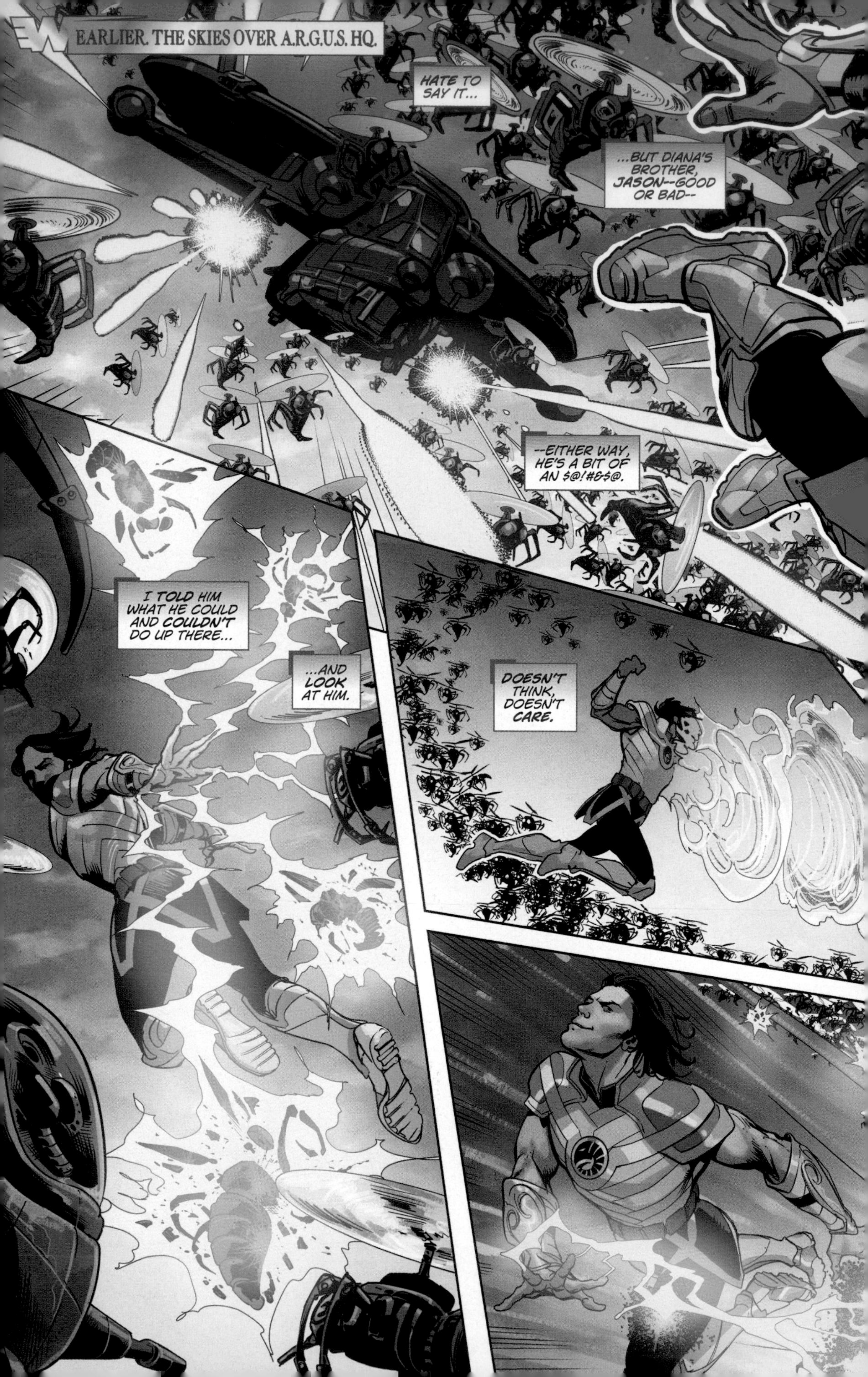
EARLIER. THE SKIES OVER A.R.G.U.S. HQ.
HATE TO SAY IT...
...BUT DIANA'S BROTHER, JASON--GOOD OR BAD--
--EITHER WAY, HE'S A BIT OF AN $@!#&$@.
I TOLD HIM WHAT HE COULD AND COULDN'T DO UP THERE...
...AND LOOK AT HIM.
DOESN'T THINK, DOESN'T CARE.

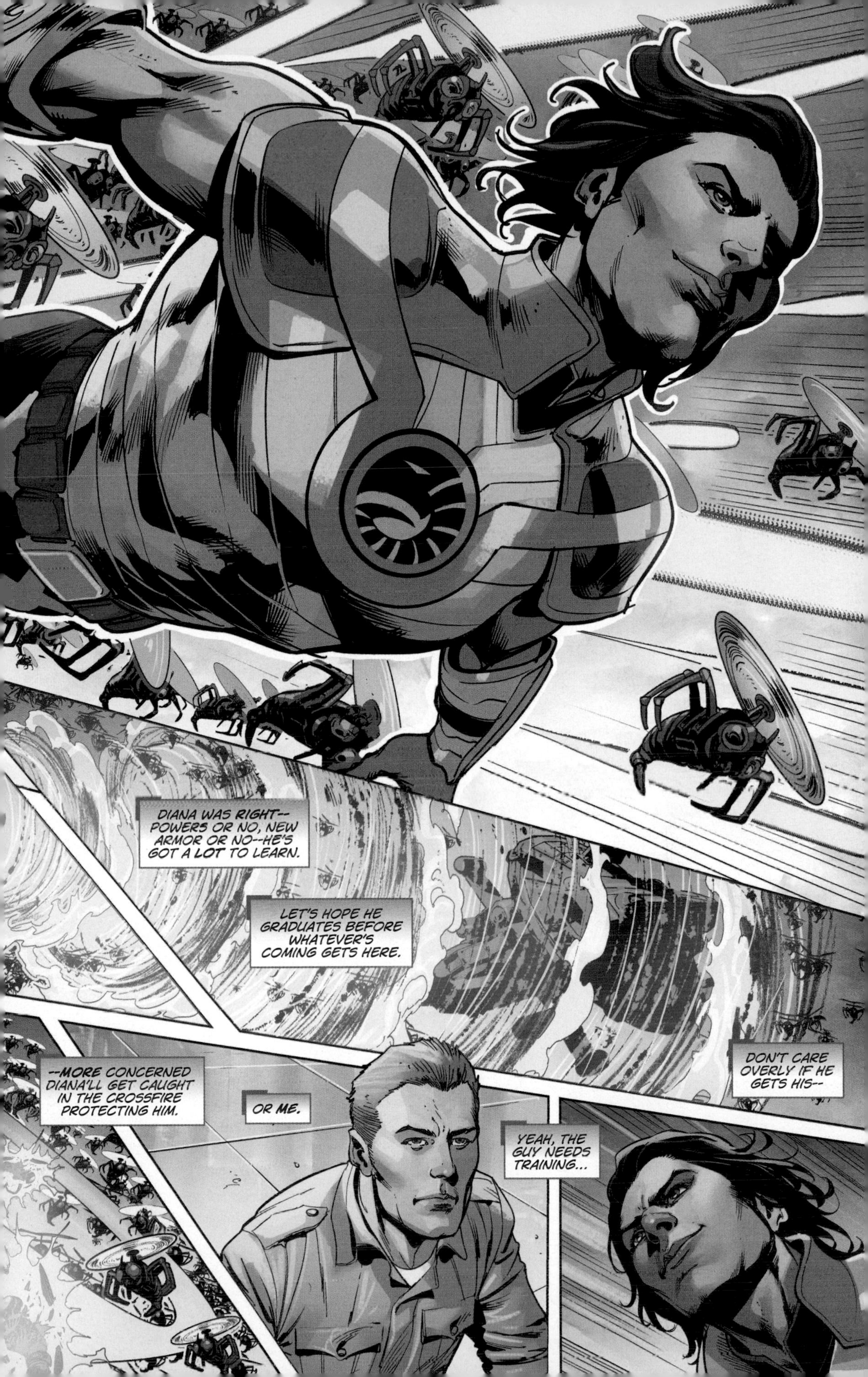
DIANA WAS RIGHT--
POWERS OR NO, NEW ARMOR OR NO--HE'S GOT A LOT TO LEARN.
LET'S HOPE HE GRADUATES BEFORE WHATEVER'S COMING GETS HERE.
DON'T CARE OVERLY IF HE GETS HIS--
--MORE CONCERNED DIANA'LL GET CAUGHT IN THE CROSSFIRE PROTECTING HIM.
OR ME.
YEAH, THE GUY NEEDS TRAINING...

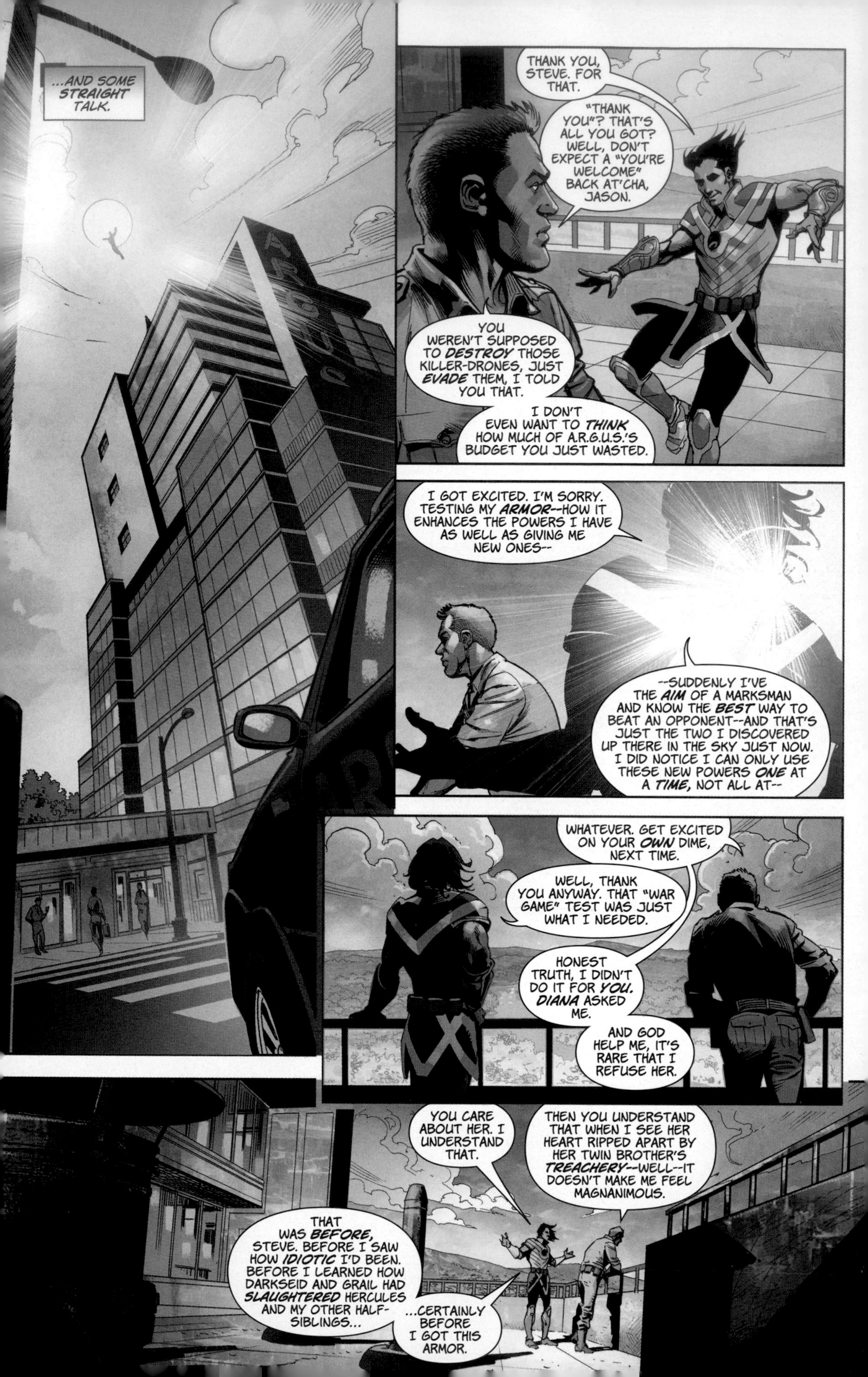
...AND SOME STRAIGHT TALK.
THANK YOU, STEVE. FOR THAT.
"THANK YOU"? THAT'S ALL YOU GOT? WELL, DON'T EXPECT A "YOU'RE WELCOME" BACK AT'CHA, JASON.
YOU WEREN'T SUPPOSED TO DESTROY THOSE KILLER-DRONES, JUST EVADE THEM, I TOLD YOU THAT.
I DON'T EVEN WANT TO THINK HOW MUCH OF A.R.G.U.S.'S BUDGET YOU JUST WASTED.
I GOT EXCITED. I'M SORRY. TESTING MY ARMOR--HOW IT ENHANCES THE POWERS I HAVE AS WELL AS GIVING ME NEW ONES--
--SUDDENLY I'VE THE AIM OF A MARKSMAN AND KNOW THE BEST WAY TO BEAT AN OPPONENT--AND THAT'S JUST THE TWO I DISCOVERED UP THERE IN THE SKY JUST NOW. I DID NOTICE I CAN ONLY USE THESE NEW POWERS ONE AT A TIME, NOT ALL AT--
WHATEVER. GET EXCITED ON YOUR OWN DIME, NEXT TIME.
WELL, THANK YOU ANYWAY. THAT "WAR GAME" TEST WAS JUST WHAT I NEEDED.
HONEST TRUTH, I DIDN'T DO IT FOR YOU. DIANA ASKED ME.
AND GOD HELP ME, IT'S RARE THAT I REFUSE HER.
YOU CARE ABOUT HER. I UNDERSTAND THAT.
THEN YOU UNDERSTAND THAT WHEN I SEE HER HEART RIPPED APART BY HER TWIN BROTHER'S TREACHERY--WELL--IT DOESN'T MAKE ME FEEL MAGNANIMOUS.
THAT WAS BEFORE, STEVE. BEFORE I SAW HOW IDIOTIC I'D BEEN. BEFORE I LEARNED HOW DARKSEID AND GRAIL HAD SLAUGHTERED HERCULES AND MY OTHER HALF-SIBLINGS...
...CERTAINLY BEFORE I GOT THIS ARMOR.

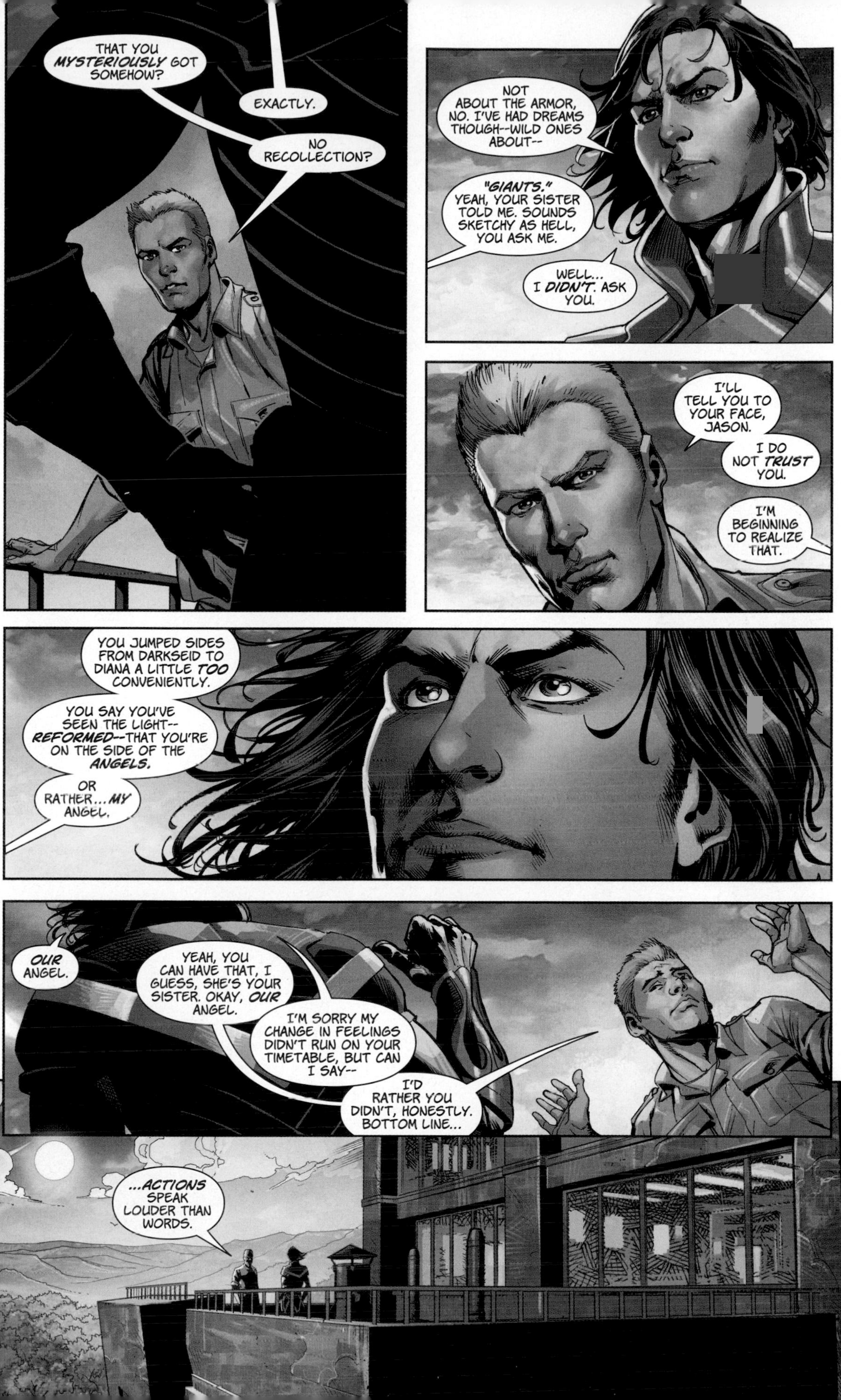
THAT YOU MYSTERIOUSLY GOT SOMEHOW?
EXACTLY.
NO RECOLLECTION?
NOT ABOUT THE ARMOR, NO. I'VE HAD DREAMS THOUGH--WILD ONES ABOUT--
"GIANTS." YEAH, YOUR SISTER TOLD ME. SOUNDS SKETCHY AS HELL, YOU ASK ME.
WELL... I DIDN'T. ASK YOU.
I'LL TELL YOU TO YOUR FACE, JASON.
I DO NOT TRUST YOU.
I'M BEGINNING TO REALIZE THAT.
YOU JUMPED SIDES FROM DARKSEID TO DIANA A LITTLE TOO CONVENIENTLY.
YOU SAY YOU'VE SEEN THE LIGHT--REFORMED--THAT YOU'RE ON THE SIDE OF THE ANGELS.
OR RATHER... MY ANGEL.
OUR ANGEL.
YEAH, YOU CAN HAVE THAT, I GUESS, SHE'S YOUR SISTER. OKAY, OUR ANGEL.
I'M SORRY MY CHANGE IN FEELINGS DIDN'T RUN ON YOUR TIMETABLE, BUT CAN I SAY--
I'D RATHER YOU DIDN'T, HONESTLY. BOTTOM LINE...
...ACTIONS SPEAK LOUDER THAN WORDS.

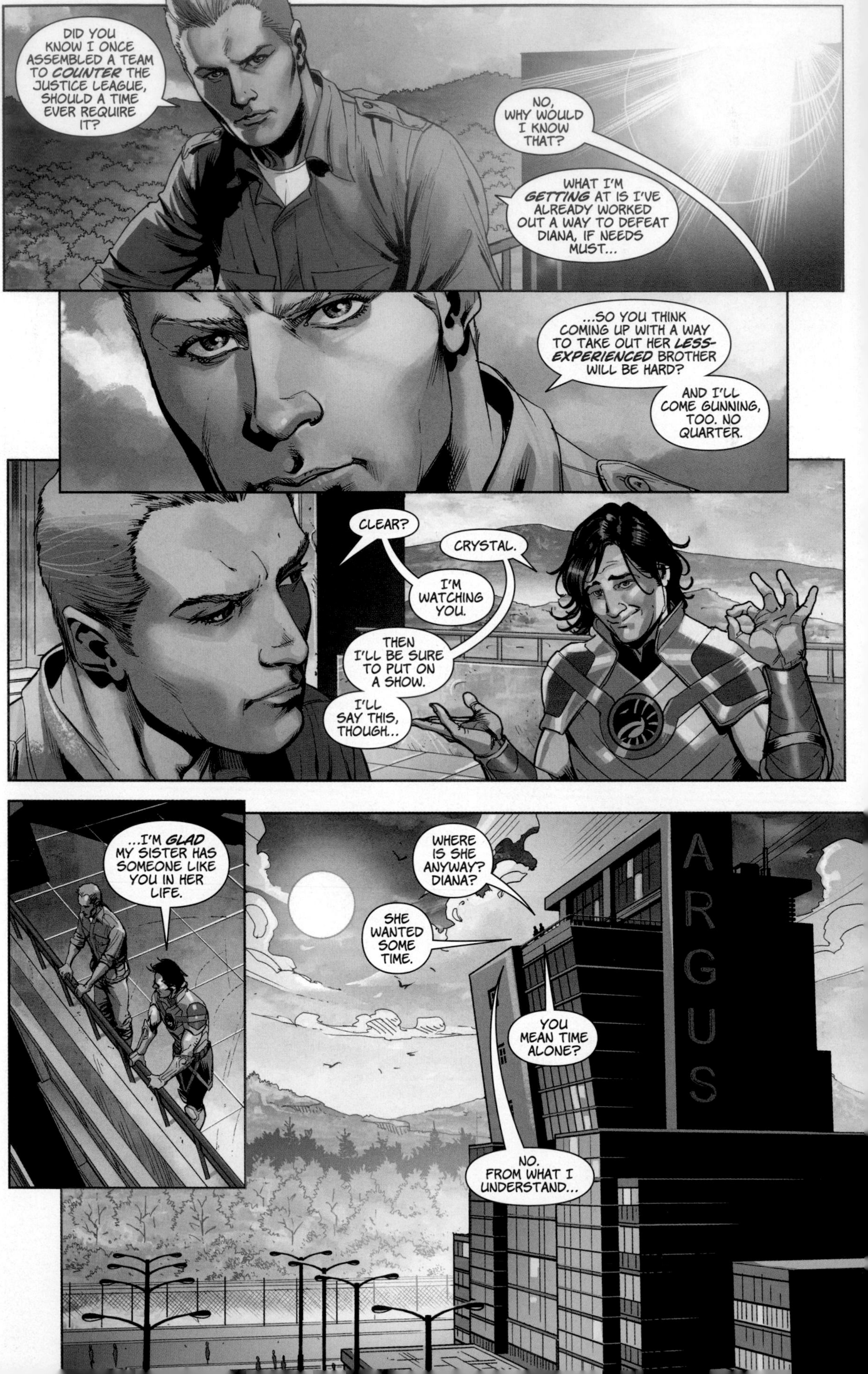
DID YOU KNOW I ONCE ASSEMBLED A TEAM TO COUNTER THE JUSTICE LEAGUE, SHOULD A TIME EVER REQUIRE IT?
NO, WHY WOULD I KNOW THAT?
WHAT I'M GETTING AT IS I'VE ALREADY WORKED OUT A WAY TO DEFEAT DIANA, IF NEEDS MUST...
...SO YOU THINK COMING UP WITH A WAY TO TAKE OUT HER LESS-EXPERIENCED BROTHER WILL BE HARD?
AND I'LL COME GUNNING, TOO. NO QUARTER.
CLEAR?
CRYSTAL.
I'M WATCHING YOU.
THEN I'LL BE SURE TO PUT ON A SHOW.
I'LL SAY THIS, THOUGH...
...I'M GLAD MY SISTER HAS SOMEONE LIKE YOU IN HER LIFE.
WHERE IS SHE ANYWAY? DIANA?
SHE WANTED SOME TIME.
YOU MEAN TIME ALONE?
NO. FROM WHAT I UNDERSTAND...
ARGUS

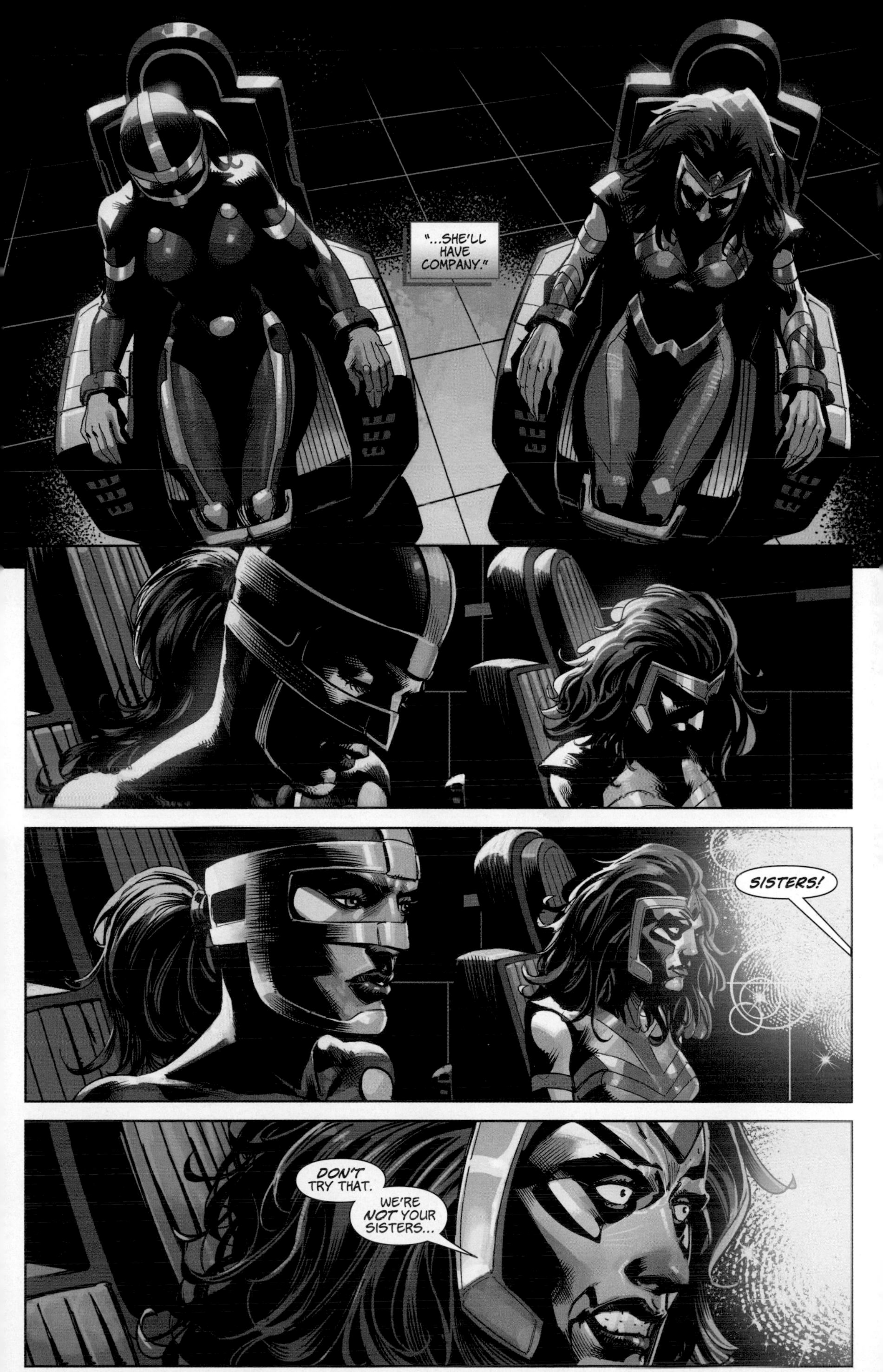
"...SHE'LL HAVE COMPANY."
SISTERS!
DON'T TRY THAT.
WE'RE NOT YOUR SISTERS...

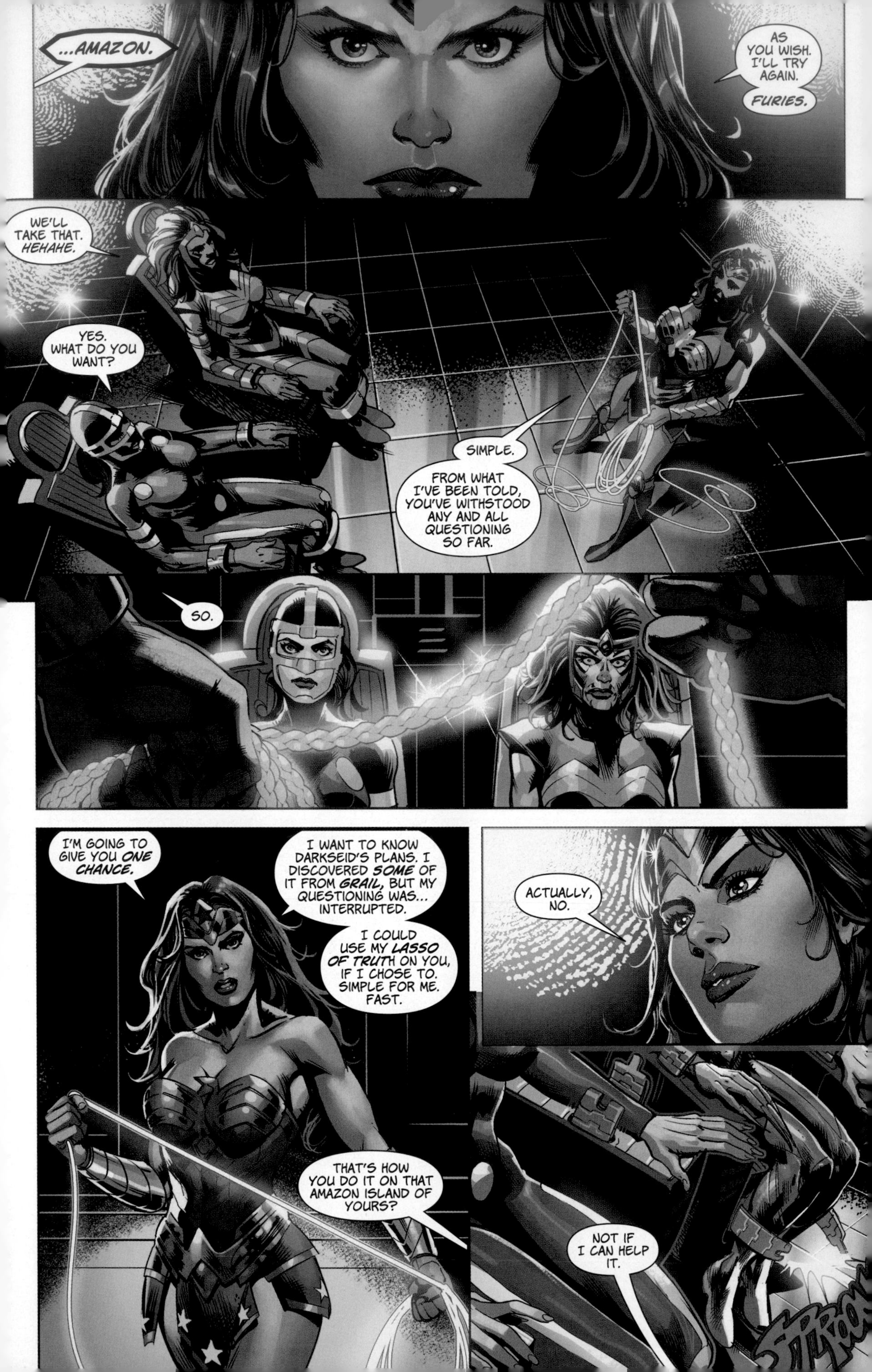
...AMAZON.
AS YOU WISH. I'LL TRY AGAIN.
FURIES.
WE'LL TAKE THAT. HEHAHE.
YES. WHAT DO YOU WANT?
SIMPLE.
FROM WHAT I'VE BEEN TOLD, YOU'VE WITHSTOOD ANY AND ALL QUESTIONING SO FAR.
SO.
I'M GOING TO GIVE YOU ONE CHANCE.
I WANT TO KNOW DARKSEID'S PLANS. I DISCOVERED SOME OF IT FROM GRAIL, BUT MY QUESTIONING WAS... INTERRUPTED.
I COULD USE MY LASSO OF TRUTH ON YOU, IF I CHOSE TO. SIMPLE FOR ME. FAST.
THAT'S HOW YOU DO IT ON THAT AMAZON ISLAND OF YOURS?
ACTUALLY, NO.
NOT IF I CAN HELP IT.

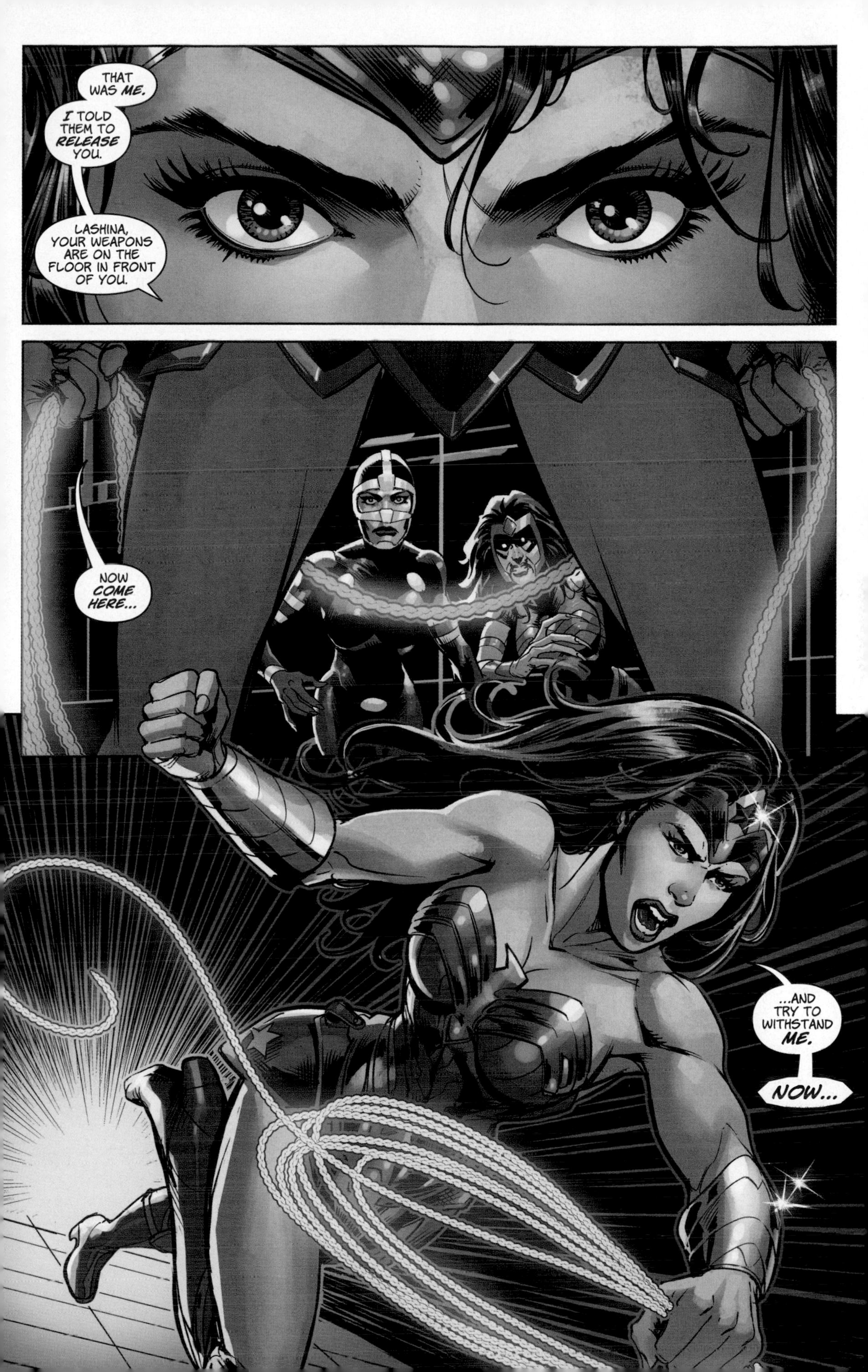
THAT WAS *ME.*
I TOLD THEM TO *RELEASE* YOU.
LASHINA, YOUR WEAPONS ARE ON THE FLOOR IN FRONT OF YOU.
NOW *COME HERE...*
...AND TRY TO WITHSTAND *ME.*
NOW...

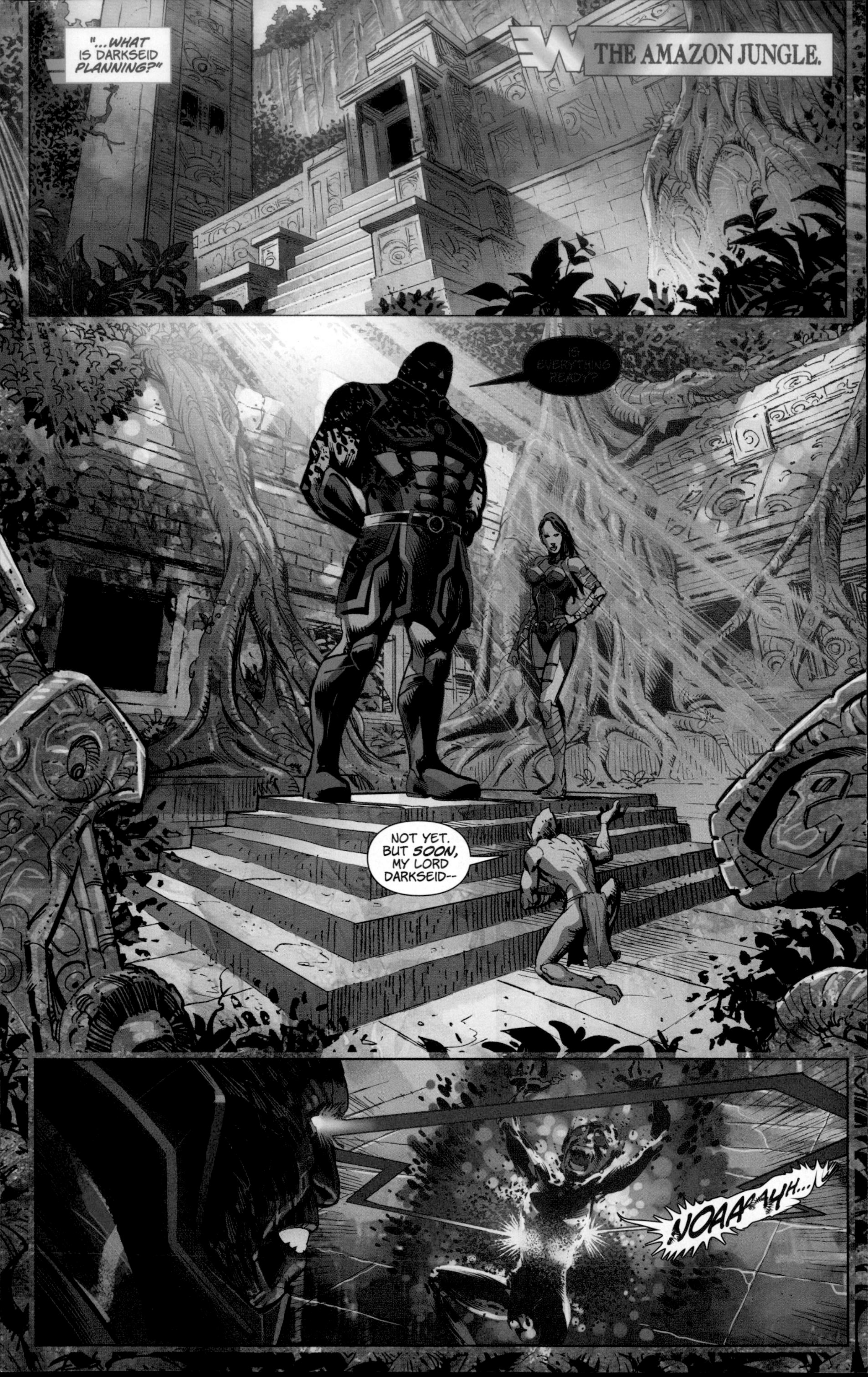
"...WHAT IS DARKSEID PLANNING?"
THE AMAZON JUNGLE.
IS EVERYTHING READY?
NOT YET. BUT SOON, MY LORD DARKSEID--
NOAAAAYH...!

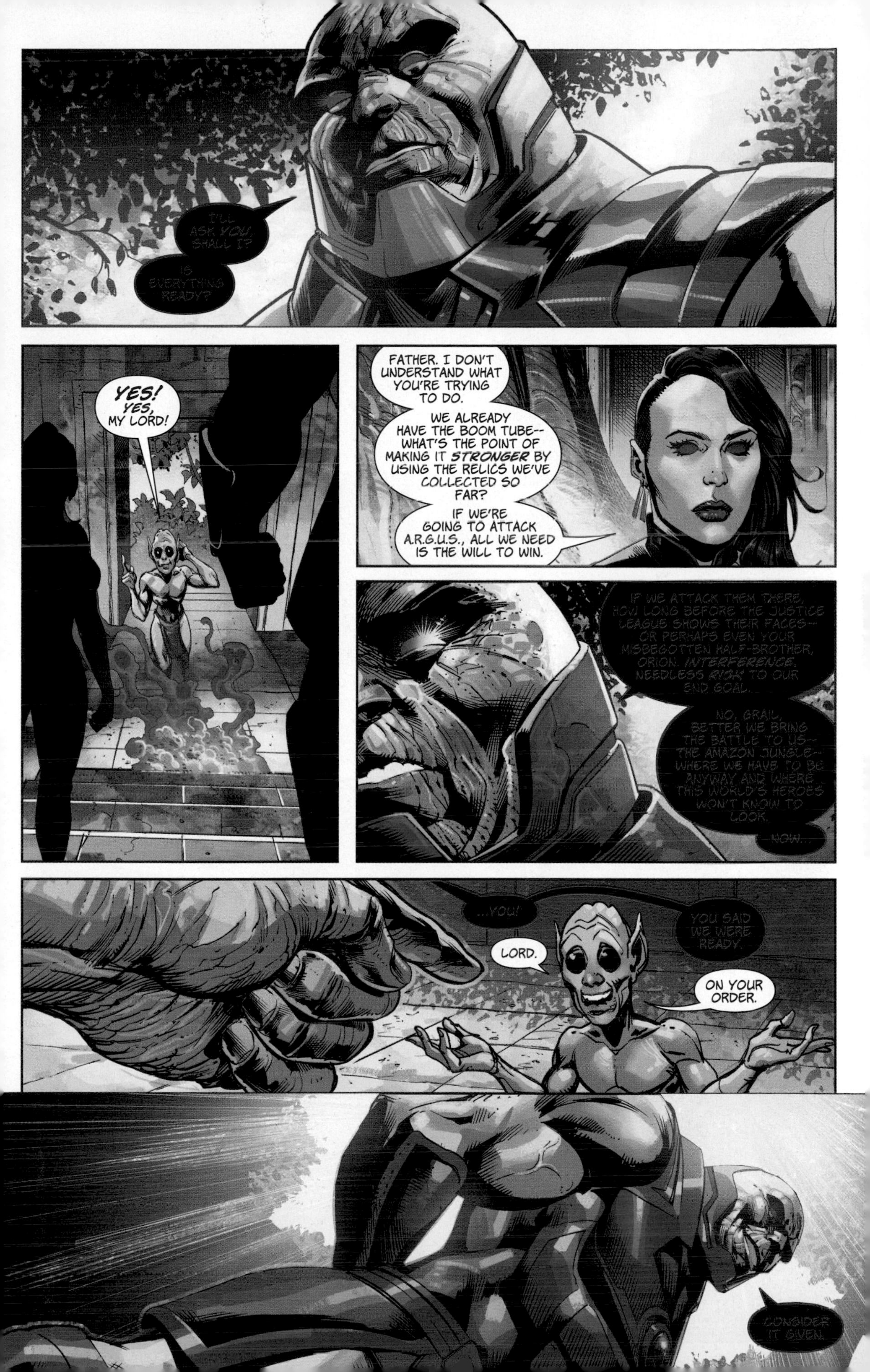

I'LL ASK *YOU*, SHALL I?
IS EVERYTHING READY?
YES! YES, MY LORD!
FATHER. I DON'T UNDERSTAND WHAT YOU'RE TRYING TO DO.
WE ALREADY HAVE THE BOOM TUBE--WHAT'S THE POINT OF MAKING IT ***STRONGER*** BY USING THE RELICS WE'VE COLLECTED SO FAR?
IF WE'RE GOING TO ATTACK A.R.G.U.S., ALL WE NEED IS THE WILL TO WIN.
IF WE ATTACK THEM THERE, HOW LONG BEFORE THE JUSTICE LEAGUE SHOWS THEIR FACES--OR PERHAPS EVEN YOUR MISBEGOTTEN HALF-BROTHER, ORION. *INTERFERENCE*. NEEDLESS *RISK* TO OUR END GOAL.
NO, GRAIL. BETTER WE BRING THE BATTLE TO US--THE AMAZON JUNGLE--WHERE WE HAVE TO BE ANYWAY AND WHERE THIS WORLD'S HEROES WON'T KNOW TO LOOK.
NOW...
...YOU!
LORD.
YOU SAID WE WERE READY.
ON YOUR ORDER.
CONSIDER IT GIVEN.

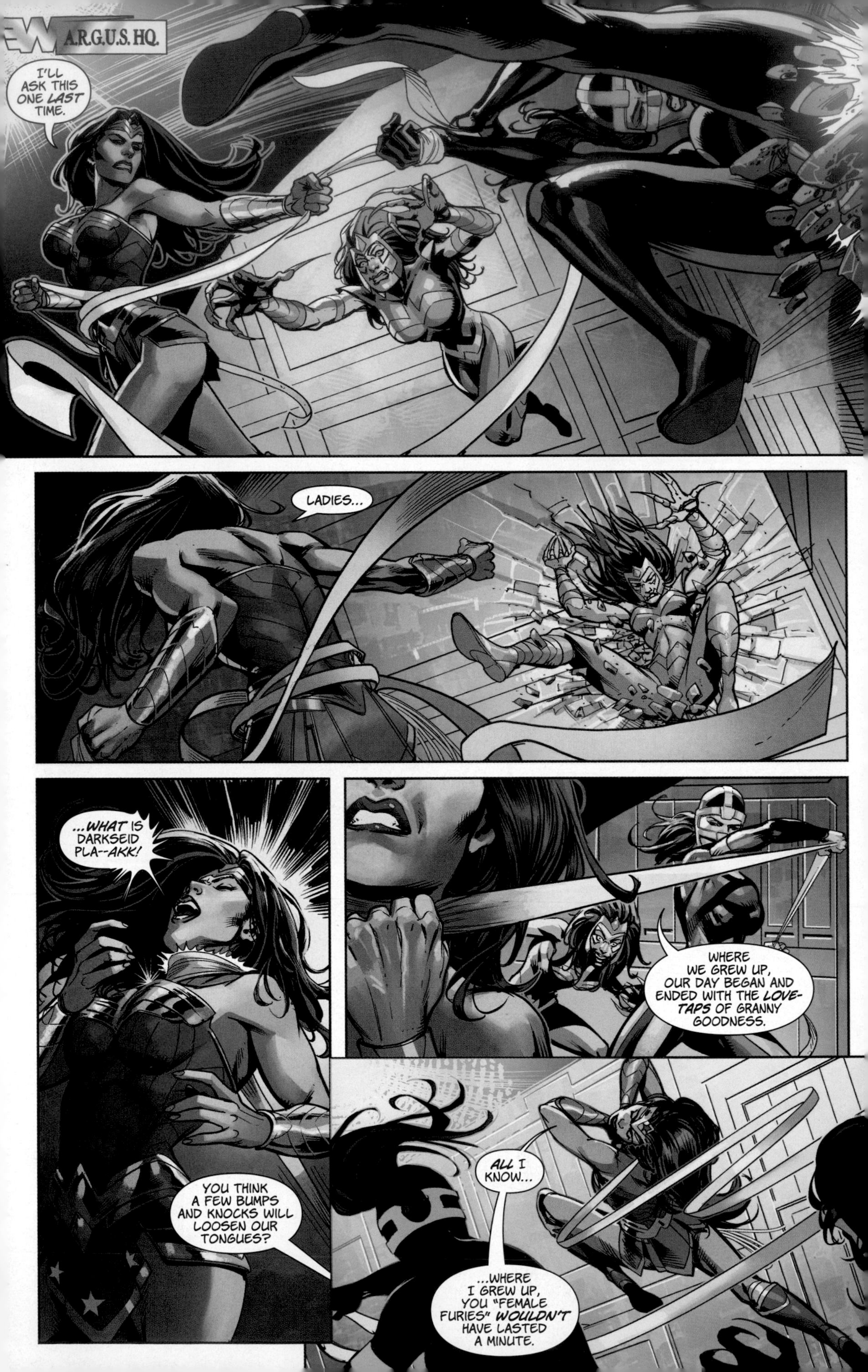
A.R.G.U.S. HQ.
I'LL ASK THIS ONE LAST TIME.
LADIES...
...WHAT IS DARKSEID PLA--AKK!
WHERE WE GREW UP, OUR DAY BEGAN AND ENDED WITH THE LOVE-TAPS OF GRANNY GOODNESS.
YOU THINK A FEW BUMPS AND KNOCKS WILL LOOSEN OUR TONGUES?
ALL I KNOW...
...WHERE I GREW UP, YOU "FEMALE FURIES" WOULDN'T HAVE LASTED A MINUTE.

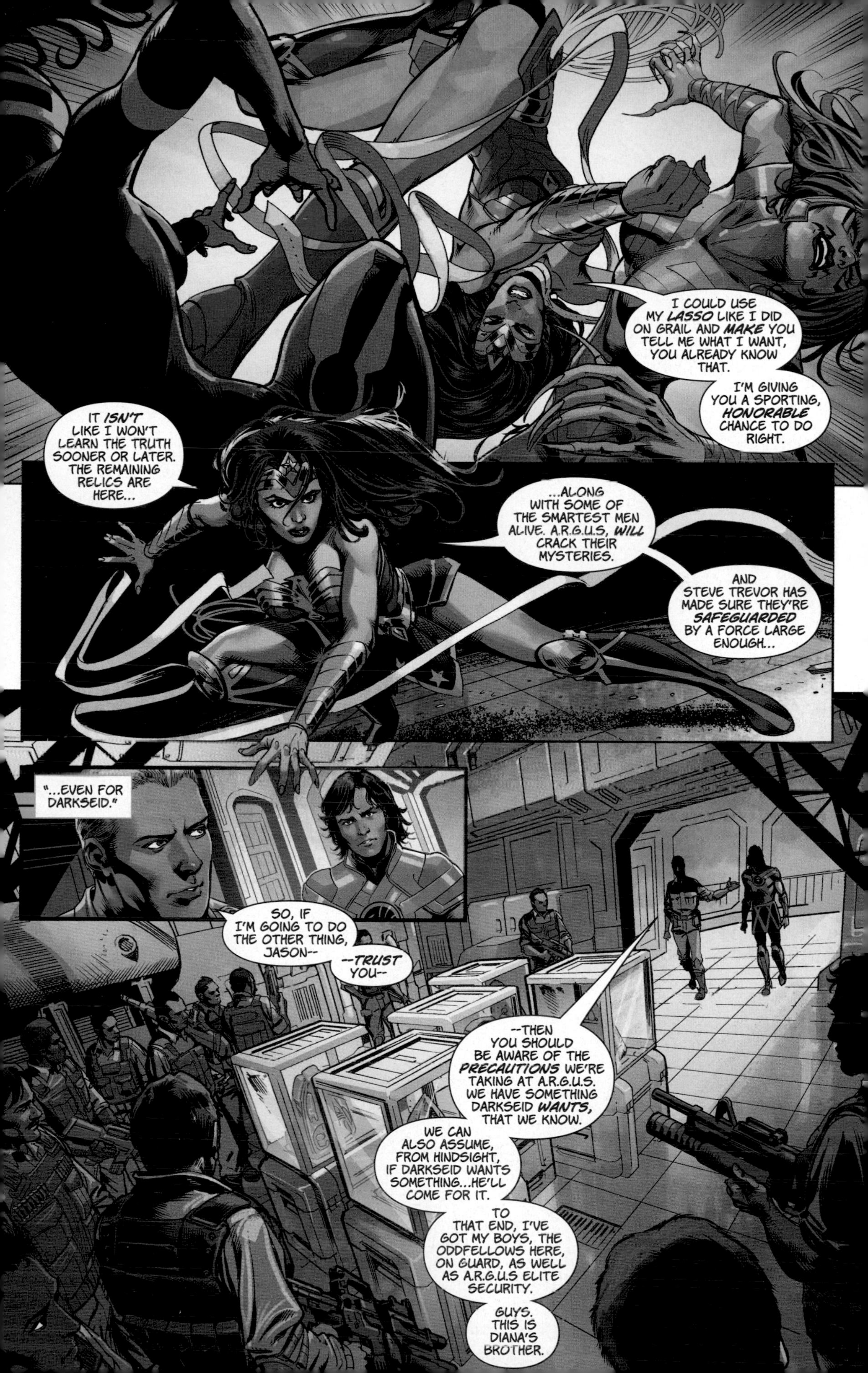
I COULD USE MY LASSO LIKE I DID ON GRAIL AND MAKE YOU TELL ME WHAT I WANT, YOU ALREADY KNOW THAT.
I'M GIVING YOU A SPORTING, HONORABLE CHANCE TO DO RIGHT.
IT ISN'T LIKE I WON'T LEARN THE TRUTH SOONER OR LATER. THE REMAINING RELICS ARE HERE...
...ALONG WITH SOME OF THE SMARTEST MEN ALIVE. A.R.G.U.S. WILL CRACK THEIR MYSTERIES.
AND STEVE TREVOR HAS MADE SURE THEY'RE SAFEGUARDED BY A FORCE LARGE ENOUGH...
"...EVEN FOR DARKSEID."
SO, IF I'M GOING TO DO THE OTHER THING, JASON--
--TRUST YOU--
--THEN YOU SHOULD BE AWARE OF THE PRECAUTIONS WE'RE TAKING AT A.R.G.U.S. WE HAVE SOMETHING DARKSEID WANTS, THAT WE KNOW.
WE CAN ALSO ASSUME, FROM HINDSIGHT, IF DARKSEID WANTS SOMETHING...HE'LL COME FOR IT.
TO THAT END, I'VE GOT MY BOYS, THE ODDFELLOWS HERE, ON GUARD, AS WELL AS A.R.G.U.S ELITE SECURITY.
GUYS. THIS IS DIANA'S BROTHER.

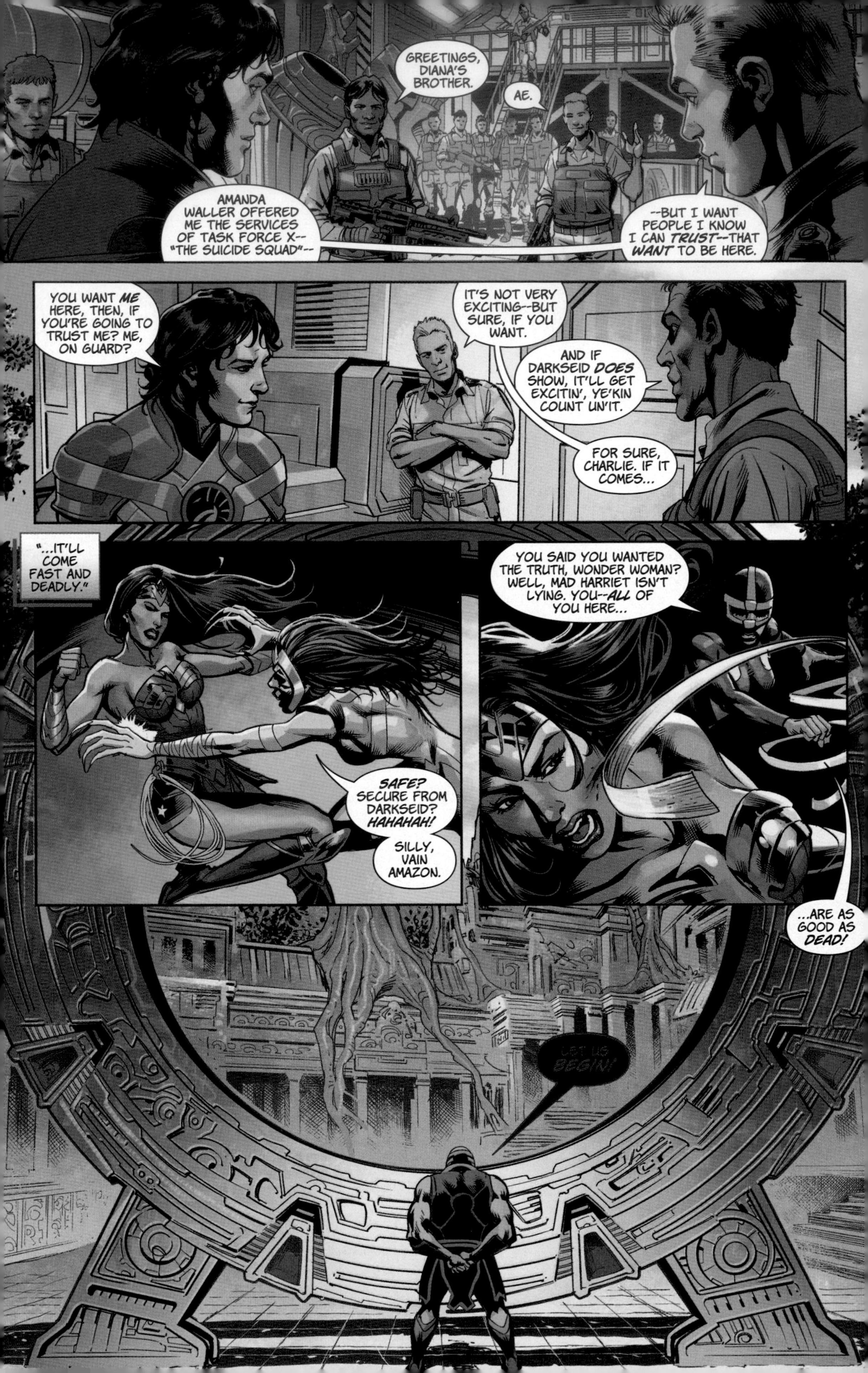
GREETINGS, DIANA'S BROTHER.
AE.
AMANDA WALLER OFFERED ME THE SERVICES OF TASK FORCE X-- "THE SUICIDE SQUAD"--
--BUT I WANT PEOPLE I KNOW I CAN TRUST--THAT WANT TO BE HERE.
YOU WANT ME HERE, THEN, IF YOU'RE GOING TO TRUST ME? ME, ON GUARD?
IT'S NOT VERY EXCITING--BUT SURE, IF YOU WANT.
AND IF DARKSEID DOES SHOW, IT'LL GET EXCITIN', YE'KIN COUNT UN'IT.
FOR SURE, CHARLIE. IF IT COMES...
"...IT'LL COME FAST AND DEADLY."
SAFE? SECURE FROM DARKSEID? HAHAHAH!
SILLY, VAIN AMAZON.
YOU SAID YOU WANTED THE TRUTH, WONDER WOMAN? WELL, MAD HARRIET ISN'T LYING. YOU--ALL OF YOU HERE...
...ARE AS GOOD AS DEAD!
LET US BEGIN!

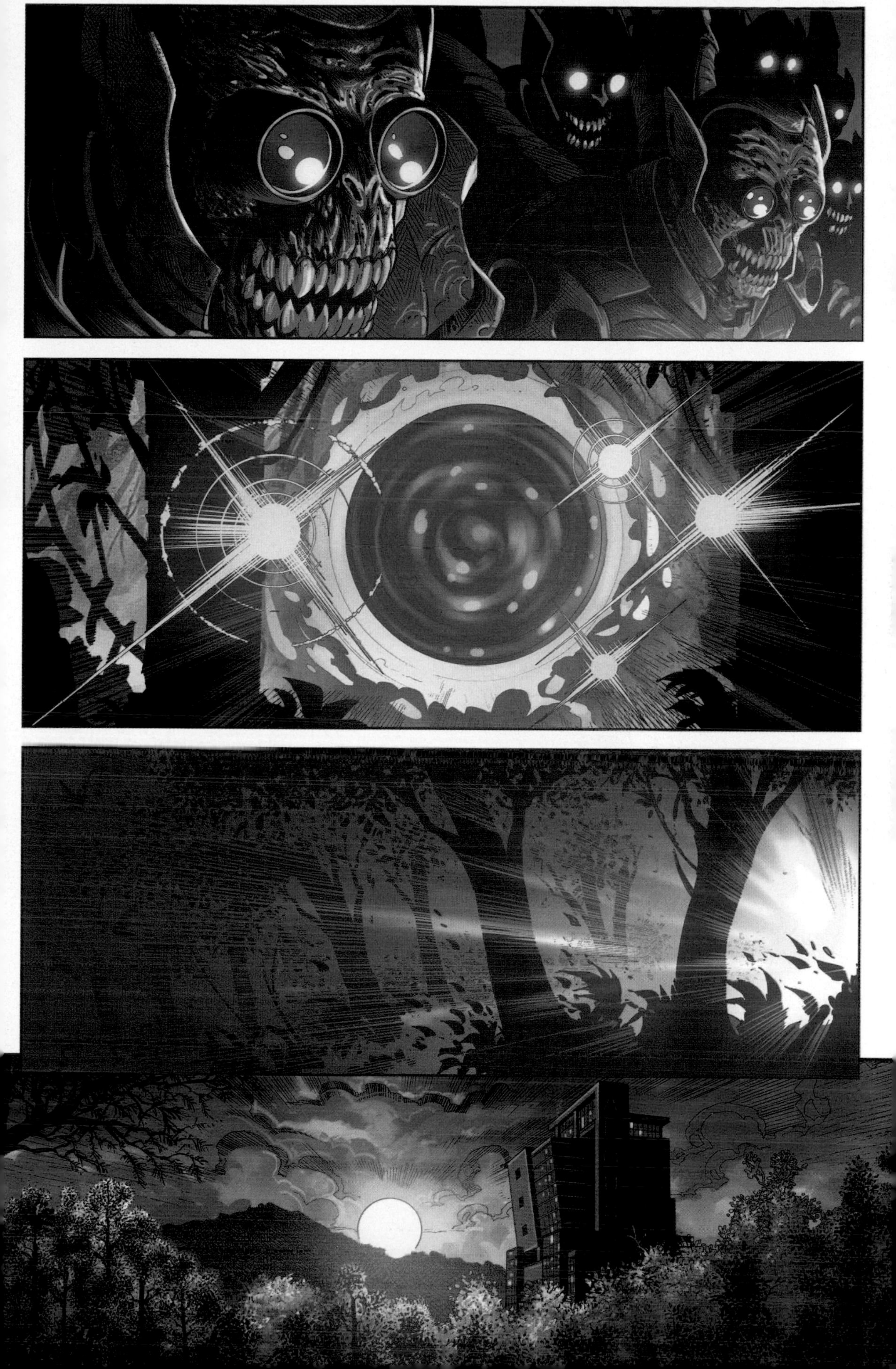

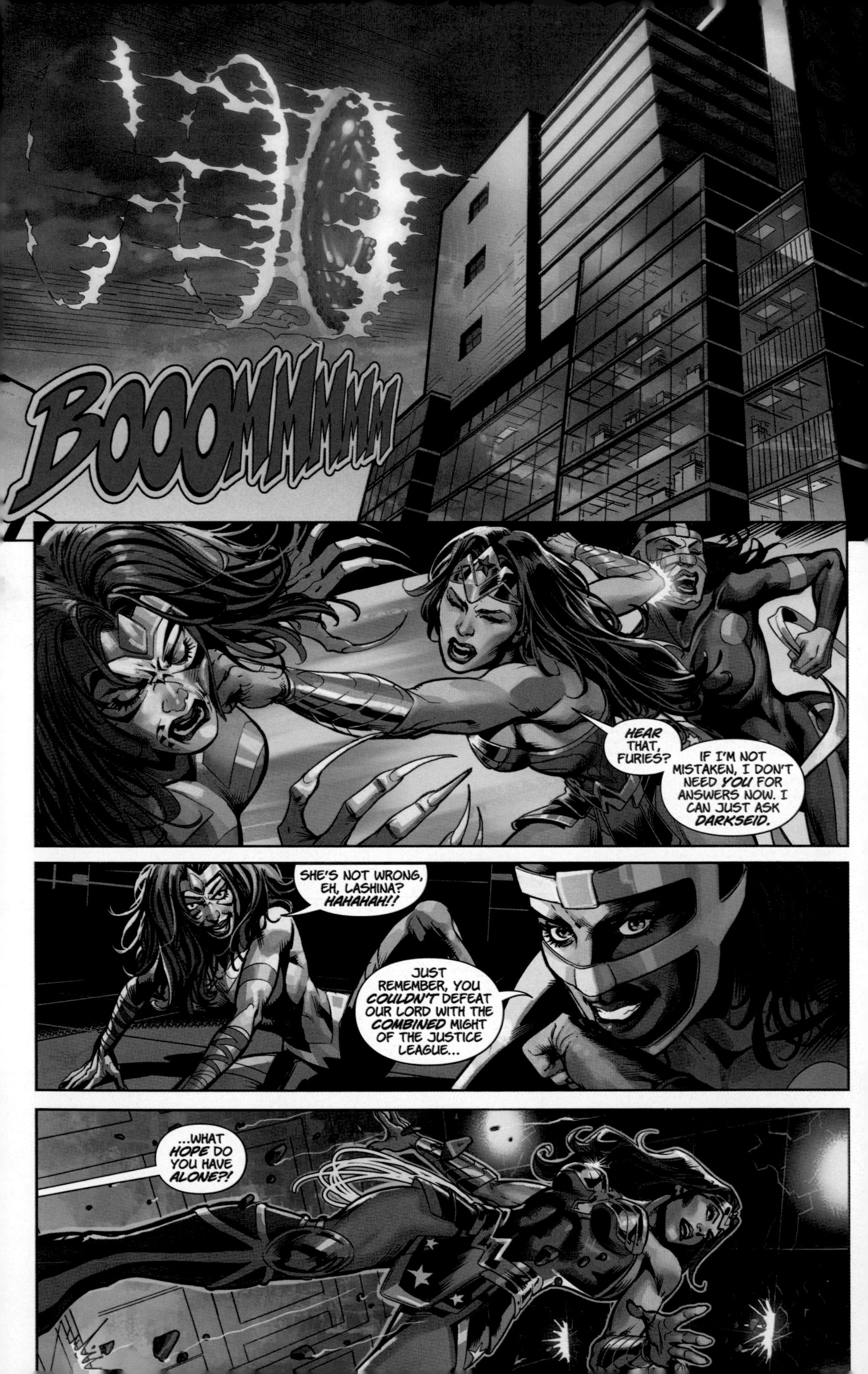
BOOOMMMMM
HEAR THAT, FURIES?
IF I'M NOT MISTAKEN, I DON'T NEED YOU FOR ANSWERS NOW. I CAN JUST ASK DARKSEID.
SHE'S NOT WRONG, EH, LASHINA? HAHAHAH!!
JUST REMEMBER, YOU COULDN'T DEFEAT OUR LORD WITH THE COMBINED MIGHT OF THE JUSTICE LEAGUE...
...WHAT HOPE DO YOU HAVE ALONE?!

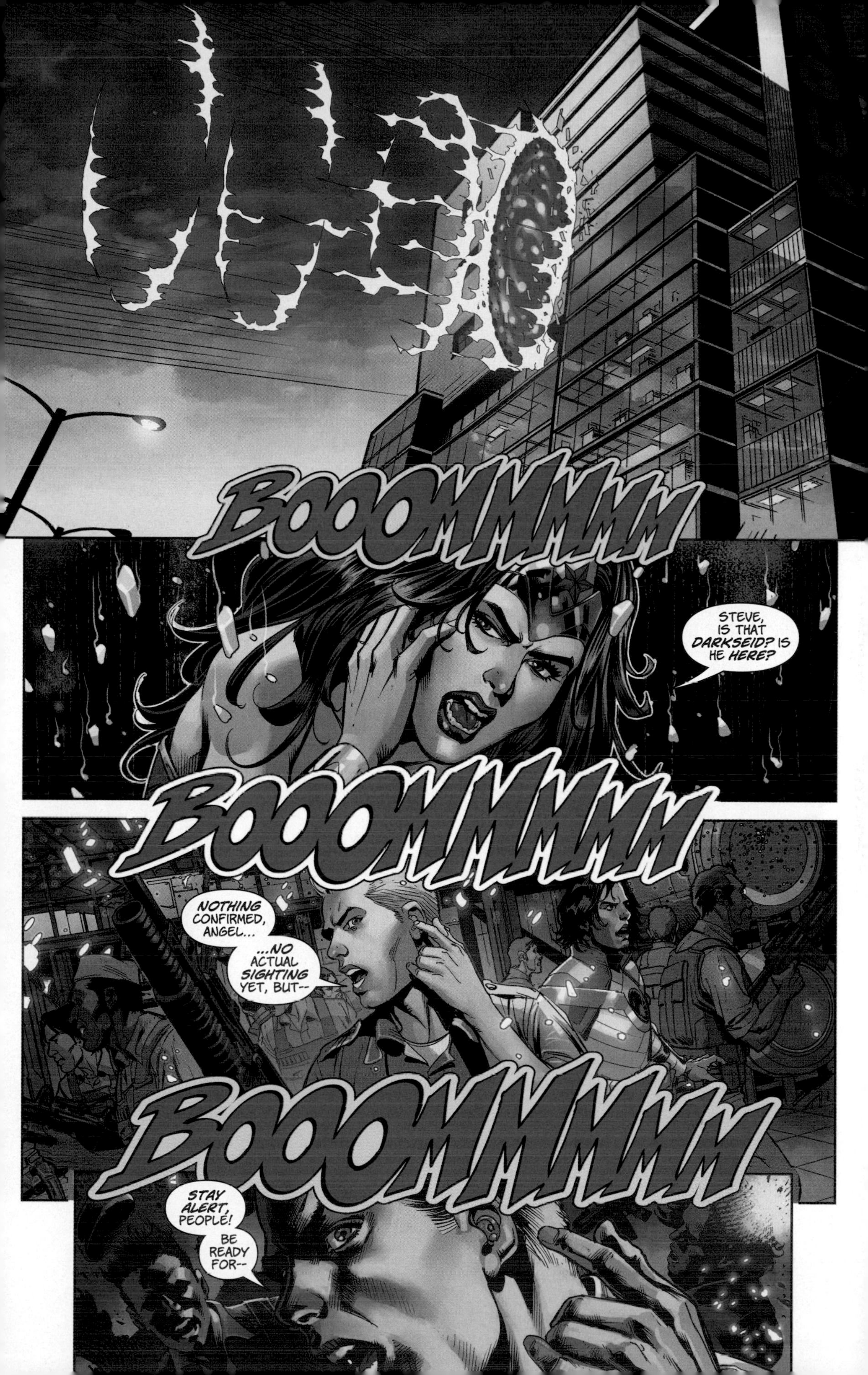
BOOOMMMMM
STEVE, IS THAT DARKSEID? IS HE HERE?
BOOOMMMMM
NOTHING CONFIRMED, ANGEL...
...NO ACTUAL SIGHTING YET, BUT--
BOOOMMMMM
STAY ALERT, PEOPLE!
BE READY FOR--

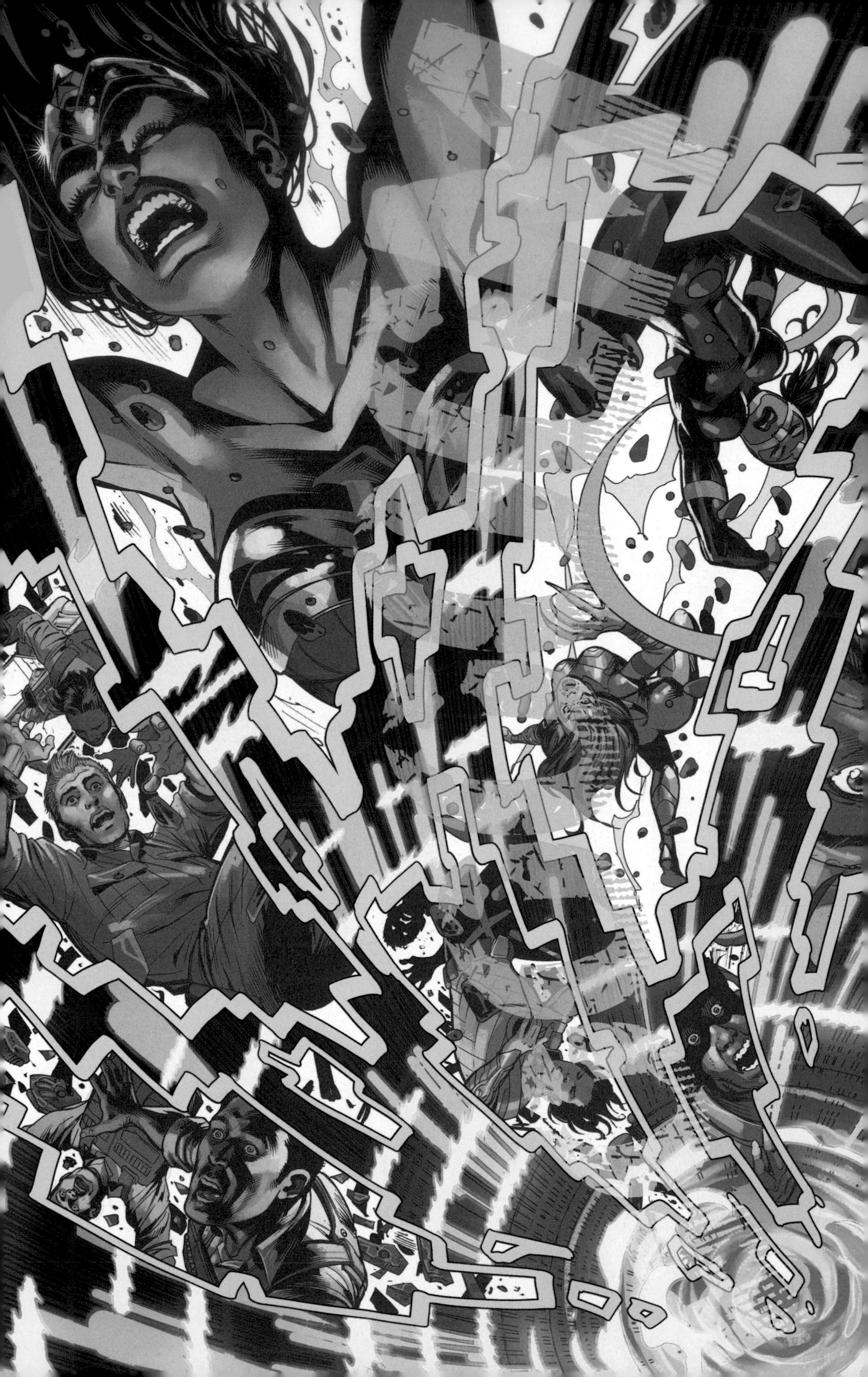

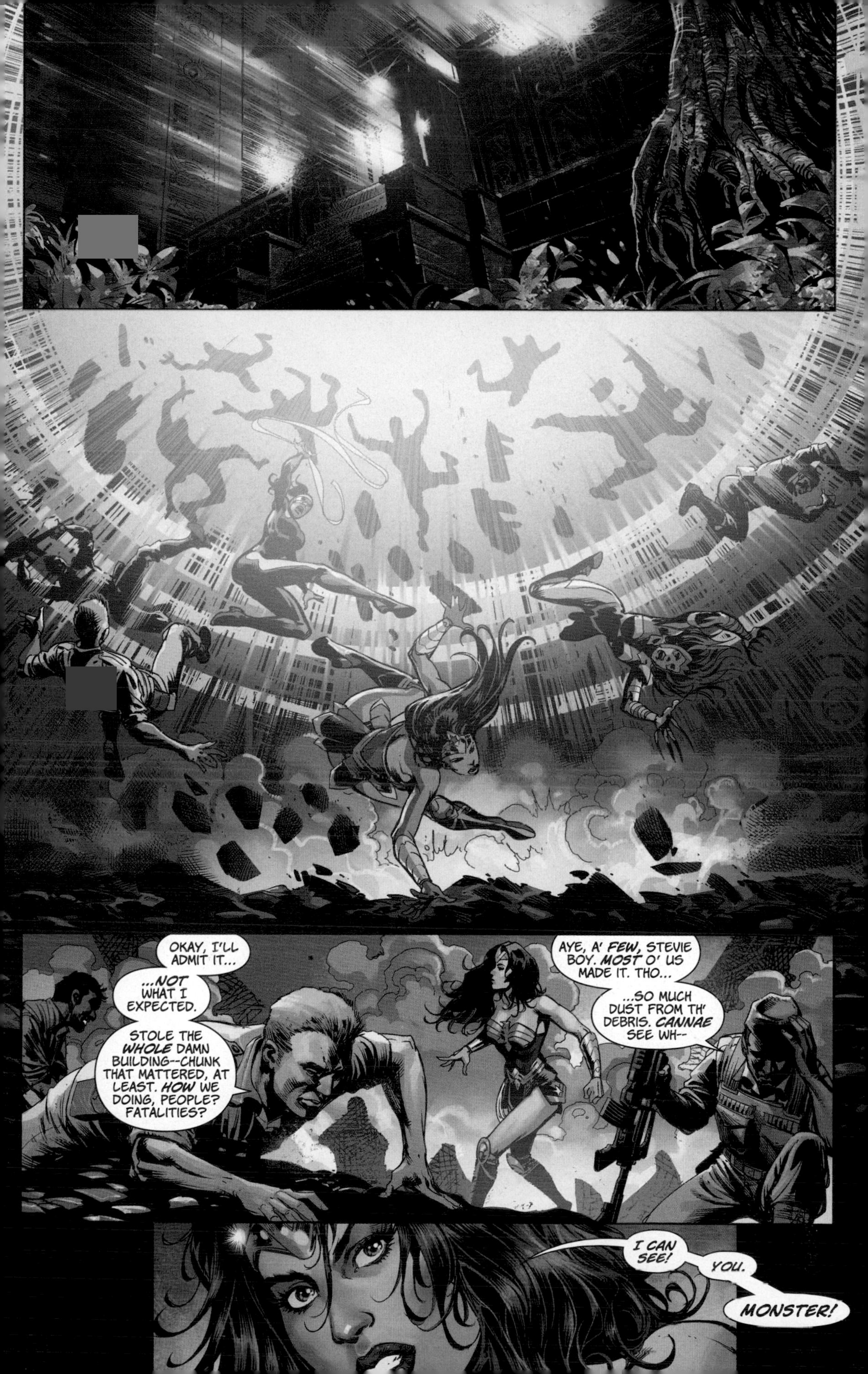
OKAY, I'LL ADMIT IT...
...NOT WHAT I EXPECTED.
STOLE THE WHOLE DAMN BUILDING--CHUNK THAT MATTERED, AT LEAST. HOW WE DOING, PEOPLE? FATALITIES?
AYE, A' FEW, STEVIE BOY. MOST O' US MADE IT. THO...
...SO MUCH DUST FROM TH' DEBRIS. CANNAE SEE WH--
I CAN SEE!
YOU.
MONSTER!

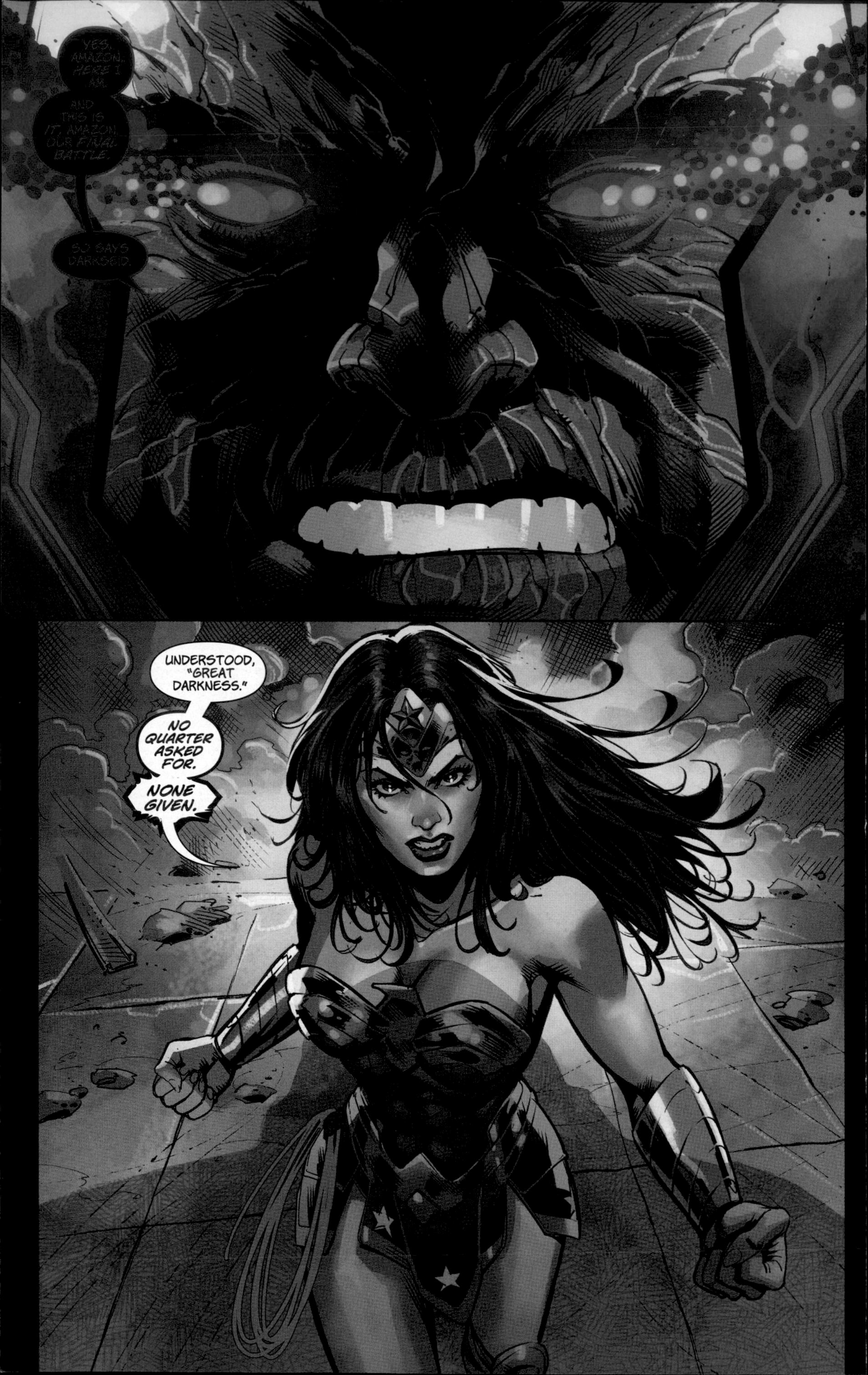
YES, AMAZON. HERE I AM.
AND THIS IS IT, AMAZON. OUR FINAL BATTLE.
SO SAYS DARKSEID.
UNDERSTOOD, "GREAT DARKNESS."
NO QUARTER ASKED FOR.
NONE GIVEN.

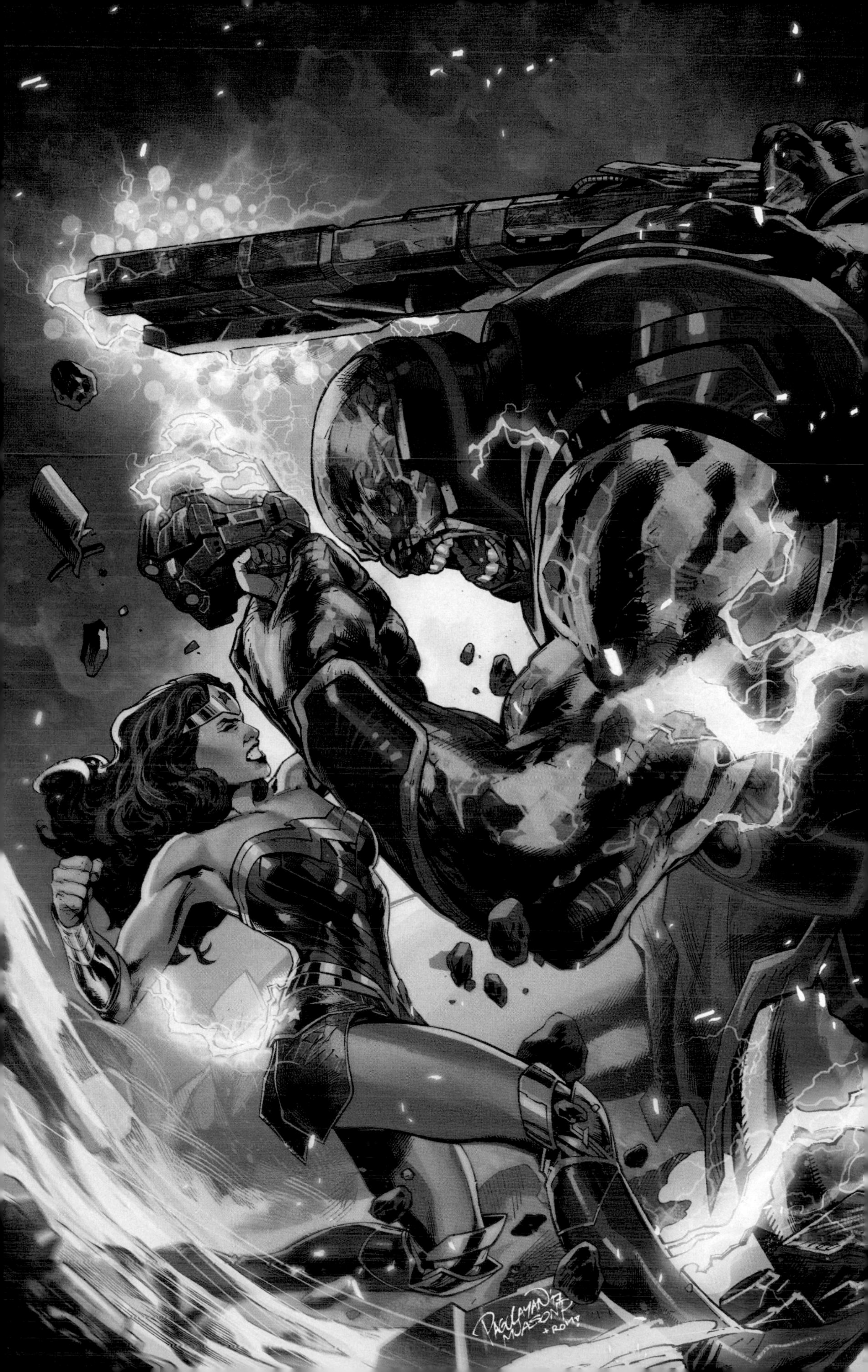

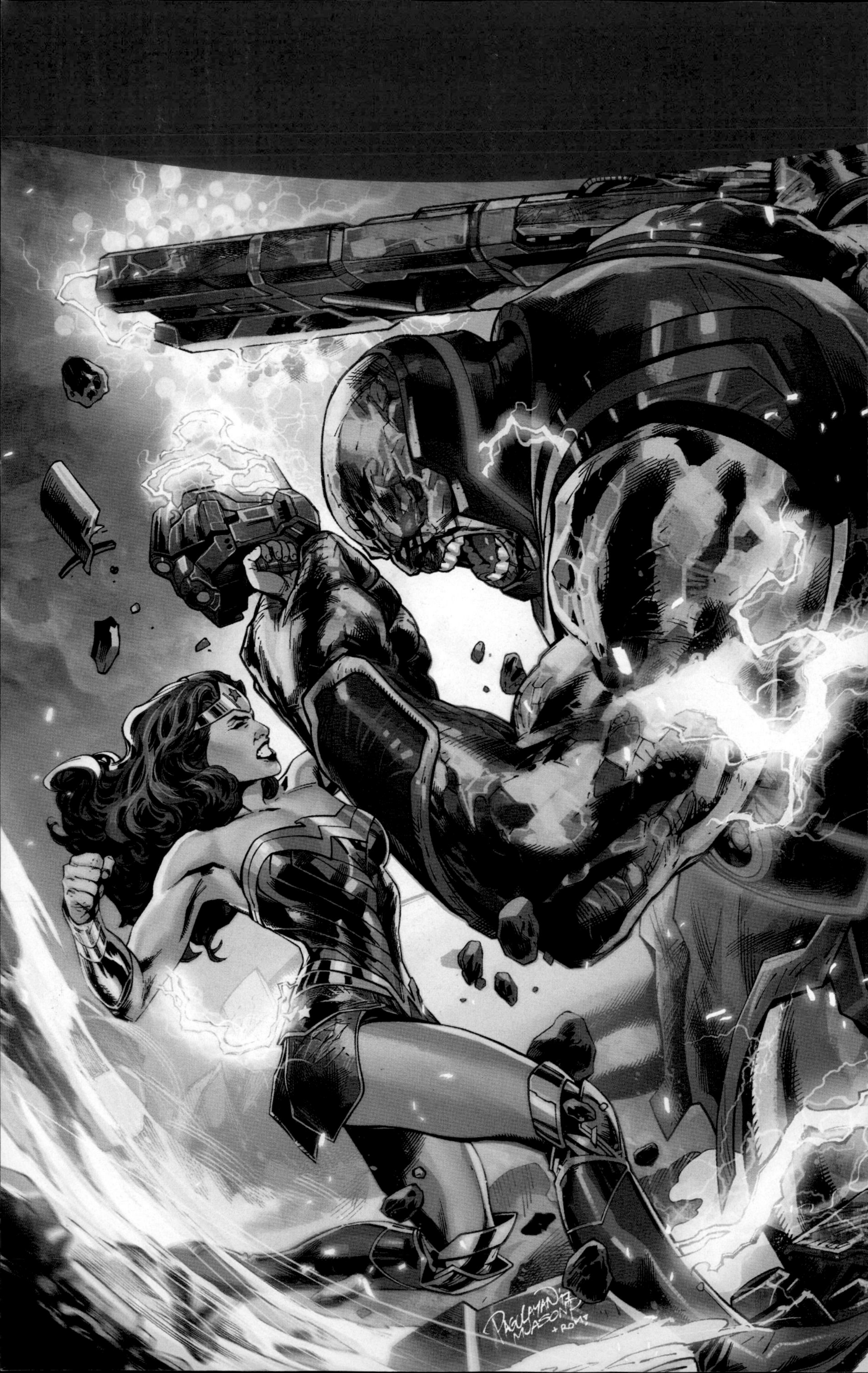

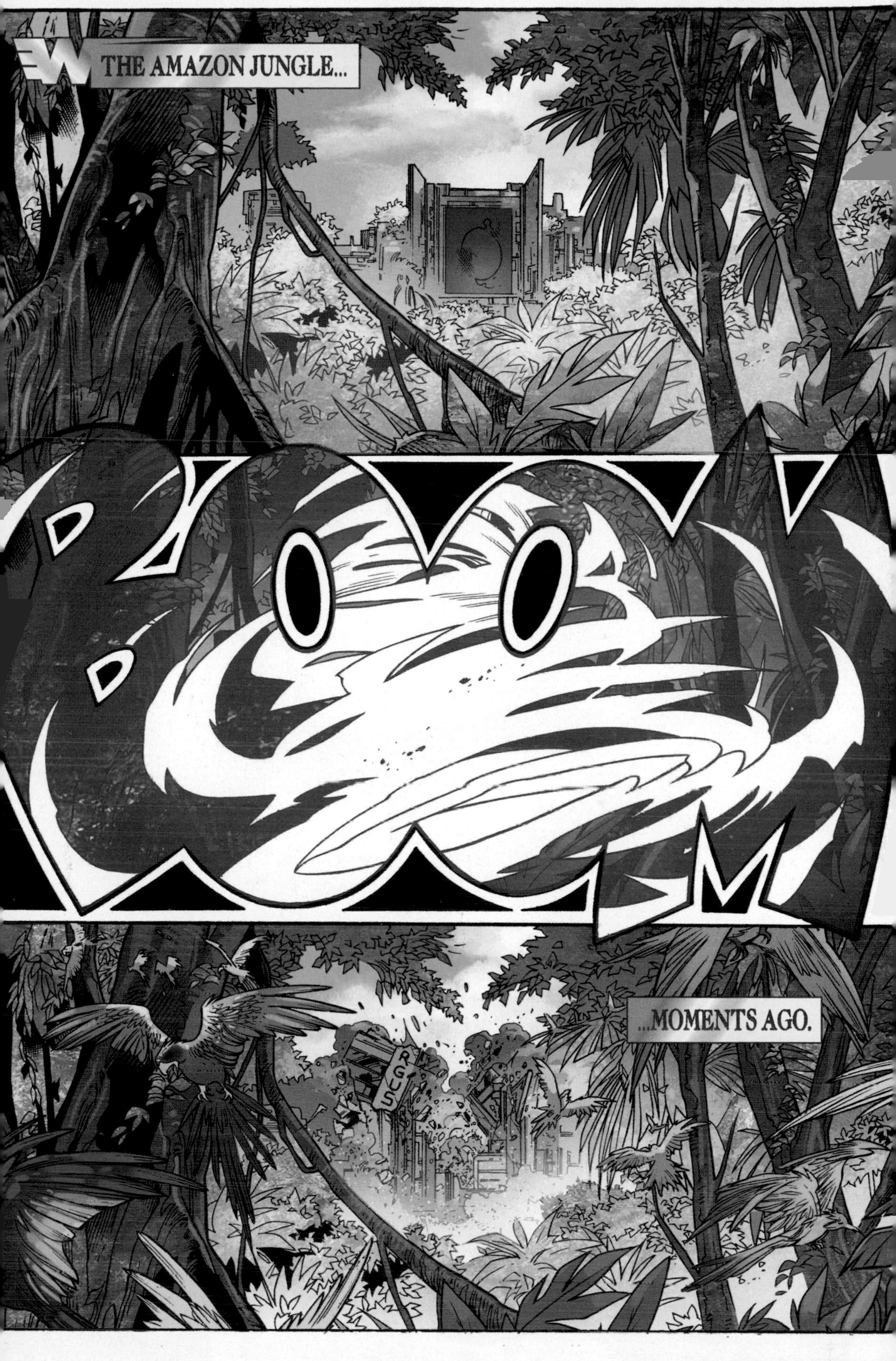
THE AMAZON JUNGLE...
BOOOM
...MOMENTS AGO.
ARGUS

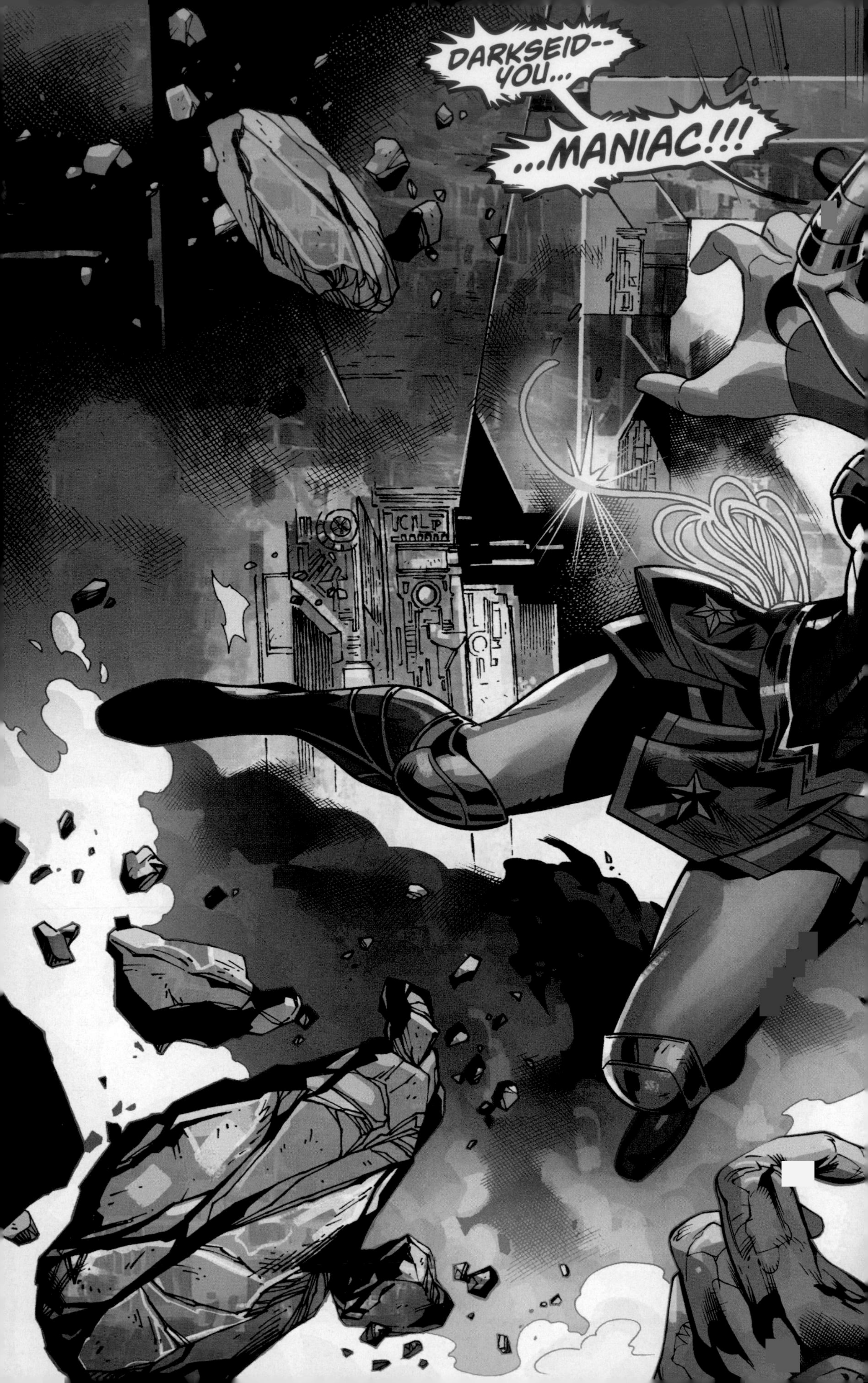
DARKSEID--
YOU...
...MANIAC!!!

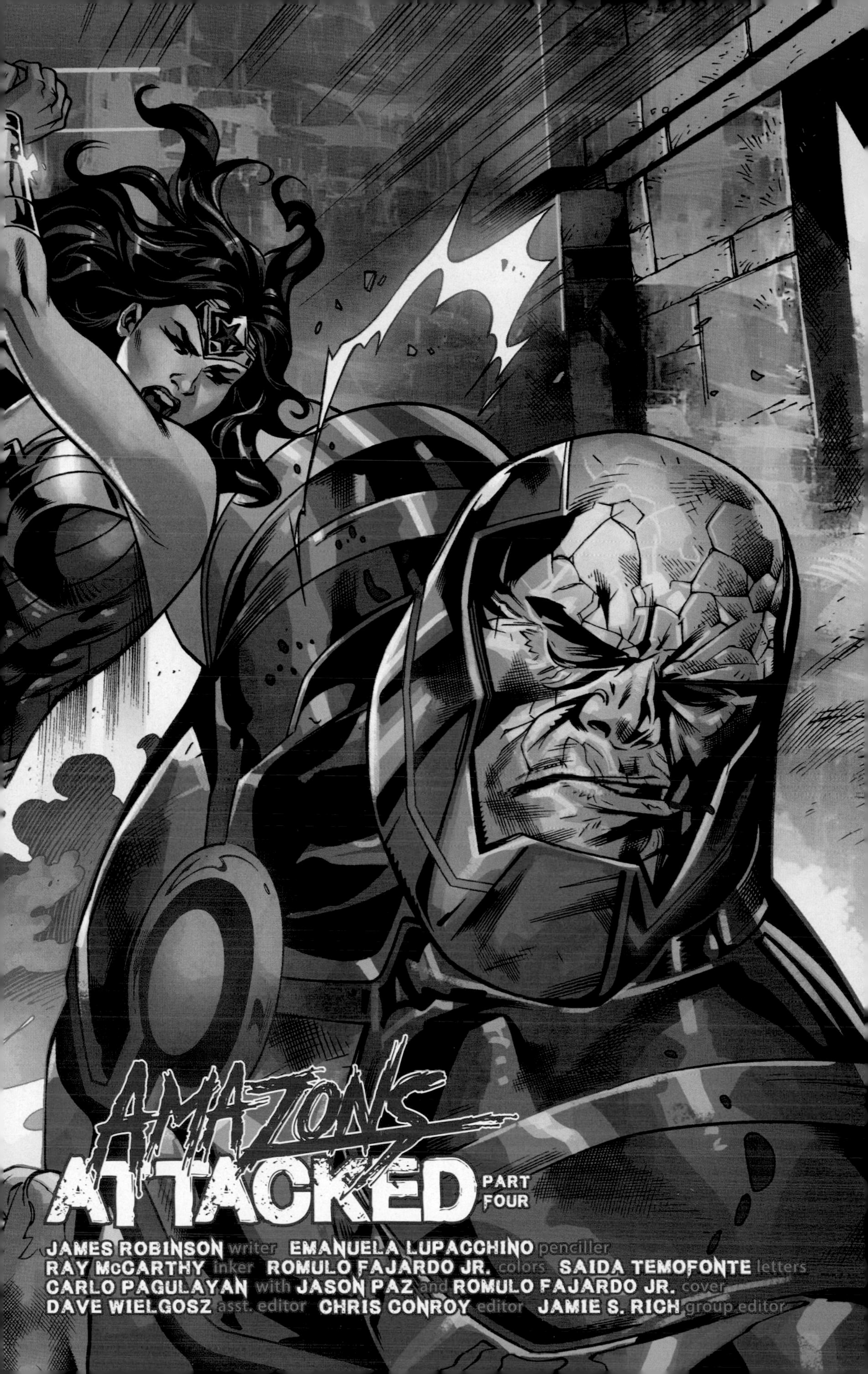
AMAZONS
ATTACKED PART FOUR
JAMES ROBINSON writer EMANUELA LUPACCHINO penciller
RAY McCARTHY inker ROMULO FAJARDO JR. colors SAIDA TEMOFONTE letters
CARLO PAGULAYAN with JASON PAZ and ROMULO FAJARDO JR. cover
DAVE WIELGOSZ asst. editor CHRIS CONROY editor JAMIE S. RICH group editor

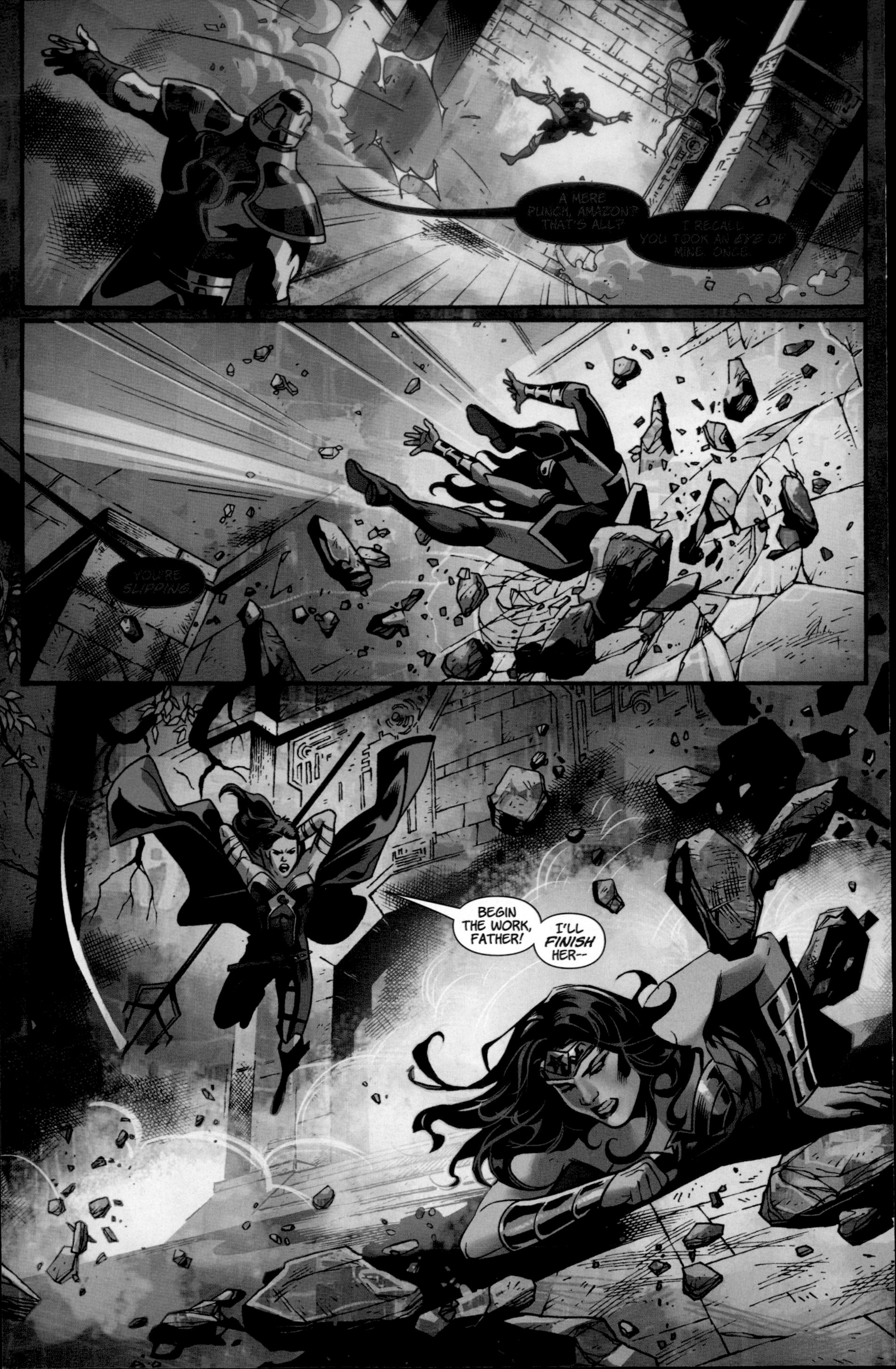
A MERE PUNCH, AMAZON? THAT'S ALL?
I RECALL YOU TOOK AN *EYE* OF MINE. ONCE.
YOU'RE SLIPPING.
BEGIN THE WORK, FATHER!
I'LL *FINISH* HER--

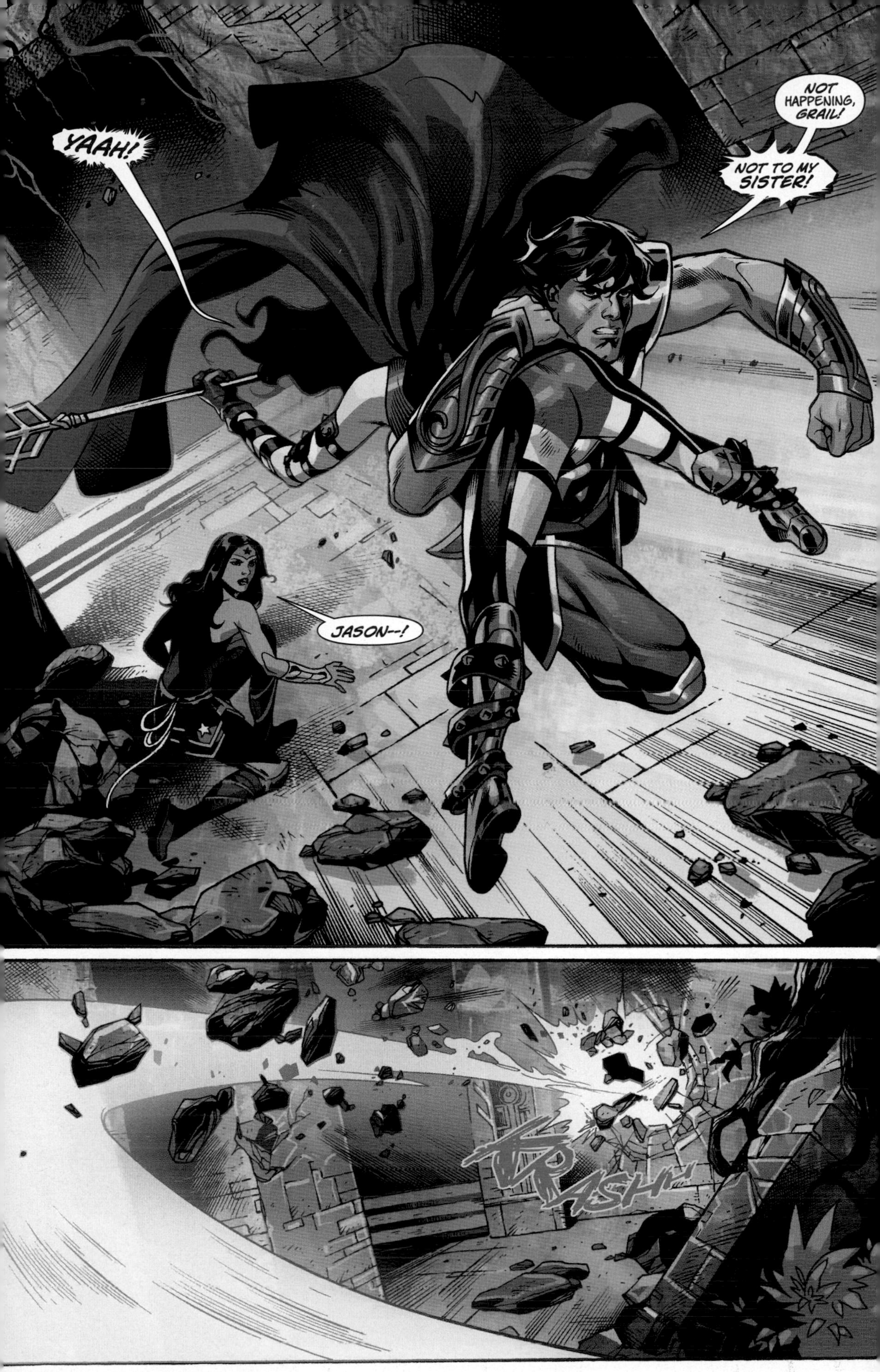
YAAH!
NOT HAPPENING, GRAIL!
NOT TO MY SISTER!
JASON--!
KRASH

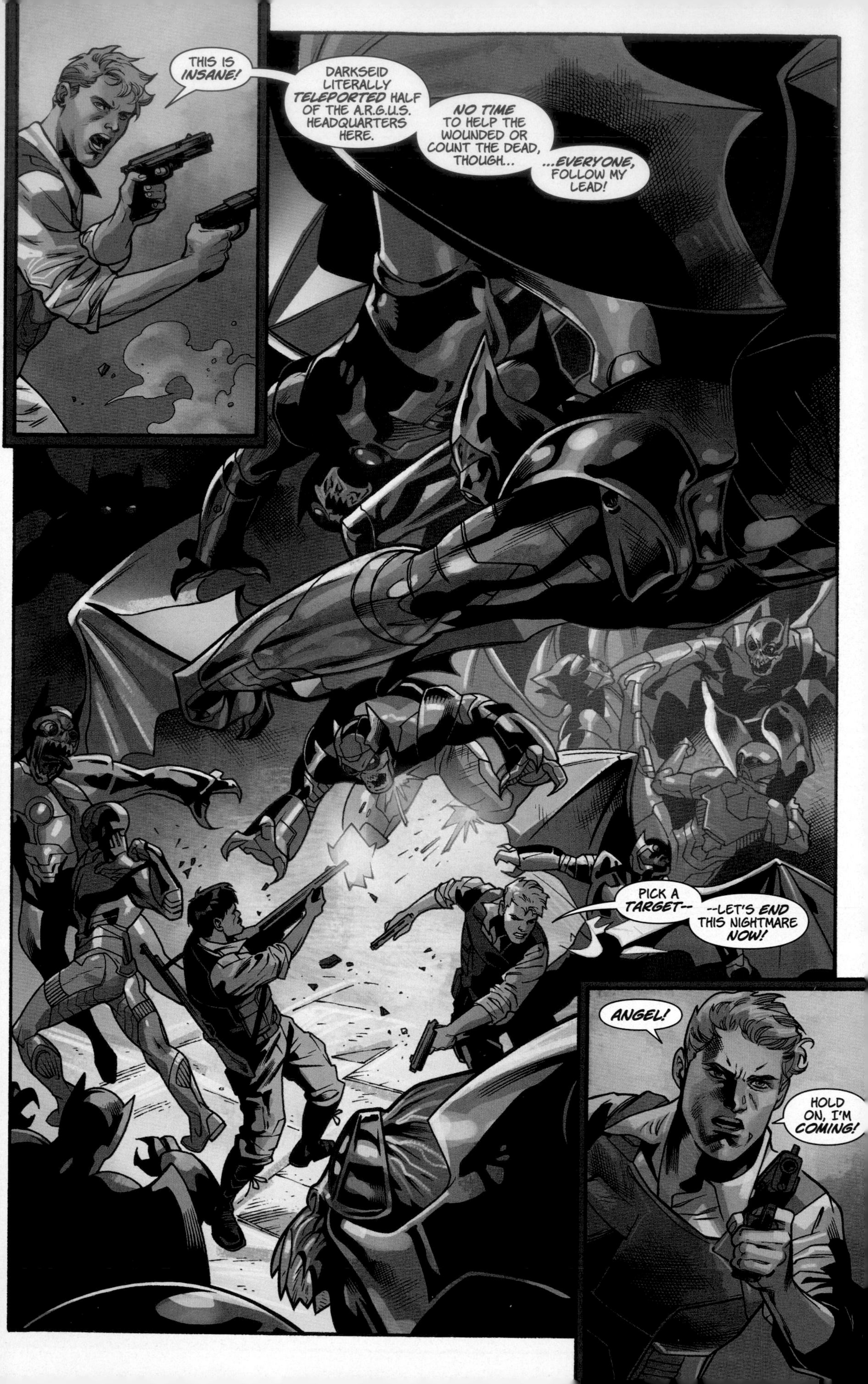
THIS IS INSANE!
DARKSEID LITERALLY TELEPORTED HALF OF THE A.R.G.U.S. HEADQUARTERS HERE.
NO TIME TO HELP THE WOUNDED OR COUNT THE DEAD, THOUGH...
...EVERYONE, FOLLOW MY LEAD!
PICK A TARGET--
--LET'S END THIS NIGHTMARE NOW!
ANGEL!
HOLD ON, I'M COMING!

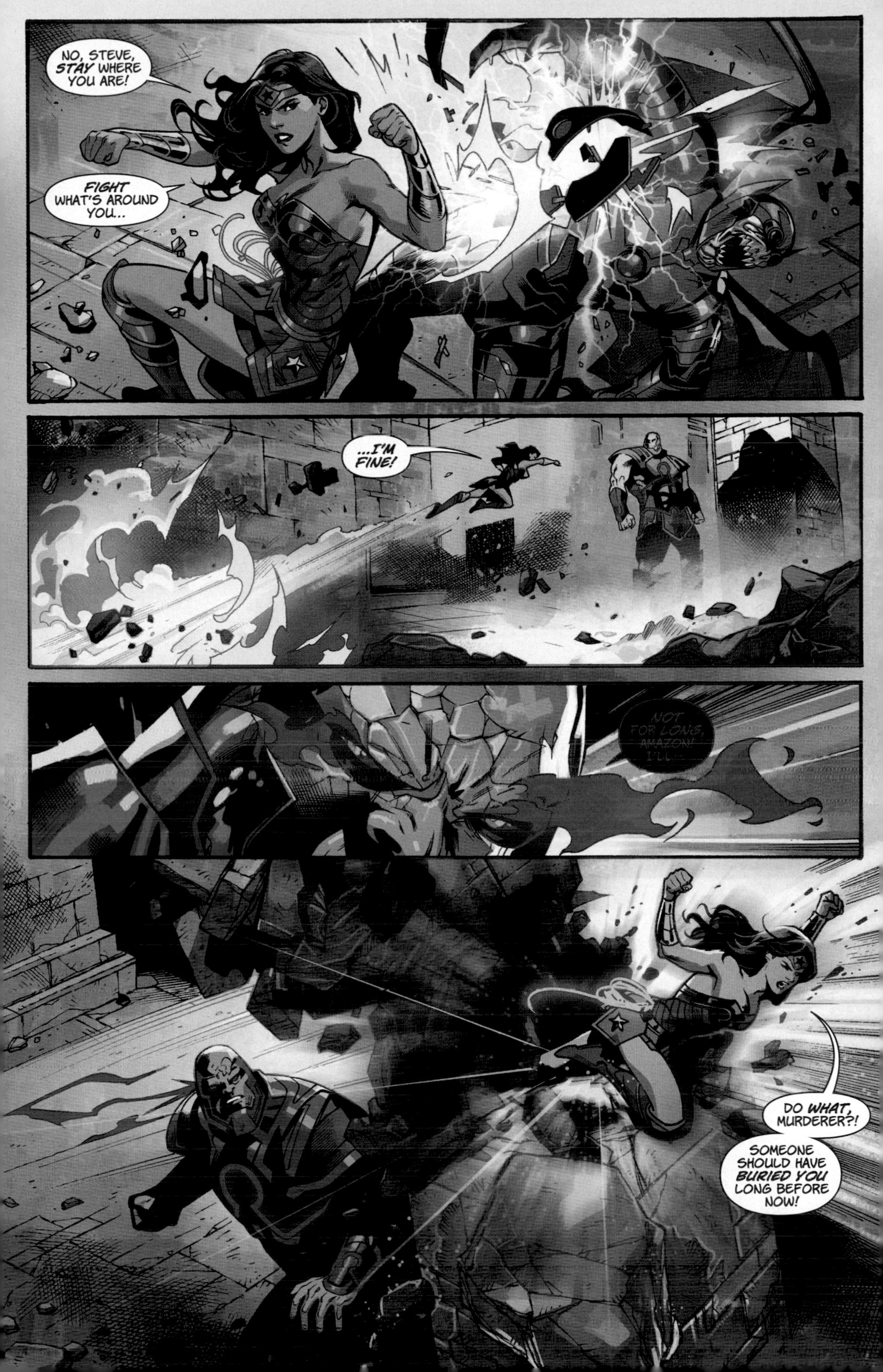

NO, STEVE, STAY WHERE YOU ARE!
FIGHT WHAT'S AROUND YOU...
...I'M FINE!
NOT FOR LONG, AMAZON! I'LL...
DO WHAT, MURDERER?!
SOMEONE SHOULD HAVE BURIED YOU LONG BEFORE NOW!

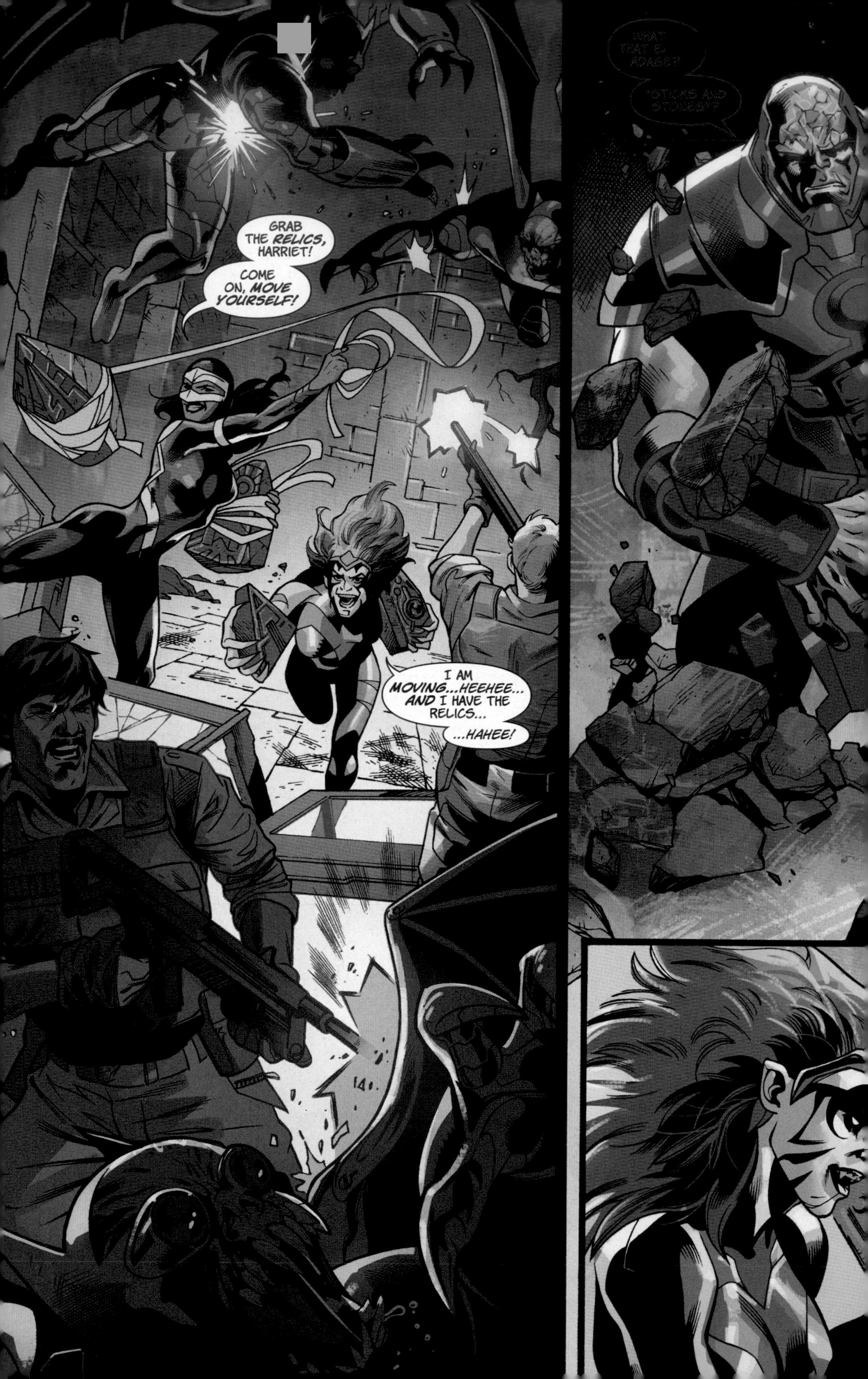
GRAB THE RELICS, HARRIET!
COME ON, MOVE YOURSELF!
I AM MOVING...HEEHEE... AND I HAVE THE RELICS...
...HAHEE!
"STICKS AND STONES"?

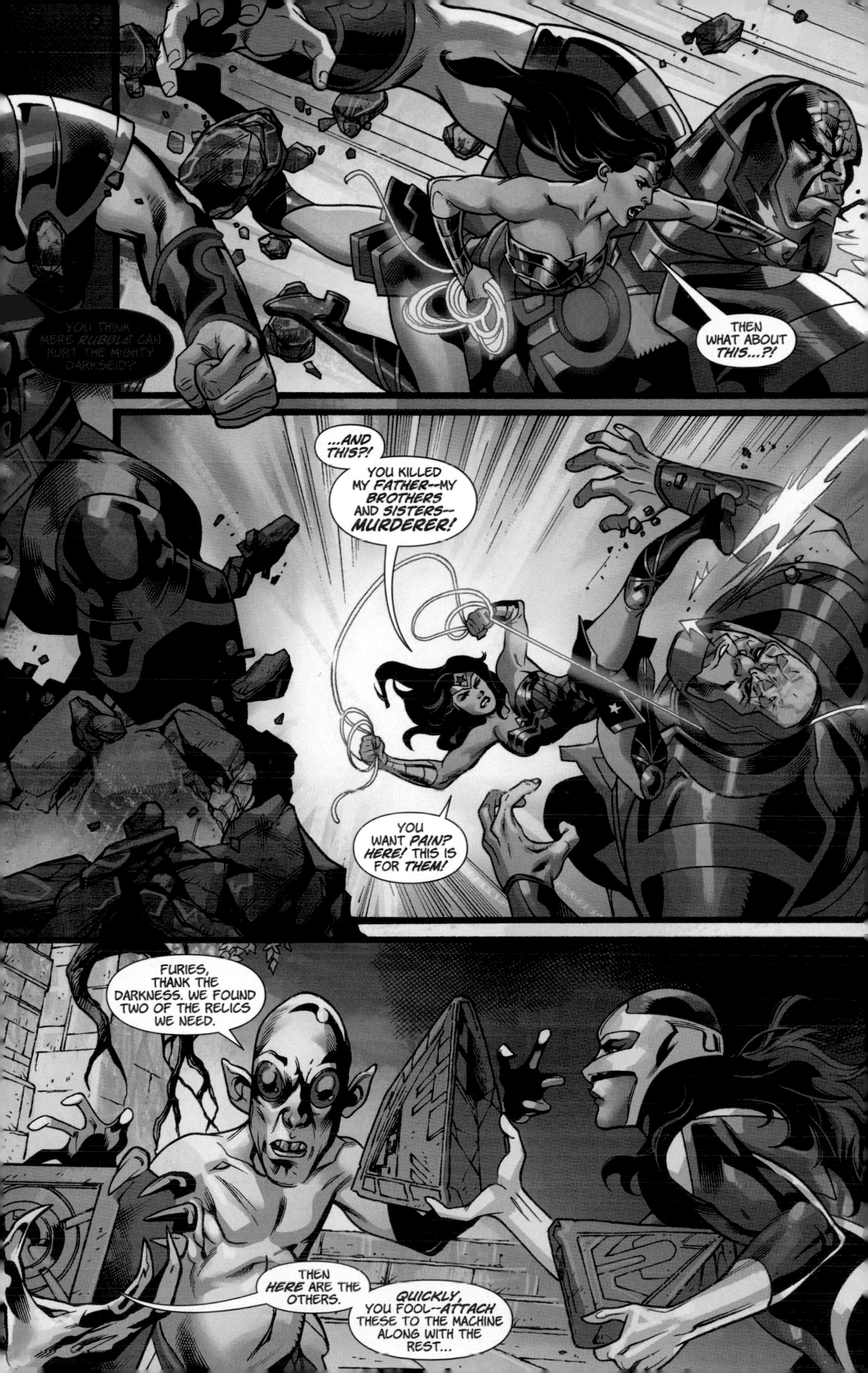
YOU THINK MERE RUBBLE CAN HURT THE MIGHTY DARKSEID?
THEN WHAT ABOUT THIS...?!
...AND THIS?!
YOU KILLED MY FATHER--MY BROTHERS AND SISTERS--MURDERER!
YOU WANT PAIN? HERE! THIS IS FOR THEM!
FURIES, THANK THE DARKNESS. WE FOUND TWO OF THE RELICS WE NEED.
THEN HERE ARE THE OTHERS.
QUICKLY, YOU FOOL--ATTACH THESE TO THE MACHINE ALONG WITH THE REST...

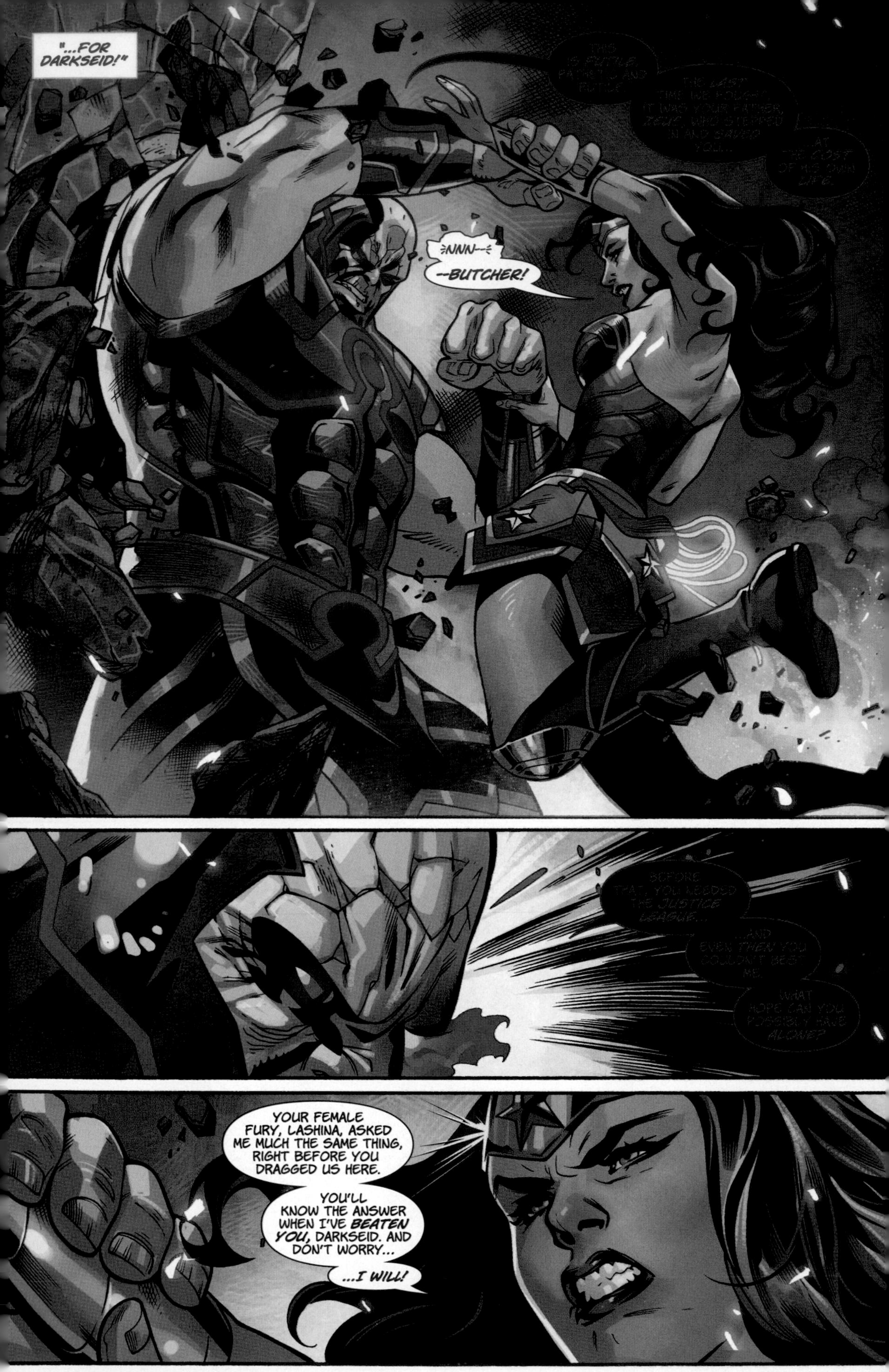
"...FOR DARKSEID!"
THIS IS FUTILE, PATHETIC AND FUTILE.
THE LAST TIME WE FOUGHT, IT WAS YOUR FATHER, ZEUS, WHO STEPPED IN AND SAVED YOU...
...AT THE COST OF HIS OWN LIFE.
NNN--
--BUTCHER!
BEFORE THAT, YOU NEEDED THE JUSTICE LEAGUE...
...AND EVEN THEN YOU COULDN'T BEST ME.
WHAT HOPE CAN YOU POSSIBLY HAVE ALONE?
YOUR FEMALE FURY, LASHINA, ASKED ME MUCH THE SAME THING, RIGHT BEFORE YOU DRAGGED US HERE.
YOU'LL KNOW THE ANSWER WHEN I'VE BEATEN YOU, DARKSEID. AND DON'T WORRY...
...I WILL!

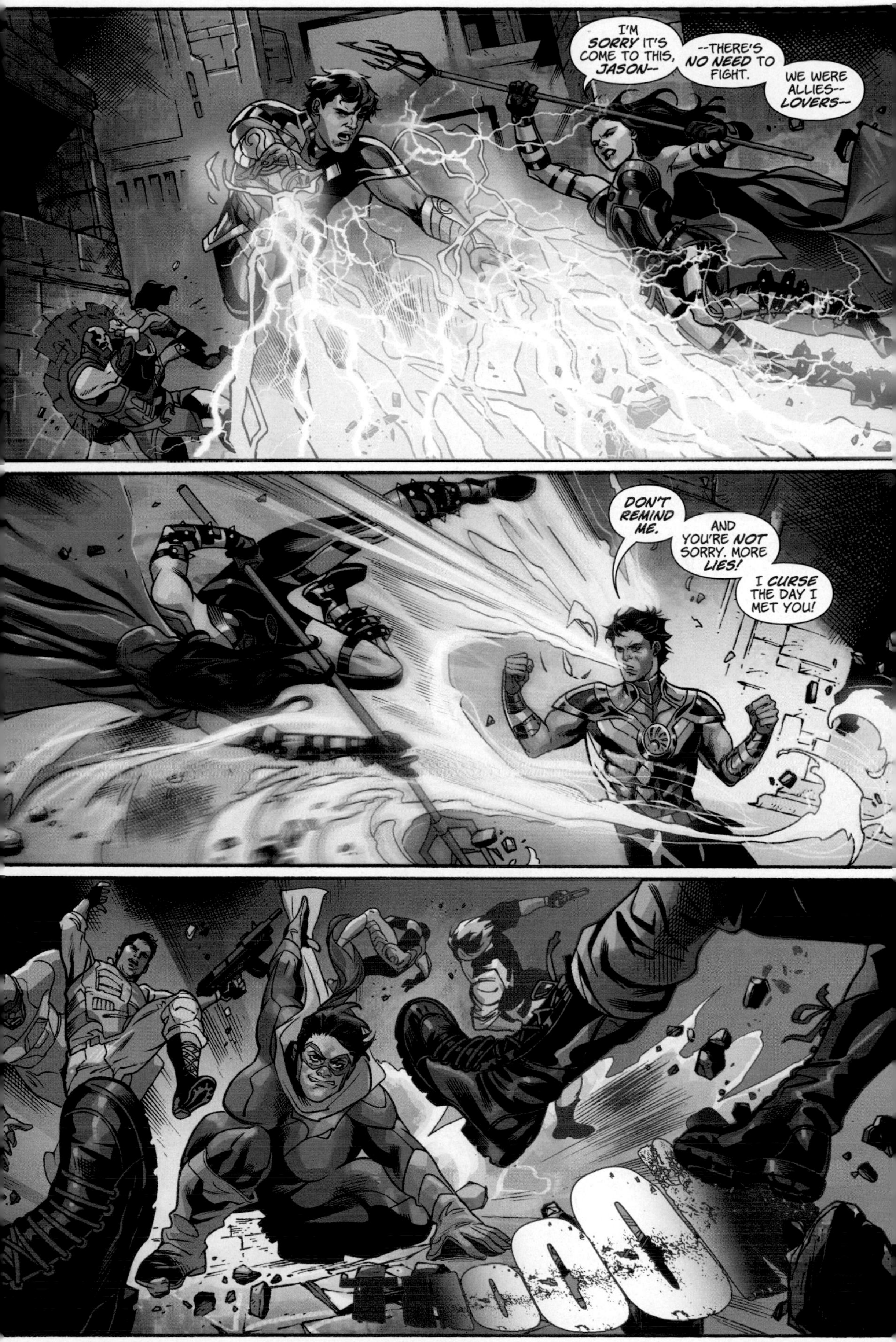
I'M SORRY IT'S COME TO THIS, JASON--
--THERE'S NO NEED TO FIGHT.
WE WERE ALLIES-- LOVERS--
DON'T REMIND ME.
AND YOU'RE NOT SORRY. MORE LIES!
I CURSE THE DAY I MET YOU!
THOOOM

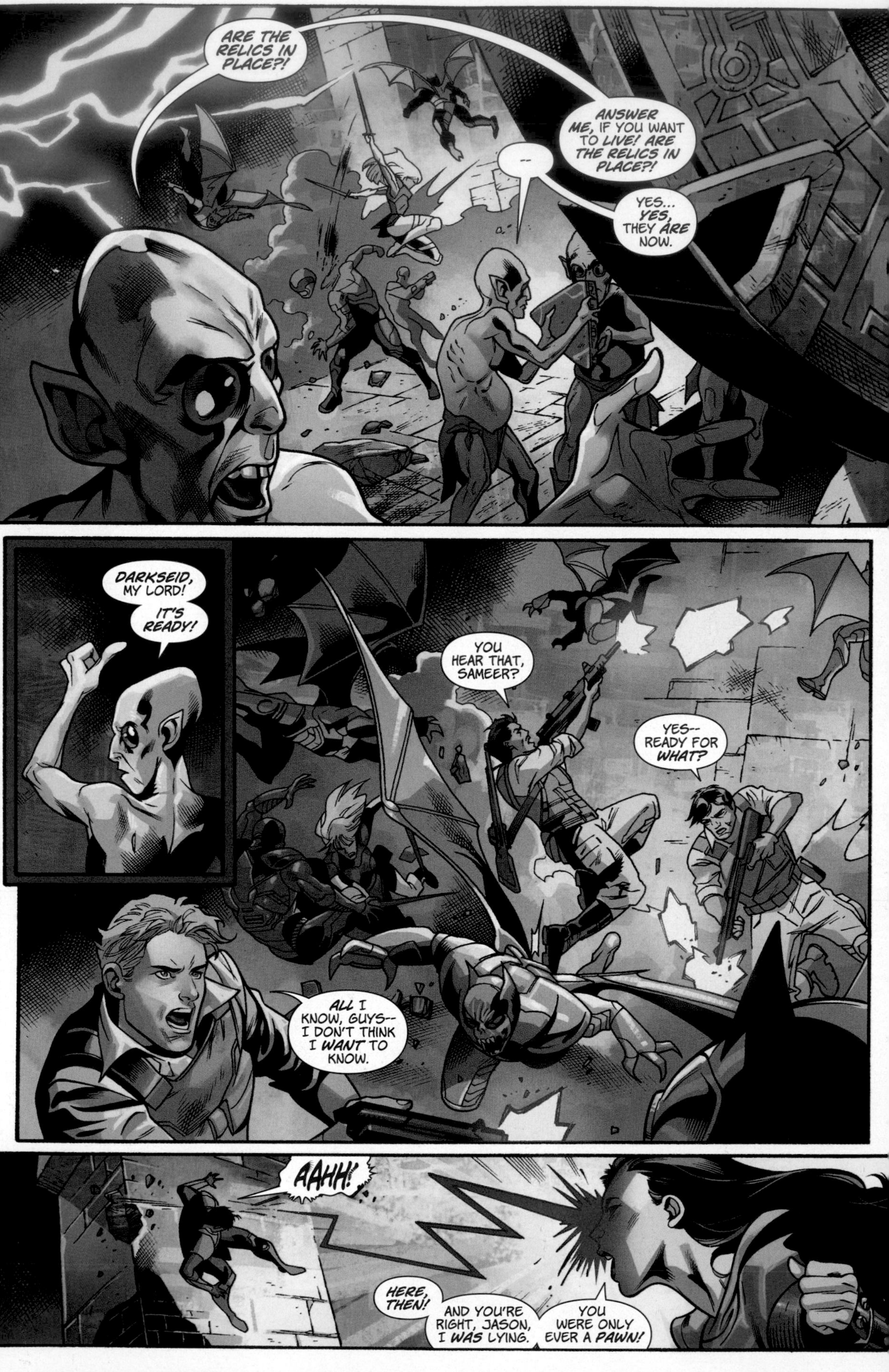
ARE THE RELICS IN PLACE?!
ANSWER ME, IF YOU WANT TO LIVE! ARE THE RELICS IN PLACE?!
--
YES... YES, THEY ARE NOW.
DARKSEID, MY LORD!
IT'S READY!
YOU HEAR THAT, SAMEER?
YES-- READY FOR WHAT?
ALL I KNOW, GUYS-- I DON'T THINK I WANT TO KNOW.
AAHH!
HERE, THEN!
AND YOU'RE RIGHT, JASON, I WAS LYING.
YOU WERE ONLY EVER A PAWN!

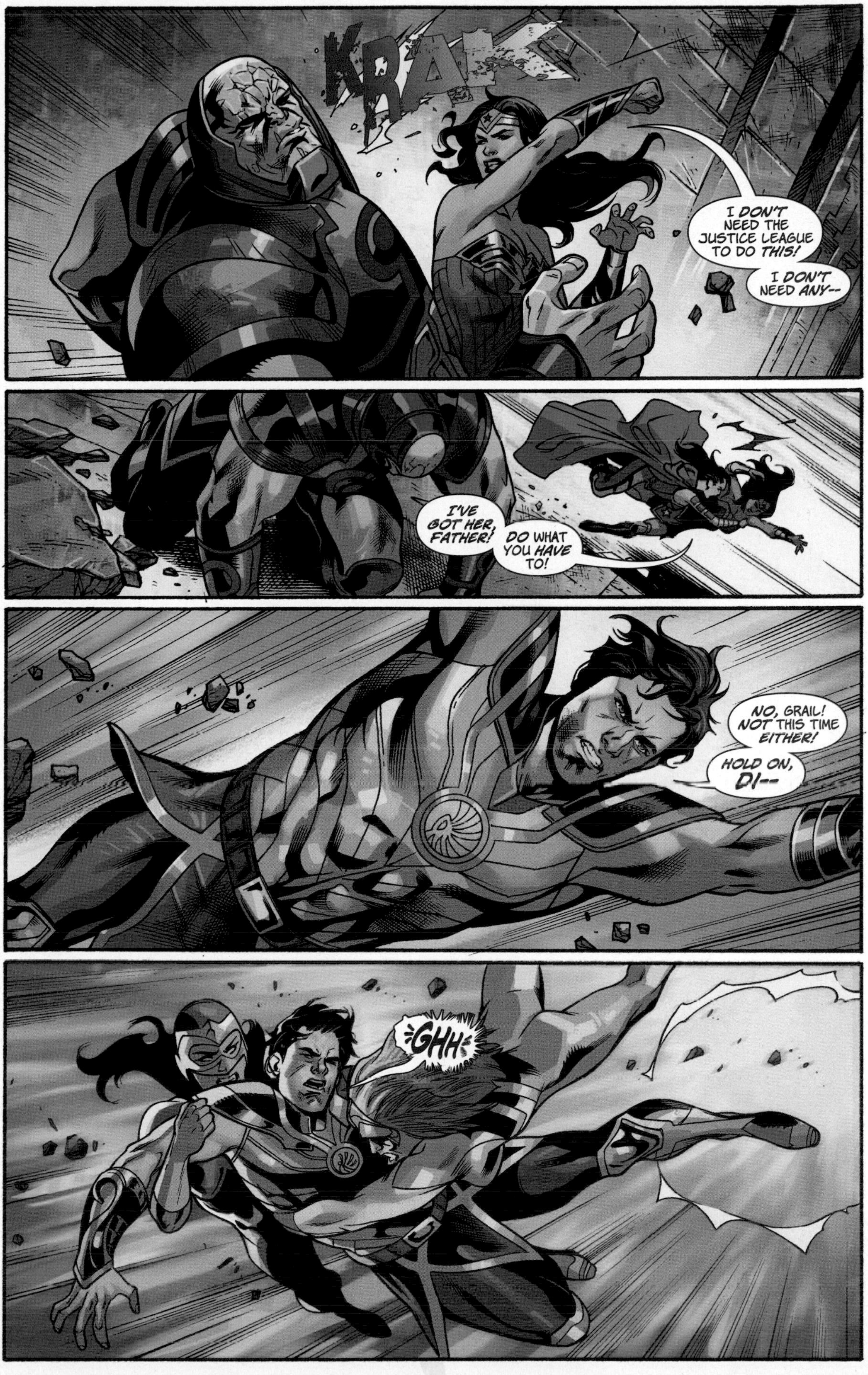
KRAK
I DON'T NEED THE JUSTICE LEAGUE TO DO THIS!
I DON'T NEED ANY--
I'VE GOT HER, FATHER!
DO WHAT YOU HAVE TO!
NO, GRAIL! NOT THIS TIME EITHER!
HOLD ON, DI--
GHH

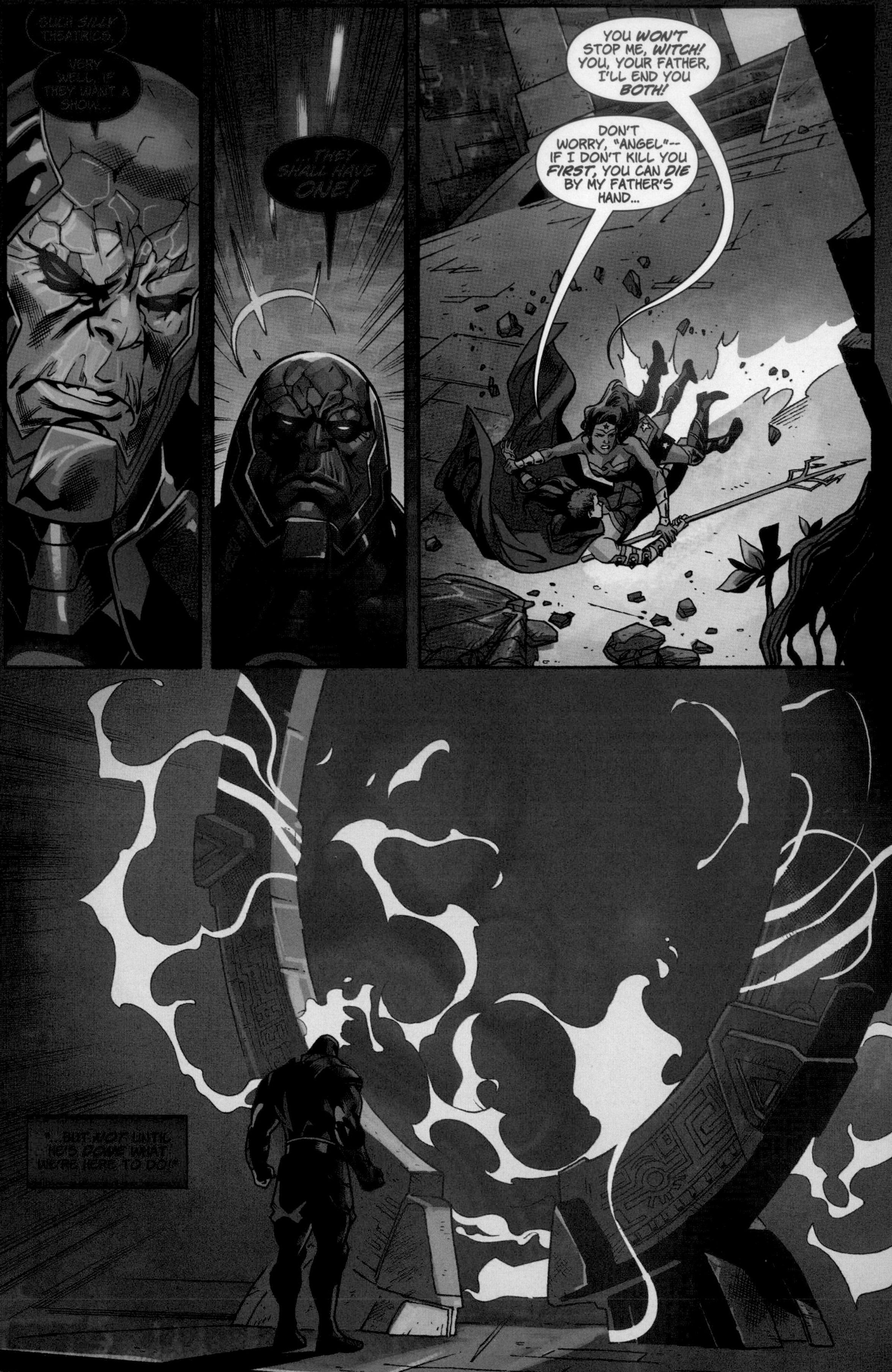
SUCH SILLY THEATRICS.
VERY WELL, IF THEY WANT A SHOW...
...THEY SHALL HAVE ONE!
YOU WON'T STOP ME, WITCH! YOU, YOUR FATHER, I'LL END YOU BOTH!
DON'T WORRY, "ANGEL"-- IF I DON'T KILL YOU FIRST, YOU CAN DIE BY MY FATHER'S HAND...
"...BUT NOT UNTIL HE'S DONE WHAT WE'RE HERE TO DO!"

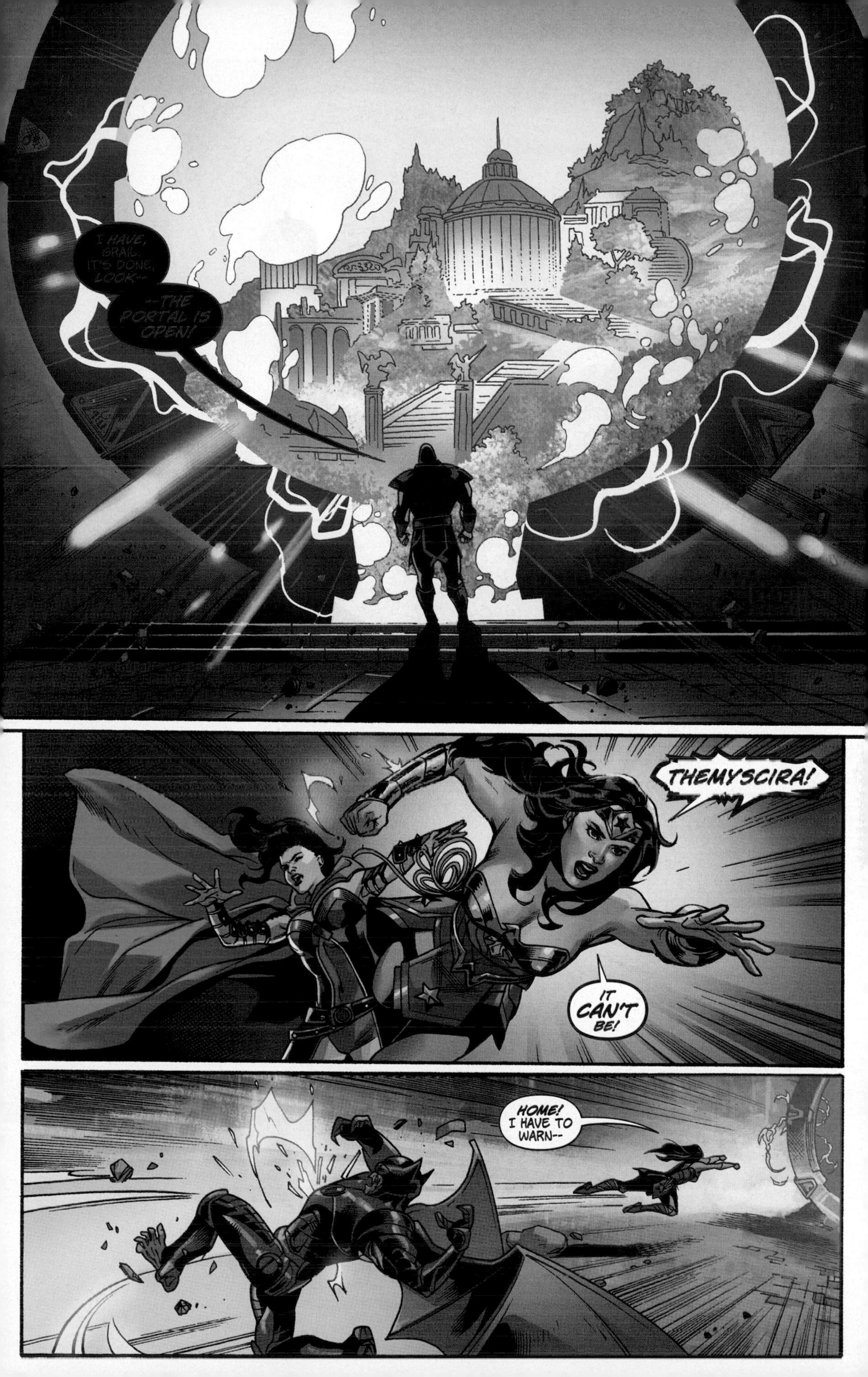

I HAVE, GRAIL. IT'S DONE. LOOK--
--THE PORTAL IS OPEN!
THEMYSCIRA!
IT CAN'T BE!
HOME! I HAVE TO WARN--

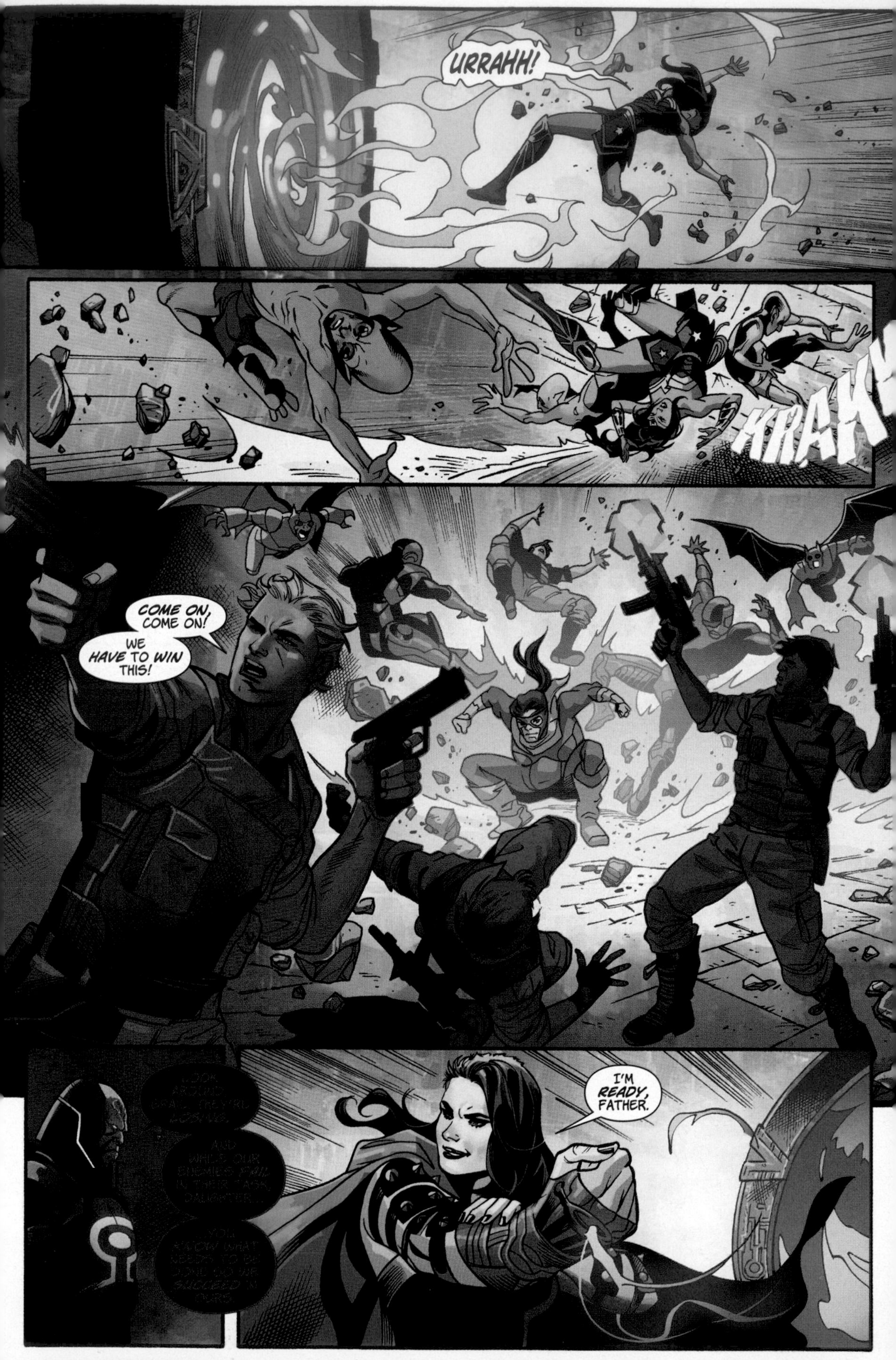
URRAHH!
KRAKK
COME ON, COME ON!
WE HAVE TO WIN THIS!
LOOK AROUND, GRAIL. THEY'RE LOSING.
AND WHILE OUR ENEMIES FAIL IN THEIR TASK, DAUGHTER...
YOU KNOW WHAT NEEDS TO BE DONE SO WE SUCCEED IN OURS.
I'M READY, FATHER.

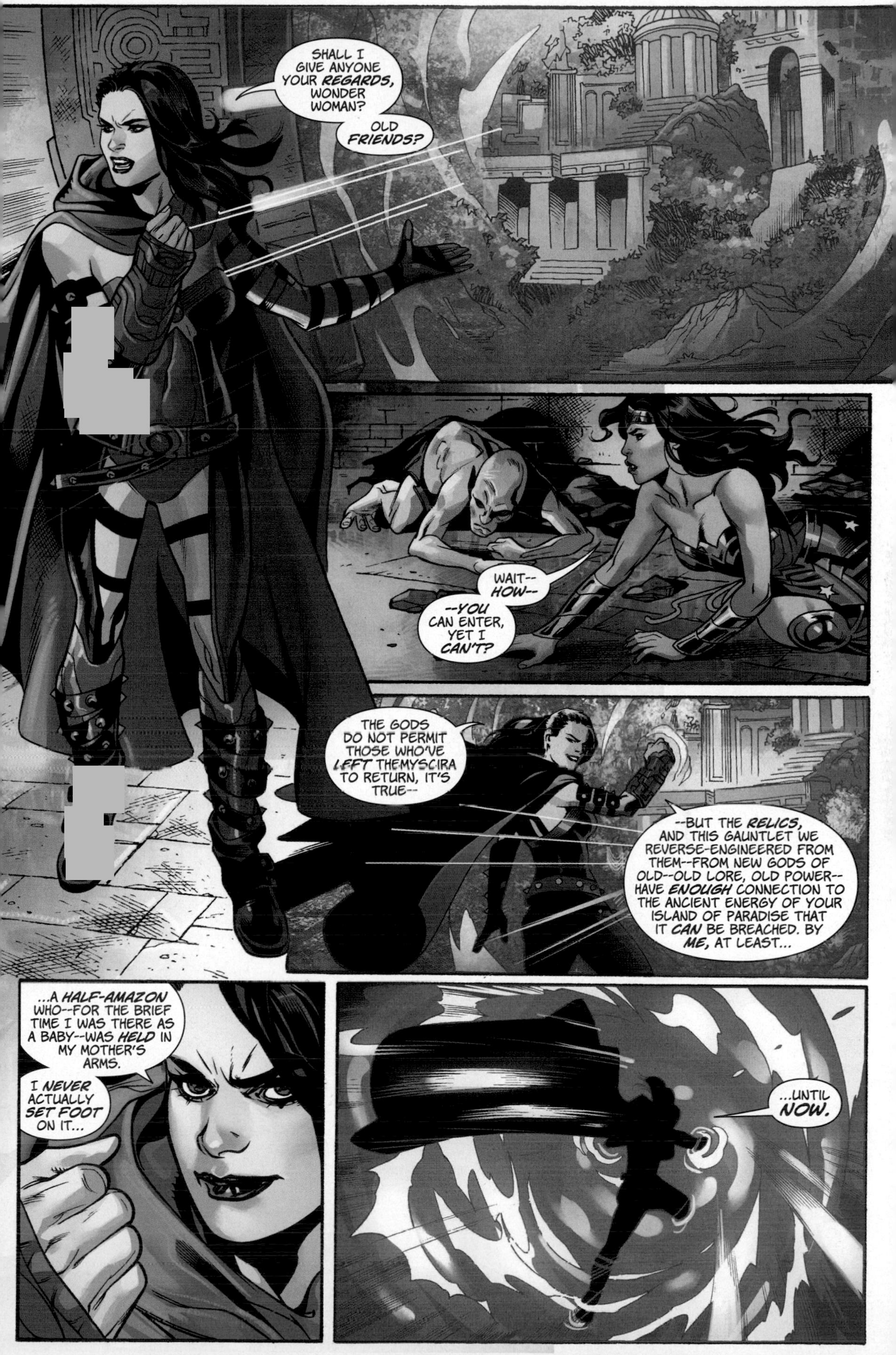
SHALL I GIVE ANYONE YOUR *REGARDS,* WONDER WOMAN?
OLD *FRIENDS?*
WAIT-- *HOW--*
--*YOU* CAN ENTER, YET I *CAN'T?*
THE GODS DO NOT PERMIT THOSE WHO'VE *LEFT* THEMYSCIRA TO RETURN, IT'S TRUE--
--BUT THE *RELICS,* AND THIS GAUNTLET WE REVERSE-ENGINEERED FROM THEM--FROM NEW GODS OF OLD--OLD LORE, OLD POWER--HAVE *ENOUGH* CONNECTION TO THE ANCIENT ENERGY OF YOUR ISLAND OF PARADISE THAT IT *CAN* BE BREACHED. BY *ME,* AT LEAST...
...A *HALF-AMAZON* WHO--FOR THE BRIEF TIME I WAS THERE AS A BABY--WAS *HELD* IN MY MOTHER'S ARMS.
I *NEVER* ACTUALLY *SET FOOT* ON IT...
...UNTIL *NOW.*

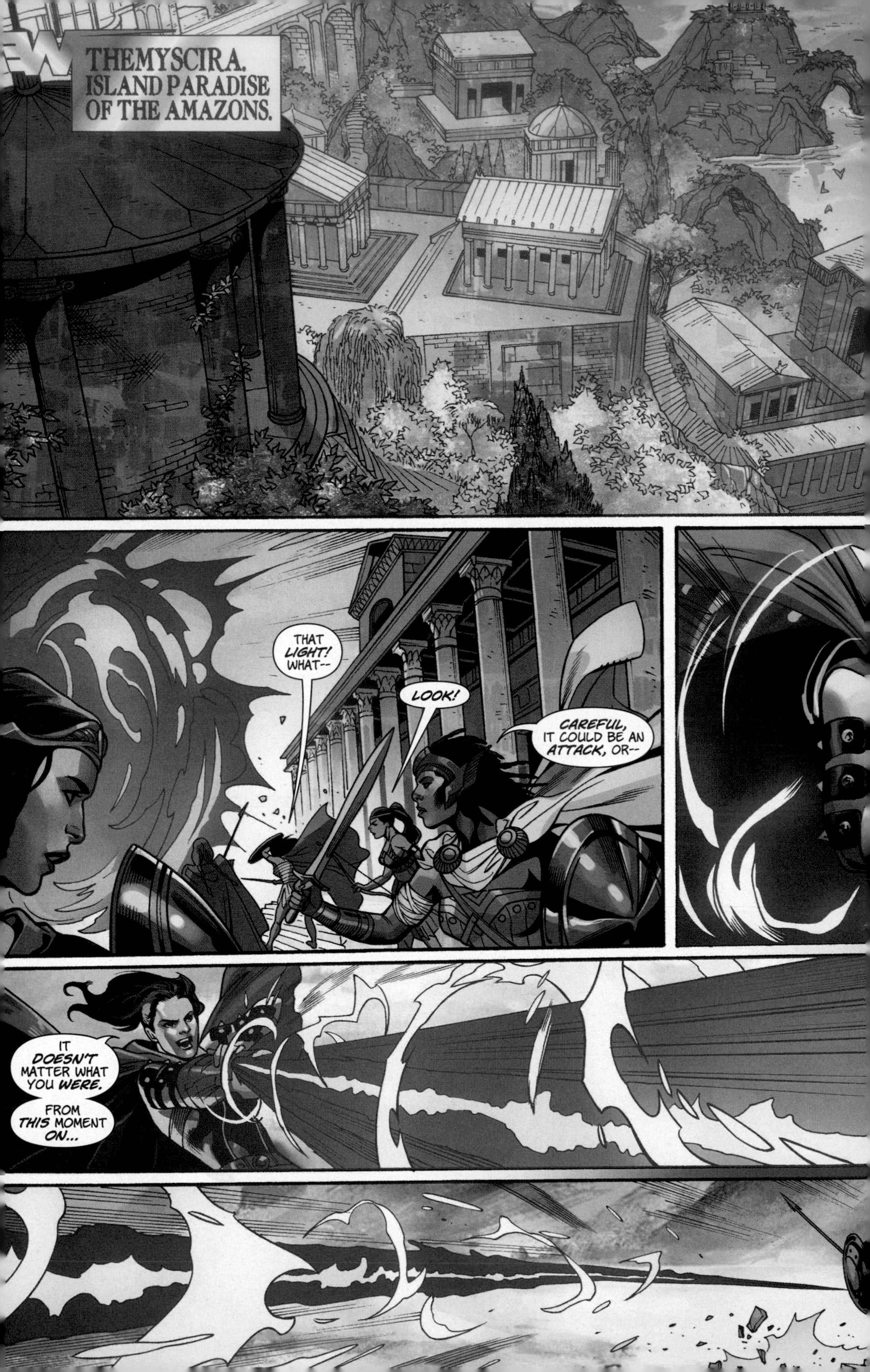
THEMYSCIRA. ISLAND PARADISE OF THE AMAZONS.
THAT LIGHT! WHAT--
LOOK!
CAREFUL, IT COULD BE AN ATTACK, OR--
IT DOESN'T MATTER WHAT YOU WERE.
FROM THIS MOMENT ON...

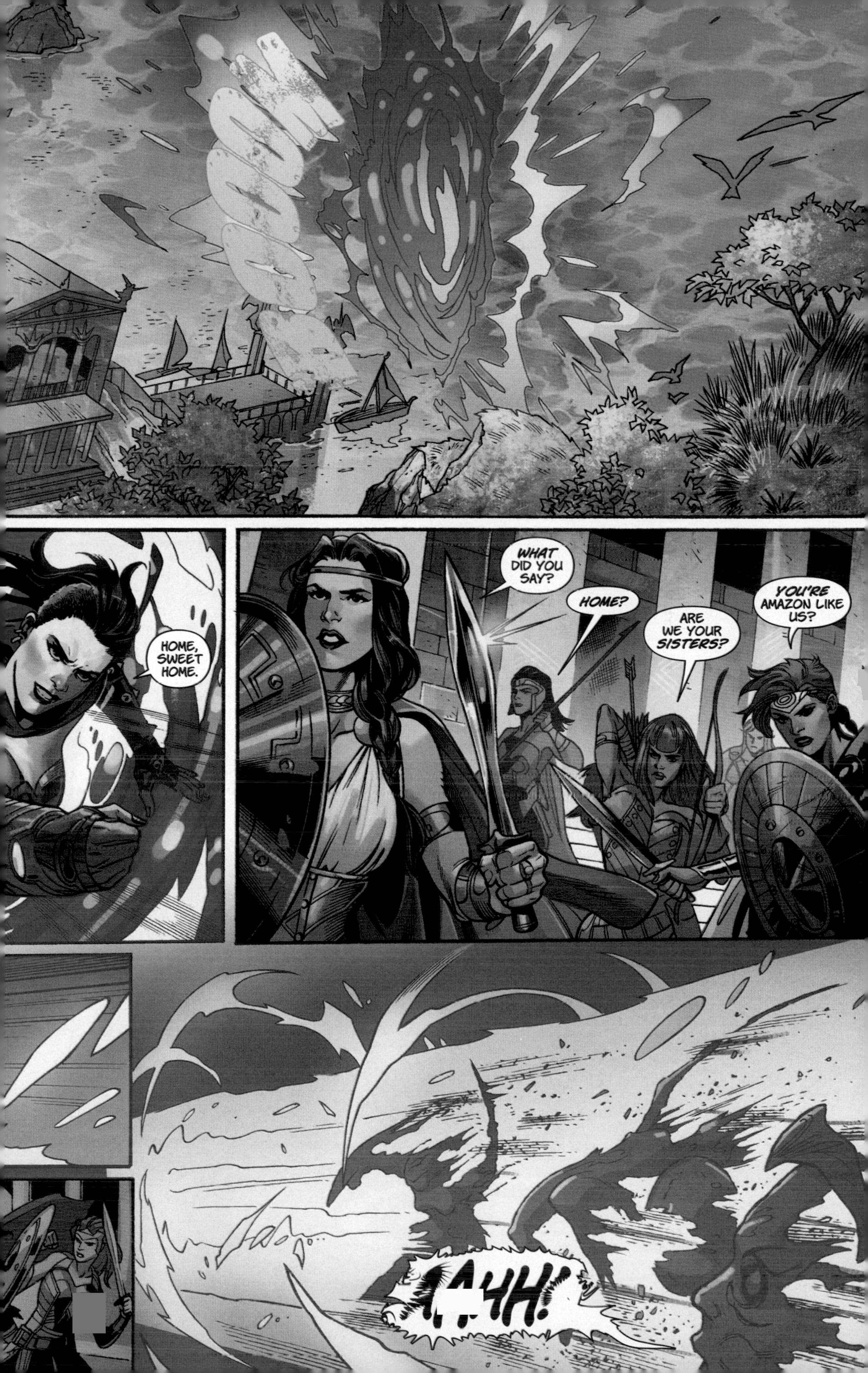
HOME, SWEET HOME.
WHAT DID YOU SAY?
HOME?
ARE WE YOUR SISTERS?
YOU'RE AMAZON LIKE US?
AHH!

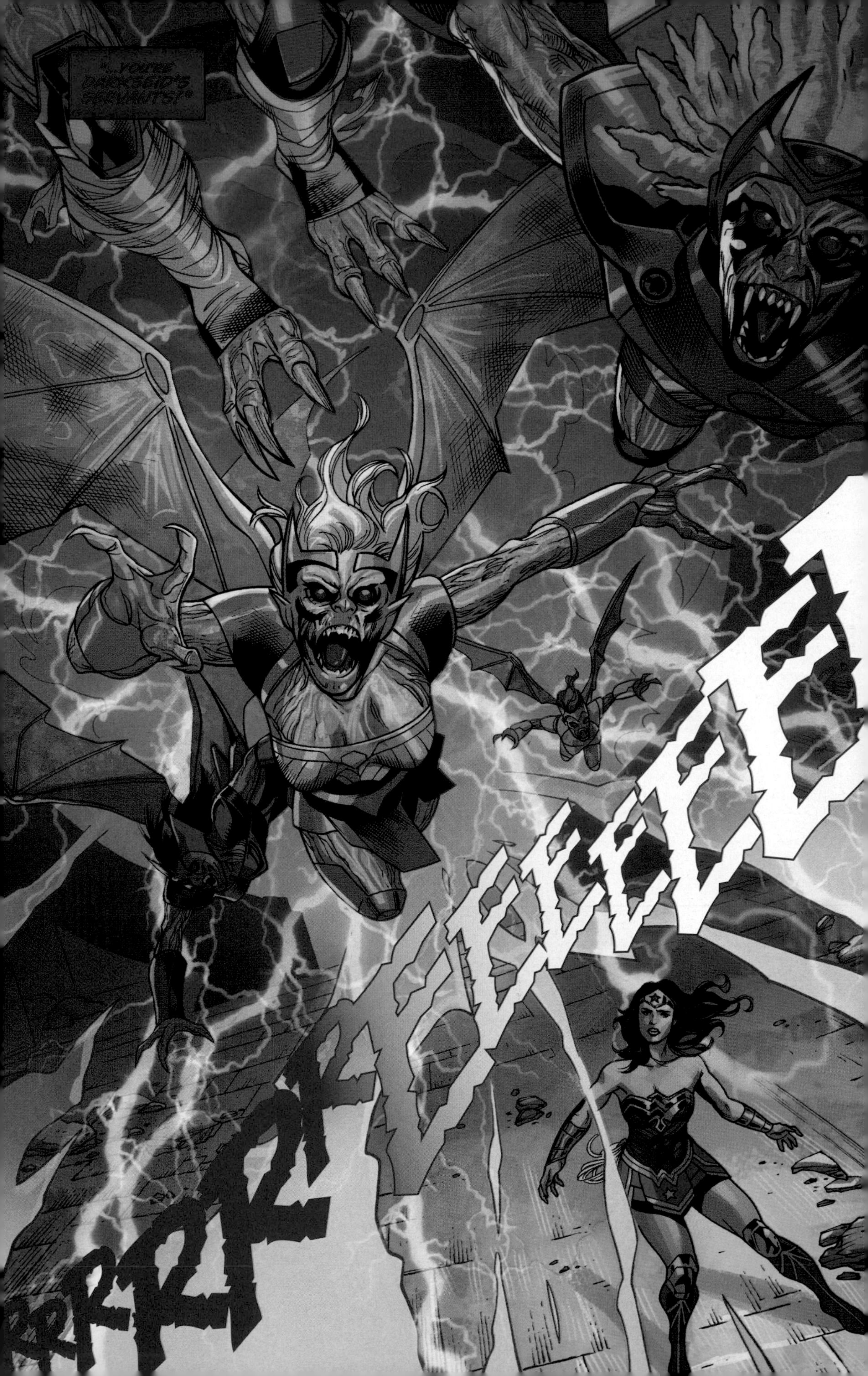
"...YOU'RE DARKSEID'S SERVANTS!"

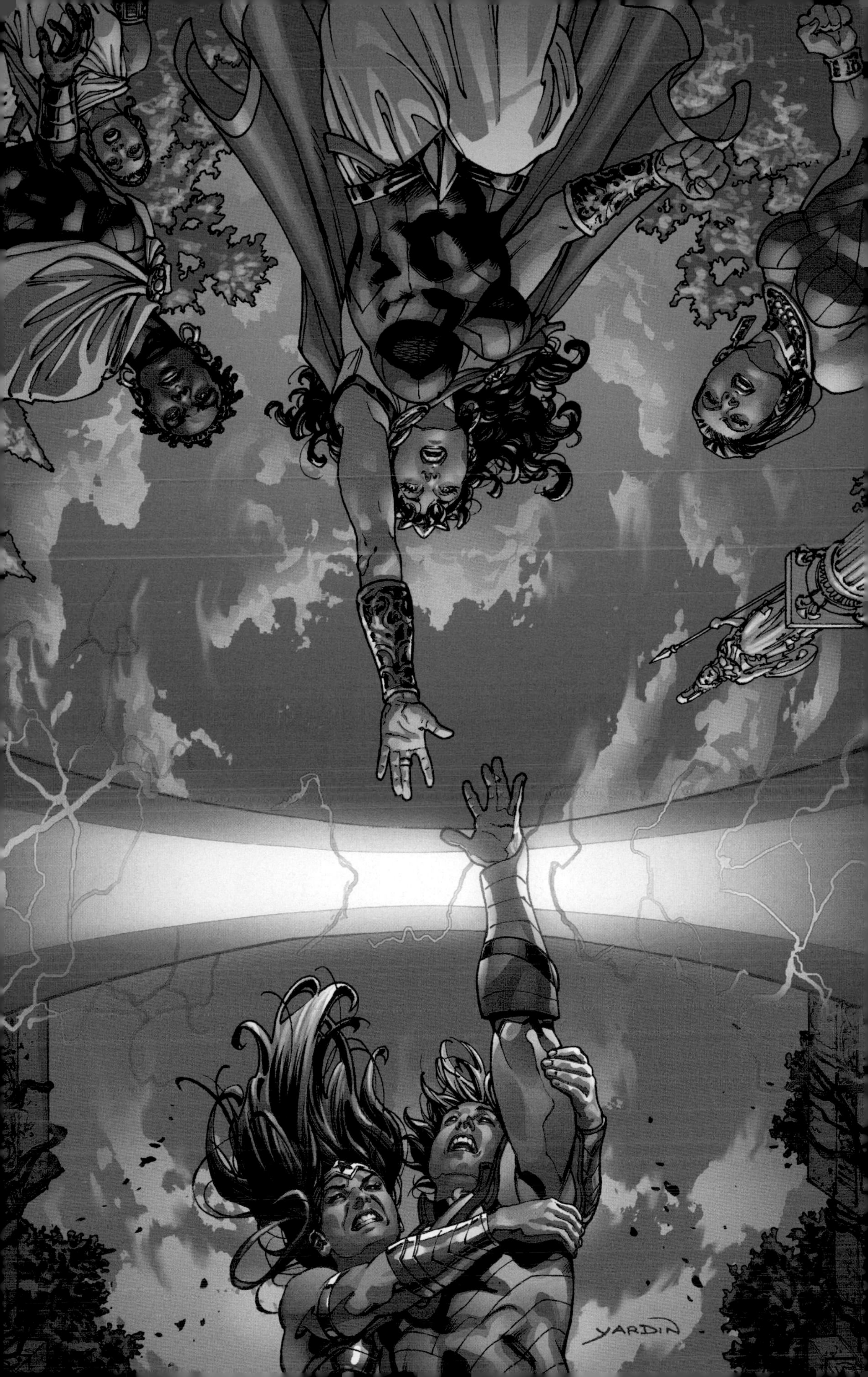
YARDIN

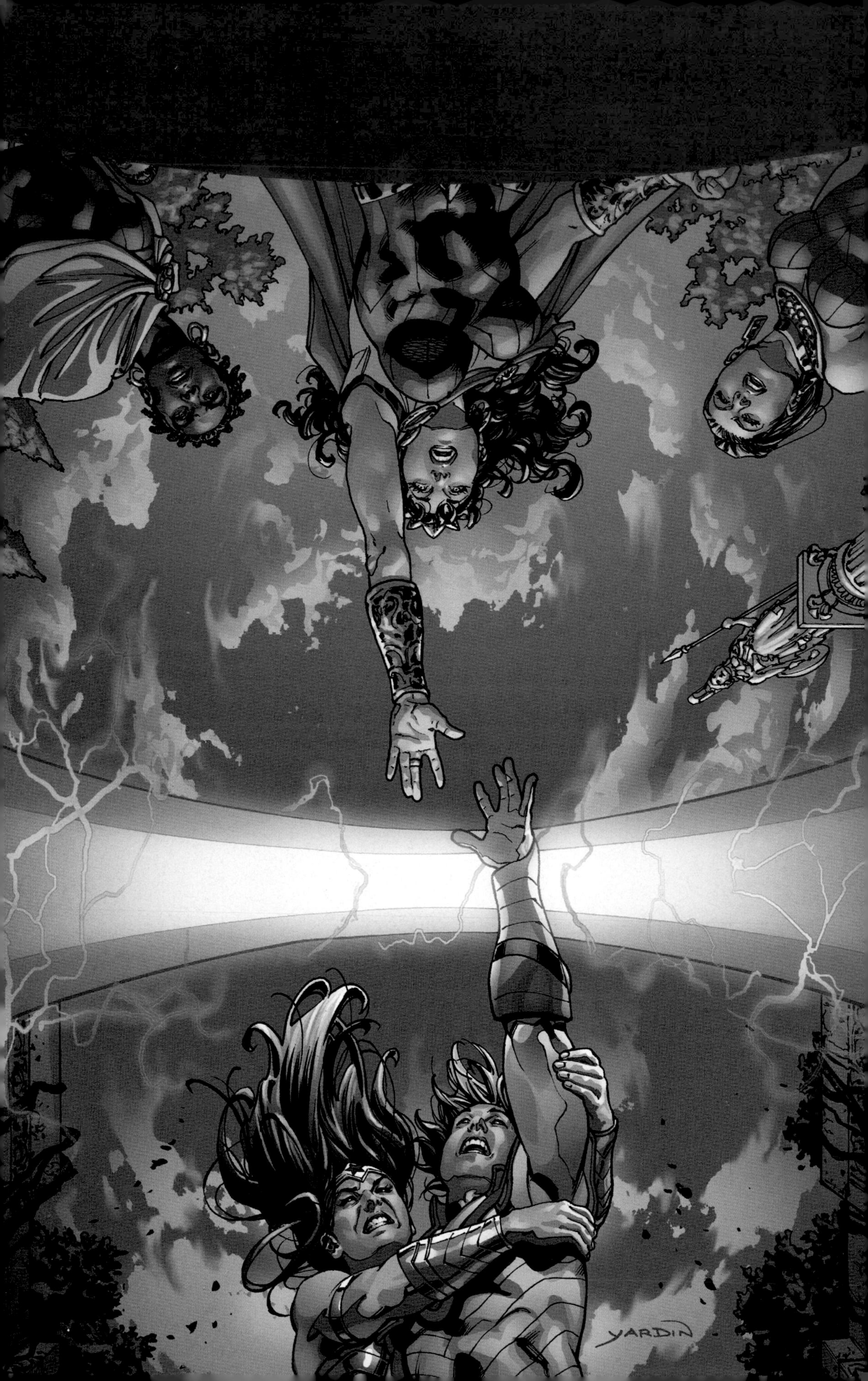
YARDIN

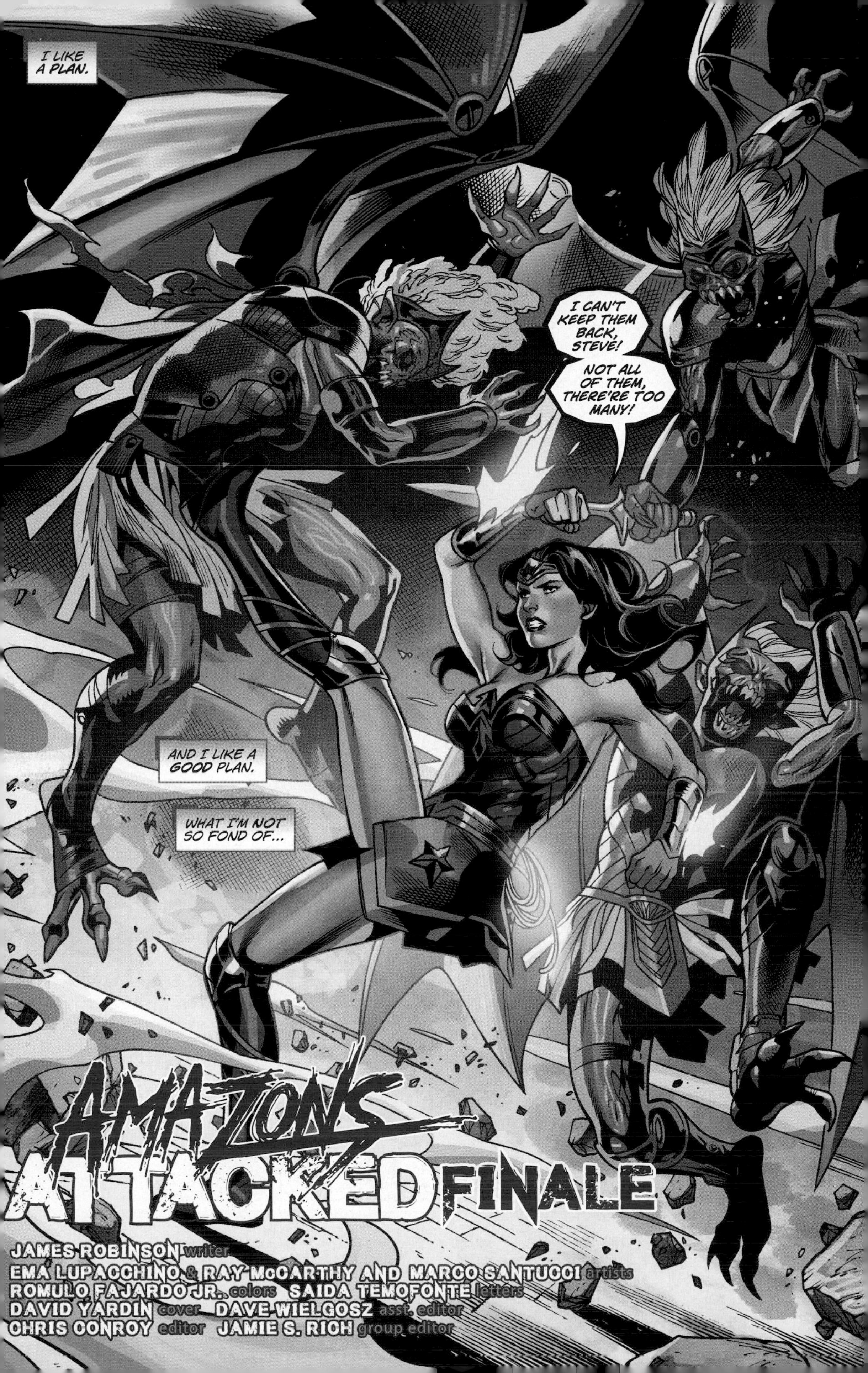
I LIKE A PLAN.
I CAN'T KEEP THEM BACK, STEVE!
NOT ALL OF THEM, THERE'RE TOO MANY!
AND I LIKE A GOOD PLAN.
WHAT I'M NOT SO FOND OF...
AMAZONS ATTACKED FINALE
JAMES ROBINSON writer
EMA LUPACCHINO & RAY McCARTHY AND MARCO SANTUCCI artists
ROMULO FAJARDO JR. colors SAIDA TEMOFONTE letters
DAVID YARDIN cover DAVE WIELGOSZ asst. editor
CHRIS CONROY editor JAMIE S. RICH group editor

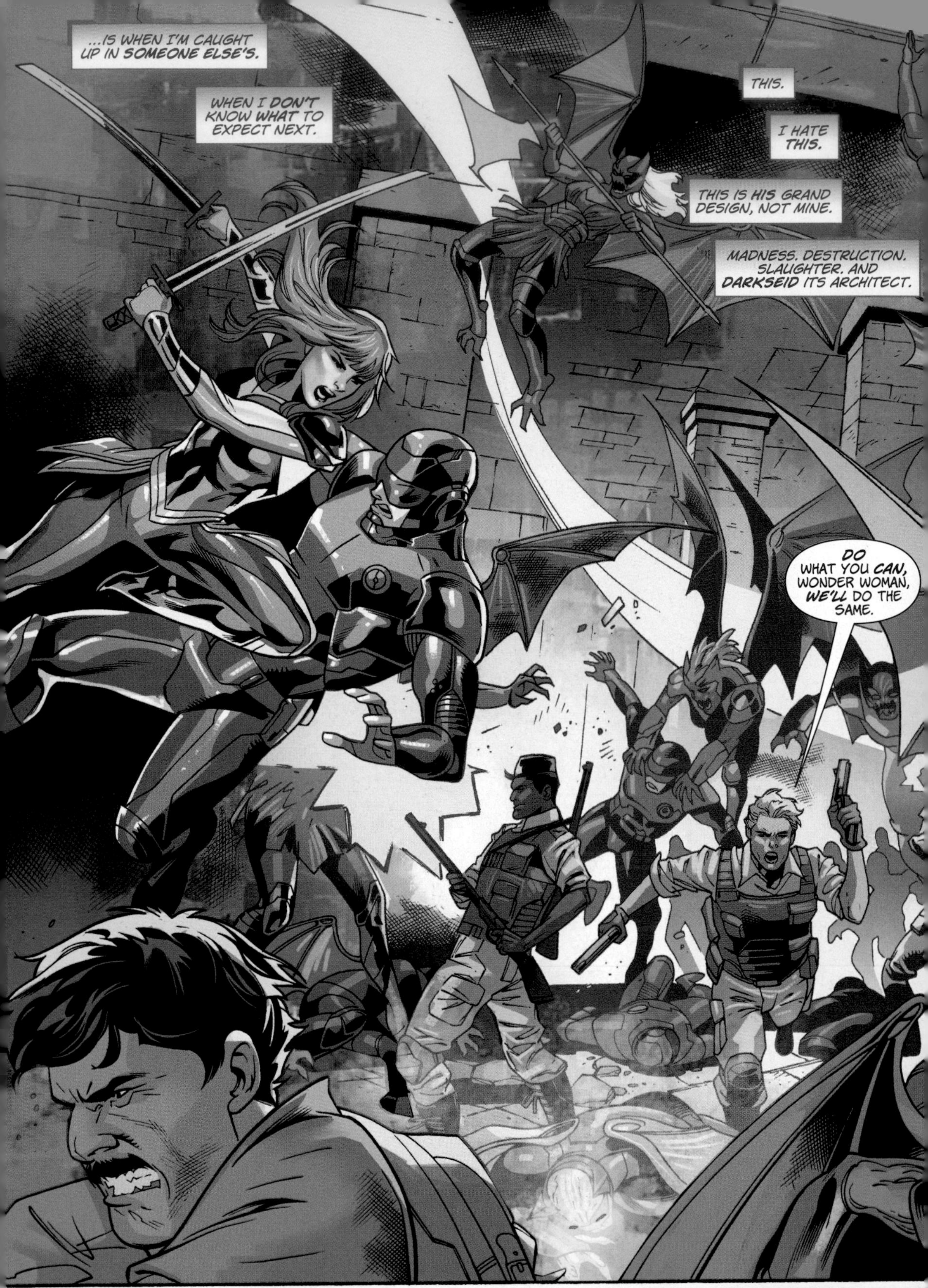

...IS WHEN I'M CAUGHT UP IN SOMEONE ELSE'S.
WHEN I DON'T KNOW WHAT TO EXPECT NEXT.
THIS.
I HATE THIS.
THIS IS HIS GRAND DESIGN, NOT MINE.
MADNESS. DESTRUCTION. SLAUGHTER. AND DARKSEID ITS ARCHITECT.
DO WHAT YOU CAN, WONDER WOMAN, WE'LL DO THE SAME.

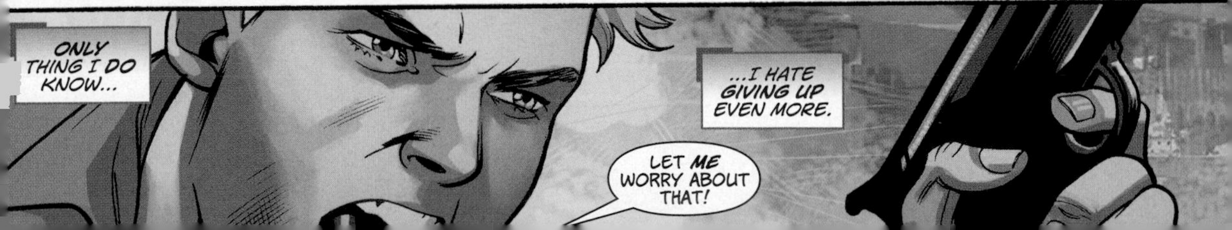

ONLY THING I DO KNOW...
...I HATE GIVING UP EVEN MORE.
LET ME WORRY ABOUT THAT!

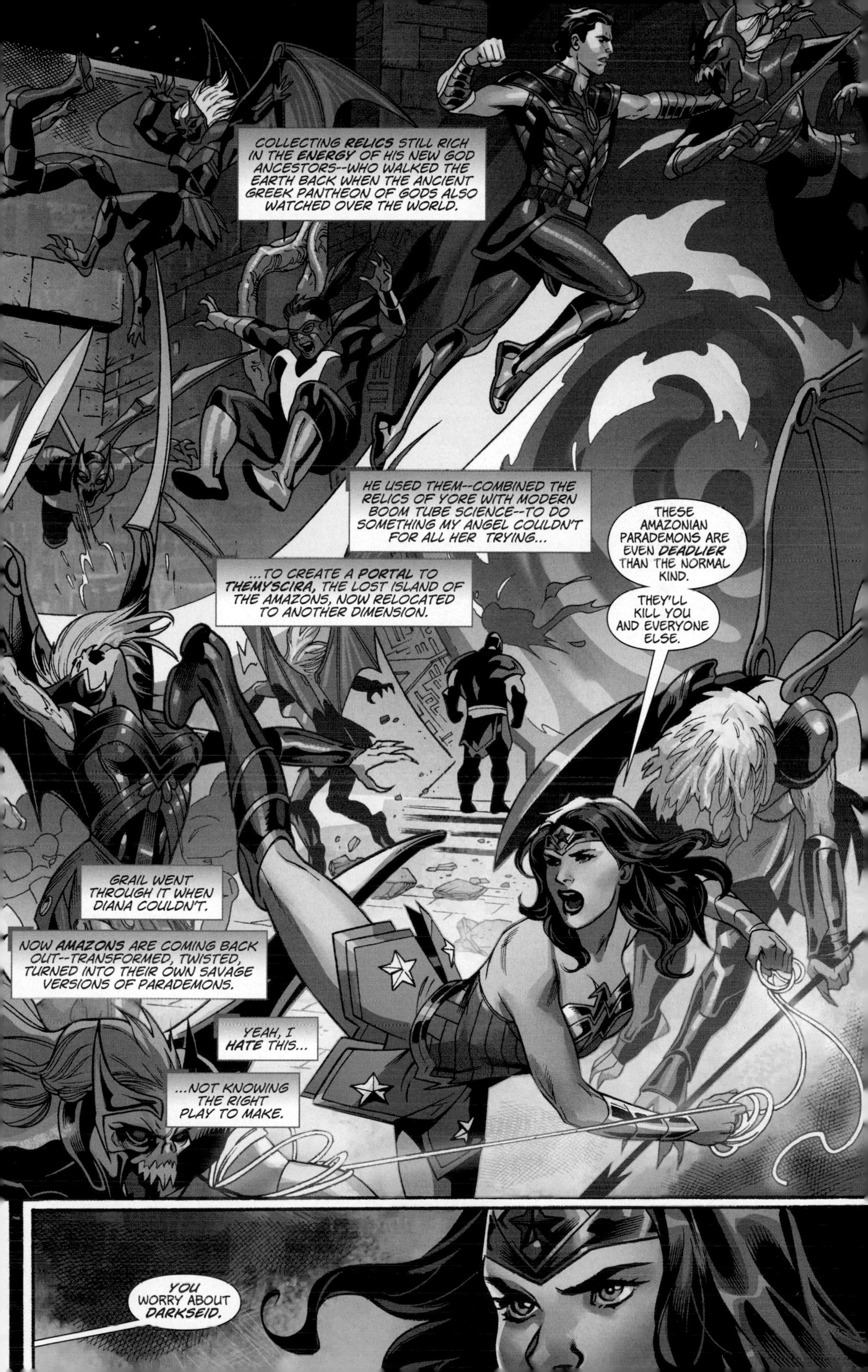
COLLECTING RELICS STILL RICH IN THE ENERGY OF HIS NEW GOD ANCESTORS--WHO WALKED THE EARTH BACK WHEN THE ANCIENT GREEK PANTHEON OF GODS ALSO WATCHED OVER THE WORLD.
HE USED THEM--COMBINED THE RELICS OF YORE WITH MODERN BOOM TUBE SCIENCE--TO DO SOMETHING MY ANGEL COULDN'T FOR ALL HER TRYING...
...TO CREATE A PORTAL TO THEMYSCIRA, THE LOST ISLAND OF THE AMAZONS, NOW RELOCATED TO ANOTHER DIMENSION.
THESE AMAZONIAN PARADEMONS ARE EVEN DEADLIER THAN THE NORMAL KIND.
THEY'LL KILL YOU AND EVERYONE ELSE.
GRAIL WENT THROUGH IT WHEN DIANA COULDN'T.
NOW AMAZONS ARE COMING BACK OUT--TRANSFORMED, TWISTED, TURNED INTO THEIR OWN SAVAGE VERSIONS OF PARADEMONS.
YEAH, I HATE THIS...
...NOT KNOWING THE RIGHT PLAY TO MAKE.
YOU WORRY ABOUT DARKSEID.

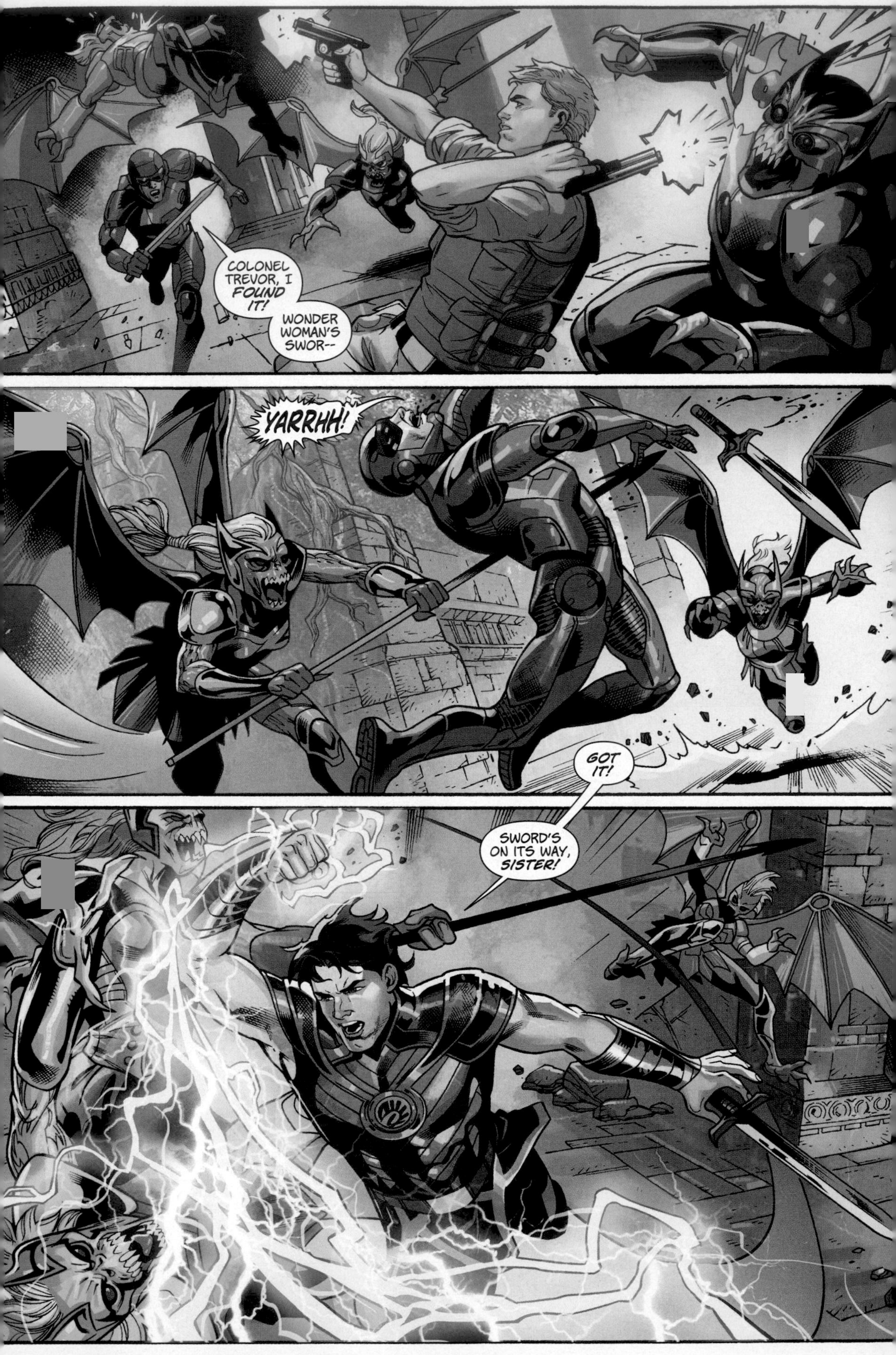
COLONEL TREVOR, I FOUND IT!
WONDER WOMAN'S SWOR--
YARRHH!
GOT IT!
SWORD'S ON ITS WAY, SISTER!

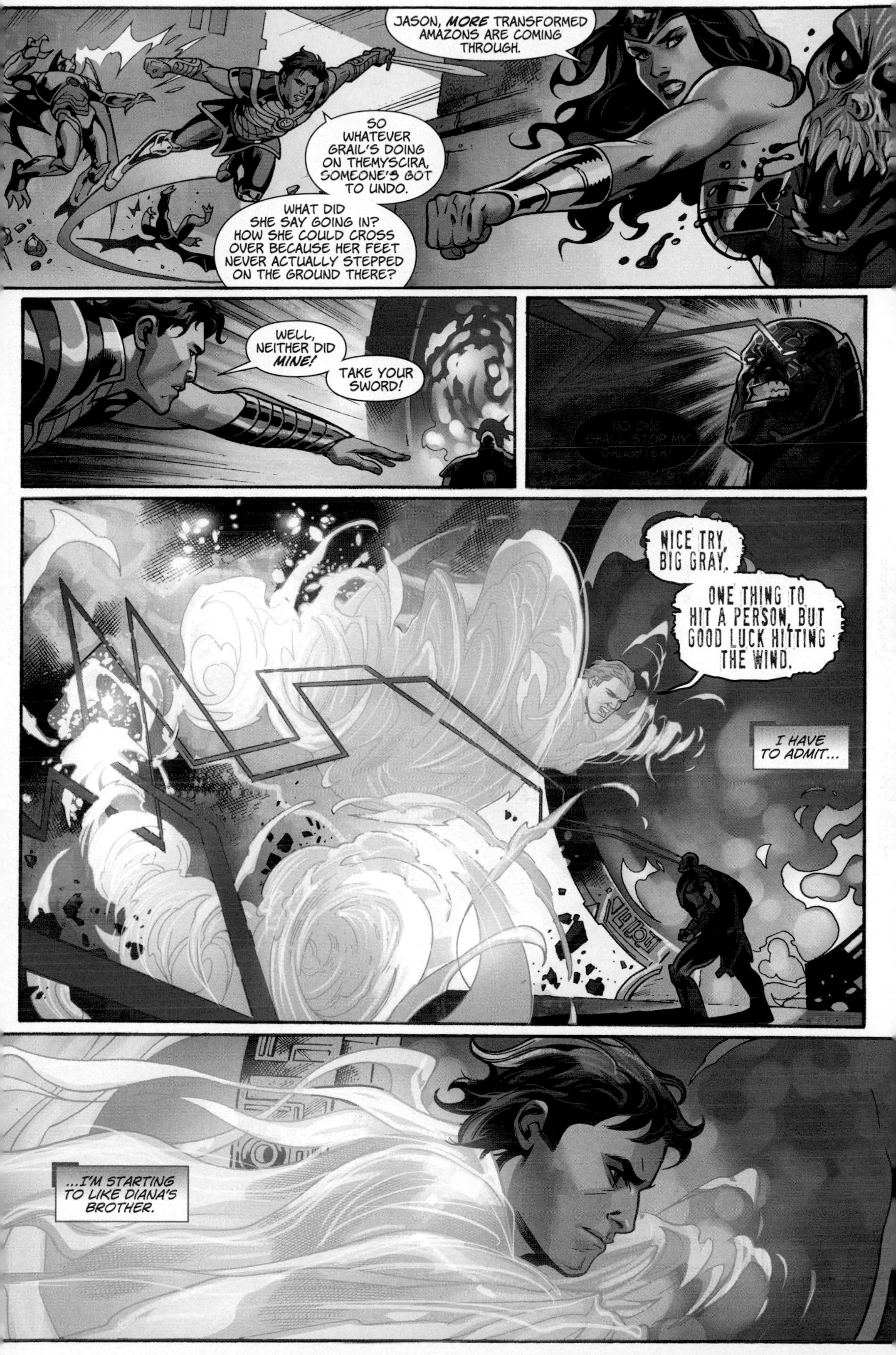

JASON, MORE TRANSFORMED AMAZONS ARE COMING THROUGH.
SO WHATEVER GRAIL'S DOING ON THEMYSCIRA, SOMEONE'S GOT TO UNDO.
WHAT DID SHE SAY GOING IN? HOW SHE COULD CROSS OVER BECAUSE HER FEET NEVER ACTUALLY STEPPED ON THE GROUND THERE?
WELL, NEITHER DID MINE!
TAKE YOUR SWORD!
NO ONE SHALL STOP MY DAUGHTER!
NICE TRY, BIG GRAY.
ONE THING TO HIT A PERSON, BUT GOOD LUCK HITTING THE WIND.
I HAVE TO ADMIT...
...I'M STARTING TO LIKE DIANA'S BROTHER.

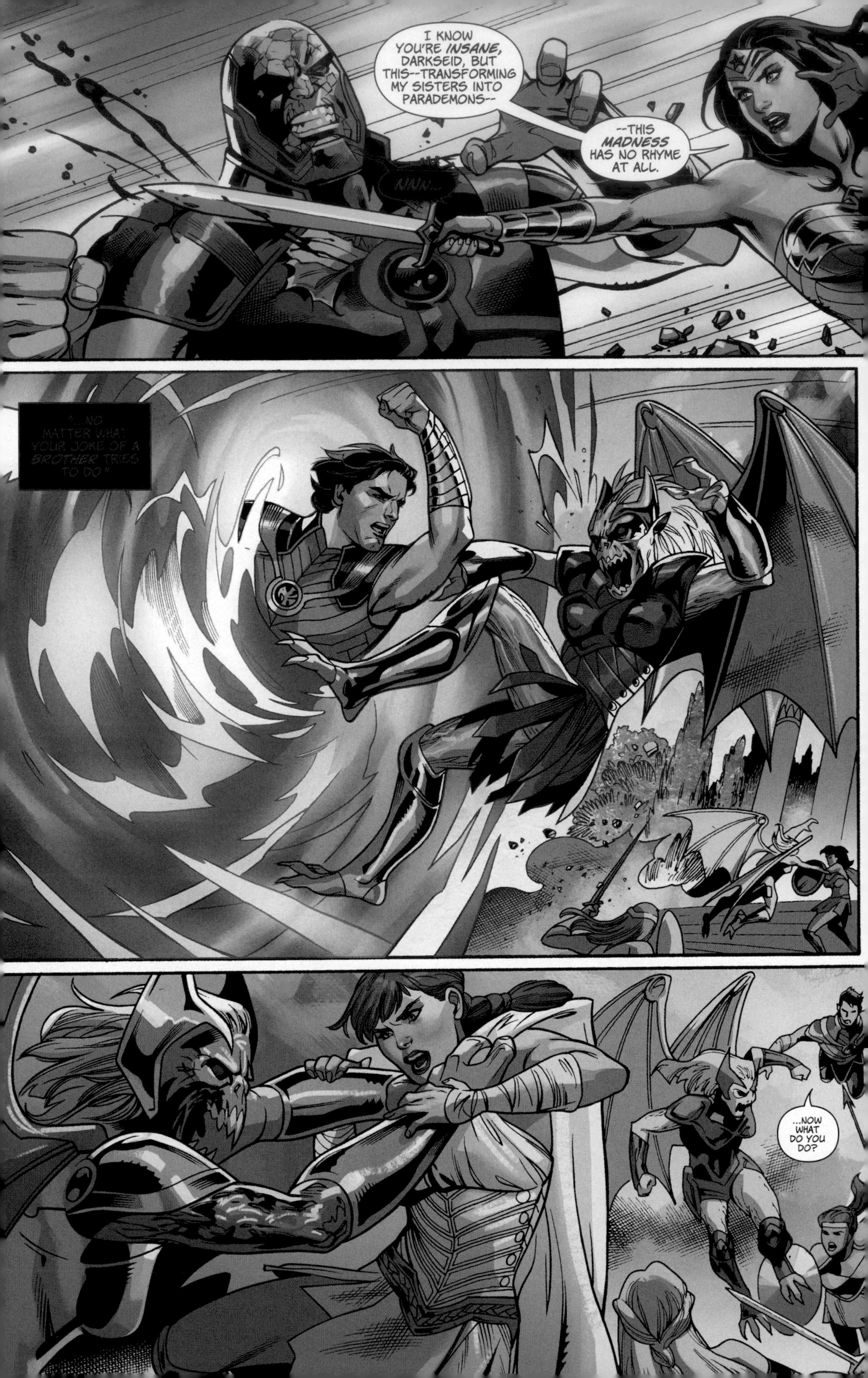
I KNOW YOU'RE *INSANE,* DARKSEID, BUT THIS--TRANSFORMING MY SISTERS INTO PARADEMONS--
--THIS *MADNESS* HAS NO RHYME AT ALL.
"...NO MATTER WHAT YOUR JOKE OF A *BROTHER* TRIES TO DO."
...NOW WHAT DO YOU DO?

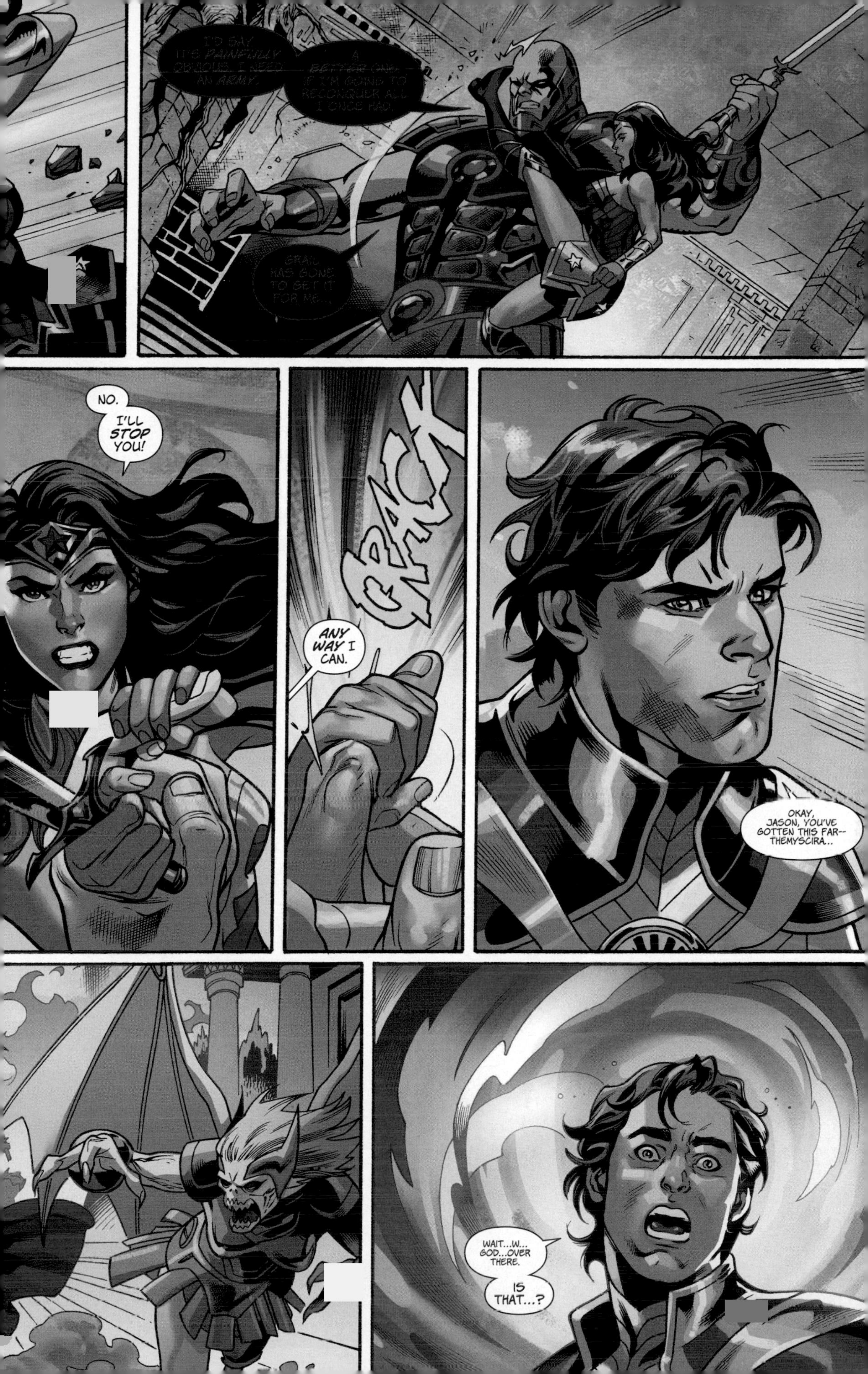
I'D SAY IT'S PAINFULLY OBVIOUS. I NEED AN ARMY.
A BETTER ONE, IF I'M GOING TO RECONQUER ALL I ONCE HAD.
GRAIL HAS GONE TO GET IT FOR ME...
NO.
I'LL STOP YOU!
CRACK
ANY WAY I CAN.
OKAY, JASON, YOU'VE GOTTEN THIS FAR--THEMYSCIRA...
WAIT...W... GOD...OVER THERE.
IS THAT...?

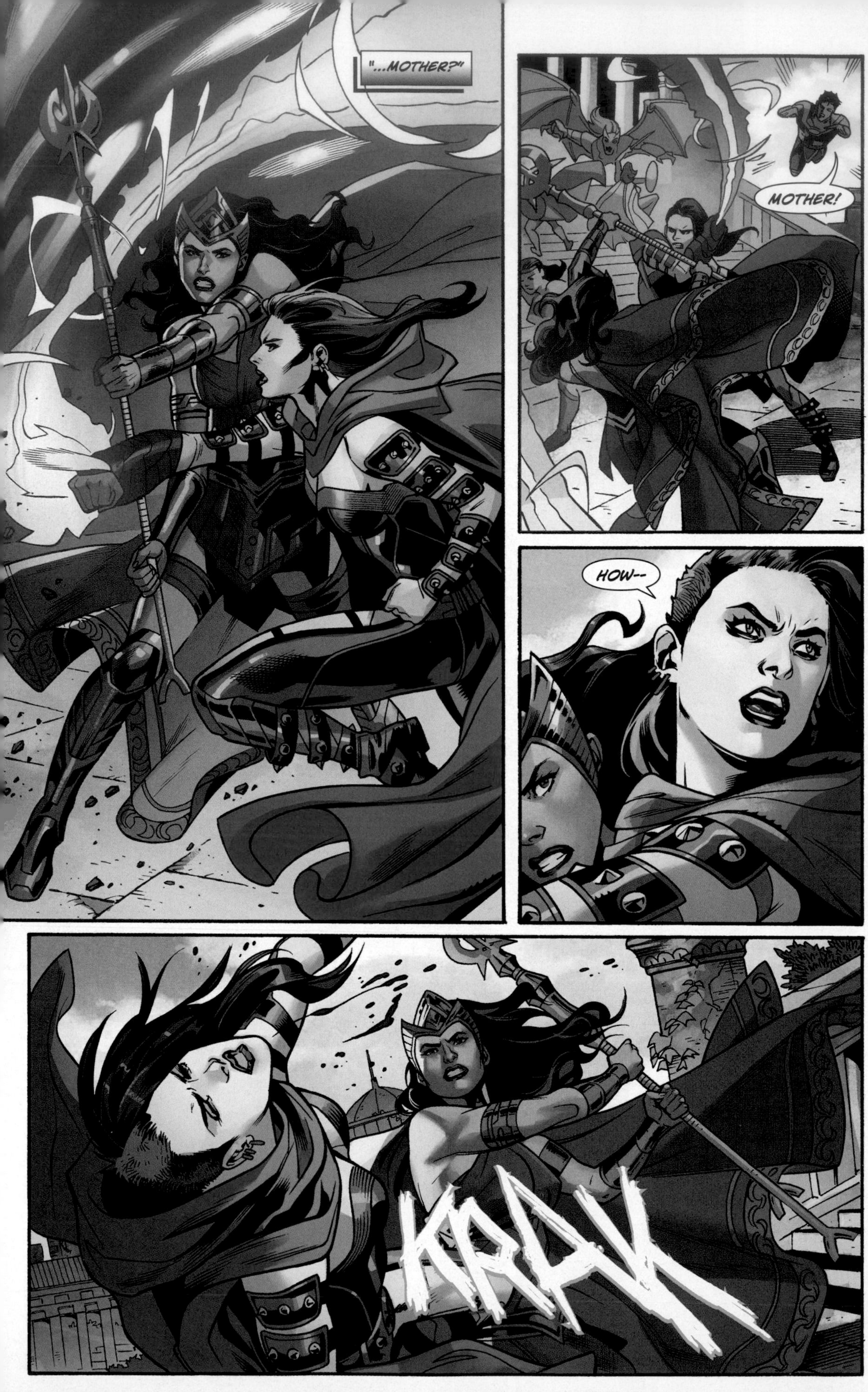
"...MOTHER?"
MOTHER!
HOW--
KRAK

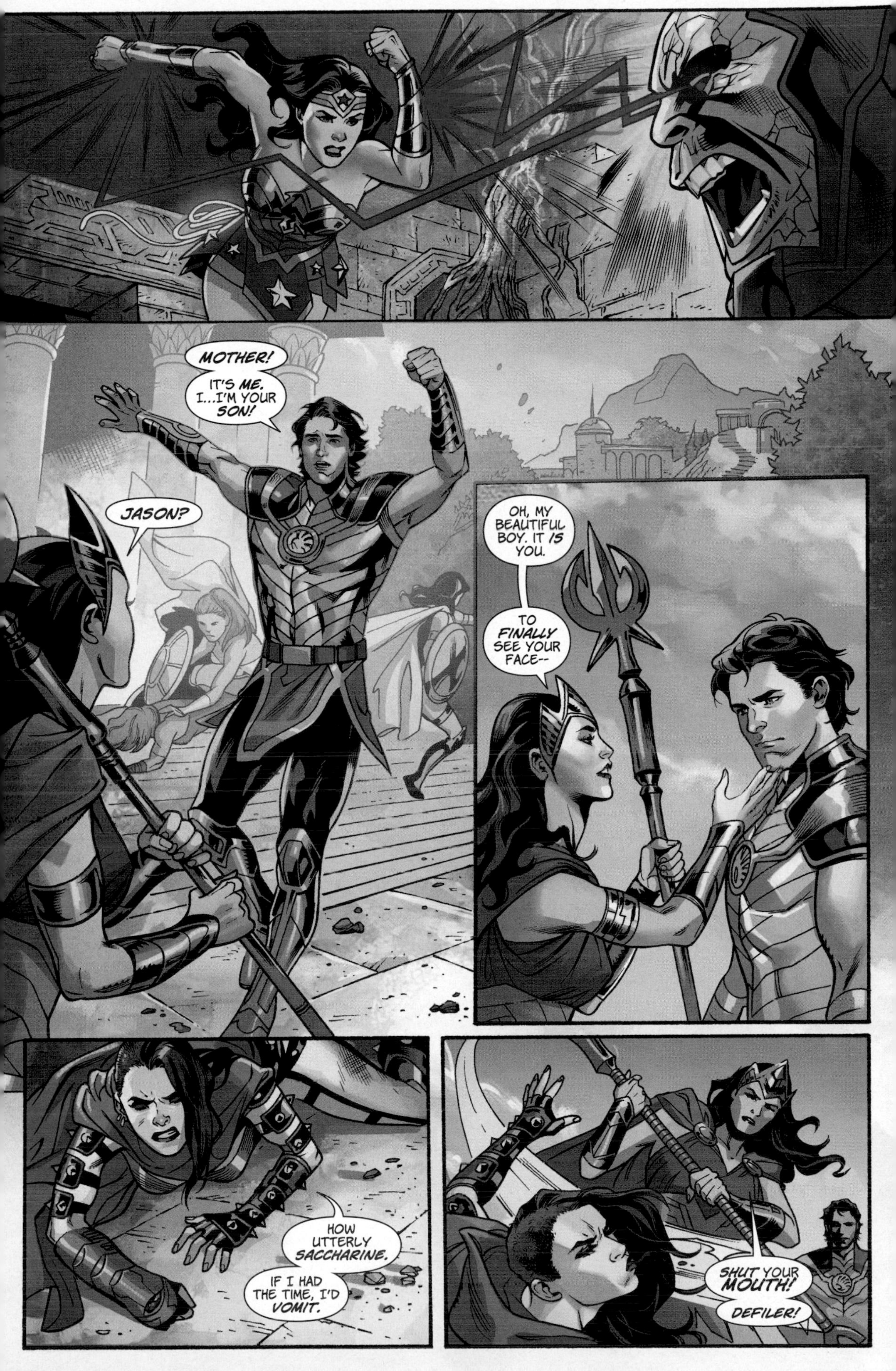
MOTHER!
IT'S ME. I...I'M YOUR SON!
JASON?
OH, MY BEAUTIFUL BOY. IT IS YOU.
TO FINALLY SEE YOUR FACE--
HOW UTTERLY SACCHARINE.
IF I HAD THE TIME, I'D VOMIT.
SHUT YOUR MOUTH!
DEFILER!

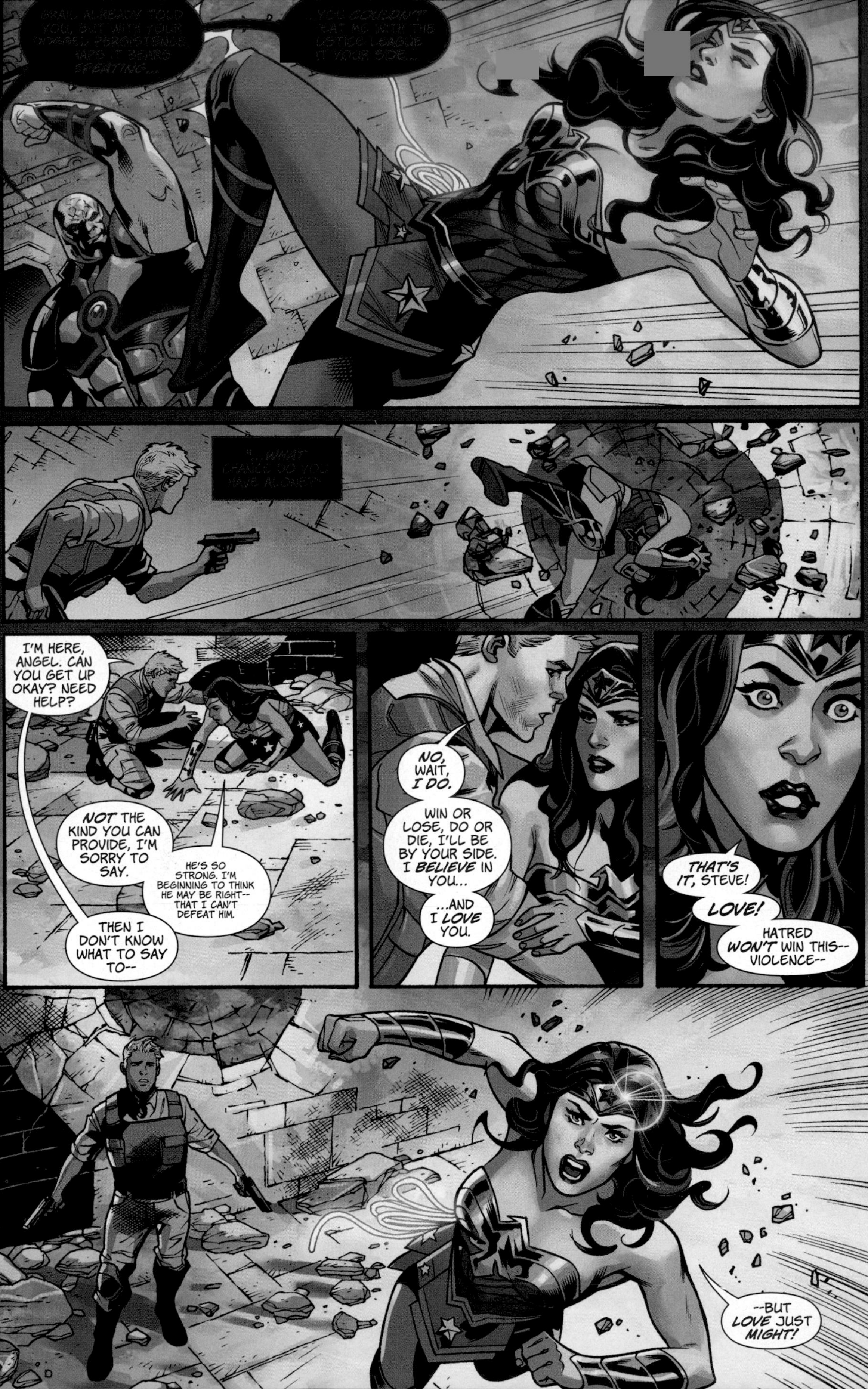

GRAIL ALREADY TOLD YOU, BUT WITH YOUR DOGGED PERSISTENCE, [redacted] APS IT BEARS [redacted] EPEATING...
...YOU COULDN'T [redacted] EAT ME WITH THE [redacted] USTICE LEAGUE [redacted] T YOUR SIDE...
"...WHAT CHANCE DO YOU HAVE ALONE?"
I'M HERE, ANGEL. CAN YOU GET UP OKAY? NEED HELP?
NOT THE KIND YOU CAN PROVIDE, I'M SORRY TO SAY.
HE'S SO STRONG. I'M BEGINNING TO THINK HE MAY BE RIGHT-- THAT I CAN'T DEFEAT HIM.
THEN I DON'T KNOW WHAT TO SAY TO--
NO, WAIT, I DO.
WIN OR LOSE, DO OR DIE, I'LL BE BY YOUR SIDE. I BELIEVE IN YOU...
...AND I LOVE YOU.
THAT'S IT, STEVE!
LOVE!
HATRED WON'T WIN THIS-- VIOLENCE--
--BUT LOVE JUST MIGHT!

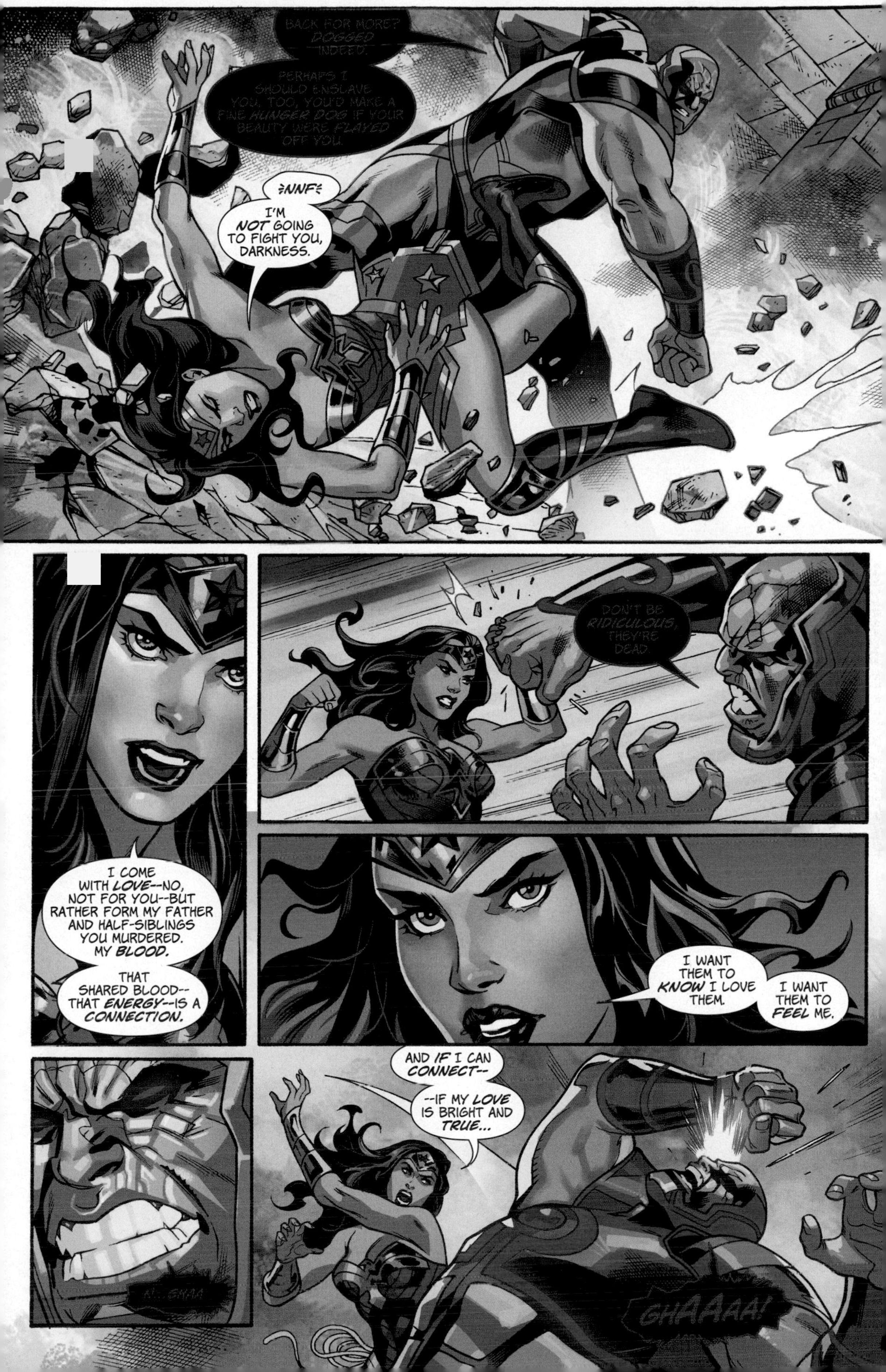
BACK FOR MORE? DOGGED INDEED.
PERHAPS I SHOULD ENSLAVE YOU, TOO. YOU'D MAKE A FINE HUNGER DOG IF YOUR BEAUTY WERE FLAYED OFF YOU.
NNF
I'M NOT GOING TO FIGHT YOU, DARKNESS.
I COME WITH LOVE--NO, NOT FOR YOU--BUT RATHER FORM MY FATHER AND HALF-SIBLINGS YOU MURDERED. MY BLOOD.
THAT SHARED BLOOD--THAT ENERGY--IS A CONNECTION.
DON'T BE RIDICULOUS, THEY'RE DEAD.
I WANT THEM TO KNOW I LOVE THEM.
I WANT THEM TO FEEL ME.
N.. GHAA
AND IF I CAN CONNECT--
--IF MY LOVE IS BRIGHT AND TRUE...
GHAAAA!

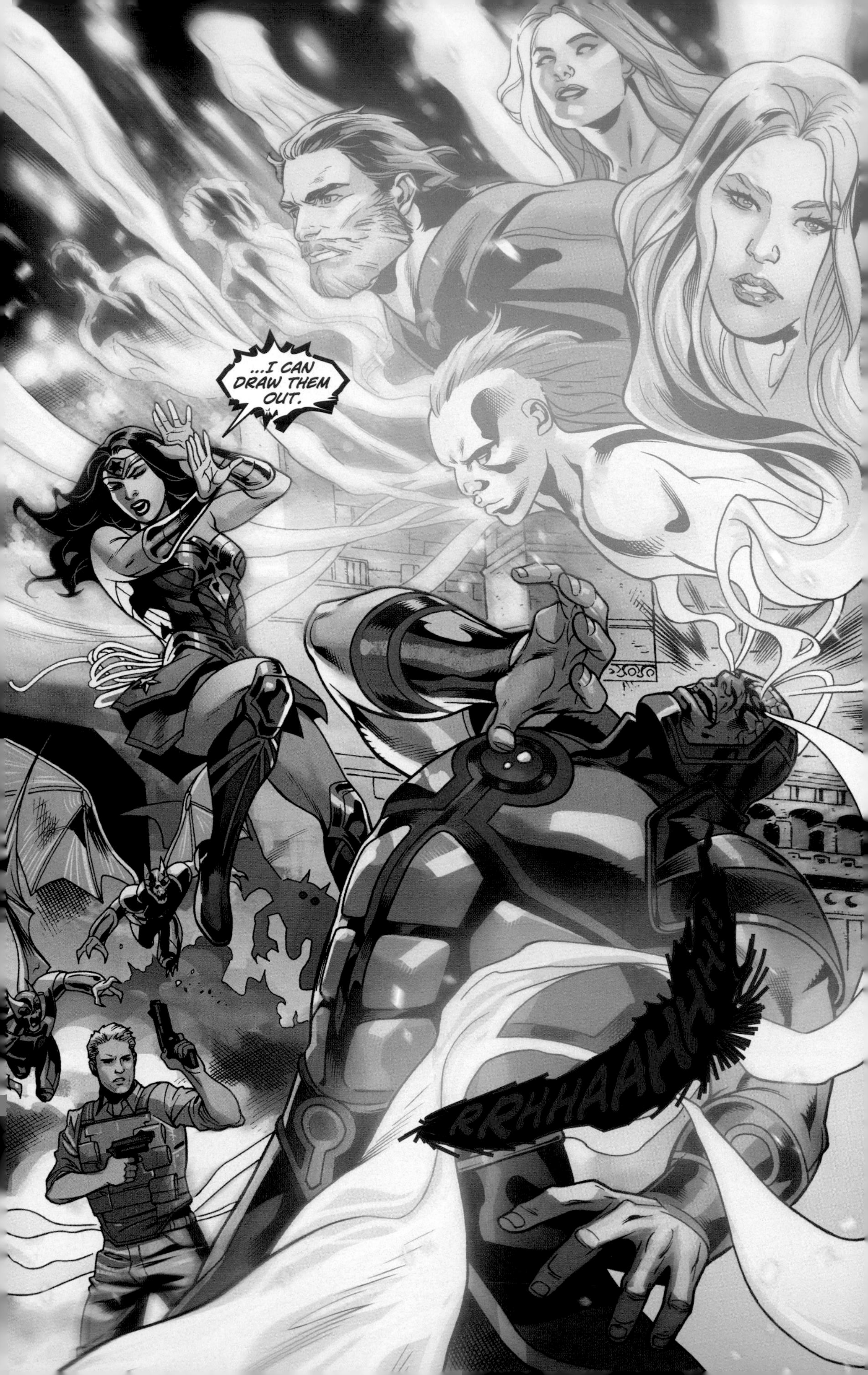
...I CAN DRAW THEM OUT.
RRHHAAAKKK!!

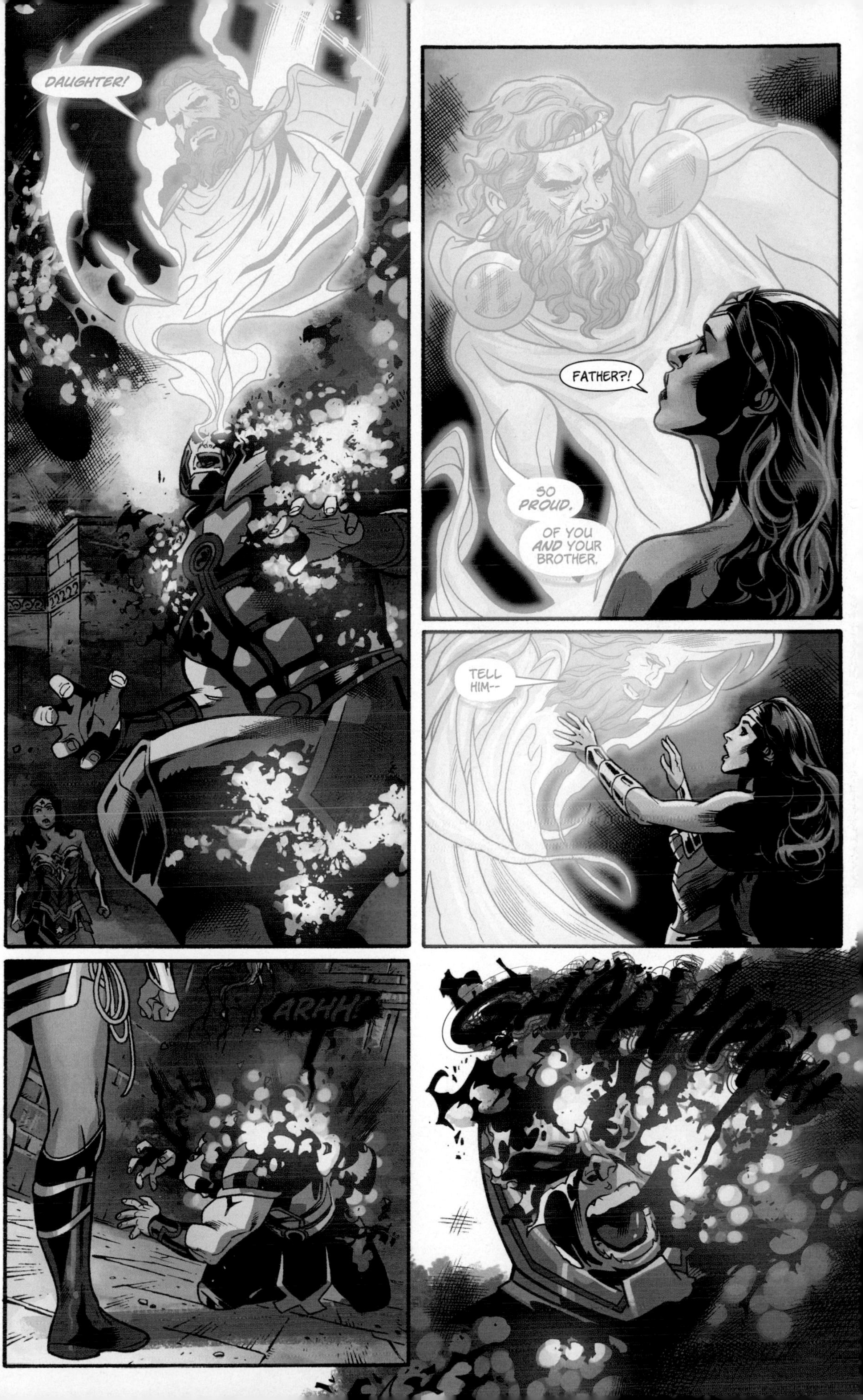
DAUGHTER!
FATHER?!
SO PROUD.
OF YOU AND YOUR BROTHER.
TELL HIM--
ARHH!

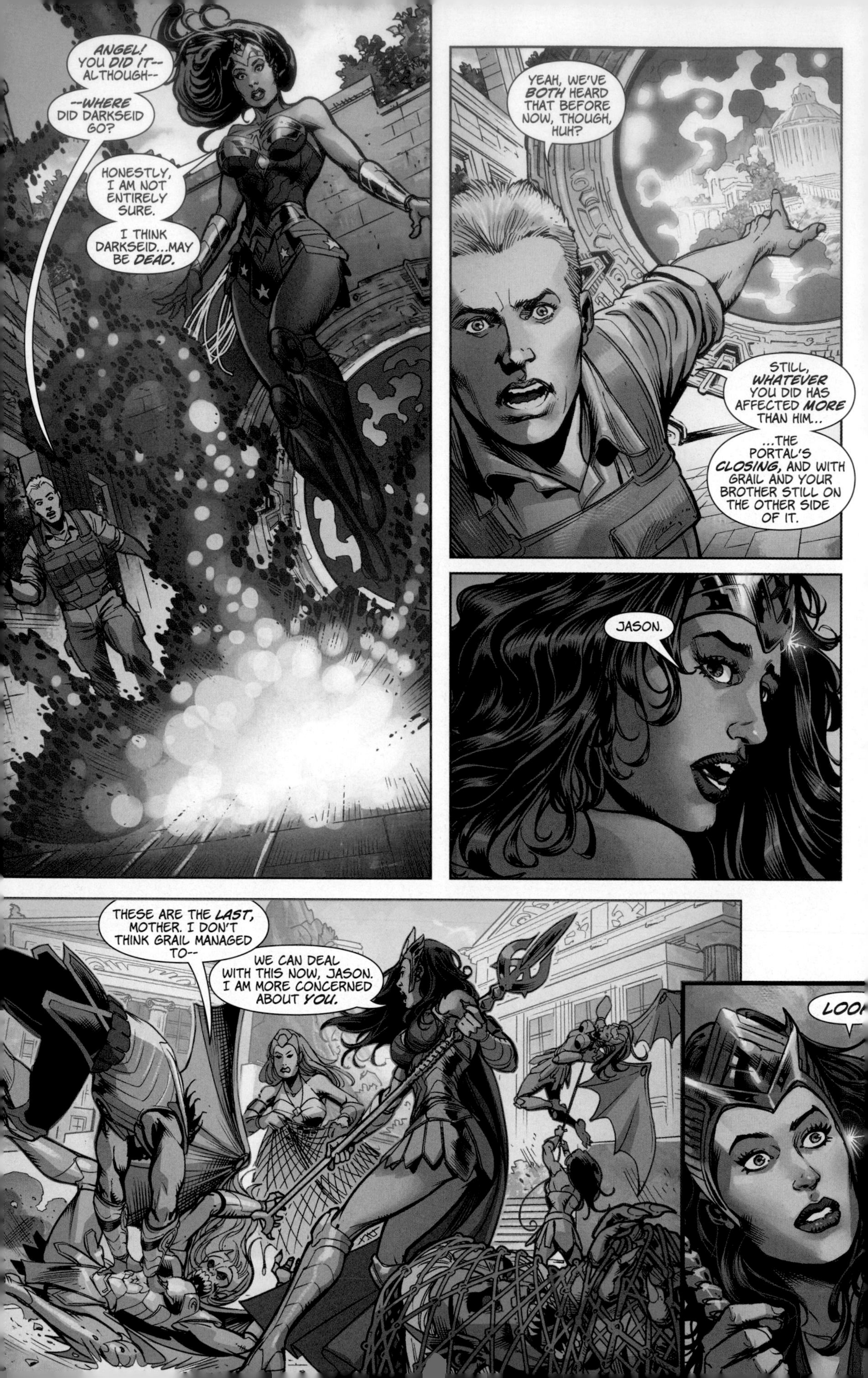
ANGEL! YOU DID IT-- ALTHOUGH--
--WHERE DID DARKSEID GO?
HONESTLY, I AM NOT ENTIRELY SURE.
I THINK DARKSEID...MAY BE DEAD.
YEAH, WE'VE BOTH HEARD THAT BEFORE NOW, THOUGH, HUH?
STILL, WHATEVER YOU DID HAS AFFECTED MORE THAN HIM...
...THE PORTAL'S CLOSING, AND WITH GRAIL AND YOUR BROTHER STILL ON THE OTHER SIDE OF IT.
JASON.
THESE ARE THE LAST, MOTHER. I DON'T THINK GRAIL MANAGED TO--
WE CAN DEAL WITH THIS NOW, JASON. I AM MORE CONCERNED ABOUT YOU.

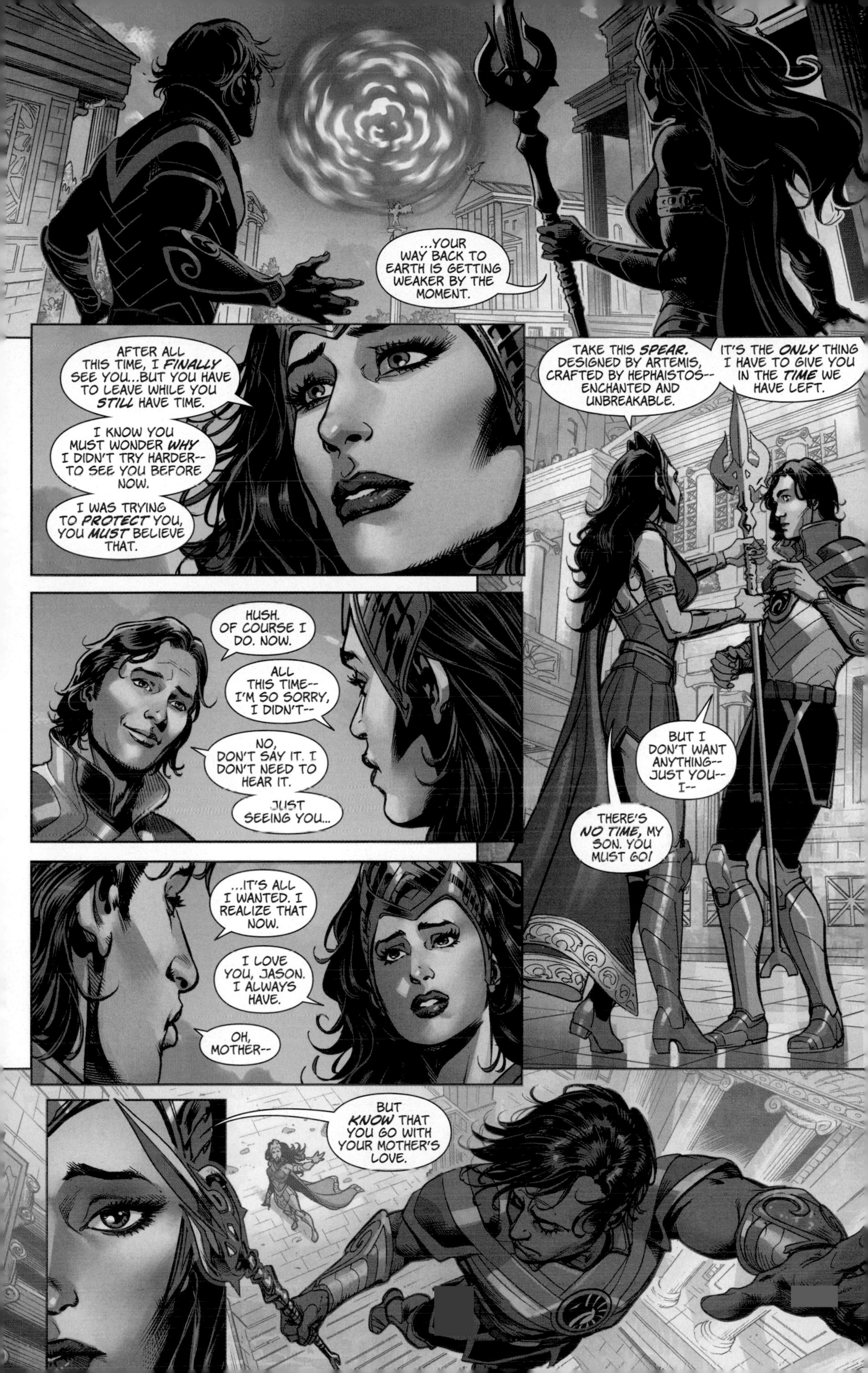
...YOUR WAY BACK TO EARTH IS GETTING WEAKER BY THE MOMENT.
AFTER ALL THIS TIME, I FINALLY SEE YOU...BUT YOU HAVE TO LEAVE WHILE YOU STILL HAVE TIME.
I KNOW YOU MUST WONDER WHY I DIDN'T TRY HARDER-- TO SEE YOU BEFORE NOW.
I WAS TRYING TO PROTECT YOU, YOU MUST BELIEVE THAT.
HUSH. OF COURSE I DO. NOW.
ALL THIS TIME-- I'M SO SORRY, I DIDN'T--
NO, DON'T SAY IT. I DON'T NEED TO HEAR IT.
JUST SEEING YOU...
...IT'S ALL I WANTED. I REALIZE THAT NOW.
I LOVE YOU, JASON. I ALWAYS HAVE.
OH, MOTHER--
TAKE THIS SPEAR. DESIGNED BY ARTEMIS, CRAFTED BY HEPHAISTOS-- ENCHANTED AND UNBREAKABLE.
IT'S THE ONLY THING I HAVE TO GIVE YOU IN THE TIME WE HAVE LEFT.
BUT I DON'T WANT ANYTHING-- JUST YOU-- I--
THERE'S NO TIME, MY SON. YOU MUST GO!
BUT KNOW THAT YOU GO WITH YOUR MOTHER'S LOVE.

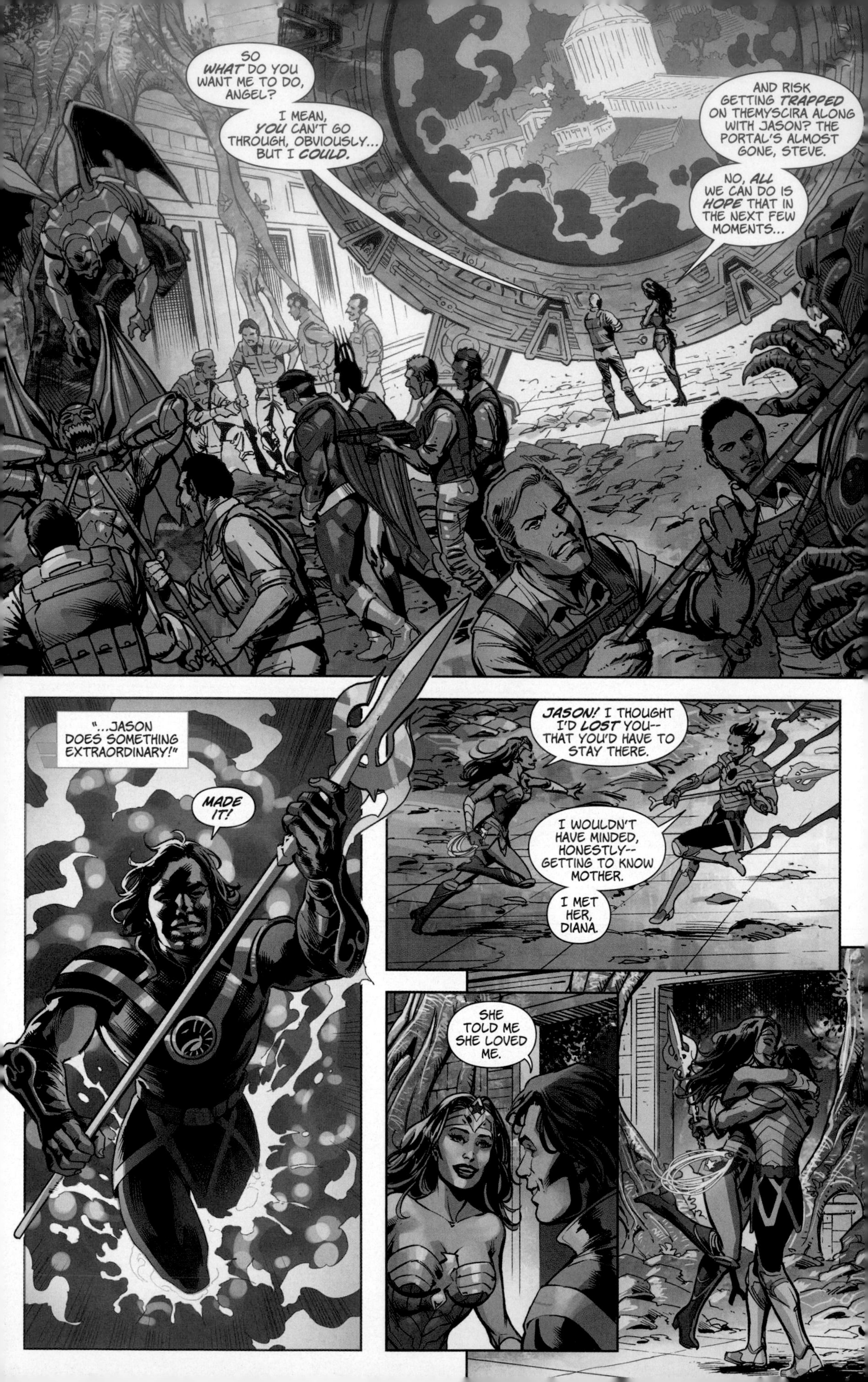

SO WHAT DO YOU WANT ME TO DO, ANGEL?
I MEAN, YOU CAN'T GO THROUGH, OBVIOUSLY... BUT I COULD.
AND RISK GETTING TRAPPED ON THEMYSCIRA ALONG WITH JASON? THE PORTAL'S ALMOST GONE, STEVE.
NO, ALL WE CAN DO IS HOPE THAT IN THE NEXT FEW MOMENTS...
"...JASON DOES SOMETHING EXTRAORDINARY!"
MADE IT!
JASON! I THOUGHT I'D LOST YOU--THAT YOU'D HAVE TO STAY THERE.
I WOULDN'T HAVE MINDED, HONESTLY--GETTING TO KNOW MOTHER.
I MET HER, DIANA.
SHE TOLD ME SHE LOVED ME.

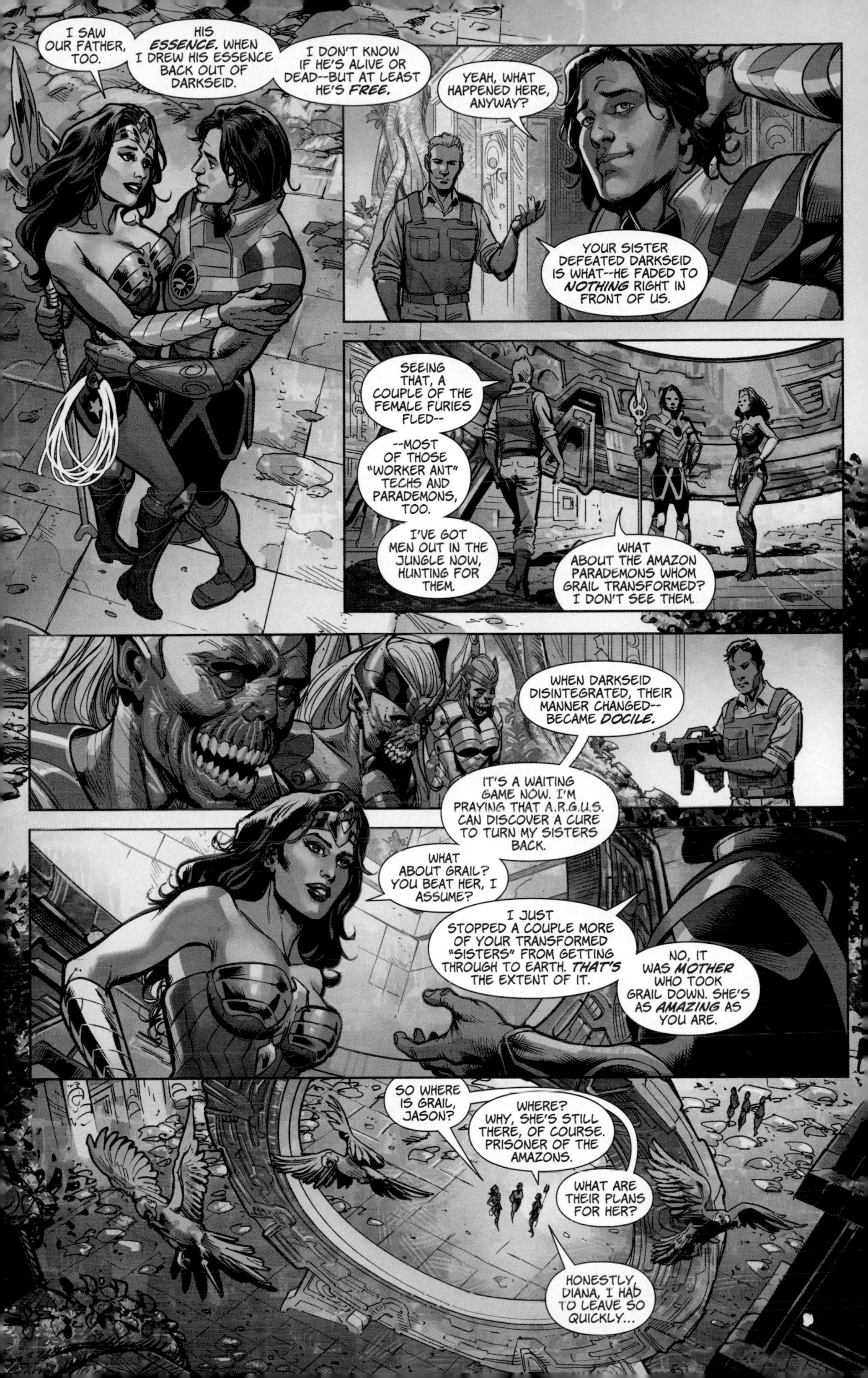
I SAW OUR FATHER, TOO.
HIS *ESSENCE.* WHEN I DREW HIS ESSENCE BACK OUT OF DARKSEID.
I DON'T KNOW IF HE'S ALIVE OR DEAD--BUT AT LEAST HE'S *FREE.*
YEAH, WHAT HAPPENED HERE, ANYWAY?
YOUR SISTER DEFEATED DARKSEID IS WHAT--HE FADED TO *NOTHING* RIGHT IN FRONT OF US.
SEEING THAT, A COUPLE OF THE FEMALE FURIES FLED--
--MOST OF THOSE "WORKER ANT" TECHS AND PARADEMONS, TOO.
I'VE GOT MEN OUT IN THE JUNGLE NOW, HUNTING FOR THEM.
WHAT ABOUT THE AMAZON PARADEMONS WHOM GRAIL TRANSFORMED? I DON'T SEE THEM.
WHEN DARKSEID DISINTEGRATED, THEIR MANNER CHANGED--BECAME *DOCILE.*
IT'S A WAITING GAME NOW. I'M PRAYING THAT A.R.G.U.S. CAN DISCOVER A CURE TO TURN MY SISTERS BACK.
WHAT ABOUT GRAIL? YOU BEAT HER, I ASSUME?
I JUST STOPPED A COUPLE MORE OF YOUR TRANSFORMED "SISTERS" FROM GETTING THROUGH TO EARTH. *THAT'S* THE EXTENT OF IT.
NO, IT WAS *MOTHER* WHO TOOK GRAIL DOWN. SHE'S AS *AMAZING* AS YOU ARE.
SO WHERE IS GRAIL, JASON?
WHERE? WHY, SHE'S STILL THERE, OF COURSE. PRISONER OF THE AMAZONS.
WHAT ARE THEIR PLANS FOR HER?
HONESTLY, DIANA, I HAD TO LEAVE SO QUICKLY...

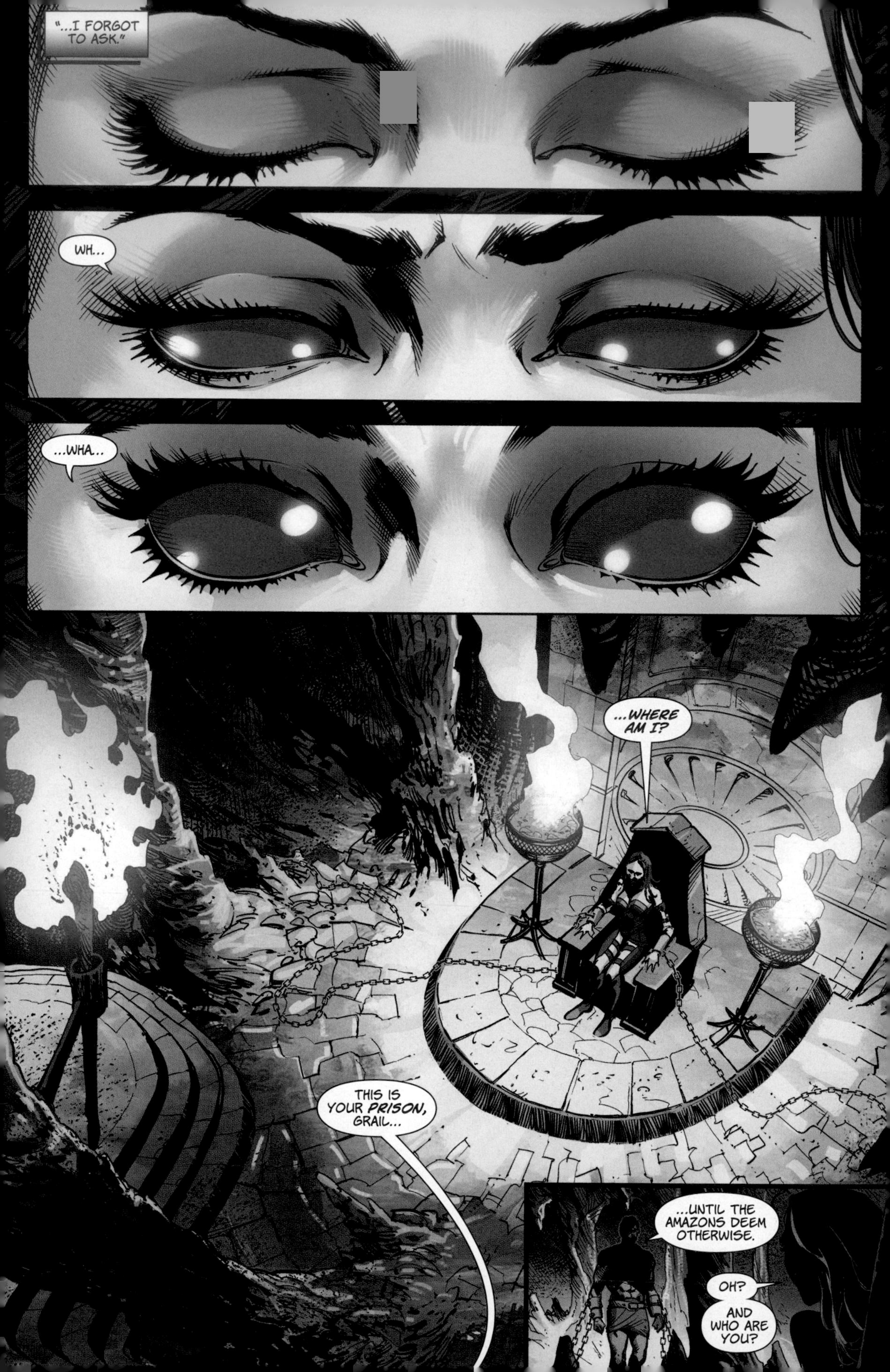
"...I FORGOT TO ASK."
WH...
...WHA...
...WHERE AM I?
THIS IS YOUR PRISON, GRAIL...
...UNTIL THE AMAZONS DEEM OTHERWISE.
OH?
AND WHO ARE YOU?

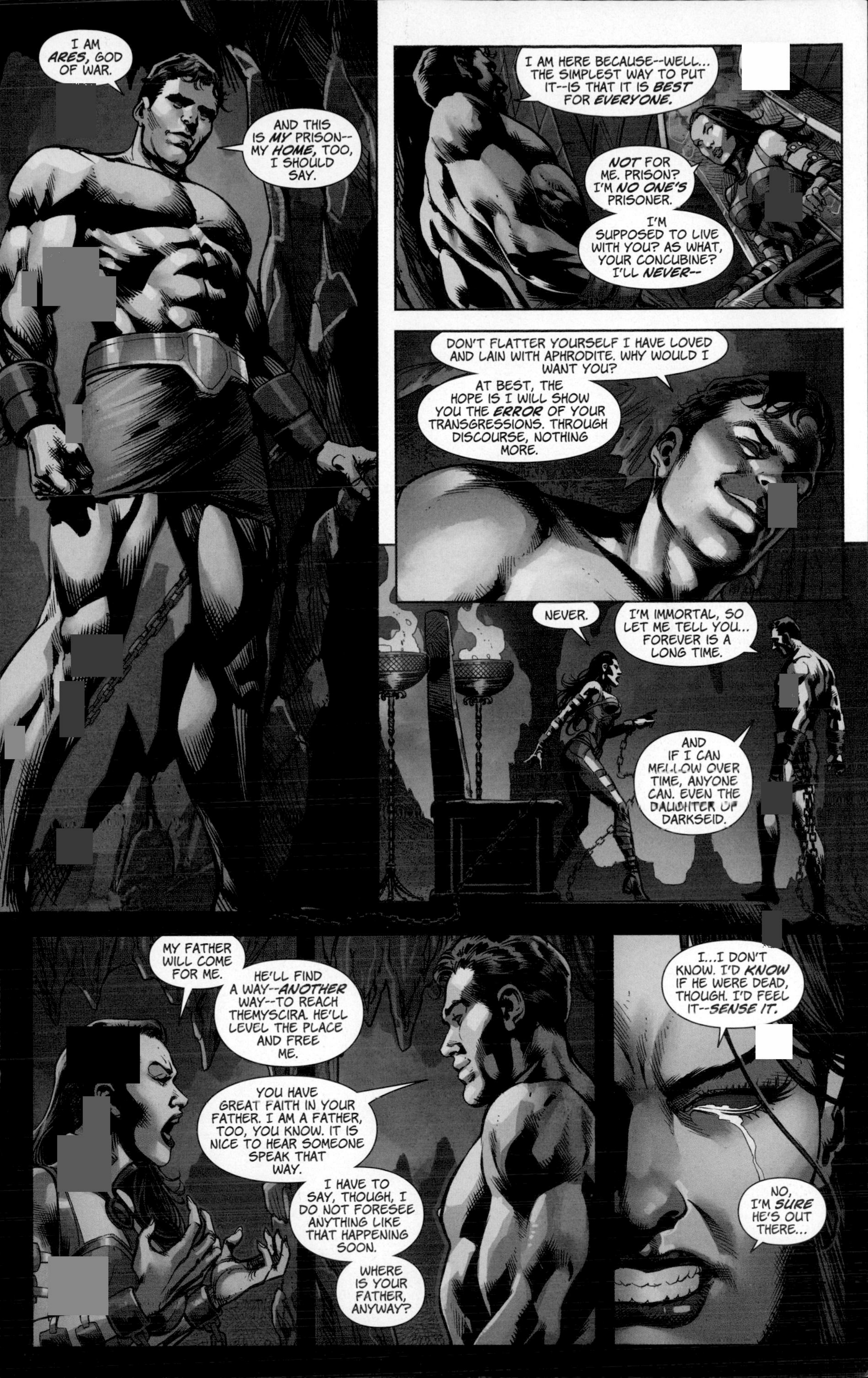

I AM ARES, GOD OF WAR.
AND THIS IS MY PRISON--MY HOME, TOO, I SHOULD SAY.
I AM HERE BECAUSE--WELL... THE SIMPLEST WAY TO PUT IT--IS THAT IT IS BEST FOR EVERYONE.
NOT FOR ME. PRISON? I'M NO ONE'S PRISONER.
I'M SUPPOSED TO LIVE WITH YOU? AS WHAT, YOUR CONCUBINE? I'LL NEVER--
DON'T FLATTER YOURSELF I HAVE LOVED AND LAIN WITH APHRODITE. WHY WOULD I WANT YOU?
AT BEST, THE HOPE IS I WILL SHOW YOU THE ERROR OF YOUR TRANSGRESSIONS. THROUGH DISCOURSE, NOTHING MORE.
NEVER.
I'M IMMORTAL, SO LET ME TELL YOU... FOREVER IS A LONG TIME.
AND IF I CAN MELLOW OVER TIME, ANYONE CAN. EVEN THE DAUGHTER OF DARKSEID.
MY FATHER WILL COME FOR ME.
HE'LL FIND A WAY--ANOTHER WAY--TO REACH THEMYSCIRA. HE'LL LEVEL THE PLACE AND FREE ME.
YOU HAVE GREAT FAITH IN YOUR FATHER. I AM A FATHER, TOO, YOU KNOW. IT IS NICE TO HEAR SOMEONE SPEAK THAT WAY.
I HAVE TO SAY, THOUGH, I DO NOT FORESEE ANYTHING LIKE THAT HAPPENING SOON.
WHERE IS YOUR FATHER, ANYWAY?
I...I DON'T KNOW. I'D KNOW IF HE WERE DEAD, THOUGH. I'D FEEL IT--SENSE IT.
NO, I'M SURE HE'S OUT THERE...

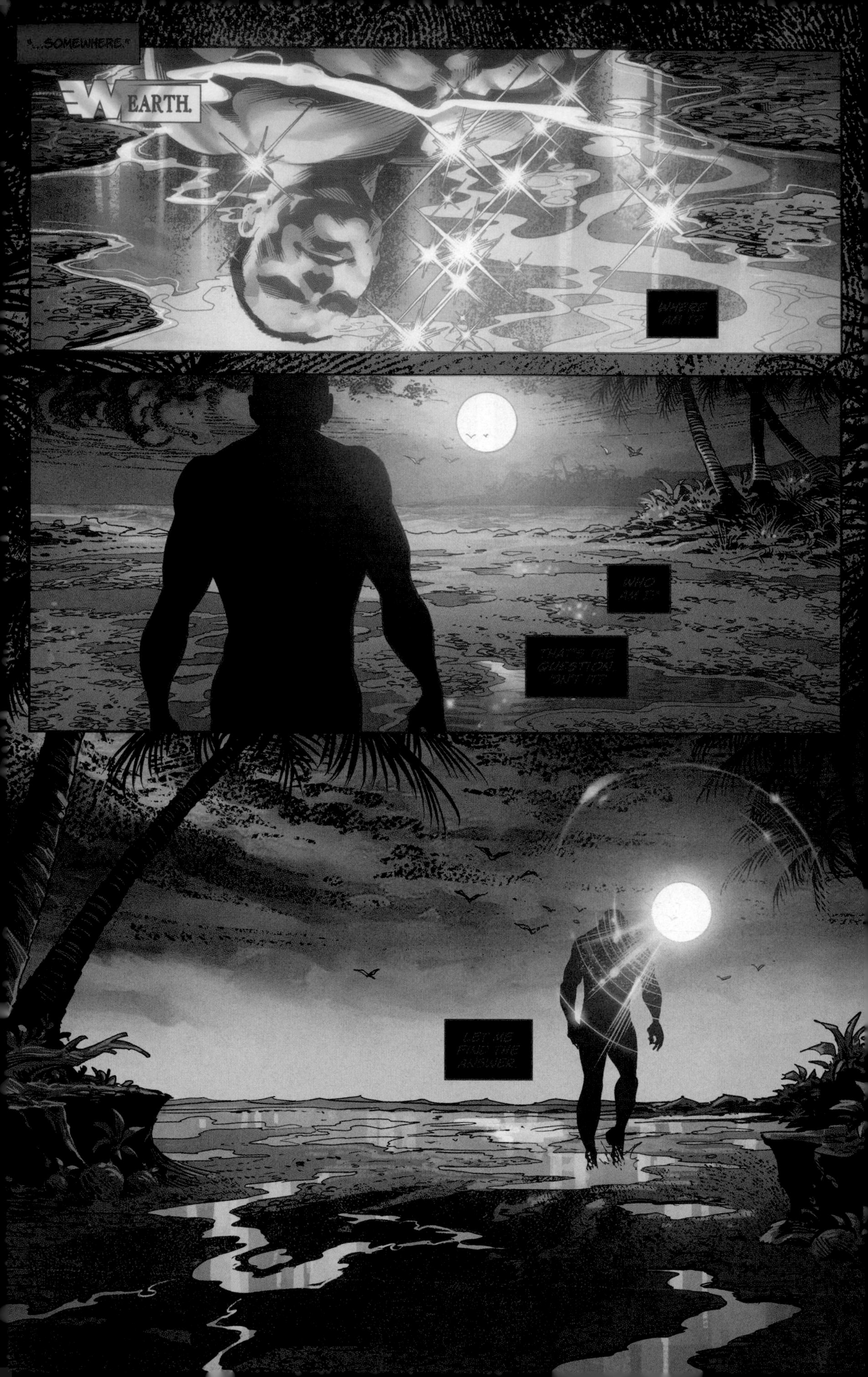
"...SOMEWHERE."
EARTH.
WHERE AM I?
WHO AM I?
THAT'S THE QUESTION, ISN'T IT?
LET ME FIND THE ANSWER.

WONDER WOMAN

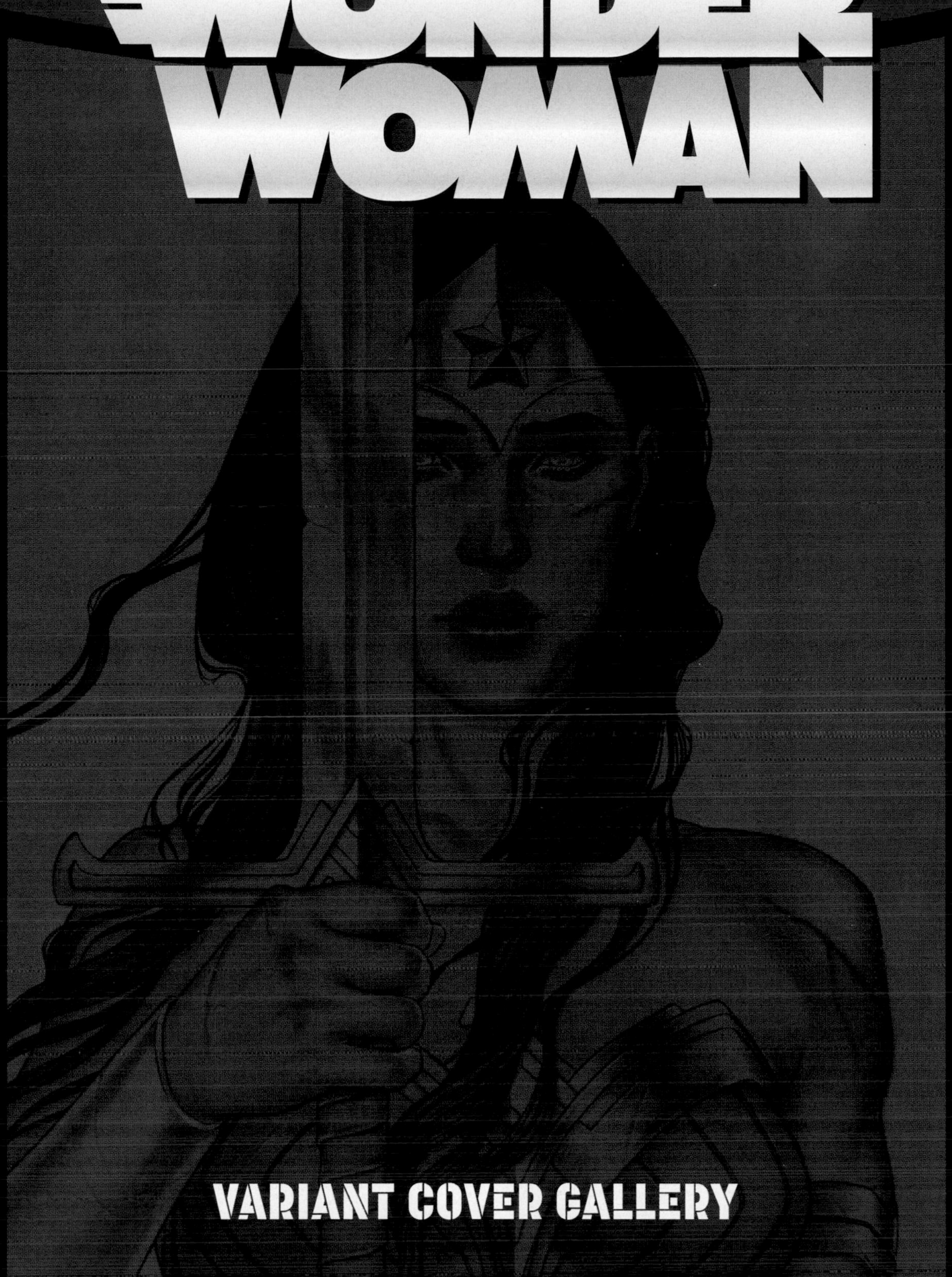

VARIANT COVER GALLERY

WONDER WOMAN #38 variant cover by JENNY FRISON

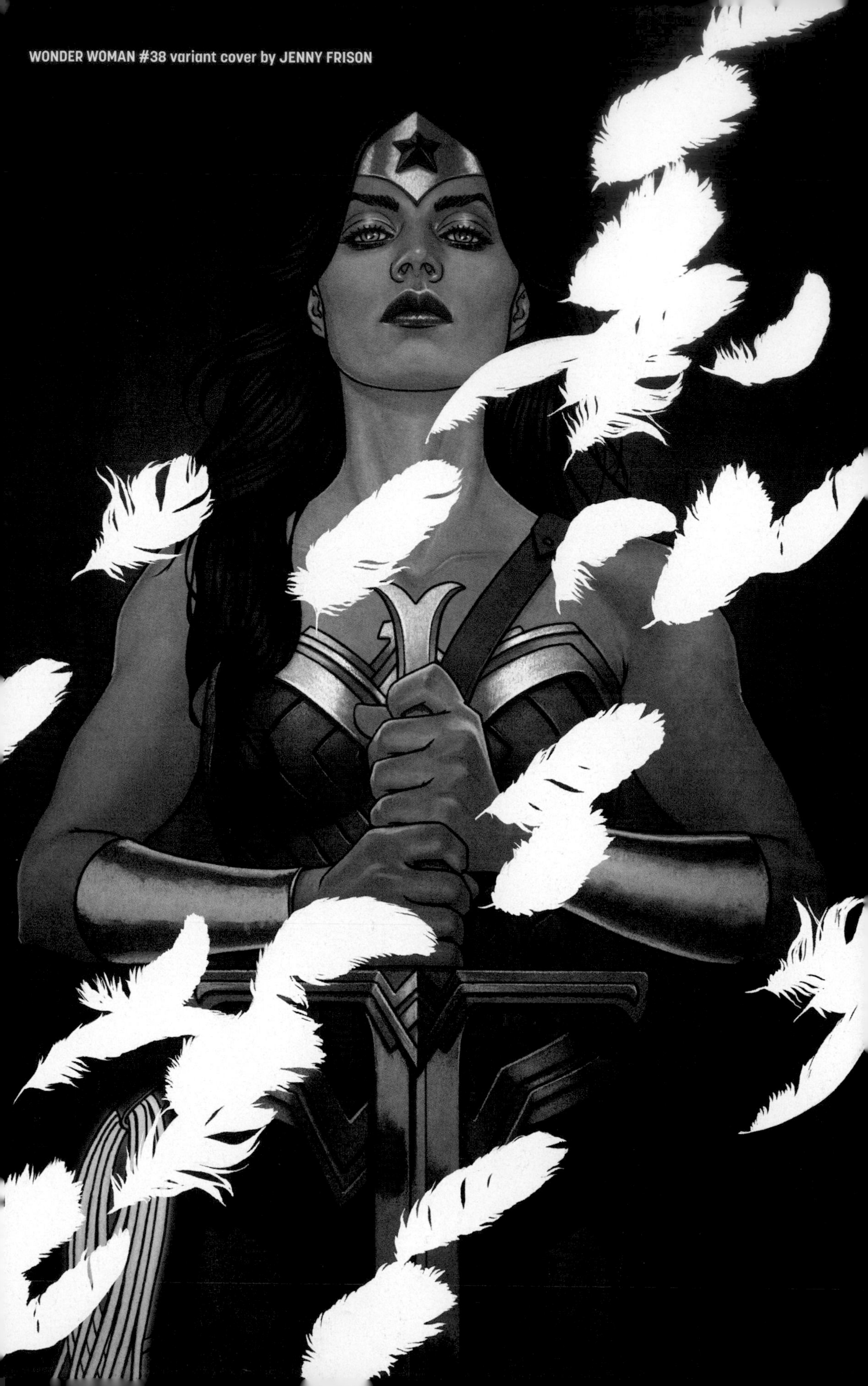

WONDER WOMAN #39 variant cover by JENNY FRISON

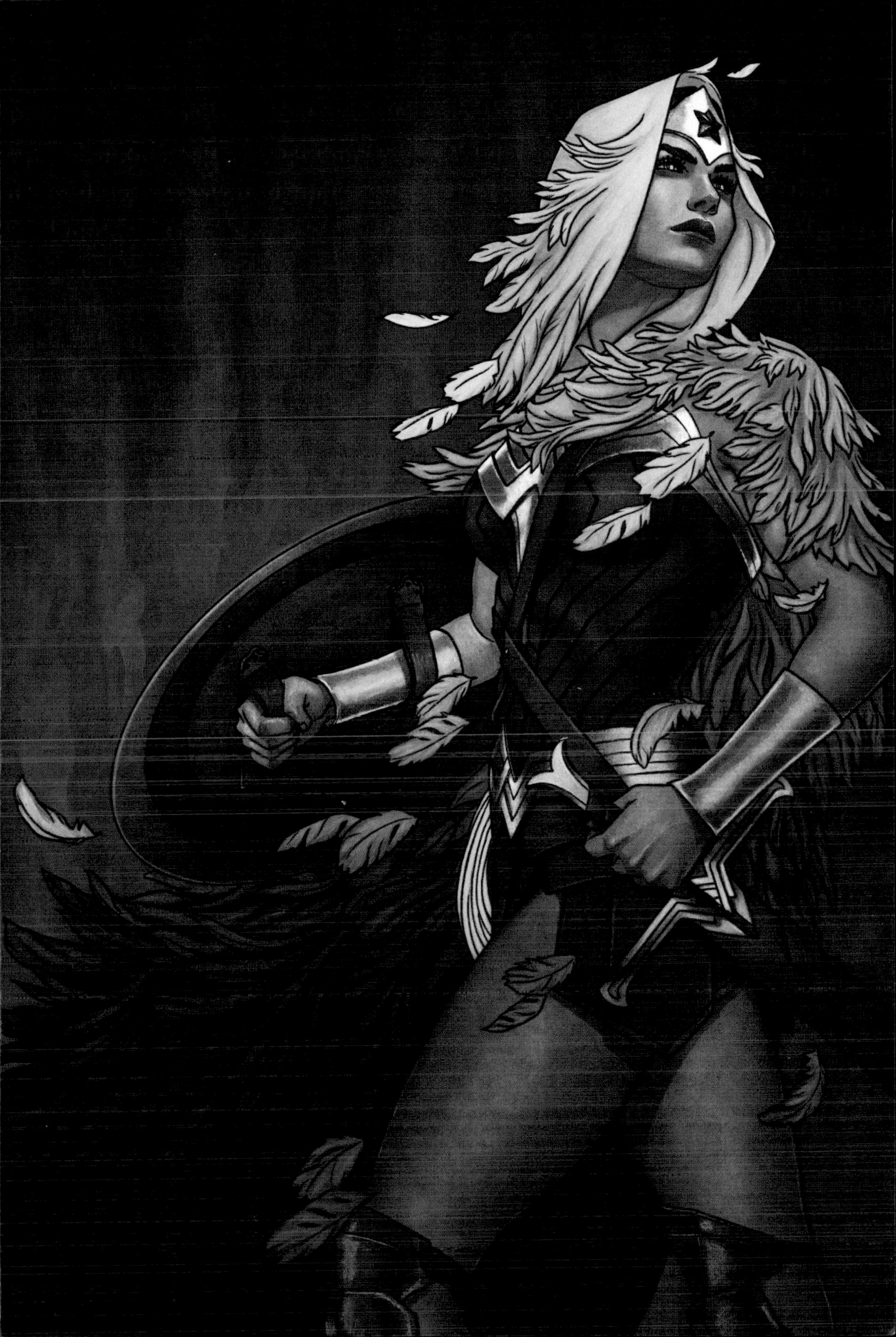

WONDER WOMAN #40 variant cover by JENNY FRISON

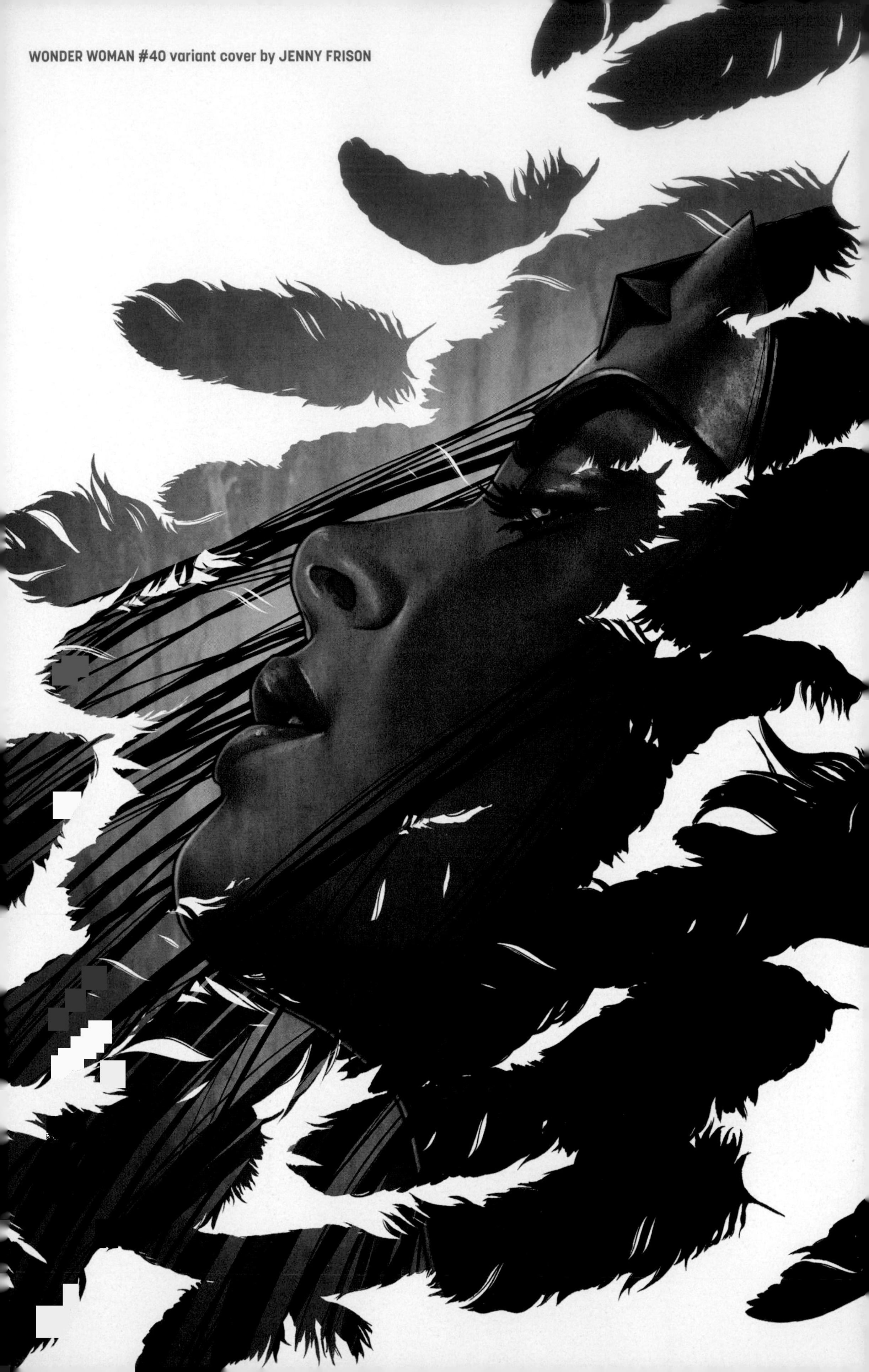

WONDER WOMAN #41 variant cover by JENNY FRISON

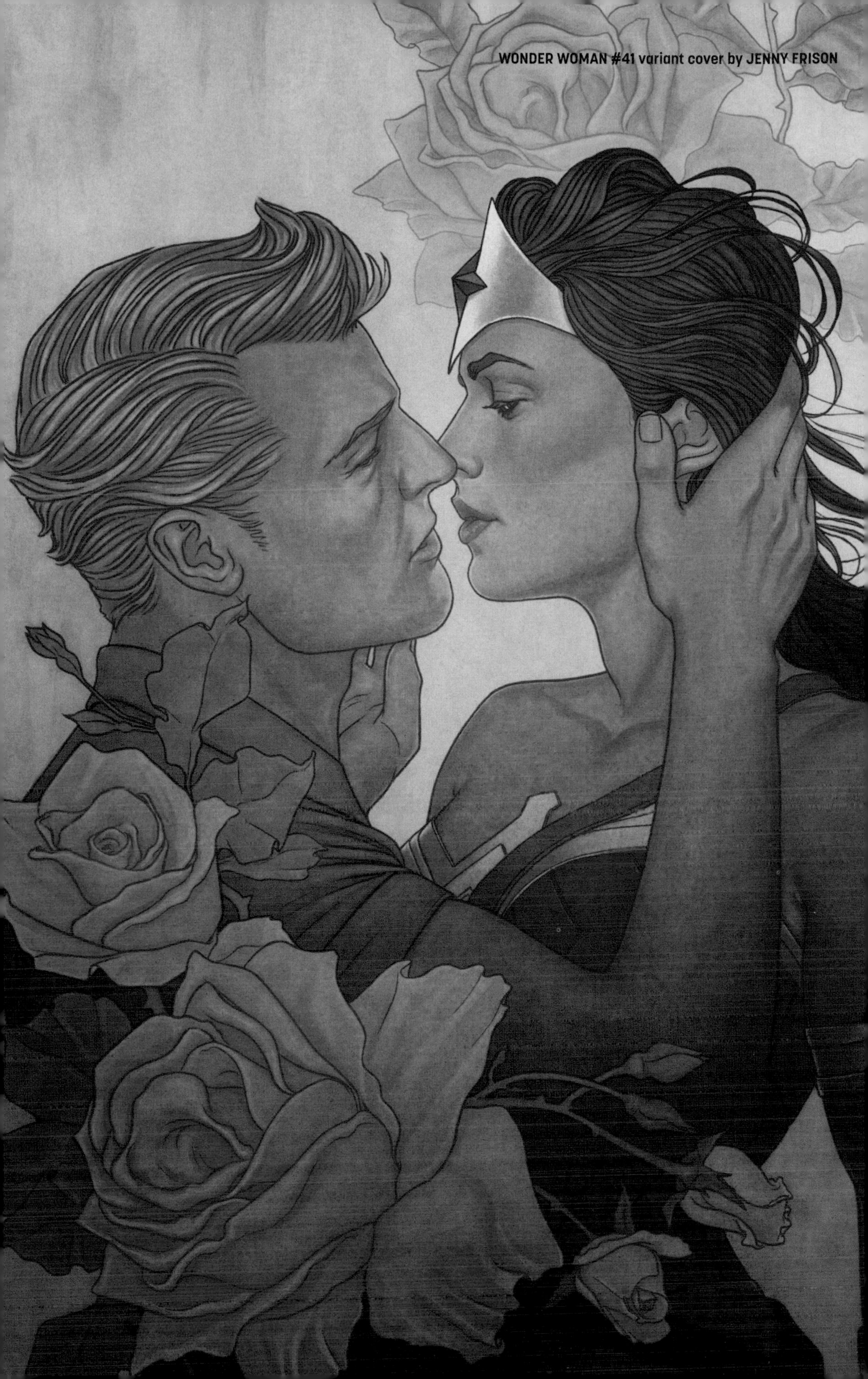

WONDER WOMAN #42 variant cover by JENNY FRISON

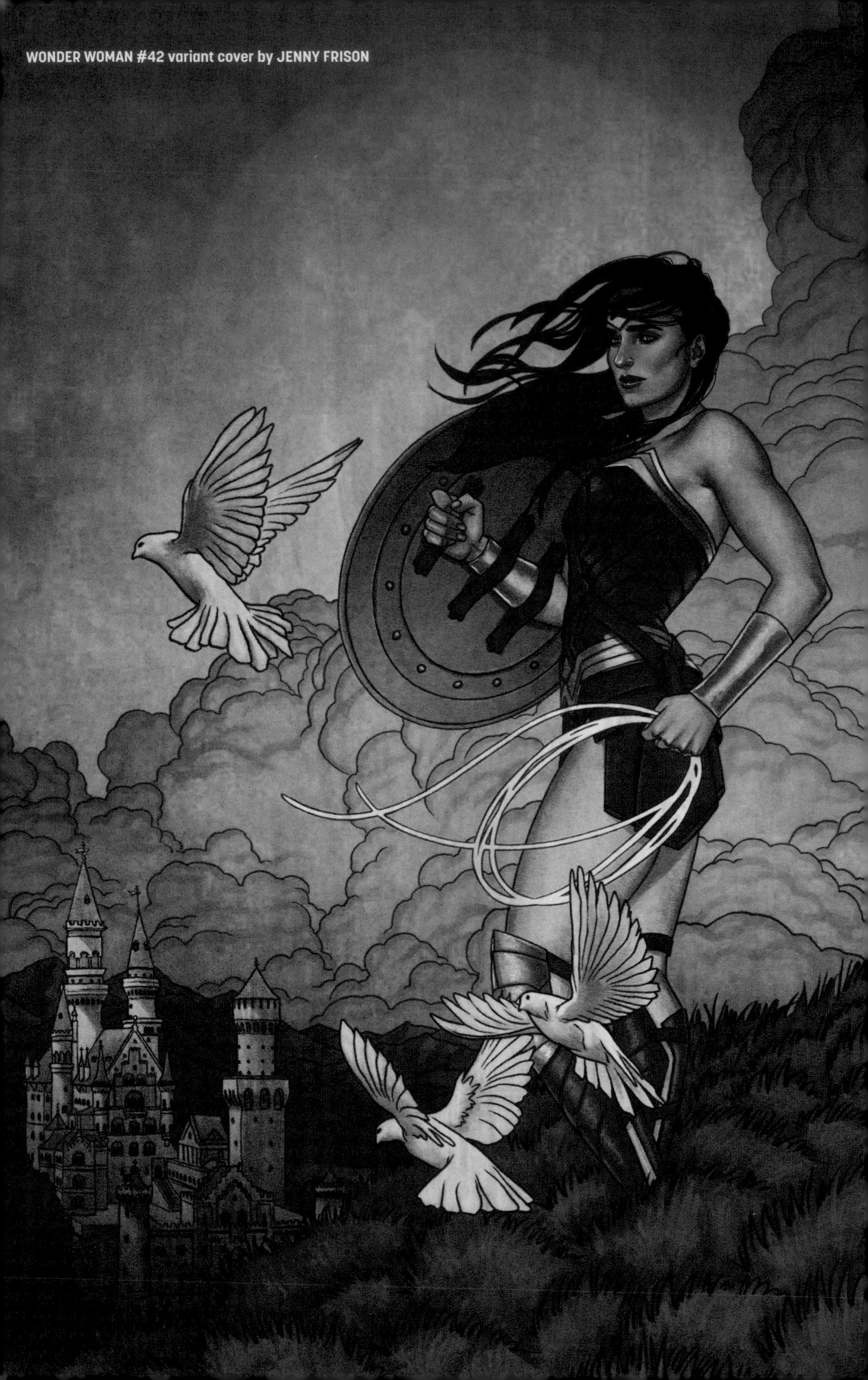

WONDER WOMAN #43 variant cover by JENNY FRISON

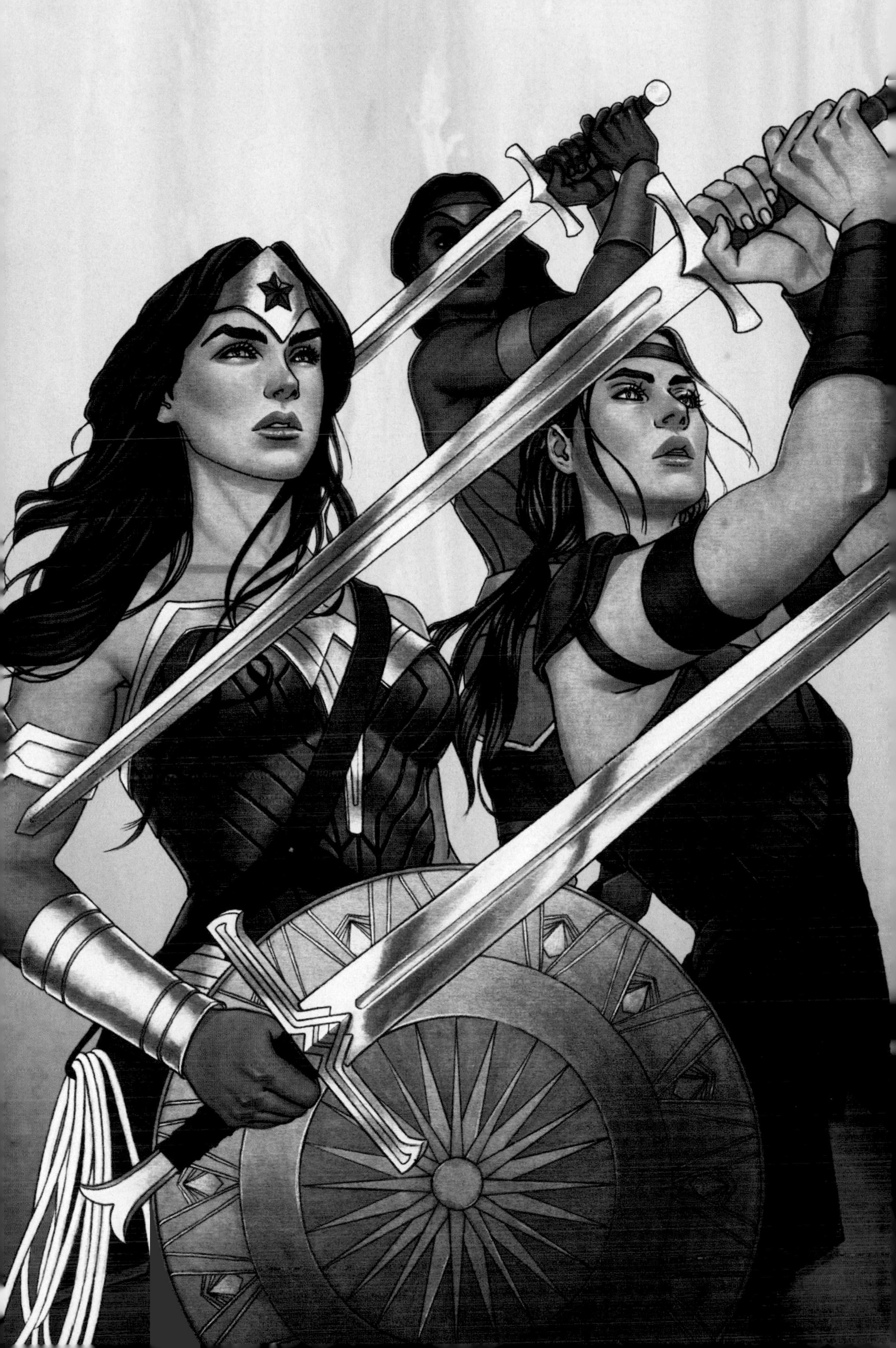

WONDER WOMAN #44 variant cover by JENNY FRISON

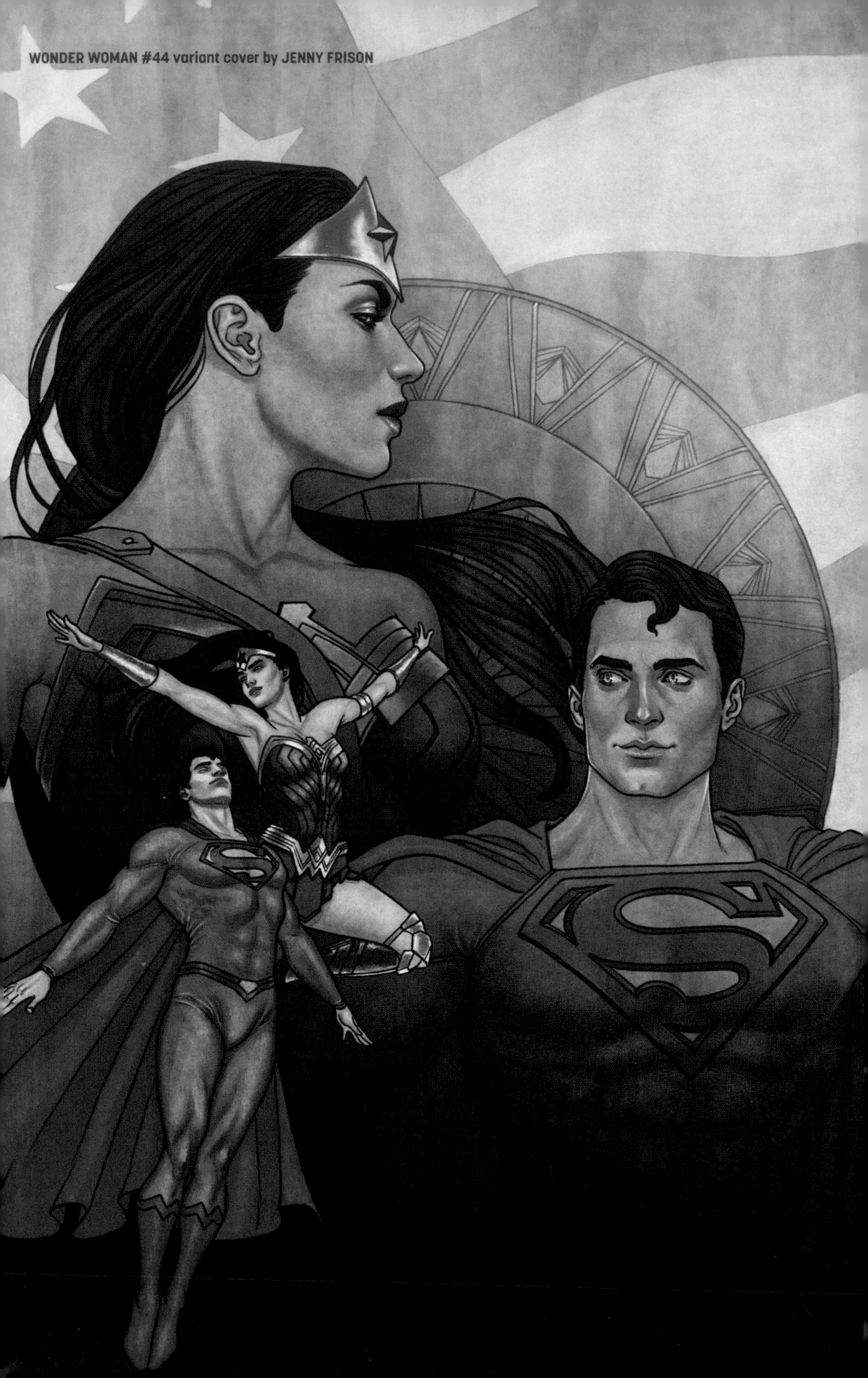

WONDER WOMAN #45 variant cover by JENNY FRISON

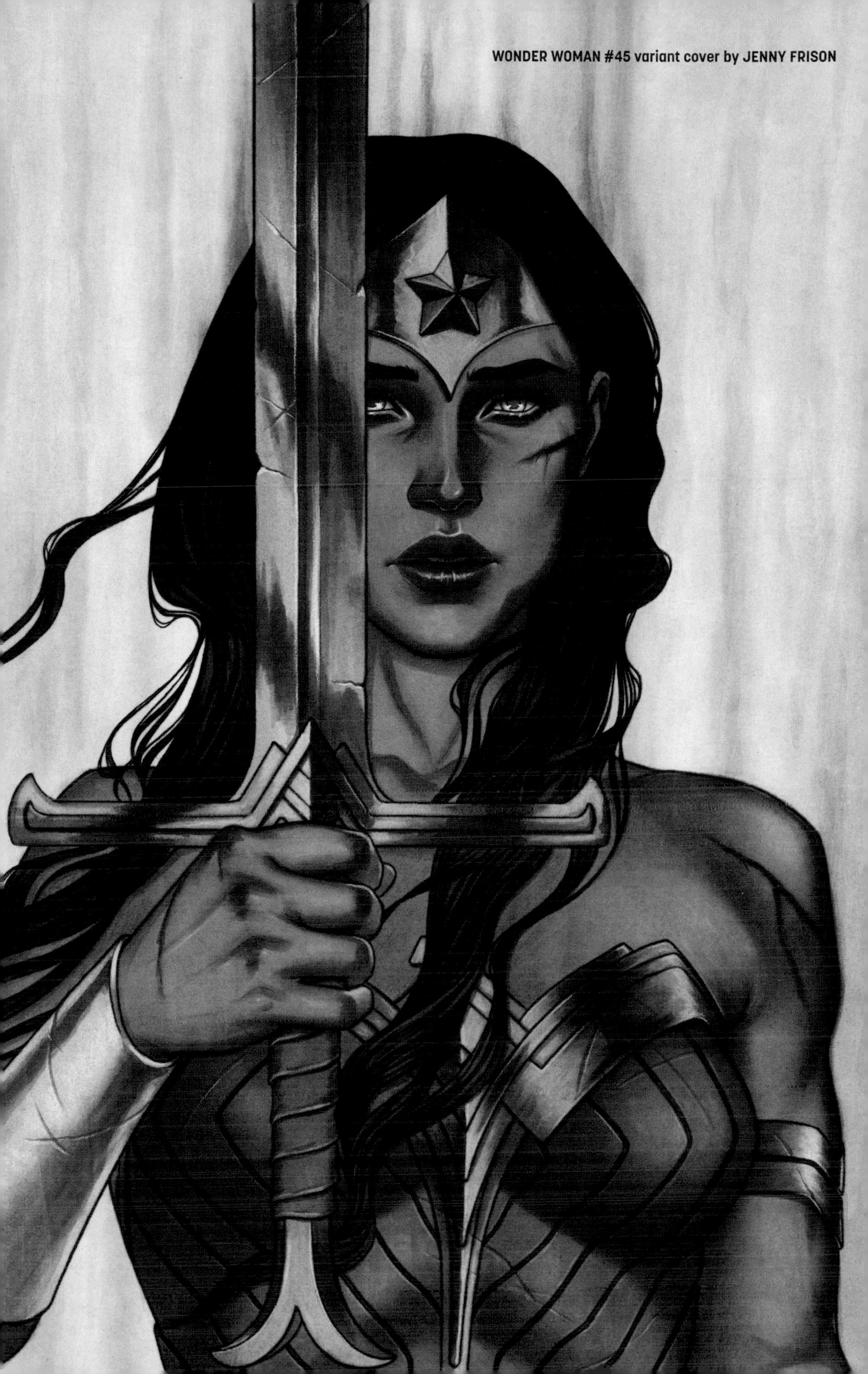

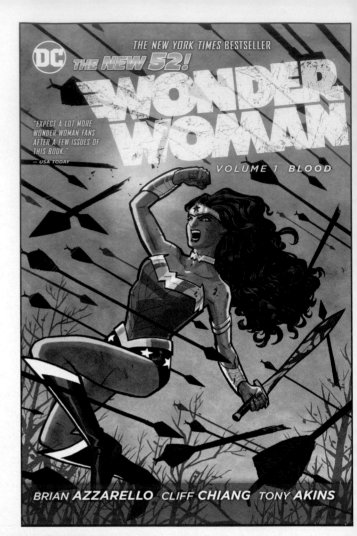

"Greg Rucka and company have created a compelling narrative for fans of the Amazing Amazon."– **NERDIST**

"(A) heartfelt and genuine take on Diana's origin."– **NEWSARAMA**

DC UNIVERSE REBIRTH

WONDER WOMAN

VOL. 1: THE LIES

GREG RUCKA
with LIAM SHARP

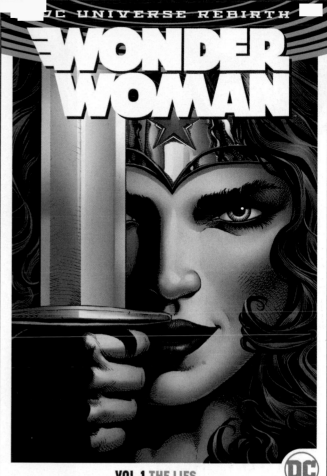

VOL.1 THE LIES
GREG RUCKA ∗ LIAM SHARP ∗ LAURA MARTIN

JUSTICE LEAGUE VOL. 1:
THE EXTINCTION MACHINES

SUPERGIRL VOL. 1:
REIGN OF THE SUPERMEN

BATGIRL VOL. 1:
BEYOND BURNSIDE

"One of the best writers for Wonder Woman in the modern era."
– NERDIST

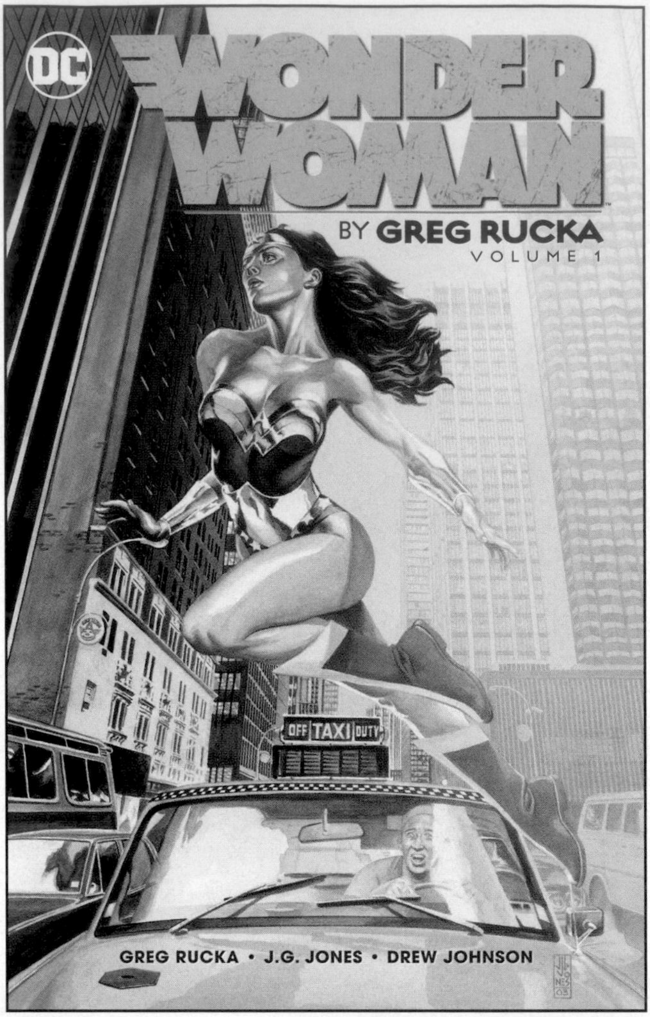
DC
WONDER WOMAN
BY GREG RUCKA
VOLUME 1
OFF TAXI DUTY
GREG RUCKA • J.G. JONES • DREW JOHNSON

WONDER WOMAN BY GREG RUCKA

with J.G. JONES & DREW JOHNSON

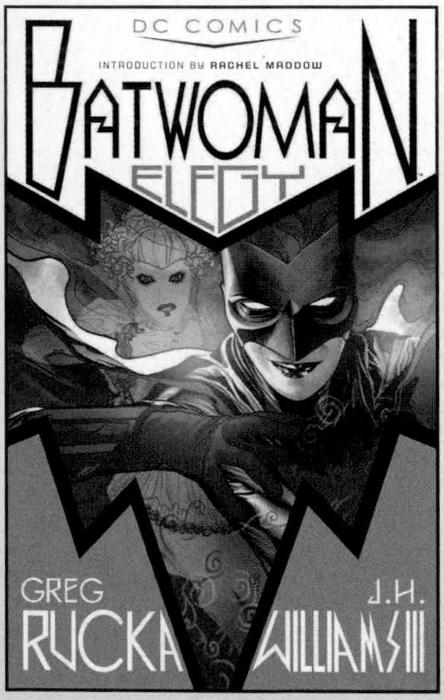
DC COMICS
INTRODUCTION BY RACHEL MADDOW
BATWOMAN
ELEGY
GREG RUCKA
J.H. WILLIAMS III

BATWOMAN: ELEGY with J.H. WILLIAMS III

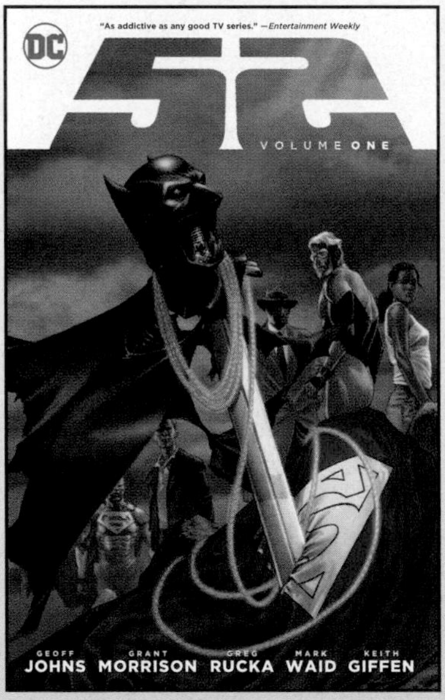
"As addictive as any good TV series." —Entertainment Weekly
DC
52
VOLUME ONE
GEOFF JOHNS
GRANT MORRISON
GREG RUCKA
MARK WAID
KEITH GIFFEN

52 VOL. 1 with VARIOUS ARTISTS

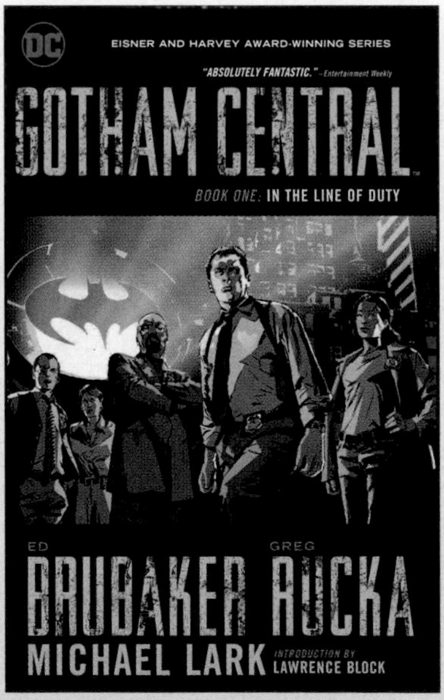
DC
EISNER AND HARVEY AWARD-WINNING SERIES
"ABSOLUTELY FANTASTIC." —Entertainment Weekly
GOTHAM CENTRAL
BOOK ONE: IN THE LINE OF DUTY
ED BRUBAKER
GREG RUCKA
MICHAEL LARK
INTRODUCTION BY LAWRENCE BLOCK

GOTHAM CENTRAL BOOK ONE with ED BRUBAKER & MICHAEL LARK

Get more DC graphic novels wherever comics and books are sold!

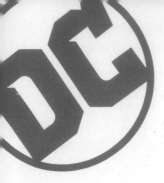